U. S. Supreme Court

U. S. SUPREME COURT

Volume 2

Furman v. Georgia —
School integration and busing

Edited by
Thomas Tandy Lewis
St. Cloud State University

SALEM PRESS, INC.
Pasadena, California   Hackensack, New Jersey

Frontispiece: *Ruth Bader Ginsburg with President Bill Clinton shortly after Ginsburg was sworn in as an associate justice on August 10, 1993.* (AP/Wide World Photos)

Essays originally appeared in *Encyclopedia of the U.S. Supreme Court* (2001). New essays and other materials have been added.

∞ The paper used in these volumes conforms to the American National Standard for Permanence of Paper for Printed Library Materials, Z39.48-1992 (R1997).

Library of Congress Cataloging-in-Publication Data
The U.S. Supreme Court / edited by Thomas Tandy Lewis.
    v. cm. – (Magill's choice)
Includes bibliographical references and indexes.
ISBN 978-1-58765-363-6 (set : alk. paper)
ISBN 978-1-58765-364-3 (vol. 1 : alk. paper)
ISBN 978-1-58765-365-0 (vol. 2 : alk. paper)
ISBN 978-1-58765-366-7 (vol. 3 : alk. paper)
1. United States Supreme Court–History. I. Lewis, Thomas T. (Thomas Tandy) II. Title: United States Supreme Court.

    KF8742.U5 2007
    347.73'2609–dc22

    2006037878

Contents

Contents

Contents

Furman v. Georgia

CITATION: 408 U.S. 238
DATE: June 29, 1972
ISSUE: Capital punishment
SIGNIFICANCE: The Supreme Court held that capital punishment as commonly practiced in 1972 constituted cruel and unusual punishment and thus violated the Eighth and Fourteenth Amendments.

By the late 1960's the majority of Americans opposed the death penalty. The Legal Defense Fund (LDF) of the National Association for the Advancement of Colored People led a legal crusade aimed at either reforming or eliminating the use of executions. In *McGautha v. California* (1971), the Supreme Court rejected the LDF's argument against the imposition of the death penalty without jury guidelines and a bifurcated trial. The next year, nevertheless, the LDF reappeared before the Court and challenged the death sentences of William Furman and two other defendants. At the time, six hundred prisoners were on death row.

A majority of five justices endorsed a short *per curiam* opinion overturning the death penalty statute of Georgia, but there was no opinion for the majority. In fact, all nine justices wrote separate opinions, totaling some 243 pages. Only two justices—William J. Brennan, Jr., and Thurgood Marshall—held that capital punishment was inherently unconstitutional. They both argued that the punishment was degrading to human dignity and that it was both unnecessary and ineffective as a deterrent to crime. In contrast, the other three justices of the majority refused to rule on the legality of capital punishment itself, but they found that the absence of clear standards for juries and judges resulted in arbitrary application of the death penalty. The four dissenters, all appointed by President Richard M. Nixon, emphasized American traditions, the Court's precedents, and the importance of federalism.

Following the *Furman* decision, thirty-five state legislatures rewrote their capital punishment statutes in an attempt to satisfy the Court's concerns. Many observers speculated that the Court would probably not approve of the revisions. In *Gregg v. Georgia* (1976), however, a 7-2 majority of the justices found that Georgia's revamped statute satisfied the requirements of the Constitution.

Thomas Tandy Lewis

SEE ALSO Capital punishment; Eighth Amendment; Fourteenth Amendment; *Gregg v. Georgia.*

Garcia v. San Antonio Metropolitan Transit Authority

CITATION: 469 U.S. 528
DATE: February 19, 1985
ISSUE: Commerce clause
SIGNIFICANCE: Using the commerce clause, the Supreme Court removed almost all limitations on Congress's power to regulate the states.

In *Garcia*, the Supreme Court had to determine whether the hour and wage provisions of the Fair Labor Standards Act (1938) applied to a public transportation system owned and operated by the city of San Antonio. The Court's ruling in *National League of Cities v. Usery* (1976) established four tests that Congress had to meet before it could regulate states under the commerce clause. These tests were unclear, and nearly ten years later they remained unclear, although the Court had made numerous rulings. By a 5-4 vote, the Court reversed *Usery* and removed almost all limitations on congressional power to regulate the states.

Justice Harry A. Blackmun, in the opinion for the Court, opted to abandon the four tests and *Usery*. He argued that the states had representatives in Congress and that these members could be counted on to defend the states' interests, pointing out the special protection states received in the Senate where every state, no matter how small, has two senators. This controversial decision was accompanied by a number of dissents expressing the hope that *Garcia* would be overturned. Lewis F. Powell, Jr., asserted that representation in Congress is an inadequate defense for the states because members of Congress, though elected from the states, become members of the federal government when they enter Congress.

Richard L. Wilson

SEE ALSO Blackmun, Harry A.; Commerce, regulation of; Federalism; *Lopez, United States v.*; States' rights and state sovereignty.

Gay and Lesbian Rights

DESCRIPTION: Constitutional and statutory protections against legal discrimination based on homosexual orientation.

SIGNIFICANCE: The Supreme Court has been slow to recognize constitutional rights on the basis of sexual orientation, and when it eventually held that states may not criminalize homosexual practices among consenting adults, the majority of the justices signaled that the ruling did not necessarily imply equal rights in areas such as marriage and the military.

Although the U.S. Constitution does not directly assign any rights to persons based on their sexual orientation, the due process clauses of the Fifth and Fourteenth Amendments prohibit the federal and state governments from arbitrarily depriving a person of liberty. Also, the equal protection clause of the Fourteenth Amendment requires the states to provide all persons with the equal protection of the laws, and the Supreme Court has construed the due process clause of the Fifth Amendment as imposing a similar requirement on the federal government. These clauses would appear to offer gays and lesbians at least some security against the kinds of legal discrimination and disability that has long been their lot.

In *Griswold v. Connecticut* (1965) and *Eisenstadt v. Baird* (1972), the Court recognized a constitutional right to privacy, or "liberty interest," that encompassed the decision to use contraceptives. In a long line of subsequent rulings, the right to privacy was expanded to protect abortion rights as well as several aspects of sexual autonomy. For many years, however, it was not clear how privacy rights related to the numerous state laws that criminalized nonviolent homosexual acts between adults in private circumstances. Before 1986, the Supreme Court denied *certiorari* for cases dealing with this issue. Finally, in *Bowers v. Hardwick* (1986), a sharply divided Court held that the constitutional right to privacy did not encompass consensual homosexual sodomy. The right was limited to matters of reproduction, traditional marriage, family intimacy, and values respected by the mainstream in the nation's history and traditions, which, in the Court's view, excluded homosexual activities. Dissenters construed the issue more broadly—as invoking a comprehensive "right to be let alone," so long as a person's actions did not cause any harm. At the time, twenty-four states had antisodomy statutes that were enforced nearly exclusively against homosexuals.

By the mid-1980's, the gay rights movement was finally achieving legislative relief from discrimination in employment, education, housing, and public accommodations. Although Congress did not amend federal civil rights laws to include the category of sexual orientation, a growing number of states, as well as cities and counties, responded with a variety of statutes and ordinances.

In Colorado, however, a backlash against such measures resulted in Amendment 2, which was added to the state constitution in a popular referendum, prohibiting any legislation protecting homosexuals from discrimination. In *Romer v. Evans* (1996), the Supreme Court decided, by a 6-3 majority, that Amendment 2 violated the equal protection clause of the Fourteenth Amendment. Although states had no obligation to enact legislative protections, Colorado's constitutional preclusion of the right even to attempt legislative protection was "inexplicable by anything but animus" against homosexuals, and it lacked "a rational relationship to legitimate state interests." However, the Court declined to recognize homosexuality as a "suspect classification," which meant that discriminatory classifications aimed at homosexuals required only a rational basis to be judged constitutional. This was a much less demanding standard than would be necessary to justify classifications based on race or gender.

Supreme Court precedents indicated that public accommodation laws prohibiting discrimination based on sexual orientation would not be applicable to private clubs that explicitly included opposition to homosexuality as integral parts of their missions. The precedents, however, did not make it clear whether the laws would be binding on large private clubs that had not explicitly advertised such views. This was the main issue in *Boy Scouts of America v. Dale* (2000), in which an assistant scoutmaster, who was dismissed when officials learned of his gay status, sued the Boy Scouts under New Jersey's antidiscrimination statute. Boy Scout leaders argued that they had always defended traditional notions of morality, and that one of their advertised purposes was to promote behavior that is "morally straight," which they asserted was widely understood by the public to be inconsistent with homosexual acts. The Supreme Court, by a 5-4 vote, accepted the argument and ruled in favor of the Scouts. The ruling was based on the doctrine of expressive association, which included the First Amendment right of a private club to control its message about its values and purposes.

Supporters of gay rights were more pleased with the ruling in *Oncale v. Sundowner Offshore Service* (1998), which held that federal law banning sexual harassment applied to situations in which harassed parties are of the same sex. The majority opinion in the case, however, included a qualification that the law would apply only to harassment that occurs "because of sex," which seemed to imply that the law would not apply to harassment based on antigay animus without any sexual or erotic element. Lower courts have differed widely in their interpretation of the *Oncale* ruling.

Historically, gays and lesbians were banned from participation in the U.S. military services. In 1993, following a heated controversy, the services agreed to a compromise that was labeled "don't ask, don't tell." This compromise continued the official ban on gay and lesbian membership in the armed services but did not require persons joining the military to say anything about their sexual orientation. However, any serviceman or woman found to have engaged in a homosexual practice would be subject to dishonorable discharge. Although many people questioned whether the policy had any rational basis, the majority of Supreme Court justices were apparently not prepared to find that the policy was unconstitutional. By 1999, the Court had refused to review five lower court rulings that upheld the don't-ask-don't-tell policy.

Many universities and law schools protested the military's discriminatory policy by refusing to allow military recruiters to use their facilities. Congress responded with the Solomon Amendment (1996), requiring recipients of federal funds to allow military recruiters access equal to that of other employers who come on campus to recruit. In a unanimous ruling in *Rumsfeld v. Forum for Academic and Institutional Rights* (2006), the Court upheld the Solomon Amendment. The Court explained that the law did not violate the First Amendment, because the act of permitting recruiters to use university facilities did not necessarily indicate any institutional endorsement for the policies of the military. Individuals were free to engage in nonviolent protests against the recruiters if they so desired.

Proponents of gay rights were pleasantly surprised with the watershed case *Lawrence v. Texas* (2003), in which the Court held by a 6-3 majority that a Texas statute criminalizing homosexual conduct between consenting adults was an unconstitutional violation of the "right to liberty under the due process clause," declaring that the statute furthered "no legitimate state interest which can justify the intrusion into the personal and private life of the individual." Also, by a 5-4 vote, the Court explicitly overturned the *Hardwick* precedent. By applying rational-basis analysis, the Court refused to recognize that homosexual practice was a fundamental right to be assessed by strict scrutiny. Only one of the justices in the majority, Sandra Day O'Connor, wanted to base the decision on the equal protection clause, which would have expanded application for the ruling. The immediate effect of the *Lawrence* decision was to strike down existing antisodomy laws in twenty-four states and the District of Columbia. However, the written opinions in the case indicated that the majority of justices were not ready to apply the ruling to the military, marriage, or other areas. In 2006, the Seventh Circuit declined to extend the reasoning of *Lawrence* to cases involving consensual adult incest.

Since the 1960's, gay and lesbian activists have argued that they should have an equal right to enter into legally recognized marriages, with the same tax benefits and other privileges that heterosexuals enjoy. They commonly point to *Loving v. Virginia* (1967), in which the Court held that the equal protection clause barred the states from prohibiting interracial marriage. In the 1990's, Hawaii's high court was poised to rule that the state constitution mandated recognition of same-sex marriages, but the quick addition of a state constitutional amendment prevented the ruling. In 1996, the U.S. Congress responded to conservative objections by passing the Defense of Marriage Act (DOMA), declaring that the states would not be required to accept either same-sex marriages or civil partnerships under the full faith and credit clause of the Constitution.

In 2000, Vermont's high court held that its state marriage laws were unconstitutional, but it accepted the legislature's enactment of civil partnerships, in which the state provided the same benefits that it gave to traditional marriages. In 2004, Massachusetts's more liberal high court ruled that its state constitution guaranteed gays and lesbians nothing less than full equality in marriage rights. In November of that year, the U.S. Supreme Court declined to review a challenge to the resulting Massachusetts statute that permitted gay and lesbian couples to marry.

In 2006, it was expected that eventually the Supreme Court would be asked to decide if other states could refuse to recognize the validity of these marriages under their laws and DOMA. In 2006, conservatives in Congress barely failed to get enough votes to initiate a constitutional amendment that would have permanently guaranteed that the full faith and credit clause would not apply. The controversial issue promised to provoke much heated debate and judicial litigation for many years into the future.

John C. Hughes
Revised and updated by the Editor

FURTHER READING

Gertsmann, Evan. *The Constitutional Underclass: Gays, Lesbians, and the Failure of Class-Based Equal Protection.* Chicago: University of Chicago Press, 1999.

Kranz, Rachel, and Tim Cusick. *Gay Rights.* New York: Facts On File, 2005.

Murdoch, Joyce. *Courting Justice: Gay Men and Lesbians v. the Supreme Court.* New York: Basic Books, 2001.

Phelan, Shane. *Sexual Strangers: Gays, Lesbians, and Dilemmas of Citizenship.* Philadelphia: Temple University Press, 2001.

Pierson, Jason. *Courts, Liberalism, and Rights: Gay Law and Politics in the United States and Canada.* Philadelphia: Temple University Press, 2005.

Richards, David. *The Case for Gay Rights: From Bowers to Lawrence and Beyond.* Lawrence: University Press of Kansas, 2005.

SEE ALSO Assembly and association, freedom of; *Boy Scouts of America v. Dale*; Certiorari, writ of; Due process, substantive; Employment discrimination; Gender issues; *Griswold v. Connecticut*; *Lawrence v. Texas*; O'Connor, Sandra Day; Privacy, right to; Scalia, Antonin.

Gender Issues

DESCRIPTION: Social questions involving and legal distinctions based on a person's sex.

SIGNIFICANCE: Supreme Court decisions on a wide range of cases involving gender issues significantly influenced many aspects of daily life. The Court's decisions provide both pragmatic and symbolic guidance on increasingly complex legal and social issues relating to gender.

In the latter half of the twentieth century, major societal changes took place in the United States. All these changes, particularly increased recognition of individual rights, the mass entry of women into the workplace, and technological advances, raised new legal issues involving gender. The Supreme Court began handling cases involving claims of differential treatment based on sex. Cases alleging de jure gender discrimination have largely, but not entirely, been supplanted by those claiming de facto discrimination.

Many of the Court's most influential decisions on gender issues occurred in cases alleging violation of the equal protection clause of the Fourteenth Amendment. History shows that this amendment was intended to remedy racial discrimination, and controversy exists as to the applicability of this clause in contexts such as sex discrimination. The disagreement centers on the extent of the Court's authority to

In 1875, the Supreme Court ruled that the Fourteenth Amendment did not extend the right to vote to women. After ratification of the Nineteenth Amendment in 1920 gave women the vote, the League of Women Voters was formed to help women make the most of their new power. (Library of Congress)

broaden the scope of equal protection; essentially, this is part of the wider controversy over the power of judicial review.

Until 1971 the Court applied a minimal level of review to all cases challenging classifications by sex as a violation of the equal protection clause. This meant that the Court focused on whether the gender distinction in the statute was rationally related to a legitimate government purpose, as embodied in the statute. Under this minimal standard, the Court did not require close congruence between government goals and statutory means, and every statutory distinction by gender that was challenged under the equal protection clause was upheld by the Court.

Reed v. Reed (1971) marked the first time the Court struck down a gender-specific statute as a violation of the equal protection clause. Although the justices purported to use the traditional minimal "rationality" standard of review, in retrospect, it was evident they had actually employed a "heightened" standard. However, this still fell far short of the strict scrutiny that plaintiff's attorney Ruth Bader Ginsburg (later Justice Ginsburg) argued should be applied.

The Court's shift toward closer scrutiny of gender issue cases and the divisions among justices on this issue became clear in *Frontiero v. Richardson* (1973). In striking down a government regulation requiring husbands, but not wives, of Air Force personnel to prove dependency in order to obtain spousal benefits, four justices argued that strict scrutiny should be applied to classifications based on sex, while four argued this was either unnecessary or unwise.

The question of what standard of review the Court should apply in gender and equal protection cases was clarified in *Craig v. Boren* (1976), in which the Court struck down a sex-specific restriction on beer purchases. In *Craig*, the Court articulated an intermediate standard that examines whether a statutory gender distinction is "substantially related to important government objectives." The Court's decision to apply this level of review to gender classifications, rather than the highest standard of strict scrutiny applied to racial classifications, marked a critical point in the legal history of gender issues cases. The Court in *Craig* reasoned that classifications by gender are *not* "inherently suspect" and thus do not require strict scrutiny, unlike classifications by race. The Court was strongly criticized for employing the less demanding standard of review for gender classifications, and the distinction also raises the question of what level of scrutiny would apply to claims of discriminatory classification on the basis of the *combination* of gender and race.

The major theme of most Supreme Court cases involving gender issues is an allegation that men and women were treated differently and thus unequally. In these cases, the Court examines the claim of differential treatment and its potential legal justifications, which vary according to the legal context in which the case is raised.

EQUAL PROTECTION CASES

The Court's analysis of cases presenting claims of gender discrimination in violation of the Fourteenth Amendment's equal protection clause focuses on whether women and men are "similarly situated" with respect to the legal issue in question. The Court's reasoning in such cases has been that differential treatment of men and women is not per se gender discrimination because equal protection requires only that persons who are "similarly situated" be treated alike. Therefore, if the Court finds that men and women are *not* similarly situated, then differential treatment may be constitutional.

Rostker v. Goldberg (1981) raised an equal protection challenge to the Military Selective Service Act requiring men to register for the draft. The Court sustained the statute on grounds that because women were not subject to the draft, men and women were not similarly situated with respect to the issue of draft registration. Justice Thurgood Marshall's dissent argued that men and women *were* similarly situated with respect to their eligibility to serve in noncombat support positions and argued that the Court majority should have applied a different analysis.

In *Michael M. v. Superior Court of Sonoma County* (1981), the Court upheld a statute specifying criminal penalties for men convicted in statutory rape cases. The challenge to the statute argued that the sex-specific provision penalizing only male participants in such encounters violated equal protection. In its decision, the Court noted that the legislative intent of the statute was deterrence of teenage pregnancies and recognized that women and men were not similarly situated with respect to the adverse consequences of such pregnancies.

The divisions among the justices on the question of whether differential treatment by gender constitutes unequal treatment offensive to the equal protection clause was highlighted in *Geduldig v. Aiello* (1974), raising an equal protection challenge to a disability statute that failed to cover pregnancy and pregnancy-related disabilities. The Court upheld the statute, reasoning that differential treatment on the basis of pregnancy was not the same as differential treatment on the basis of gender. The Court noted that although only women become pregnant, nonpregnant women and men received the same benefits under the statute. In dissent, Justices William J. Brennan, Jr., William O.

Douglas, and Thurgood Marshall noted that the statute did provide coverage for disabilities unique to men and asserted that differential treatment of pregnancy was essentially sex discrimination.

TITLE VII CASES

In cases arising in a statutory context, the Court examines the issues in terms of the requirements and limitations of the applicable statute. Title VII of the 1964 Civil Rights Act, which prohibits discrimination in the terms, conditions, and privileges of employment, has been a source of several significant Court cases.

In *California Federal Savings and Loan Association v. Guerra* (1985), the Court examined whether Title VII's prohibitions on sex discrimination conflicted with a California provision requiring private employers to provide leave for childbirth. A receptionist seeking to enforce her right to maternity leave under the state statute was denied by her employer. The employer asserted that because the state statute provided a benefit for pregnant employees, it was inconsistent with, and thus preempted by, the federal provisions of Title VII prohibiting discrimination on the basis of sex distinctions (including pregnancy and childbirth). The Court rejected this theory and supported the state provision, finding that the legislative intent of Title VII was to prevent discrimination against pregnant employees, not place limits on preferential treatment for them. The Court noted that the state statute supported equal employment opportunities and therefore was consistent with the purposes of Title VII.

Title VII was interpreted by the Court as prohibiting both disparate treatment and disparate impact types of discrimination. A plaintiff alleging that an employer's policies illustrate disparate treatment must prove that the employer had discriminatory intent. If proven, the employer may justify the gender classification as a bona fide occupational classification. For example, in *Dothard v. Rawlinson* (1977), the Court upheld state prison regulations requiring male guards in some sections of men's prisons. In claims of disparate impact, the employer's intent is not relevant to the issue of whether the employer's policy has a disproportionately adverse impact.

GENDER DIFFERENCES

The Court's decisions in cases involving claims that differential treatment by gender is required or justified by differences between women and men illustrate the justices' attempts to distinguish between claims based on gender stereotypes and those based on actual gender differences, whether biological, economic, or sociocultural. In *Craig v. Boren* (1976), Justice William J. Brennan, Jr., wrote: "It was necessary that the legislatures choose either to realign their substantive laws in a gender neutral fashion, or to adopt procedures for identifying those instances where the sex centered generalization actually comported to fact."

In *Mississippi University for Women v. Hogan* (1982), the Court rejected the university's claim that its single-sex admissions policy was intended to offer women a choice of a female-only educational environment. The majority opinion by Justice Sandra Day O'Connor reasoned that barring male applicants to the university's nursing education program would not only restrict men's educational choices but could perpetuate stereotypes about nursing as a strictly female occupation.

The reaction of the Court to purported gender differences has varied greatly depending on the case and the legal philosophy of individual justices. The Court's opinions reveal disagreement between justices on the issue of whether ostensible gender differences are based on gender stereotypes or reflect biological or social facts and also on the issue of whether a particular gender difference is a legally supportable rationale for differential treatment.

The variation in the justices' perspectives on gender issues is exemplified by their opinions in cases employing protectionistic rationales for differential treatment by gender. Paternalism has been employed as part of the rationale for allowing differential treatment that clearly harmed women's interests by denying them equal opportunities or legal status, such as denial of the right to practice law (*Bradwell v. Illinois*, 1873).

Another example is *Automobile Workers v. Johnson Controls* (1991), which challenged a workplace policy that prohibited female employees capable of childbearing from occupying positions involving exposure to lead as a violation of Title VII. The employer asserted that its concern was prevention of reproductive problems, but plaintiffs argued that this protectionistic policy deprived women of the right to make their own choices, and the Court agreed.

However, paternalistic reasons also were often used as rationales for differential treatment by gender that ostensibly (although often not actually) benefited women. In *Muller v. Oregon* (1908), the Court supported legislation authorizing shorter work hours for women than men, accepting the argument that women's physical constitution and reproductive role required reduced hours. As the following cases illustrate, the Court has often reviewed claims that differential treatment benefits women.

"BENIGN" SEX CLASSIFICATIONS

Historically, the Court has labeled gender distinctions that actually or ostensibly favor women relative to men as "benign" sex classifications. A major question the Court has grappled with is whether benign gender distinctions are in fact harmless or whether they have potentially adverse consequences or ramifications for men, women, or both.

In *Kahn v. Shevin* (1974), a widower challenged a state statute allowing only widows a property tax exemption as a violation of equal protection. The Court upheld the statute, noting that economic differences between women and men made it reasonable to support a policy distinction between widows and widowers. In dissent, Justices William J. Brennan, Jr., and Thurgood Marshall asserted that the statute was both overinclusive in its application to all widows regardless of financial status and underinclusive in its disregard for widowers in need. Brennan and Marshall reasoned that the statute should target surviving spouses who demonstrated financial need, regardless of gender.

In *Schlesinger v. Ballard* (1975), the Court upheld a U.S. Navy policy granting women a longer time period in which to obtain promotion or else face discharge. In its reasoning, the Court emphasized that women and men in the Navy were not similarly situated with respect to the opportunities available for service (and thus promotion). Similarly, the Court upheld Social Security provisions giving women an advantage in computing their base income (and thus their benefits) in *Califano v. Webster* (1977), citing Congress's intent to compensate women for historically unequal economic treatment. Some observers of the Court hailed these decisions as appropriate redress for economic gender inequalities, and others raised questions about the fairness of such policies and their potential to engender backlash or stereotyping of women.

In contrast, three weeks before in *Califano v. Goldfarb* (1977), the Court struck down Social Security provisions awarding widows automatic benefits based on their husbands' earnings but awarding widowers benefits only after they showed that they had received at least half their support from their wives. Some justices found the provision violated equal protection by discriminating against widowers receiving fewer benefits; however, some justices also found discrimination against the deceased women wage earners.

OTHER GENDER ISSUES

The workplace and gender cases considered by the Court have significantly influenced most aspects of private and public employment. A prominent example is *Meritor Savings Bank v. Vinson* (1986), in which the Court distinguished between the "voluntariness" and the "welcomeness" of conduct in recognizing the coercive power of fear of job loss in sexual harassment cases. This distinction has resonated throughout subsequent cases addressing sexual harassment claims in the workplace and educational arenas.

The Court's decision in *Roe v. Wade* (1973), legalizing abortion subject to certain restrictions, remains the landmark case in the area of gender and reproductive rights. *Roe* is significant not only for its substantive decision but also for its role in the Court's reasoning on the right to privacy. As such, *Roe* has implications for many types of cases grounded at least partially in the right to privacy. The Court's decisions on gender and reproductive rights serve as the legal framework for legislation and lower court cases addressing specific aspects of such rights, such as restrictions on abortion and abortion funding, access to contraception, and sterilization.

Legislation and cases in the area of family law (also known as domestic relations law) reflect both the influence of relevant Court decisions and the scope and rapidity of societal and technological changes in the late twentieth century. Gender issues are often raised in cases involving marriage, divorce, paternity, parental rights, custody, adoption, and related topics such as same-sex marriage, custody, and adoption. Changes in reproductive technology such as surrogate parenting, sex-selection techniques, and egg and sperm viability raised a host of other legal questions.

Some cases involve crimes or civil offenses that raise issues of differential treatment of one gender or that have differential implications for one gender. The Court's decisions on constitutional and statutory questions such as the scope of due process in a wide variety of cases (whether originally presenting a gender dimension or not) are applicable to many issues raised with respect to gender and criminal or civil offenses.

One example is *DeShaney v. Winnebago County Department of Social Services* (1989), in which the Court affirmed that the due process clause represents a limitation on governmental power, rather than an affirmative guarantee of government protection of an individual's safety. This reasoning has been applied in subsequent cases establishing that police do not have a constitutional duty to protect victims of domestic violence.

The question of whether differential treatment violates equal protection has been raised in cases comparing the treatment of male and female offenders and cases challenging gender-specific definitions of crimes such as rape. The Court's reasoning regarding fetuses and legal personhood in *Roe v. Wade* has been revisited in cases contesting the legality of prosecuting pregnant substance abusers for child endangerment or abuse. A major source of cases raising claims of differential impact by gender are cases concerning the definition, First Amendment status, and impact of pornography. Such cases raise broad gender issues for the Court because of allegations that some pornographic depictions of women may cause women psychological or physical harm.

Gender and education issues involving Court decisions include the constitutionality of single-sex educational institutions, the comparability of men's and women's sports programs at coeducational schools, and policies and practices concerning sexual harassment in schools. In *United States v. Virginia* (1996), the Court rejected the Virginia Military Institute's (VMI) proposal to preserve its historic status as a men-only educational institution by creating a separate but "substantively comparable" institute for women. The majority opinion by Justice Ruth Bader Ginsburg found that VMI failed to demonstrate that maintaining its men-only admission policy would serve an important government purpose such as contributing to educational diversity and also determined that the proposed facility for female cadets could not offer resources comparable to those of VMI.

The Court has addressed a wide range of cases alleging civil rights violations on the basis of gender. These include cases alleging discrimination against patrons in public accommodations, challenging the membership restrictions of private groups, and challenging the exclusion of women from participation in civic duties such as jury service.

The Court's decisions in cases involving gender issues reflect a mixture of adherence to precedent together with awareness of changing societal values, with the ratio of these elements varying according to the historical context, the nature of the case, and the legal philosophy of individual justices. The substance of the Court's rulings and the opinions expressed by the justices in these cases both reflect and significantly shape gender relations.

Diana R. Grant

FURTHER READING

An excellent starting point is Joanne Belknap's *The Invisible Woman: Gender, Crime, and Justice* (3d ed. Belmont, Calif.: Thomson/Wadsworth, 2006). *Class, Race, Gender and Crime: Social Realities of Justice in America* (Los Angeles: Roxbury, 2002) by Gregg Barak, Jeanne M. Flavin, and Paul S. Leighton provides broad overviews of gender and other justice issues. Mary Becker, Cynthia Grant Bowman, and Morrison Torrey's *Taking Women Seriously: Cases and Materials* (St. Paul, Minn.: West Publishing, 1994) is a collection of essays and excerpts from cases and articles on feminist perspectives on gender issues.

Joan Hoff's *Law Gender and Injustice: A Legal History of U.S. Women* (New York: New York University Press, 1991) provides a detailed and comprehensive look at the incomplete legal rights afforded women by the Constitution. Hoff's discussion clearly illustrates the concept of equal protection as "an umbrella with holes." *Feminist Jurisprudence*, edited by Patricia Smith (New York: Oxford University Press, 1993), is a rich anthology providing excellent analyses of gendered perspectives in legal reasoning, including some selections on how relationships between gender, ethnicity, and class influence legal action on gender issues.

A thought-provoking look at how political and religious norms are interwoven with legal and social issues of gender, race, and sexual identity is provided in *Law's Promise, Law's Expression: Visions of Power in the Politics of Race, Gender, and Religion* by Kenneth Karst (New Haven, Conn.: Yale University Press, 1993).

The Criminal Justice System and Women, edited by Barbara Price and Natalie Sokoloff (3d ed. New York: McGraw-Hill, 2004) includes theoretical and empirical articles on women offenders, victims, and employees of the legal system. *Women, Law, and Social Control*, edited by Alida V. Merlo and Joycelyn M. Pollock (Newton, Mass.: Allyn & Bacon, 1995) examines the experiences of women workers in the legal system, as well as women offenders and victims. The latter two selections include insightful discussions of women who are both victims and offenders.

Anne M. Butler's *Gendered Justice in the American West: Women Prisoners in Men's Penitentiaries* (Chicago: University of Illinois Press, 2000) provides an interesting historical perspective by looking at the treatment of female prisoners in nineteenth century male-inmate dominated prisons.

SEE ALSO Americans with Disabilities Act; Birth control and contraception; *Bradwell v. Illinois*; *Buck v. Bell*; Employment discrimination; Equal protection clause; Fourteenth Amendment; Ginsburg, Ruth Bader; Judicial scrutiny; Race and discrimination; *Reed v. Reed*; *Roe v. Wade*.

General Welfare Clause

DATE: 1789

DESCRIPTION: First clause of Article I, section 8, of the U.S. Constitution, authorizing Congress to collect taxes and spend money for the common defense and the general welfare.

SIGNIFICANCE: After 1936, the Supreme Court sometimes used the general welfare clause to provide constitutional justification for expanding congressional powers.

There have been two major interpretations of the general welfare clause, which is also called the taxing and spending clause. James Madison made a narrow construction of the clause, so that it was a summary of congressional power to tax and spend money for those purposes specifically enumerated in section 8. In contrast, Alexander Hamilton and Justice Joseph Story argued that the clause was a separate grant of power, authorizing Congress to use broad discretion in

Alexander Hamilton, the first secretary of the treasury, argued that the general welfare clause granted Congress broad spending and taxing powers. (National Portrait Gallery, Smithsonian Institution, Gift of Cabot Lodge)

511

taxing and spending for the general welfare.

In *United States v. Butler* (1936), Justice Owen J. Roberts's majority opinion cautiously endorsed most of the Hamilton/Story position on the general welfare clause. The next year, in *Steward Machine Co. v. Davis* and *Helvering v. Davis*, the Supreme Court expanded on Butler in sustaining the constitutionality of the Social Security Act. Justice Benjamin N. Cardozo's two majority opinions emphasized the idea that Congress had broad authority to determine which policies promote the welfare of the nation. In *South Dakota v. Dole* (1987), the Court allowed Congress to withhold federal funds for the purpose of putting pressure on states to maintain a uniform drinking age, because the policy was "reasonably calculated to advance the general welfare." The general welfare clause usually overlaps with the commerce clause. Given the Court's expansive definition of commerce, it is unlikely that the Court will ever overturn a federal statute as contrary to the general welfare clause.

Thomas Tandy Lewis

SEE ALSO Cardozo, Benjamin N.; Commerce, regulation of; Income tax; New Deal; Story, Joseph.

Gerrymandering

DESCRIPTION: The practice of drawing contorted electoral district boundaries with the intent of favoring a particular party or group.

SIGNIFICANCE: The outcome of elections can be strongly influenced by the way electoral districts are drawn. Gerrymandering can threaten the fairness and very legitimacy of representative democracy, and in most cases the Supreme Court ruled it to be unconstitutional.

Put simply, gerrymandering is the drawing of electoral districts in order to favor a political party or other group. In practice, gerrymandering results in contorted district boundaries that include "desirable" demographic groups (whose members are inclined to vote for a particular party) and exclude "undesirable" groups. Although the practice violates the intended purpose of redistricting, a case has been made for maintaining "cohesive" voting blocs within electoral districts.

REDISTRICTING

The citizens of the United States are divided into 435 congressional districts, with each district electing one legislator to the U.S. House of Representatives. Each state is allocated a certain number of districts, based on its relative population. Every ten years the 435 congressional seats are "reapportioned" among the states, according to new population figures from the latest census. The states (primarily the state legislatures) then draw new district boundaries, both to permit an increase or decrease in their allotment of congressional seats and to ensure that all districts include approximately the same number of voters.

The term "gerrymander" was coined in 1812, when the Massachusetts legislature created a contorted state senate district to favor the Democratic-Republican party. The district was said to resemble a salamander, and was dubbed a "Gerrymander" in reference to Governor Elbridge Gerry, who approved it.

CONSTITUTIONAL ISSUES

Various manifestations of gerrymandering have been found to be unconstitutional on several grounds. One concerns the equality of constituency size. A disproportionately large population might be consolidated into one district, thus diluting the political strength of its voters relative to the voters in smaller districts. (This would occasionally be done to dilute the voting strength of African Americans.) In *Wesberry v. Sanders* (1964), the Court decreed that congressional representation must be based on the one person, one vote principle. That is, districts must be created "as nearly as practicable" with roughly equal numbers of voters.

Yet simply creating districts with numerically comparable populations does not ensure that the one person, one vote principle is observed. With knowledge of certain voting indicators (such as party affiliation), a district can be drawn that is heavily weighted toward a particular political party or group. The Court found this type of gerrymander to be unconstitutional in *Gomillion v. Lightfoot* (1960).

In this case, the Alabama legislature had altered a local election district to virtually exclude African Americans. The Court found that the district violated the equal protection clause of the Fourteenth Amendment.

Although many gerrymandered districts were based on attempts to disfranchise minority voters, many others simply favored a political party, irrespective of ethnic considerations. The Court found, in *Davis v. Bandemer* (1986), that these, too, violate the equal protection clause of the Fourteenth Amendment.

MAJORITY-MINORITY DISTRICTS

Although the Court consistently stood against redistricting schemes that seek to disenfranchise minorities, for a period in the 1970's and 1980's it ruled that race-based districts may be necessary to ensure the voting strength of minority groups. In fact, federal courts ordered some states to create districts containing a majority of ethnic or racial minority groups in order to uphold the 1965 Voting Rights Act. In essence, it was assumed that the voting strength of racial and ethnic groups could be increased by concentrating their votes in individual districts. The approach was bolstered by a 1982 amendment to the Act that upheld the right of African Americans and Hispanics "to elect representatives of their choice."

In the 1990's the notion of majority-minority districts came under increasing, powerful attack. Although many leaders of minority groups continued to defend such districts as a necessary mechanism for increasing minority representation, the public mood and the Court turned against the idea.

A watershed was reached with the *Shaw v. Reno* decision in 1993. In this case, two predominantly African American districts in North Carolina were at issue. Under pressure from the U.S. Department of Justice, the North Carolina legislature created the districts in an attempt to ensure that the state, whose population was 22 percent African American, would elect its first black congressional representatives in more than a century. Both districts did indeed elect African Americans in 1992. However, five white voters in one of the districts sued the state, claiming that they had been effectively "disenfranchised" by the reapportionment plan. The case reached the Court, whose 5-4 majority opinion instructed the lower courts to reconsider the constitutionality of the district, which had a "bizarre" shape and bore an "uncomfortable resemblance to political apartheid." Although the lower courts again upheld the district (while making findings to satisfy the Court), *Shaw* opened the door for more legal challenges to majority-minority districts.

In 1995 the Court more definitively rejected the notion of race-based districts in *Miller v. Johnson*. In this case, the Court rejected redistricting plans in which "race was the predominant factor motivating the legislature's decision to place a significant number of voters within or without a particular district." *Miller* forced the Georgia legislature to amend its reapportionment plan, and subsequent decisions forced other states to do the same. A number of incumbent minority legislators found themselves running for reelection in districts that no longer had a high proportion of minority voters. Many minority groups saw this as a reversal in their quest for greater representation. Some even claimed that *Miller* was akin to the 1857 *Scott v. Sandford* decision, which held that African Americans "had no rights which the white man was bound to respect." However, in a significant development, many of those same legislators were in fact reelected in their newly white-dominated districts.

The case of *League of United Latin American Citizens v. Perry* (2006) involved a mid-decade redistricting plan that had been drawn by Texas Republicans with the transparent partisan goal of increasing their representation in Congress and the state legislature. Upholding most of the plan, the Court concluded that the scheme was no more partisan than were most redistricting plans drawn at the beginning of new decades following census returns. However, the Court disallowed the dismantling of one district with a Latino majority in southwest Texas. In this case, the Court ruled that the dilution of the Latino vote violated the Voting Rights Act of 1965.

Steve D. Boilard
Updated by the Editor

FURTHER READING

Bernstein, Mark F. "Racial Gerrymandering." *The Public Interest* (Winter, 1996): 59-70.

DiClerico, Robert E. *Voting in America: A Reference Handbook.* Santa Barbara, Calif.: ABC-Clio, 2004.

Rush, Mark E., ed. *Voting Rights and Redistricting in the United States.* Westport, Conn.: Greenwood Press, 1998.

Savage, David G. "The Redistricting Tangle." *State Legislatures* (September, 1995): 20-24.

Swain, Carol M. "Limited Racial Gerrymandering." *Current* (January, 1996): 3-6.

Zelden, Charles L. *Voting Rights on Trial: A Handbook with Cases, Laws, and Documents.* Santa Barbara, Calif.: ABC-Clio, 2002.

SEE ALSO Fifteenth Amendment; Fourteenth Amendment; Political questions; Poll taxes; Representation, fairness of.

Gibbons v. Ogden

CITATION: 22 U.S. 1
DATE: March 2, 1824
ISSUE: Commerce clause
SIGNIFICANCE: In this watershed ruling, the Supreme Court supported the federal license of a steamboat operator over a state monopoly license holder, thus expanding federal control through the Constitution's commerce clause.

Aaron Ogden had a New York license giving him the exclusive right to operate a steamship between New Jersey and the port of New York City. The license had been purchased from Robert Fulton and Robert Livingston, who had earlier been awarded a monopoly to operate steamships on New York waterways. However, Thomas Gibbons began operating a competing steamship under a federal license. Ogden sued Gibbons to keep him out of New York waters, and the New York state courts accepted the validity of Ogden's monopolistic license. In 1824, the case reached the U.S. Supreme Court. In representing Gibbons, Daniel Webster argued that the New York license interfered with Congress's exclusive prerogative to regulate interstate commerce. Ogden's lawyer countered that navigation was not covered by the commerce clause and that it had traditionally been regulated by the states.

In the Court's first serious attempt to interpret the meaning of the commerce clause, the justices unanimously overturned the New York courts and ruled in favor of Gibbons. Writing the opinion for the Court, Chief Justice John Marshall held that a federal license necessarily took precedence over a state license. Commerce, moreover, included more than buying and selling merchandise; it referred to "every species of commercial intercourse," including travel and navigation on interstate waterways. Marshall went on to assert that Congress had plenary powers over its delegated functions in the Constitution. Probably because of the increasing controversy over regulation of the slave trade, he did not declare that Congress's authority over interstate commerce was exclusive. In a concurring opinion, however, William Johnson, a southern justice with strong nationalist convictions, argued that Congress possessed exclusive powers in this domain, meaning that the states were prohibited from placing any restraints on "the free intercourse among the states," even in the absence of a federal statute.

The issues of commerce raised by this steamboat ruling would become increasingly controversial during the next quarter century. After several inconclusive attempts to formulate an approach acceptable to various interests, the Court would finally arrive at an enduring compromise in *Cooley v. Board of Wardens of the Port of Philadelphia* (1852), affirming the doctrine of selective exclusiveness, based on the view that some aspects of commerce required uniform national regulation while others were best left up to the states.

Richard L. Wilson
Revised and updated by the Editor

FURTHER READING

Baxter, Maurice G. *The Steamboat Monopoly: Gibbons v. Ogden.* New York: Alfred Knopf, 1972.
Levinson, Isabel Simone. *"Gibbons v. Ogden": Controlling Trade Between States.* Springfield, N.J.: Enslow Publishers, 1999.

SEE ALSO Commerce, regulation of; Federalism; Johnson, William; Marshall, John; States' rights and state sovereignty.

Gideon v. Wainwright

CITATION: 372 U.S. 335
DATE: March 18, 1963
ISSUE: Right to counsel
SIGNIFICANCE: In this landmark case, the Supreme Court ruled that counsel must be provided for indigents accused of serious crimes.

Clarence Earl Gideon had convictions for petty crimes as a young man but no criminal convictions when he was arrested for breaking into a poolroom to steal coins and beverages. He requested an attorney be appointed for him, but the judge declined because Florida state law provided court-appointed attorneys only in capital cases. Although Gideon represented himself perhaps better than the average layperson, he was convicted and sentenced as a habitual criminal to five years in prison. While in prison, he filed an *in forma pauperis* (pauper's) petition for a writ of habeas corpus.

In *Betts v. Brady* (1942), the Supreme Court required that states provide counsel only if special circumstances existed, but many states had developed legislation that provided court-appointed counsel for indigents. After 1951, the Court had consistently found "special circumstances" in every case involving states that failed to provide counsel for indigents, and many believed the *Betts* holding was ripe to be overturned. The Court appointed a well-known Washington, D.C., lawyer, Abe Fortas, who later became a Supreme Court justice, to represent Gideon. Fortas obtained a broad overturning of the *Betts* ruling. The Court unanimously reversed earlier decisions, including *Betts v. Brady*, that allowed states to fail to provide counsel to indigents accused of serious crimes by applying the Sixth Amendment to the states through incorporation.

When the case was returned to Florida, a newly appointed local attorney successfully attacked the prosecution's case and demonstrated the wisdom of the Court's requirement by showing that the most likely perpetrators of the crime were the very witnesses the prosecution had called against Gideon. *Gideon* laid the ground work for the far more controversial *Escobedo v. Illinois* (1964) and *Miranda v. Ar-*

izona (1966), which involved police interrogations without the presence of legal counsel.

Richard L. Wilson

See also Black, Hugo L.; Counsel, right to; Due process, procedural; Fortas, Abe; Goldberg, Arthur J.; Incorporation doctrine; *Rompilla v. Beard*; Sixth Amendment.

Ruth Bader Ginsburg

Identification: Associate justice (August 10, 1993-   )
Nominated by: Bill Clinton
Born: March 15, 1933, Brooklyn, New York
Significance: As the second female appointee to the Supreme Court, Ginsburg acquired the reputation of being a moderately liberal justice and continued to pursue her earlier commitment to use law to combat gender discrimination.

The daughter of Russian Jewish immigrants, Ruth Bader Ginsburg completed her undergraduate studies at Cornell University in 1954 and received her law degree from Columbia University in 1959. Although she tied for first place in her class and served on her school's law review staff, she was unable to obtain employment in a major law firm after she graduated. Her experiences with gender discrimination early in her career were similar to those of Justice Sandra Day O'Connor, the first woman to be appointed to the Supreme Court. Recognizing the barriers that lay between her and the private practice of law, Ginsburg sought and obtained a clerkship with a federal district judge, Edmund Palmieri. She then joined the law faculties at Rutgers University and Columbia University.

Ginsburg's commitment to eradicating gender discrimination became evident while she was teaching at Columbia University. As a faculty member, she headed the Women's Rights Project for the American Civil Liberties Union, and she also coauthored a pioneering book, *Text, Cases, and Materials on Sex-Based Discrimination* (1974). As a legal pioneer in the area of gender discrimination, Ginsburg helped put the issue on the legal agenda. Between 1971 and 1976, she argued six gender discrimination cases before the Supreme Court, winning five of them. One of her victories was *Frontiero v. Richardson* (1973), in which the Court overturned a federal law that automatically awarded supplementary benefits to married men but not to married women in the military. The justices declined by only one vote to classify gender as a suspect classification, which would have meant the application of strict scrutiny in cases involving gender discrimination.

President Jimmy Carter appointed Ginsburg to the U.S. Court of Appeals for the District of Columbia in 1980. Serving on the court with Antonin Scalia and Clarence Thomas, both of whom would precede her to the Supreme Court, Ginsburg became known for her scholarly and balanced opinions and her ability to get along with both the liberal and conservative wings of the Court. She advocated gradual change when adjudicating either constitutional law or the

Ruth Bader Ginsburg with President Bill Clinton after her investiture. (AP/Wide World Photos)

common law, observing that "doctrinal limbs too swiftly shaped, experience teaches, may prove unstable."

APPOINTMENT TO THE SUPREME COURT

The moderate political ideology that Ginsburg demonstrated as a circuit court judge matched that of President Bill Clinton, who nominated her to the Supreme Court in 1993. She received the highest recommendation of the American Bar Association. With Democrats having a majority in the Senate, her confirmation hearings lasted only four days, with only one hostile witness allowed to testify. Committee chairman Joseph Biden advised her not to answer any questions that she did not feel comfortable answering. She was then confirmed by a Senate vote of ninety-six to three on August 3, 1993, and became the Court's second female justice.

Unlike many newcomers who apparently suffer from freshman anxiety, Ginsburg seemed comfortable on the Court from the beginning. She quickly acquired the reputation of being an energetic and enthusiastic questioner during oral arguments. Some Court observers labeled her as "aggressive" in this role because of her apparent willingness to interrupt her more senior colleagues in their questioning efforts. Nevertheless known for her politeness, she has never made sarcastic comments or strong attacks on the legal reasoning of others. In her opinions, she has given meticulous attention to details. Her major concern has always been the practical application of the law, giving minimal interest to the historical background of issues. She was soon regarded as the Court's expert on civil procedure, a subject that she had taught for many years.

JURISPRUDENCE AND DECISIONS

Ginsburg had long been a strong advocate of the right of women to terminate unwanted pregnancies, although she argued that the Court should have grounded the right in the equal protection principle rather than in the concept of personal liberty. Informed observers were not surprised when she joined the Court's majority in *Stenberg v. Carhart* (2000), striking down Nebraska's restrictive law on partial-birth abortions. She also could be counted on to support other claims of privacy and liberty interests, such as *Lawrence v. Texas*

(2003), which ruled that states could not outlaw homosexual practices between consenting adults.

The area of sex discrimination is the only area in which Ginsburg
has been a zealous crusader. One of her most controversial opinions
was the majority opinion in *United States v. Virginia* (1996), in which the
Court declared unconstitutional the male-only admission policy at the
publicly supported Virginia Military Institute. When examining claims
of sex discrimination by government, she wrote that the court would
henceforth apply a standard of heightened "skeptical scrutiny," requiring government to demonstrate an "exceedingly persuasive justification" in order to maintain sex-based distinctions. She has firmly -
rejected rationales based on presumptions of "inherent" sex differences
or stereotypes of what was appropriate for "most women."

Ginsburg has not been sympathetic toward claims of "reverse discrimination" when reviewing affirmative action programs designed
to enhance the opportunities of minorities or women. When considering the constitutionality of such programs, she has advocated the
standard of minimal scrutiny. Thus, she dissented in *Adarand Constructors v Peña* (1995), when a 5-4 majority applied the strict scrutiny
standard to racial preferences in federal programs. Likewise, in the
cases of *Grutter v. Bollinger* and *Gratz v. Bollinger* (2003), Ginsburg endorsed race-based preferences, whether based on individualized assessment or not, based on the goal of diversity. Drawing a sharp distinction between classifications that were aimed at "exclusions" and
those aimed at "inclusion," she quoted a United Nations document
approving race-based measures designed to accelerate de facto equality for categories of people.

This practice of looking to international law and foreign courts as a
source of guidance became a matter of some controversy after the
Court's decision in *Roper v. Simmons* (2005), in which a 5-4 majority
held that the execution of minors was unconstitutional. The opinion
for the Court, which Ginsburg joined, took into account current international law on the issue. Justice Antonin Scalia disagreed, expressing
opposition to giving "like-minded foreigners" a role in interpreting the
U.S. Constitution. Likewise, the House of Representatives passed a resolution declaring that foreign laws and pronouncements should never
be used as a source for understanding the U.S. Constitution. Ginsburg

expressed her disagreement with the resolution in a speech before the American Society of International Law. Acknowledging that foreign sources were not authoritative for the Court's decisions, she argued that Americans should be willing to learn from the experiences and "good thinking" of foreigners.

Many commentators have viewed Ginsburg as an advocate of judicial restraint, and it is true that she has frequently declared that legislative acts should be respected whenever possible. When discussing the abortion issue, she even wrote that it would have been preferable if the right to abortion had been gradually accomplished through legislation, even though the process would have taken many years. When she dissented in the controversial case of *Bush v. Gore* (2000), which stopped the recount of presidential ballots in Florida, she blasted the majority for not following the precedent of allowing a state court to interpret the state's laws. Her praise for judicial restraint, however, did not prevent her from voting to strike down some laws in which the question of constitutionality was ambiguous. In *Zelman v. Simmons-Harris* (2002), for example, she joined the minority that opposed the use of tax-supported vouchers in parochial schools, even though the program involved no coercion and only indirectly helped religious institutions.

Paula C. Arledge
Revised and updated by the Editor

FURTHER READING

Bayer, Linda N. *Ruth Bader Ginsburg.* Philadelphia: Chelsea House Publishers, 2000.

Cooper, Phillip J. *Battles on the Bench: Conflicts Inside the Supreme Court.* University Press of Kansas, 1995.

Frederick, David C. *Supreme Court and Appellate Advocacy.* Foreword by Ruth Bader Ginsburg. St. Paul, Minn.: West Group, 2003.

Ginsburg, Ruth Bader. "Remarks for the American Law Institute Annual Dinner." *St. Louis University Law Journal* 38 (Summer, 1994): 884.

Hensley, Thomas R. *The Rehnquist Court: Justices, Rulings, and Legacy.* Santa Barbara, Calif.: ABC-Clio, 2006.

Smith, Christopher E., Joyce Ann Baugh, Thomas R. Hensley, and

Scott Patrick Johnson. "The First-Term Performance of Justice Ruth Bader Ginsburg." *Judicature* 78 (1994): 74-80.

Tushnet, Mark. *A Court Divided: The Rehnquist Court and the Future of Constitutional Law.* New York: W. W. Norton, 2005.

Yarbrough, Tinsley. *The Rehnquist Court and the Constitution.* New York: Oxford University Press, 2000.

SEE ALSO *Bush v. Gore*; Gender issues; *Gratz v. Bollinger/ Grutter v. Bollinger*; Judicial review; O'Connor, Sandra Day; Rehnquist, William H.; *Roper v. Simmons*; *Virginia, United States v.*; *Zelman v. Simmons-Harris.*

Gitlow v. New York

CITATION: 268 U.S. 652
DATE: June 8, 1925
ISSUE: Freedom of speech
SIGNIFICANCE: Although the Supreme Court upheld the conviction of a man for writing and distributing a socialist pamphlet, it determined that the First Amendment guarantee of freedom of speech is so central to the notion of due process under the Fourteenth Amendment that it must be required of the states under the incorporation doctrine.

Justice Edward T. Sanford wrote the opinion for the 7-2 majority upholding the conviction of a socialist, Benjamin Gitlow, for writing and distributing a pamphlet advocating strikes, socialism, and class action in "any form." American Civil Liberties Union attorney Walter H. Pollak defended Gitlow, making a strong case for freedom of expression and succeeding in persuading a unanimous Court to apply the freedom of speech and press sections of the First Amendment to the states through the incorporation doctrine of the Fourteenth Amendment. He failed, however, to get his client's conviction overturned because the majority thought that Gitlow's pamphlet could be a "spark" that could create a real danger to society.

Justice Oliver Wendell Holmes dissented, arguing that Gitlow's pamphlet was not likely to incite action and using his clear and present danger doctrine, which distinguished between speech and action. Justice Louis D. Brandeis joined Holmes's dissent. *Gitlow* remained a theoretical issue until the Court struck down a state law for violating free speech rights in *Stromberg v. California* (1931).

Richard L. Wilson

SEE ALSO Bad tendency test; *Brandenburg v. Ohio*; Censorship; Fourteenth Amendment; Incorporation doctrine; *Schenck v. United States*; Seditious libel; Speech and press, freedom of.

Arthur J. Goldberg

IDENTIFICATION: Associate justice (October 1, 1962-July 25, 1965)
NOMINATED BY: John F. Kennedy
BORN: August 8, 1908, Chicago, Illinois
DIED: January 19, 1990, Washington, D.C.
SIGNIFICANCE: Although he served on the Supreme Court for only three terms, Goldberg provided an articulate and highly influential voice on individual liberties, labor issues, and social justice. He was a key player in several significant decisions by Earl Warren's court, especially those that expanded constitutional rights.

The eleventh and last child of immigrant Russian Jews, Arthur J. Goldberg grew up in one of the poorest sections of Chicago. He worked his way through college and then Northwestern Law School, where he graduated summa cum laude and first in his class. At age twenty, Goldberg was technically too young to be admitted to the Illinois bar; he sued, argued his own case, and won when the judge waived the age restriction for the young lawyer.

ASSOCIATION WITH ORGANIZED LABOR

Despite his outstanding academic record and obvious intelligence, Goldberg was not offered a position with any of the more prestigious Chicago law firms because of anti-Semitic prejudice. He began work with a firm that specialized in property law, including foreclosure on mortgages. Goldberg, who knew firsthand the devastation that the

Great Depression was causing, detested the work, and in 1933 he left to form his own law office, specializing in labor law cases.

Goldberg soon had established what would be a long and close association with organized labor in the United States. In 1938 and 1939 Goldberg was lead counsel for the Newspaper Guild in its bitter battle against the two Chicago newspapers owned and run by William Randolph Hearst. The strike finally ended in May, 1940, but soon after, the Hearst papers closed. However, Goldberg had established his credentials with organized labor and soon was heavily involved with groups such as the Steelworkers Organizing Committee and the Congress of Industrial Organizations. As Goldberg rose higher in the counsels of labor, he was called on more frequently to act as a negotiator, especially in difficult or complex issues.

During the years before World War II (1941-1945), Goldberg took a more active role in civic affairs, for example, joining the Chicago chapter of the White Committee, a group formed by liberal Republican newspaper editor William Allen White to support aid to Great Britain and the other powers fighting Nazi Germany. As member of the White Committee, Goldberg came to know Adlai Stevenson, then a rising star in the Democratic Party.

When World War II began, Goldberg enlisted and served in the Office of Strategic Services, where he helped organize and supply French labor unions in their efforts to resist Nazi occupation of their country.

SERVICE ON THE COURT

Goldberg, a strong supporter of Stevenson during the 1952 and 1956 presidential elections, backed John F. Kennedy in his quest for the Democratic nomination and then the presidency in 1960. When Kennedy was elected, he appointed Goldberg to serve as secretary of labor. Just a year later, on August 28, 1962, Kennedy selected Goldberg to take the seat of Felix Frankfurter, who was retiring from the Supreme Court. Goldberg was approved by the Senate at the end of September.

As a justice, Goldberg quickly showed himself a champion of individual liberties and civil rights. A strong supporter of nonenumerated rights (those not specifically named but clearly implied in the U.S. Constitution, 1789), Goldberg sought to expand these rights even further, especially those associated with the Ninth Amendment. A dependable ally of Chief Justice Earl Warren, Goldberg helped lead the Court to take a decisive stand in a number of major cases, three of them in particular with lasting constitutional impact.

In *Gideon v. Wainwright* (1963), the Court held that a criminal defendant could not be denied legal representation simply because he or she could not afford to pay for an attorney. One of the most famous and influential cases in U.S. legal history, *Gideon* fundamentally transformed the nation's criminal justice system. Taking the lead in *Escobedo v. Illinois* (1964), Goldberg argued that coerced confessions, such as that gained from the suspect in this case, were unconstitutional. Finally, in his concurrence in the Court's ruling on *Griswold v. Connecticut* (1965), Goldberg joined with his brethren to affirm the constitutional right to privacy, in this case marital privacy involving contraception and birth control. Eight years later, in 1973, the Court would look back on Griswold as a significant precedent in its decision to legalize abortion in *Roe v. Wade*.

LIFE AFTER THE COURT

In August, 1965, at the urging of President Lyndon B. Johnson, Goldberg resigned from the Supreme Court to take the position of U.S. ambassador to the United Nations. Although many wondered at the decision, Goldberg explained he felt a sense of public duty, especially in efforts to negotiate an end to the escalating conflict in Vietnam. However, he was unsuccessful in his efforts and, finding himself increasingly at odds with the Johnson administration's use of ever greater military force, Goldberg resigned on April 23, 1968.

In 1970 Goldberg narrowly won the Democratic primary nomination for governor of New York. However, the campaign was a difficult one, and Goldberg was decisively defeated by Republican Nelson A. Rockefeller, who won his fourth term in the November election. Leaving partisan politics, Goldberg remained active in public life and in 1977 and 1978 served as ambassador at large for President Jimmy Carter. Carter honored Goldberg with the Presidential Medal of Freedom in 1978. Goldberg returned to the practice of law and died in Washington, D.C., in 1990.

Michael Witkoski

FURTHER READING

Bader, William H., and Roy M. Mersky, eds. *The First One Hundred Eight Justices.* Buffalo, N.Y.: William S. Hein, 2004.

Cushman, Clare, ed. *The Supreme Court Justices: Illustrated Biographies.* 2d ed. Washington, D.C.: Congressional Quarterly, 1995.

Stebenne, David. *Arthur J. Goldberg: New Deal Liberal.* New York: Oxford University Press, 1996.

Urofsky, Melvin I. *The Warren Court: Justices, Rulings, and Legacy.* Santa Barbara, Calif.: ABC-Clio, 2001.

SEE ALSO Birth control and contraception; Counsel, right to; Fortas, Abe; *Gideon v. Wainwright*; *Griswold v. Connecticut*; Ninth Amendment; Resignation and retirement; Warren, Earl.

Good News Club v. Milford Central School

CITATION: 533 U.S. 98
DATE: June 11, 2001
ISSUES: Equality for religious expression; separation of church and state
SIGNIFICANCE: The Supreme Court held that all public schools must open their doors for after-school religious activities on the same basis that school policy permits other after-hours activities.

In an earlier decision, *Lamb's Chapel v. Center Moriches Union Free School District* (1993), the Supreme Court had held that public high school property must be open to groups with religious messages so long as they could be used by other groups. Since the *Lamb's Chapel* case had involved an adult activity during evening hours, the Court had not addressed whether the same analysis would apply to activities involving young children as soon as the regular school day ends. When a school district in New York followed a policy of not allowing "quintessentially religious" subjects to be taught in elementary school buildings, an evangelical Christian organization for young boys and girls, the Good News Club, sued the district in federal court. The appeals court in Manhattan ruled in favor of the district, emphasizing the special susceptibility of young children to indoctrination.

Reversing the lower court's ruling by a 6-3 vote, the Supreme Court reaffirmed that the expression of religious viewpoints is protected by the First Amendment against discrimination on school property. Writing for the majority, Justice Clarence Thomas relied on the Court's well-established neutrality principle, and he argued that the danger that young children might misperceive an open-door policy as an endorsement of religion was no greater "that they might perceive a hostility toward the religious viewpoint if the club were excluded from the public forum." With Justice Stephen Breyer writing an equivocal concurring opinion, five members of the Court appeared not to make any distinctions among religious speech, worship services, and recruitment activities.

Thomas Tandy Lewis

SEE ALSO Breyer, Stephen G.; Religion, establishment of; Religion, freedom of; Thomas, Clarence

Grandfather Clause

DESCRIPTION: Legal provision enacted in some southern states after the passage of the Fifteenth Amendment that exempted men who could vote before 1866 and their descendants from suffrage restrictions such as literacy tests and poll taxes.

SIGNIFICANCE: Until the Supreme Court struck down grandfather clauses as a violation of the Fifteenth Amendment to the U.S. Constitution, states used this as a method to disenfranchise blacks and allow illiterate white men to vote.

The Fifteenth Amendment, adopted in 1870, guaranteed that citizens of the United States could not be denied their right to vote by the federal or state government on account of race, color, or previous condition of servitude. However, many southern states passed laws, including grandfather clauses, designed to disenfranchise African Americans through literacy tests or poll taxes.

Guinn v. United States (1915) involved an Oklahoma law that required all voters to prove that they or a direct ancestor could vote before 1866 or to pass a literacy test. The Supreme Court found the grandfather clause to be an unconstitutional evasion of the Fifteenth Amendment. Although the Oklahoma provision did not directly cite race, most white men could prove that an ancestor could vote. Therefore, it was mostly people of color who were forced to take the literacy test. In *Lance v. Wilson* (1939), the Court ruled that literacy tests were also unconstitutional.

Siobhan McCabe
Matthew Lindstrom

SEE ALSO Civil Rights movement; Fifteenth Amendment; Gerrymandering; Poll taxes; Reconstruction; Slavery.

Gratz v. Bollinger/ Grutter v. Bollinger

CITATION: 539 U.S 306; 539 U.S. 244
DATE: June 23, 2003
ISSUES: Affirmative action; civil rights
SIGNIFICANCE: Declaring that government has a compelling interest in promoting student diversity, the Supreme Court upheld the constitutionality of narrowly tailored affirmative action programs for admissions into highly competitive universities.

In the seminal case of *Regents of the University of California v. Bakke* (1978), the Supreme Court endorsed admissions programs that provided limited preferences for members of underrepresented groups. The use of such programs became one of the most controversial issues in American society. The future of the programs became doubtful after the Court in *Adarand Constructors v. Peña* (1995) held that the programs would henceforth be evaluated according to the strict scrutiny standard. Applying this standard in 1996, the Court of Appeals for the Fifth Circuit announced that all race-based admissions policies were unconstitutional. The Supreme Court declined to review the decision.

The admissions policy at the University of Michigan Law School continued to provide racial preferences in order to achieve a "critical mass" of underrepresented minority students. After Barbara Grutter, a white student with a 3.8 undergraduate grade point average and an LSAT score of 161, failed to gain admission to the school, she sued with the argument that the preferences violated the equal protection clause and the 1964 Civil Rights Act. Although she won at the district court level, the appellate court upheld the university's affirmative action policy.

In a 5-4 decision, to the surprise of many observers, the Supreme Court also upheld the policy. Delivering the majority opinion, Justice Sandra Day O'Connor argued that the policy was "narrowly tailored" to further a compelling interest in seeking the benefits of a diverse student body. She emphasized that each student was individually reviewed, that factors other than race and ethnicity were considered, that the goal of a "critical mass" was not equivalent to a quota, and that the preferences did "not unduly harm majority students." Finally, she wrote of her expectation that the preferences would no longer be necessary after the passage of twenty-five years.

On the same day that the *Grutter* ruling was announced, the Court also announced *Gratz v. Bollinger,* in which the university's admissions policy for minorities was found unconstitutional by a 6-3 margin. For selecting undergraduates, the university had simply added a 20 percent increase in the number of points to every underrepresented minority applicant without any individualized assessment. Chief Justice William H. Rehnquist declared that because the automatic preferences were not narrowly tailored, they did not survive a review according to the strict scrutiny standards.

Thomas Tandy Lewis

SEE ALSO Affirmative action; O'Connor, Sandra Day; Race and discrimination; *Regents of the University of California v. Bakke;* Rehnquist, William H.

Horace Gray

IDENTIFICATION: Associate justice (January 9, 1882-September 15, 1902)

NOMINATED BY: Chester A. Arthur

BORN: March 24, 1828, Boston, Massachusetts

DIED: September 15, 1902, Washington, D.C.

SIGNIFICANCE: Gray brought considerable judicial experience and wide legal learning to the Supreme Court, especially in the area of common law. Writing more than 450 Court opinions, he strongly promoted the right of states to enact legislation.

After graduating from Harvard Law School in 1851, Horace Gray served as reporter of the Massachusetts Supreme Court from 1854 to 1861. He was one of the early organizers of the Free-Soil Party and later the Republican Party in Massachusetts. Frequently, he provided advice to Massachusetts governor John Andrew on legal problems

Horace Gray.
(Library of Congress)

arising from the Civil War. Andrew named Gray to the state supreme court in 1864, and he remained on that bench for seventeen years, serving the last eight as chief justice.

Gray was appointed to the Supreme Court by President Chester A. Arthur in 1881 and was confirmed in 1882. Although often overshadowed by some better-known colleagues, he brought considerable legal experience to the Court, particularly his expertise in common law and his command of precedent. His most notable case, one of the *Legal Tender Cases*, was *Juilliard v. Greenman* (1884), which validated the continued circulation of Civil War notes. In the *United States v. Wong Kim Ark* (1898), Gray wrote that the Fourteenth Amendment made citizenship a birthright regardless of the race or national origin of a person who applied for naturalization.

Alvin K. Benson

SEE ALSO Bail; Clerks of the justices; Common law; Fuller, Melville W.; Judicial review; Waite, Morrison R.

Gregg v. Georgia

CITATION: 428 U.S. 153
DATE: July 2, 1976
ISSUE: Capital punishment
SIGNIFICANCE: The Supreme Court held that the use of capital punishment, with proper procedures and safeguards, is not inconsistent with the requirements of the Eighth and Fourteenth Amendments.

The Court ruled in *Furman v. Georgia* (1972) that capital punishment as commonly practiced in 1972 violated the U.S. Constitution. In response, thirty-five state legislatures and Congress revised their capital punishment statues in order to eliminate as much arbitrariness and unfairness as possible. The state of Georgia amended its statute to include three requirements: consideration of both aggravating and mitigating circumstances before a death sentence is rendered, a bifurcated trial for the separate determinations of guilt and punishment, and an automatic appeal to the state's highest court to examine whether a sentence of death might have been imposed in an arbitrary or disproportionate manner. After Troy Leon Gregg was sentenced to death under the new law, his lawyers appealed the case to the Supreme Court.

By a 7-2 vote, the Court upheld Georgia's statute. Justice Potter Stewart's plurality opinion argued that the use of the death penalty was not cruel and unusual in and of itself. Stewart emphasized American traditions and the intent of the constitutional Framers, and he noted that current public opinion was reflected in the capital punishment statues that had been passed by the majority of the states. He insisted, moreover, that legislatures did not have the burden of proving that capital punishment was an effective deterrent and that retribution was neither a forbidden objective nor inconsistent with respect for human dignity. The two dissenters, Justices William J. Brennan, Jr., and Thurgood Marshall, insisted that capital punishment was inherently unconstitutional. Marshall wrote that capital punishment was not necessary as a deterrent to crime and that the public, if it were informed, would reject the practice as "morally unacceptable."

The same day the Court announced *Gregg*, it announced *Woodson v. North Carolina* (1976), which stuck down a state law requiring a mandatory death sentence for select crimes. Following the *Gregg* and *Woodson* holdings, the Court decided many issues regarding the circumstances in which capital punishment was permissible. By the late 1980's the Court appeared to reflect public opinion as it increasingly took a prodeath penalty stance. In *McCleskey v. Kemp* (1987), for example, the Court rejected a challenge to capital punishment based on evidence of disparate racial impact. In 1995 a record fifty-six people were executed and more than three thousand inmates were on death row.

Thomas Tandy Lewis

SEE ALSO Capital punishment; Due process, procedural; Eighth Amendment; Fourteenth Amendment; *McCleskey v. Kemp*; *Payne v. Tennessee*.

Robert C. Grier

IDENTIFICATION: Associate justice (August 10, 1846-January 31, 1870)
NOMINATED BY: James K. Polk
BORN: March 5, 1794, Cumberland County, Pennsylvania
DIED: September 25, 1870, Philadelphia, Pennsylvania
SIGNIFICANCE: A Supreme Court justice noted for his forthright and scholarly opinions, Grier typically upheld the power of the states. In 1863 his opinion extended the president's powers by providing legal authority for the chief executive's use of emergency power before congressional authorization.

Robert C. Grier graduated from Dickinson College in 1812 and was admitted to the Pennsylvania bar in 1817. He enjoyed notable success in law and was appointed president judge of the district court of Allegheny County in 1833. In 1846 he was appointed to the Supreme

Robert C. Grier. (Handy Studios/Collection of the Supreme Court of the United States)

Court by President James K. Polk to fill the vacancy left by the death of Henry Baldwin.

Although a Democrat, Grier was an avid supporter of President Abraham Lincoln during the Civil War. He concurred in *Scott v. Sandford* (1857), and in his most important opinion, he spoke for the Court in the 1863 *Prize Cases*, validating President Lincoln's proclamation of a blockade of Confederate ports and the subsequent seizure of neutral shipping. Grier did not consider armed opposition to the Fugitive Slave Act to be treason because it did not amount to levying war. He concurred with the Court's decision in *Cummings v. Missouri* (1867), which denied the legal requirement that certain job applicants had to swear an oath that they had not opposed the Union during the Civil War.

Alvin K. Benson

See also Baldwin, Henry; Bradley, Joseph P.; Civil War; Presidential powers; *Scott v. Sandford*.

Griggs v. Duke Power Co.

Citation: 401 U.S. 424
Date: March 8, 1971
Issue: Employment discrimination
Significance: The Supreme Court interpreted Title VII of the 1964 Civil Rights Law so that if employment practices have an adverse effect on minorities or women, employers are required to show that the practices are clearly related to job performance.

On July 2, 1965, the day that Title VII took effect, Duke Power instituted a new policy of requiring high school graduation and minimum grades on aptitude tests as requirements for jobs previously reserved for whites. Although the requirements applied to all races, the effect was to disqualify a disproportionate number of African Americans. Only 12 percent of African Americans in North Carolina had completed high school, compared with 34 percent of whites in the state.

By an 8-0 vote, the Supreme Court ruled that the power company's requirements violated Title VII. Chief Justice Warren E. Burger explained that the purpose of the law was "to achieve equality of employment opportunities and remove barriers that have operated in the past to favor an identifiable group of white employees over other employees." Whenever qualifications for employment have a disparate impact on minority groups, the employer has the burden of demonstrating that the qualifications are a reasonable measure of potential job performance.

Because of the cost and difficulty in validating job requirements, critics argue that the landmark *Griggs* decision put pressure on employers to discard reasonable requirements or to adopt hiring quotas. *Wards Cove Packing Co. v. Atonio* (1989) shifted the burden of proof to the plaintiff to show that employment practices were discriminatory, but the Civil Rights Act of 1991 returned the burden to employers.

Thomas Tandy Lewis

SEE ALSO Affirmative action; Burger, Warren E.; Employment discrimination; Race and discrimination.

Griswold v. Connecticut

CITATION: 381 U.S. 479
DATE: June 5, 1965
ISSUES: Birth control; right to privacy; substantive due process; unenumerated rights
SIGNIFICANCE: While overturning a Connecticut statute that had prohibited the use of contraceptives in this case, the Supreme Court explicitly recognized constitutional protection for a generic right to privacy.

According to the doctrine of substantive due process, which was implicitly utilized in *Griswold v. Connecticut*, the due process clauses of the Fifth and Fourteenth Amendments prohibited government from depriving persons of liberty arbitrarily or without adequate justification. From 1897 to 1937, the Court consistently used the doctrine to protect a liberty of contract, thus limiting the government's power to regulate the economy in the public interest. For this reason, liberal justices, such as Hugo L. Black and William O. Douglas, distrusted the doctrine. Nevertheless, the Court several times had applied the doctrine in protecting noneconomic liberties not mentioned in the Constitution, as in *Pierce v. Society of Sisters* (1925), which affirmed the right of parents to send their children to private schools.

A Connecticut statute of 1879 criminalized the use and dissemination of contraceptives. In *Tileston v. Ullman* (1943) and *Poe v. Ullman* (1961), the Court refused to make a ruling on the law's constitutionality because of the issues of ripeness and standing. Estelle Griswold, director of the Planned Parenthood League of Connecticut, was one of the leaders in the movement to repeal the law, which was primarily being utilized to prevent the operation of birth-control clinics. After she and an associate opened a clinic, they were arrested and convicted of misdemeanors under the 1879 statute. The convictions were upheld by Connecticut's high court.

On appeal, the U.S. Supreme Court reversed the convictions by a 7-2 vote. Delivering the opinion of the Court, Justice William O. Douglas argued that the specific protections in the Bill of Rights had penumbras, or emanations extending beyond the literal words of the amendments. He referred to a series of precedents, including *National Association for the Advancement of Colored People v. Alabama* (1958), which had broadly interpreted the First Amendment to imply a right of association. Douglas asserted that another protected penumbra was the right to privacy, which included protection for intimate marital relationships. He asked rhetorically: "Would we allow the police to search the sacred precincts of marital bedrooms for tell-tale signs of the use of contraceptives?"

Other justices wrote three concurring opinions and two dissenting opinions. Justice Arthur Goldberg, joined by William J. Brennan, Jr., argued that the Ninth Amendment demonstrated the framers' belief in fundamental rights not enumerated in the Constitution. Justice John Marshall Harlan relied more openly on the doctrine of substantive due process, writing that the Connecticut law violated the "basic values implicit in the concept of ordered liberty." Similarly, Justice Byron R. White declared that the statute had deprived married couples "of 'liberty' without due process of law." Dissenting, Justice Hugo L.

Black argued that it was just as wrong for justices to impose their personal preferences in matters of personal liberty as in matters of economic relations. Justice Potter Stewart joined Black's dissent, although he observed that the law was "uncommonly silly."

The *Griswold* ruling did not attract much attention from the public at the time it was issued. Eight years later, however, the logic of the ruling provided the foundation for *Roe v. Wade*, which recognized the right of women to terminate unwanted pregnancies. Afterward, the right of privacy was extended to several related areas, such as the right to refuse any medical services (*Cruzan v. Missouri Dept. of Health*, 1990) and the right of consenting adults to engage in homosexual practices in their private homes (*Lawrence v. Texas*, 2003). During the early twenty-first century, many justices preferred to speak of "liberty interests" rather than the right of privacy.

Thomas Tandy Lewis

SEE ALSO Abortion; Birth control and contraception; Fifth Amendment; First Amendment; Fourth Amendment; *Lawrence v. Texas*; Ninth Amendment; *Pierce v. Society of Sisters*; Privacy, right to; *Roe v. Wade*.

Guarantee Clause

DATE: 1789

DESCRIPTION: Clause in Article IV, section 4, of the U.S. Constitution empowering the national government to guarantee to each state a republican form of government.

SIGNIFICANCE: This clause was important in the development of the political question doctrine. The Supreme Court held that the clause provides no basis for judicial review of presidential or congressional action or inaction or of claims that state laws violate the U.S. Constitution.

As a basis of national power, the guarantee clause has seldom been invoked. President Abraham Lincoln relied on it for authority to suppress the rebellion of the Southern states during the Civil War, and Congress, with the subsequent support of the Supreme Court

(*Texas v. White*, 1869), used it to justify the post-Civil War Reconstruction laws. Its principal significance in constitutional law has been in the Court's nonjusticiability jurisprudence. In a trespass action arising out of Dorr's Rebellion (1842), the Court faced the vexing problem of determining which of the warring factions was the legitimate government of Rhode Island when the alleged trespass occurred. Instead of deciding, the Court, in *Luther v. Borden* (1849), said that the guarantee clause left to Congress alone the task of deciding "what government is the established one in a State." For more than a century, Luther became the leading case, and the guarantee clause the primary example, for the principle that certain issues were, nonjusticiable because they posed political questions properly left to the political branches. Similarly, the court rejected challenges to Oregon's initiative and referendum procedures in *Pacific States Telephone and Telegraph Co. v. Oregon* (1912) and Kentucky's election procedures in *Taylor v. Beckham* (1900).

In *Baker v. Carr* (1962), the Court reaffirmed that a challenge to state legislative apportionment was nonjusticiable under the guarantee clause, which was not "a repository of judicially manageable standards which a court could utilize independently in order to identify a state's lawful government." Nevertheless, the Court allowed the challenge to proceed under the equal protection clause of the Fourteenth Amendment, reaffirming the Court's position that its reluctance to apply the guarantee clause is based not on deference to state governments but on its relationship to the coordinate branches of the federal government; in other words, it is a question of separation of powers, not one of federalism.

It has long been argued that the Court should invoke the guarantee clause to protect state autonomy against federal interference and to protect individuals against state tyranny. The Court's use of the Tenth Amendment to accomplish the former in *New York v. United States* (1992), following the use of the equal protection clause to accomplish the latter in *Baker,* gave new impetus to the case for a guarantee clause jurisprudence that would give federal courts an active role on both fronts while maintaining appropriate deference to the president, Congress, and the states.

William V. Dunlap

FURTHER READING

Bonfield, Arthur. "The Guarantee Clause of Article IV, Section 4: A Study in Congressional Desuetude." *Minnesota Law Review* 46, no. 513 (1962).

Merritt, Deborah Jones. "The Guarantee Clause and State Autonomy: Federalism for a Third Century." *Columbia Law Review* 88 (1988).

Wiecek, William M. *The Guarantee Clause of the U.S. Constitition.* Clark, N.J.: Lawbook Exchange, 2004.

SEE ALSO *Baker v. Carr;* Judicial review; Political questions; State action; States' rights and state sovereignty.

Habeas Corpus

DESCRIPTION: Right of prisoners to have the constitutionality of their imprisonment reviewed by a federal court.

SIGNIFICANCE: Although the right of habeas corpus is guaranteed by both the U.S. Constitution and federal statutes, the Supreme Court has played a significant role in determining the scope and limits of habeas review.

Habeas corpus, literally "you have the body," originated as a common-law writ in England. In the United States, the writ of habeas corpus was guaranteed in Article I of the U.S. Constitution. Federal statutes enacted in 1789 and 1867 empowered federal courts to hear habeas cases for federal and state prisoners.

Habeas corpus, often called a collateral attack, is a limited right. Its basic purpose is to ensure that a person's constitutional right to liberty is not being violated. It is available only to people who are in custody and who have already exhausted the direct appeals of their conviction. It is technically a civil action rather than criminal, and the prisoner's actual guilt or innocence is not the issue. Instead, the prisoner must prove that something about his or her incarceration violates the Constitution. Most frequently, the prisoner will claim constitutional errors occurred during the original trial (for example, that the jury was improperly chosen) or that there is something unconstitutional about the sentence given (for example, that it is cruel and unusual punishment). Prisoners who succeed with their habeas claims are not typically set free but instead are given a new trial or new sentence. Significantly, even if the prisoner was convicted and incarcerated by a state, habeas corpus proceedings may be brought in federal court.

THE WARREN COURT

Although the right to habeas corpus is as old as the Constitution, the rules relating to the scope of habeas review were primarily set by the Supreme Court during the second half of the twentieth century. During the years when Earl Warren was chief justice of the Supreme Court (1953-1969), the Court took an expansive view of the right. A majority of the justices believed that this was necessary because of the extreme importance of the right to liberty. Broad reviews of trial courts' decisions would protect the right to liberty and ensure that correct decisions were reached.

An example of the Warren Court's approach to habeas is the case of *Fay v. Noia* (1963), in which the Court upheld Noia's habeas challenge of his felony murder conviction. Noia's conviction had been based entirely on a confession that had been coerced in violation of his Fifth Amendment rights. Justice William J. Brennan, Jr., writing for the majority, stated that habeas was the "ultimate remedy" in the struggle for personal liberty.

Not all jurists and legal scholars agreed with the Warren Court's approach to habeas law. In fact, during the tenures of Chief Justices Warren E. Burger and William H. Rehnquist, a majority of the justices adopted a considerably narrower view of the scope of habeas corpus relief. The primary reason was their concern over the number of habeas cases federal courts were compelled to hear. In addition to burdening the courts, this interfered with the finality of decisions, encouraged frivolous claims, and contributed to the drawing out of legal proceedings. In death penalty cases, for example, habeas challenges could delay executions for decades. Furthermore, these justices believed, federalism required that federal courts give great respect to state courts' decisions.

A CHANGING VIEW

One of the most significant post-Warren habeas decisions was *Stone v. Powell* (1976). Defendants in two different cases challenged their convictions on the grounds that the trial courts had admitted evidence that was the product of unconstitutional searches and seizures. The Court held that prisoners cannot raise Fourth Amendment issues in habeas cases if they had a fair chance to litigate those issues in the state courts.

The Court further limited habeas rights in *Teague v. Lane* (1989), a case that dealt with the retroactivity of court decisions. If a federal court announces a new rule of criminal procedure after a prisoner's conviction is final, that prisoner may not take advantage of that rule in subsequent habeas claims. The reason given for this decision was the interest in preserving the finality of decisions; without such a rule, it was argued, established convictions would be perpetually subject to review as the law evolved.

In 1993 in *Herrera v. Collins*, the Court again endorsed a restricted view of the right to habeas corpus. Herrera had been sentenced to death for murdering a police officer. Several years after he had exhausted his direct appeals and after he had filed several unsuccessful habeas petitions, he brought a new habeas claim in federal court, claiming that new evidence had appeared that would prove his actual innocence of the crime. The Court held that he was not entitled to habeas relief based solely on a claim of actual innocence; because he could point out no procedural errors at his original trial, his death sentence was affirmed.

By the end of the twentieth century, the Court's conservative approach to habeas corpus was well established. This approach was supported by Congress, which in 1996 passed the Anti-Terrorism and Effective Death Penalty Act. Among other things, the act required that habeas claims be brought no more than one year after a claimant had exhausted his or her state appeals and generally limited prisoners to a single habeas petition.

Phyllis B. Gerstenfeld

FURTHER READING

Del Carmen, Rolando V. *Criminal Procedure: Law and Practice.* 6th ed. Belmont, Calif.: Thomson/Wadsworth, 2004.

Del Carmen, Rolando V., Mary Parker, and Frances P. Reddington. *Briefs of Leading Cases in Juvenile Justice.* Cincinnati: Anderson, 1998.

Emanuel, S. L. *Criminal Procedure.* Aspen, Colo.: Aspen Publishing, 2003.

Samaha, Joel. *Criminal Procedure.* 6th ed. Belmont, Calif.: Wadsworth, 2005.

Stahlkopf, Deborah. "A Dark Day for Habeas Corpus: Successive Petitions under the Antiterrorism and Effective Death Penalty Act of 1996." *Arizona Law Review* 40 (1998): 1115.

Wood, Horace G. *A Treatise on the Legal Remedies of Mandamus and Prohibition: Habeas Corpus, Certiorari, and Quo Warranto.* 3d ed. Revised and enlarged by Charles F. Bridge. Littleton, Colo.: Fred B. Rothman, 1997.

SEE ALSO Brennan, William J., Jr.; Civil War; *Debs, In re*; Due process, substantive; Military and the Court; *Milligan, Ex parte*; Warren, Earl.

Hamdan v. Rumsfeld

CITATION: 548 U.S. ___
DATE: June 29, 2006
ISSUE: Military commissions for trials of foreign nationals
SIGNIFICANCE: In this ruling, the Supreme Court held that the president did not have the authority to establish military commissions to try foreign nationals without congressional authorization. In addition, the Court held that foreign detainees had the rights guaranteed by the Geneva Convention on Prisoners of War.

After the terrorist attacks of September 11, 2001, the Bush administration launched its war on terrorism, targeting members of the al-Qaeda organization in Afghanistan. The U.S. military captured hundreds of foreign nationals, many of whom were taken to the U.S.

military base at Guantanamo Bay, Cuba. The administration argued that these prisoners lacked prisoner of war status because they were not fighting in uniform for an organized country. The administration insisted that the prisoners were therefore not entitled to the protections of the Geneva Convention of 1949. The prisoners were kept in indefinite detention, without counsel and usually without specific charges of illegal acts. In *Rasul v. Bush* (2004), the Court ruled that the detainees had the right to petition for writs of habeas corpus relief in federal courts.

In a presidential order of 2001, the Bush administration had made plans to have foreign nationals accused of war crimes to be tried before special military commissions. To defend the legality of the order, the administration referred to the inherent powers of the president as commander in chief and to the congressional Authorization for the Use of Military Force (AUMF) of 2001. In addition, administration lawyers pointed to the precedents of World War II, when the Court had approved trials of such a policy. Civil libertarians disliked several aspects of the commissions. They noted that the commissions were not entirely independent of the executive; in addition, the commissions could use evidence obtained by torture, as well as secret evidence that the defendant's lawyer could not examine. The commissions' verdicts, moreover, could not be appealed to civilian courts.

Salim Ahmed Hamdan, a Yemeni national who had worked as a driver for Osama bin Laden, was one of the suspected terrorists captured in Afghanistan and detained at Guantanamo. He and nine other detainees were charged with conspiracy to commit acts of terrorism. Hamdan's lawyers petitioned for a writ of habeas corpus, arguing that the commissions were illegal, that Hamdan was entitled to all the protections of a prisoner of war under the Geneva Convention, and that he should not be tried until his status was determined. The district court partly ruled in his favor, but the Court of Appeals endorsed the government's position.

Reviewing Hamdan's habeas corpus petition, the Supreme Court rendered the administration a major setback in *Hamdan v. Rumsfeld* (2006), which held, by 5-3 vote, that the special commissions were illegal under both the Geneva Convention and the Uniform Code of Military Justice (UCMJ). Writing the majority opinion, Justice John

Military prison housing hundreds of foreign nationals at Guantanamo Bay U.S. Naval Base in June, 2006. (AP/Wide World Photos)

Paul Stevens further found that Congress's AUMF did not expand presidential war powers. Even if special commissions were later to be authorized by congressional authority, they would have to include all the procedures of the UCMJ and the Geneva Convention. Stevens firmly rejected the administration's claim that the detainees did not merit the protections of the Geneva Convention because they lacked the status of lawful combatants. He insisted that each detainee was entitled to the convention's full protections until a court ruled him not to be a prisoner of war. The three dissenting justices were sharply critical of the majority's ruling.

Although most observers expected that Congress would eventually authorize the creation of military commissions, the Court's 2006 decision was still important, for it helped to clarify the constitutional prerogatives of the president as commander in chief of the military.

Thomas Tandy Lewis

SEE ALSO Habeas corpus; Presidential powers; Stevens, John Paul; Thomas, Clarence; War powers.

Hammer v. Dagenhart

CITATION: 247 U.S. 251

DATE: June 3, 1918

ISSUE: Regulation of manufacturing

SIGNIFICANCE: Striking down federal restrictions on child labor, the Supreme Court held that Congress could regulate only interstate commerce, not the manufacturing of goods destined for such commerce.

Influenced by the Progressive movement, Congress in 1916 passed the Keating-Owen Child Labor Act, which banned from interstate commerce any goods made in a plant using child labor. By a 5-4 vote, the Supreme Court ruled that the statute was unconstitutional. Using the same reasoning as in *United States v. E. C. Knight Co.* (1895), Justice William R. Day based his opinion on a distinction between manufacturing and commerce, in combination with the doctrine of dual federalism. The states, under their police powers and the Tenth Amendment, possessed broad authority to regulate manufacturing, but the federal government, under the commerce clause, could only regulate those goods and services directly related to interstate commerce.

In a spirited dissent, Justice Oliver Wendell Holmes accused the majority of reading their own economic prejudices into the Constitution, and he insisted that there was an adequate connection between manufacturing and commerce to justify the law. Despite a public outcry, the Court overturned a second child labor law in *Bailey v. Drexel Furniture Co.* (1922). The two decisions were finally overturned in *United States v. Darby Lumber Co.* (1941).

Thomas Tandy Lewis

SEE ALSO Clarke, John H.; Commerce, regulation of; *Darby Lumber Co., United States v.*; Day, William R.; Federalism; Progressivism; Tenth Amendment.

John M. Harlan II

IDENTIFICATION: Associate justice (March 28, 1955-September 23, 1971)

NOMINATED BY: Dwight D. Eisenhower

BORN: May 20, 1899, Chicago, Illinois

DIED: December 29, 1971, Washington, D.C.

SIGNIFICANCE: As an associate on the Supreme Court, Harlan was regarded as the Court's conservative conscience. He believed that the content of constitutional provisions changed and moved with the times and was the author of the constitutional right to privacy.

The family of John M. Harlan II was noted for public service. A Quaker forebear, George Harlan, came to America in 1687 and later became governor of Delaware. His grandfather, John Marshall Harlan, for whom he was named, was a Supreme Court justice from 1877 to 1911. His father, John Maynard Harlan, practiced law and served as a city alderman in Chicago. The young Harlan graduated with honors in 1920 from Princeton and spent three years as a Rhodes Scholar at Oxford, taking an A.B. with a first in jurisprudence in 1923.

LEGAL CAREER

After returning from England, Harlan joined the prestigious New York City law firm of Root, Clark, Buckner, and Howland and began studying at the New York Law School. Harlan earned his L.L.B. in 1924, was admitted to the New York bar in 1925, and became a partner in his firm in 1931. Eighteen months after joining the firm, one of Harlan's superiors and his mentor, Emory R. Buckner, was named U.S. Attorney in Manhattan. Buckner served two years in that position and took Harlan with him for the duration. Harlan became the head of the Prohibition Division, enforcing the Volstead Act, the federal law implementing Prohibition.

After becoming a partner in his law firm, Harlan meticulously represented some of the top corporations in the United States. During World War II (1941-1945), he served as a colonel in the U.S. Army Air Force, in charge of the operations analysis section of the Eighth

Bomber command in England. In 1951 Governor Thomas E. Dewey appointed Harlan chief counsel to a state commission investigating links between organized crime and state government in New York.

In January, 1954, President Dwight D. Eisenhower nominated Harlan to the Second U.S. Circuit Court of Appeals. Harlan was confirmed on February 9, 1954, but in October, 1954, Justice Robert H. Jackson died, and Eisenhower sent Harlan's name to the Senate. On March 28, 1955, the Senate voted 71 to 11 to confirm Harlan's nomination. He remained on the Court until September 23, 1971, when he resigned because of failing health.

CONSTITUTIONAL PHILOSOPHY

Harlan served on the Court during a time when a majority of the Court was determined to use the power of the federal courts to help remedy societal ills. Because Harlan generally opposed this mission, he is sometimes thought to have held a restrictive view of federal court remedial power. Harlan dissented from many of the sweeping decisions of Earl Warren's court, such as the one person, one vote ruling in *Reynolds v. Sims* (1964). "The Constitution [1789] is not a panacea for every blot upon the public welfare," Harlan wrote, "nor should this Court, ordained as a judicial body, be thought of as a general haven for reform movements." Although he was cautious in exercising judicial power, he nevertheless held a very expansive and generous view of federal court authority to grant traditional damage and equitable remedies. Harlan favored traditional implication standards, which involved implying or inferring an appropriate remedy from a statute whenever the statute did not expressly state a remedy. He believed that a jurisdiction to give effect to the policy of the legislature is inherent in the courts of equity.

Harlan's conservatism had two key aspects: his respect for the legislature and his refusal to view the Court as a legitimate engine of political reform. These qualities are revealed in his dissenting opinions in such cases as *Miranda v. Arizona* (1966), *Baker v. Carr* (1962), and *Mapp v. Ohio* (1961). In these dissents, he defined his conservatism by such characteristics as an arduous dedication to analyzing the record of the case, a refusal to twist the historical truth to reach a desired result, a respect for adjacent institutions, and a vision of a judicial opinion as a ruling tailored to address the specific legal issues presented to the Court in a given case.

PRIVACY AND OTHER RIGHTS

Although Harlan was perceived as a conservative, he wrote an opinion establishing freedom of private association as a fully guaranteed right in *National Association for the Advancement of Colored People v. Alabama* (1958) and ruled for the Court that indigent women have the right to sue for divorce at state expense in *Boddie v. Connecticut* (1971). He also concluded that the First Amendment's free speech provision is broad enough to protect a man wearing a jacket embroidered with a common obscenity denouncing the draft in public in *Cohen v. California* (1971). In addition, Harlan is regarded as the author of the constitutional right to privacy with his dissenting opinion in *Poe v. Ullman* (1961). Justice William O. Douglas cited this dissent as the source of his "penumbra" of privacy in his opinion for the Court in *Griswold v. Connecticut* (1965), which firmly put the right of privacy into constitutional law.

Dana P. McDermott

FURTHER READING

Bader, William H., and Roy M. Mersky, eds. *The First One Hundred Eight Justices*. Buffalo, N.Y.: William S. Hein, 2004.

Friedman, Leon, and Fred L. Israel, eds. *The Justices of the United States Supreme Court: Their Lives and Major Opinions*. 5 vols. New York: Chelsea House, 1997.

Hensley, Thomas R. *The Rehnquist Court: Justices, Rulings, and Legacy*. Santa Barbara, Calif.: ABC-Clio, 2006.

Urofsky, Melvin I. *The Warren Court: Justices, Rulings, and Legacy*. Santa Barbara, Calif.: ABC-Clio, 2001.

Yarbrough, Tinsley E. *The Burger Court: Justices, Rulings, and Legacy*. Santa Barbara, Calif.: ABC-Clio, 2000.

_____. *John Marshall Harlan: Great Dissenter of the Warren Court*. New York: Oxford University Publishers, 1992.

_____. *The Rehnquist Court and the Constitution*. New York: Oxford University Press, 2000.

SEE ALSO *Baker v. Carr*; Douglas, William O.; *Griswold v. Connecticut*; Harlan, John Marshall; *Mapp v. Ohio*; Privacy, right to; *Reynolds v. Sims*; Warren, Earl.

John Marshall Harlan

IDENTIFICATION: Associate justice (December 10, 1877-October 14, 1911)
NOMINATED BY: Rutherford B. Hayes
BORN: June 1, 1833, Boyle County, Kentucky
DIED: October 14, 1911, Washington, D.C.
SIGNIFICANCE: An early champion of modern American constitutional law, Harlan is remembered as the "Great Dissenter" on the Supreme Court for his crusade for a nationalistic interpretation of the Fourteenth Amendment broad enough to protect the rights of African Americans and to apply the first eight amendments to the states.

As a Kentuckian and former slave owner, John Marshall Harlan was an unlikely candidate for a position as the Supreme Court's defender of black rights in the late nineteenth century. Harlan had opposed emancipation and objected to the Civil War amendments. However, like the great chief justice (John Marshall) for whom he was named, Harlan was a nationalist at heart.

Harlan, like his father, was a staunch Whig. He completed his undergraduate work at Centre College, studied law at Transylvania University in Lexington, then read law in his father's office. Following his admission to the bar in 1853, he rose quickly in Whig ranks. Harlan affiliated with the Know-Nothings when the Whig Party ceased to exist, serving a one-year term on the Franklin County bench. He served the Union army as a lieutenant colonel, returning to his father's law practice when the elder Harlan died in 1863. From 1863 to 1867 he was attorney general of Kentucky, serving under the Constitutional Unionist banner.

Harlan's conversion to Republican Party principles could not have been easy. Like most of his fellow Kentuckians, he found uncompen-

551

sated emancipation a bitter pill to swallow. However, Harlan was a devout Christian with a paternalistic regard for the well-being of the former slaves. When the Constitutional Unionist Party died, he was forced to choose between Democratic terrorism and the Republican principle of equality before the law. After choosing Republicanism, Harlan ran unsuccessfully for governor in 1871 and 1875.

A CAREER OF DISSENT

Harlan, head of the Kentucky delegation to the 1876 Republican Party convention, secured the presidential nomination for Hayes with his vote and those of the other delegates. When the contested election results were finally settled and Hayes inaugurated, he rewarded Harlan with a Supreme Court seat.

Harlan's nationalism ran counter to the philosophy of the other justices. During his long tenure, the Court used the Fourteenth Amendment to protect the property rights of the rich, ignoring the civil rights protections the amendment afforded to African Americans. Not one to compromise or negotiate where he held strong convictions, Harlan castigated the Court for its errors, often accompanying his dissents with table thumping and finger wagging.

In the *Civil Rights Cases* (1883) and again in *Plessy v. Ferguson* (1896), Harlan stood alone in seeking a generous interpretation of the Civil War amendments. The *Civil Rights Cases* struck down the Civil Rights Act of 1875, which provided African Americans equal access to hotels, theaters, and other privately owned places of business that were open to the public. The law was unconstitutional, Justice Joseph P. Bradley ruled, because there was no discriminatory state action; the Fourteenth Amendment did not reach private discrimination. Harlan's eloquent dissent—written with the same pen and inkwell Chief Justice Roger Brooke Taney used for *Scott v. Sandford* (1857)—criticized the majority for a formalistic interpretation that sacrificed the "substance and spirit" of the recent amendments. Similarly, when the rest of the justices established the separate but equal doctrine in *Plessy*, Harlan objected to the legalization of caste through the "thin disguise" of what were termed equal accommodations. Insisting that the Constitution is color-blind, Harlan predicted that the *Plessy* case would eventually prove as pernicious as *Scott v.*

Sandford, a prophecy that was eventually justified in *Brown v. Board of Education* (1954).

Harlan's commitment to racial equality did not completely overcome his background, however. In *Pace v. Alabama* (1883), Harlan agreed with a unanimous decision that interracial fornication could be punished more severely than that within a race as long as the punishment was identical for each offender, a position that is difficult to square with Harlan's notion of a color-blind Constitution.

Harlan spoke for the future once again in *Hurtado v. California* (1884). His dissent maintained that the due process clause of the Fourteenth Amendment made the provisions of the Bill of Rights applicable to the states. Harlan held this position consistently throughout his long judicial career, but it was not until 1925 that the Supreme Court began its piecemeal process of nationalizing the Bill of Rights.

John Marshall Harlan.
(Library of Congress)

ECONOMIC ISSUES

In the economic sphere, Harlan generally—although somewhat inconsistently—opposed the majority's growing tendency to favor the interests of business and capital. He scolded the Court in *United States v. E. C. Knight Co.* (1895), for example, for making an artificial distinction between manufacturing and commerce that threatened to leave the federal government helpless in its attempts to control monopolies. Dissenting again in the income tax case *Pollock v. Farmers' Loan and Trust Co.* (1895), Harlan complained bitterly that the majority ruling against the constitutionality of the federal income tax was a gross injustice to ordinary citizens. Harlan's view was vindicated with the Sixteenth Amendment in 1913.

Harlan grounded his bitter denunciation of the majority opinion in *Lochner v. New York* (1905) in concrete evidence regarding the health hazards of baking. He argued that the police powers of the state overrode the freedom of contract, the idea that the Fourteenth Amendment forbade government interference between employer and employee. In contrast, Harlan wrote the majority opinion in *Adair v. United States* (1908), which struck down a federal law outlawing yellow dog (antiunion) contracts on interstate railroads. He asserted the equality of bargaining power between employer and employee and pronounced the law an "arbitrary interference with the liberty of contract."

During his final year on the bench, Harlan continued to protest the Court's support for big business. Although he agreed with the majority's trust-busting efforts in *Standard Oil Co. v. United States* (1911), he denounced the rule of reason, which the case wrote into the Sherman Antitrust Act (1890) as "judicial legislation." *Standard Oil*, along with a similar dissent in *United States v. American Tobacco Co.* (1911), brought him public acclaim.

Until the civil rights era of the twentieth century, Harlan was underrated as a Supreme Court justice. Fellow justices jokingly claimed he was afflicted with "dissent-ery," and legal scholars considered him eccentric and out of tune with his time. His reputation soared after *Brown v. Board of Education* (1954), although it is difficult to reconcile Harlan's insistence on a color-blind Constitution with affirmative action.

Lou Falkner Williams

FURTHER READING

Bader, William H., and Roy M. Mersky, eds. *The First One Hundred Eight Justices.* Buffalo, N.Y.: William S. Hein, 2004.

Beth, Loren P. *John Marshall Harlan: The Last Whig Justice.* Lexington: University Press of Kentucky, 1992.

Ely, James W., Jr. *The Fuller Court: Justices, Rulings, and Legacy.* Santa Barbara, Calif.: ABC-Clio, 2003.

Shoemaker, Rebecca S. *The White Court: Justices, Rulings, and Legacy.* Santa Barbara, Calif.: ABC-Clio, 2004.

Stephenson, Donald Grier, Jr. *The Waite Court: Justices, Rulings, and Legacy.* Santa Barbara, Calif.: ABC-Clio, 2003.

Westin, Alan F. "John Marshall Harlan and the Constitutional Rights of Negroes: The Transformation of a Southerner." *Yale Law Journal* 66 (April, 1957): 637-710.

White, G. Edward. *The American Judicial Tradition: Profiles of Leading American Judges.* New York: Oxford University Press, 1988.

Yarbrough, Tinsley. *Judicial Enigma: The First Justice Harlan.* New York: Oxford University Press, 1995.

SEE ALSO *Civil Rights Cases*; Fourteenth Amendment; Fundamental rights; Incorporation doctrine; *Plessy v. Ferguson*; Reconstruction; State action.

Hate Speech

DEFINITION: Communications intended to insult, degrade, intimidate, or create animosity against a person or persons belonging to a particular race, ethnicity, gender, religion, disability, or sexual orientation.

SIGNIFICANCE: The First Amendment broadly prohibits government from restricting the content of communications, with the exception of particular categories of expression, such as defamation, "fighting words," threats to physically harm another parson, and incitement of violent behavior. Hate speech must be distinguished from hate crimes, which are deeds that are not protected by the Constitution.

The Supreme Court has long accepted the principle that a number of narrowly defined categories of communication are not protected by the First Amendment. In *Chaplinsky v. New Hampshire* (1942), for example, the Court declared that one of these categories was the use of "fighting words," or a face-to-face declaration of extremely offensive words that "by their very utterance inflict injury or tend to incite an immediate breach of the peace." Although the *Chaplinsky* ruling has been reaffirmed in principle, the Court applied the category of fighting words so narrowly that it became almost impossible to draft a law or ordinance that is enforceable.

In *Gooding v. Wilson* (1972) and *Lewis v. New Orleans* (1974), the Court struck down ordinances that used the term "opprobrious language," which Justice William J. Brennan, Jr., argued was overly broad

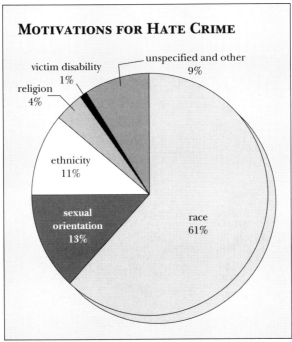

MOTIVATIONS FOR HATE CRIME

victim disability 1%
religion 4%
ethnicity 11%
sexual orientation 13%
unspecified and other 9%
race 61%

Source: U.S. Bureau of Justice Statistics, 2005. Data are based on nearly 3,000 incidents of hate crime reported to the National Incident-Based Reporting System (NIBRS) in 1997-1999. Because of rounding, percentages do not add up to 100.

because it might be applied to constitutionally protected speech.

The Court appeared to endorse the criminalization of some forms of hate speech in the almost forgotten case of *Beauharnais v. Illinois* (1952). The defendants in the case had been showing offensive lithographs of African Americans when petitioning for racial segregation, and they were convicted under a statute that made it a crime to expose persons to "contempt, derision, or obloquy" because of their race, creed, or religion. The official opinion of the Court argued that measures against criminal libels had been sanctioned by centuries of Anglo-American law. Even though the *Beauharnais* ruling has never been formally overturned, the Court's rulings since 1952 have made it manifestly clear that it is no longer a binding precedent.

The main problem with Justice Oliver Wendell Holmes's clear and present danger test was its vagueness, which left it susceptible to so many different interpretations and applications. The Court presented a modified version of the test in *Brandenburg v. Ohio* (1968), a case involving a Ku Klux Klan leader who was convicted of suggesting, in a televised rally, that violent actions might be necessary or desirable. In overturning his conviction, the Court allowed government to punish advocacy of illegal conduct only when "such advocacy is directed to inciting or producing imminent lawless action and is likely to incite or produce such action."

Brandenburg's so called "imminent and likely danger" test clearly distinguished between the expression of an idea and the commission of a crime, making it impossible to punish persons for hate speech except when there is a direct and immediate linkage between the speech and a criminal act. The constitutional right to express unpopular, even intolerant, ideas was further strengthened in the case of *Smith v. Collins* (1978), when the Supreme Court refused to review the Seventh Circuit's decision that authorized the American Nazi Party to march on a public street in the predominantly Jewish community of Skokie, Illinois.

During the late 1980's and 1990's, more than thirty states and numerous communities and colleges enacted speech codes or laws prohibiting speech communicating various kinds of hate or bias. College speech codes tended to be especially broad, and when challenged, they were almost invariably found to violate the First Amendment in lower courts. In the case of *R.A.V. v. City of St. Paul* (1992), the Supreme Court examined an antibias criminal ordinance that prohibited the display of a symbol that "arouses anger, alarm, or resentment in others on the basis of race, color, creed, religion, or gender." Robert A. Viltora and another teenager were punished for disobeying the ordinance after they burned a cross on a black family's lawn. In their review of the case, the Supreme Court justices unanimously voted to strike down the ordinance, but they based their conclusions on different rationales. Justice Antonin Scalia, for example, argued that the ordinance violated the First Amendment because of its "viewpoint discrimination," punishing some expressions of hostility and allowing others. A majority of the justices agreed that a narrowly drawn law punishing race-based "fighting words" would be constitutional. Following the ruling, many states and communities, and colleges, attempted to establish new rules in content-neutral language.

The state of Virginia enacted a statute that made it a felony to burn a cross with the intent to "intimidate" a person or group of persons. The statute also specified that any act of cross-burning would be taken as "prima facie evidence" of a person's intent to intimidate. In reviewing the cases of three persons convicted under the statute in *Virginia v. Black* (2002), the Supreme Court issued two 6-3 rulings. First, the Virginia statute was constitutional so long as it was construed to punish a person for the act of intimidating or threatening another person. Secondly, the Court found that the First Amendment forbade the state to punish a cross-burner whose intent was simply to communicate a pro-Ku Klux Klan idea, without sufficient evidence that he intended to intimidate a particular person. The ruling in *Virginia v. Black* implicitly recognized that individuals have the constitutional right to communicate messages of hatred or disdain toward social groups or individuals if they are so inclined.

Thomas Tandy Lewis

FURTHER READING

Greenawalt, Kent. *Fighting Words: Individuals, Communities, and Liberties of Speech.* Princeton, N.J.: Princeton University Press, 1995.

Sturm, Philippa. *When the Nazis Came to Skokie: Freedom for the Speech We Hate.* Lawrence: University Press of Kansas, 1999.

Walker, Samuel. *Hate Speech: The History of an American Controversy.* Lincoln: University of Nebraska Press, 1994.

SEE ALSO *Brandenburg v. Ohio*; Libel; Scalia, Antonin; Speech and press, freedom of; Symbolic speech; *Virginia v. Black.*

Heart of Atlanta Motel v. United States

CITATION: 379 U.S. 241
DATE: December 14, 1964
ISSUE: Desegregation
SIGNIFICANCE: In a landmark decision, the Supreme Court upheld the public accommodations section of the 1964 Civil Rights Act and enjoined a motel from refusing to serve African Americans.

An Atlanta motel owner, whose clientele was largely interstate travelers, refused to rent rooms to African Americans as required by Title II, the public accommodations provision of the Civil Rights Act of 1964. The owner argued that Congress had exceeded its power to regulate private business under the commerce clause. The Supreme Court unanimously held that the services rendered to guests at the motel were a part of interstate commerce and therefore could be properly regulated by Congress. Justice Tom C. Clark wrote the unanimous decision upholding the validity of the public accommodations provision. Justices Hugo L. Black, William O. Douglas, and Arthur J. Goldberg wrote separate concurrences.

Richard L. Wilson

SEE ALSO *Civil Rights Cases*; Clark, Tom C.; Commerce, regulation of; *Plessy v. Ferguson*; Race and discrimination; State action.

Oliver Wendell Holmes

IDENTIFICATION: Associate justice (December 8, 1902-January 12, 1932)

NOMINATED BY: Theodore Roosevelt

BORN: March 8, 1841, Boston, Massachusetts

DIED: March 6, 1932, Washington, D.C.

SIGNIFICANCE: In the course of his twenty-nine years on the Supreme Court, Holmes wrote 873 opinions, and several of his eloquently argued dissents on free speech and due process are now treated as precedents. Holmes preferred common law over natural law and was strongly reluctant to interfere with state legislation that was not expressly prohibited by the Constitution.

Oliver Wendell Holmes was born into a distinguished Boston Brahmin family, a son of the famous raconteur and medical doctor, Dr. Oliver Wendell Holmes. He attended Harvard College for four years before enlisting in 1861 in the Fourth Battalion, Massachusetts Militia. As a first lieutenant, Holmes saw much heavy fighting and was wounded three times: at Ball's Bluff, Virginia, in 1861, at Antietam Creek in 1862, and at Chancellorsville in 1863. His military service ended in July, 1864, and it left an indelible mark on him, as evidenced in his 1895 Harvard Memorial Day address on "The Soldier's Faith." In 1866 Holmes received a law degree from Harvard. He was admitted to the Massachusetts bar in 1867, and three years later, he became coeditor of the *American Law Review* and began lecturing at Harvard College. In 1873 he became a partner in the new firm of Shattuck, Holmes, and Munroe.

THE MASSACHUSETTS LEGAL SCHOLAR

Holmes's scholarly career began in 1873 when the twelfth edition of *Kent's Commentaries* appeared with Holmes as the sole editor. The Lowell Lectures that Holmes delivered in 1880 were published in 1881 as *The Common Law*, his interpretation of the legal principles that the courts had developed over centuries, and the following year, he abandoned his law practice to teach at Harvard Law School for a few months before being appointed to the supreme judicial court of Massachusetts in December, 1882. Holmes soon became known for his dictum that "except so far as expressly or by implication [a legislative act] is prohibited by the Constitution—that the question always is where do you find the prohibition—not where do you find the power."

Nothing did more to establish Holmes's reputation as the "Great Dissenter" than his dissent in the Massachusetts court's 6-1 ruling in 1896 on *Vegelahn v. Guntner.* The furniture manufacturer Frederick O. Vegelahn resisted the upholsterers' union (represented by George M. Guntner) in their demands for a raise and a nine-hour workday. When the upholsterers picketed, Vegelahn went to the Massachusetts court and won a ruling that the picketing constituted "unlawful interference" with an employer's right to hire anyone who wanted to work for him and his employees' right to stay employed by anyone who would hire them. In his dissent, Holmes supported Vegelahn in disallowing the picketers the right to any violent behavior, including obstructing access to the factory entrance, but he refused to forbid peaceful picketing or boycotting.

APPOINTMENT TO WASHINGTON

When Theodore Roosevelt became president in 1901, the United States was experiencing a struggle between big business and the rights of individuals. The first blow had been struck in 1890 by the federal government with the Sherman Antitrust Act, but the barons were still powerful and Roosevelt knew that he had to fight them. In 1902 when Roosevelt was to make his first Supreme Court appointment, the strong advocacy of Holmes's fellow Boston Brahmin, Henry Cabot Lodge, won Holmes the seat. Holmes's first opinion, in *Otis v. Parker* (1902), supporting the California state constitution in its law prohibiting the sale of stocks on margin, was delivered when he had been sworn in less than a month, and it established his consistent respect for his proclamation in *The Common Law* that the "first requirement of a sound body of law is that it should correspond with the actual feelings and demands of the community, whether right or wrong." *Otis* was soon followed by *Bleistein v. Donaldson Lithographing Co.* (1903), a landmark case in U.S. copyright law, in which Holmes argued that a circus advertising poster could be copyrighted, whatever its merit as art.

Holmes, Oliver Wendell

DEFENDER OF STATE LEGISLATURES

The Fourteenth Amendment, added to the U.S. Constitution in 1868, featured in many of the cases in Holmes's career on the Court. Unfortunately for African Americans, although the Fourteenth Amendment was intended to provide relief from racial injustice, the amendment's equal protection clause usually served business interests instead. Holmes's devotion to laws shaped by the people's will did not usually serve justice for African Americans well, and in 1903, his first year on the Court, he wrote two majority opinions rebuffing African Americans in *Brownfield v. South Carolina* and *Giles v. Harris*. In *Swift and Co. v. United States* (1905), however, Holmes went against big business, finding that Swift's intent to monopolize interstate commerce in beef violated the Sherman Antitrust Act (1890). Holmes's argument hinged on his postulation of a "stream of commerce" in which live animals moved into an area and were shipped out as meat, an interpretation that was to become important in New Deal legislation.

Business interests continued to cite the Fourteenth Amendment in their defense in cases such as *Lochner v. New York* (1905). New York had enacted in 1895 a law controlling conditions in the many small cellar bakeries and limiting the workweek to sixty hours. When Joseph Lochner of Utica was fined fifty dollars for letting an employee work more than sixty hours, he carried his case to the Supreme Court after losing in the New York appeals courts. Lochner argued that the Fourteenth Amendment protected him from the Bakeshop Act by guaranteeing that he could not be deprived of his liberty of contract without due process. The Court decided in Lochner's favor in a 5-4 vote, with Holmes and Justice John Marshall Harlan dissenting. Justice Rufus W. Peckham wrote the majority opinion, ruling that the right to buy and sell labor was guaranteed by the Fourteenth Amendment. In his dissent, Holmes claimed that state laws should not be overruled unless it was obvious to any rational person that some constitutional principle was being violated, and his clear understanding of what was going on emerged in his scolding that "A constitution is not intended to embody a particular economic theory."

Adkins v. Children's Hospital (1923) was a minimum-wage case with parallels to *Lochner.* A 1918 federal law had guaranteed women a

Oliver Wendell
Holmes.
(Library of Congress)

minimum wage in the District of Columbia on the grounds that low
wages were detrimental to health and contributed to poor morals.
Children's Hospital filed suit, alleging that the law was unconstitutional because it fixed wages in clear violation of the freedom of
contract, a position upheld by the Court, with Holmes joining Chief
Justice William H. Taft in dissent. Justice George Sutherland's opinion for the 5-3 majority agreed with Children's Hospital and also
found the minimum-wage law burdened employers with welfare responsibilities more properly left to society as a whole. Holmes dar-
ingly challenged the freedom of contract doctrine, pointing out that
law quite generally forbade people from doing as they pleased.
Despite the eloquent dissents of Taft and Holmes, the Court's support of laissez-faire constitutionalism continued until its striking setbacks under the New Deal, notably in the case of *West Coast Hotel Co. v.
Parrish* (1937), which overruled *Adkins* and upheld a Washington
minimum-wage law for women.

CIVIL RIGHTS

On January 3, 1911, the Court handed down two opinions gratifying to Progressives. In the first, *Noble State Bank v. Haskell*, Holmes wrote the unanimous opinion rejecting the bank's claim. The Oklahoma legislature had voted to protect bank depositors with a Depositors' Guaranty Fund built up by assessing banks 5 percent of their average daily deposits, and the Noble State Bank resorted to the due process clause of the Fourteenth Amendment to seek relief from the levy. Acknowledging that the bank had a case, Holmes nevertheless asserted that the Court should not subvert the state legislature's attempt to provide for the public welfare without clear evidence of a law's lack of public support.

However, if liberals were pleased with Holmes's observations in this opinion, his dissent in the second case decided that day, *Bailey v. Alabama*, enraged them. Alabama was one of several southern states with so-called peonage laws by which a worker who quit a job while still owing the employer money could be prosecuted. *Bailey v. Alabama* took up the case of Lonzo Bailey, an illiterate African American who had left his job as a farmhand while still owing his employer $13.75. Bailey's case reached the Court in 1908 but was sent back to Alabama. In the Court's second round of deliberations, Chief Justice Charles Evans Hughes wrote for the majority that the Alabama law was coercive and that the Thirteenth Amendment had outlawed involuntary servitude. However, Holmes, faithful defender of the rights of state legislatures and believer in the sanctity of state statutes, found Bailey clearly guilty of breach of contract and fraud and therefore subject to punishment by the law. His fellow justices, Holmes stated, expected that the law would be followed differently in Alabama than it would be in New York.

Holmes's first important free speech case was *Schenck v. United States* (1919), which tested the federal government's right under the Espionage Act (1917) to prosecute draft resisters. Holmes relied on the doctrine of clear and present danger in limiting the speeches and leaflets that the government found threatening, an argument that was used to support subsequent convictions of draft obstructors. As it turned out, only the prosecutors had any success arguing for the threat of a clear and present danger, and in *Abrams v. United States*, also decided for the government in 1919, Holmes dissented on the grounds that the doctrine could not be used against political dissidents who were merely exercising a right guaranteed by the First Amendment: "The best test of truth is the power of the thought to get itself accepted in the competition of the market."

Frank Day

FURTHER READING

Edward G. White's *Oliver Wendell Holmes, Jr.* (New York: Oxford University Press, 2006) is a detailed study of Holmes's entire life that is particularly well suited for young adult readers. Catherine Drinker Bowen's *Yankee from Olympus: Justice Holmes and His Family* (Boston: Little, Brown, 1945) is a readable, admiring book that became a bestseller. Samuel J. Konefsky's *The Legacy of Holmes and Brandeis* (New York: Macmillan, 1956) is a study in the influence of ideas. Another specialist study is Jeremy Cohen's *Congress Shall Make No Law: Oliver Wendell Holmes, the First Amendment, and Judicial Decision Making* (Ames: Iowa State University Press, 1989), an exploration of the famous First Amendment case *Schenck v. United States.*

In *Justice Oliver Wendell Holmes: The Proving Years, 1870-1882* (Cambridge, Mass.: Harvard University Press, 1963), Mark DeWolfe Howe studies the period in which Holmes was formulating his philosophy of law. The first of three excellent modern biographies is Sheldon M. Novick's *Honorable Justice: The Life of Oliver Wendell Holmes* (Boston: Little, Brown, 1989), which includes a useful chronology. Liva Baker's *The Justice from Beacon Hill: The Life and Times of Oliver Wendell Holmes* (New York: HarperCollins, 1991) combines close attention to the man with sharp analysis of the legal scholar. G. Edward White's *Justice Oliver Wendell Holmes: Law and the Inner Self* (New York: Oxford University Press, 1993) is an excellent biography that sees an understanding of Holmes's life as basic to understanding the jurist.

Bernard Schwartz's supremely readable *A History of the Supreme Court* (New York: Oxford University Press, 1993) provides knowledgeable commentary on Holmes's Court decisions. Holmes's judicial career may also be studied in the context of the chief justices under whom he served. ABC-Clio's reference series on chief justices is especially useful for this purpose. Its volumes include *The Fuller Court: Jus-*

tices, Rulings, and Legacy (Santa Barbara, Calif.: ABC-Clio, 2003) by James W. Ely, Jr.; *The White Court: Justices, Rulings, and Legacy* (Santa Barbara, Calif.: ABC-Clio, 2004) by Rebecca S. Shoemaker; *The Taft Court: Justices, Rulings, and Legacy* (Santa Barbara, Calif.: ABC-Clio, 2003) by Peter G. Renstrom; and *The Hughes Court: Justices, Rulings, and Legacy* (Santa Barbara, Calif.: ABC-Clio, 2002) by Michael E. Parrish.

SEE ALSO Antitrust law; Bad tendency test; *Buck v. Bell*; Common law; Constitutional law; Contract, freedom of; Espionage acts; First Amendment; Fourteenth Amendment; *Lochner v. New York*; Rule of reason; *Schenck v. United States*; Seditious libel.

Housing Discrimination

DESCRIPTION: Attempt by government entities or private parties to bar the sale or rental of housing to members of minority groups.

SIGNIFICANCE: The Supreme Court declared both public and private housing discrimination to be unconstitutional or illegal, although it allowed some practices that indirectly result in residential segregation. Its rulings did not, however, lead to significant integration in residential patterns.

The first type of housing discrimination addressed by the Supreme Court was attempts by cities and towns to establish separate residential areas for different races. In *Buchanan v. Warley* (1917), the Court struck down such policies as unconstitutional, holding that they violated the equal protection clause of the Fourteenth Amendment by forcing property owners to sell or rent only to certain groups.

Housing discrimination persisted, however, through restrictive covenants (contractual agreements by property owners that they would never sell or rent property to nonwhites). In 1926 the Court let stand a lower court decision upholding their legality. Discrimination in this form continued undisturbed until the Court declared in *Shelley v. Kraemer* (1948) that these agreements denied minority groups their constitutional right to equal protection of the law. Although restrictive covenants were not forbidden, it was held that state and federal courts could no longer execute them. This decision was broadened in a 1953 ruling that monetary damages could not be sought when such contracts were breached. Therefore, although restrictive covenants remained as a tool of private housing discrimination, they were no longer legally enforceable.

During the late 1960's and 1970's the Court began to focus on private acts of discrimination. In *Reitman v. Mulkey* (1967), the Court ruled on an amendment to the California constitution that declared the state could not limit the right of citizens to discriminate in the sale or rental of their property. The amendment was struck down, as it was found to overly involve the state in such actions. A year later the Court made a more sweeping decree, holding in *Jones v. Alfred H. Mayer Co.* (1968) that public and private acts of housing discrimination had been banned by the Civil Rights Act of 1866, even though that provision had never been enforced.

In 1968 Congress passed a fair housing act that clearly restricted private and public acts of housing discrimination. After its enactment, the Court's role was increasingly to rule on cases involving more subtle attempts to exclude particular groups. For example, the refusal of cities and towns to approve the construction of low-income housing or apartments was challenged as indirect discrimination against minorities. However, in several cases in the 1970's, the most notable of which was *Arlington Heights v. Metropolitan Housing Development Corp.* (1977), the Court refused to limit such zoning restrictions, finding that acts that have the effect of excluding particular residents do not amount to proof of an intent to discriminate.

Francine Sanders Romero

FURTHER READING

Hall, Kermit L. *Freedom and Equality: Discrimination and the Supreme Court.* New York: Garland, 2000.

Klarman, Michael J. *From Jim Crow to Civil Rights: The Supreme Court and the Struggle for Racial Equality.* New York: Oxford University Press, 2006.

Rasmussen, R. Kent. *Farewell to Jim Crow: The Rise and Fall of Segregation in America.* New York: Facts On File, 1997.

Rosenberg, Gerald N. *The Hollow Hope.* Chicago: University of Chicago Press, 1991.

Vose, Clement. *Caucasians Only.* Berkeley: University of California Press, 1973.

SEE ALSO Contract, freedom of; Fourteenth Amendment; Race and discrimination; Restrictive covenants; *Shelley v. Kraemer;* Zoning.

Housing of the Court

DESCRIPTION: Places where the Supreme Court met and held court.

SIGNIFICANCE: Because the judiciary was considered a relatively unimportant branch of the government, the Court met in a variety of places until a dedicated building was constructed in 1935.

Although the Framers of the U.S. Constitution agreed to a tripartite division of the federal government, the judiciary received the least emphasis. The Judiciary Act of 1789 established a Supreme Court

Entrance to the Supreme Court building, which was completed in 1935. (Library of Congress)

consisting of a chief justice and five associate justices. Most of the Court's time would be devoted to the circuit courts.

Two sessions were held in 1790 in the Merchants Exchange building in New York City before the government moved to Philadelphia. In 1791 the Court met in Independence Hall; from 1791 to 1800, it met in Philadelphia's City Hall. After the 1800 term, the Court moved to the new capital city of Washington, D.C. The north wing of the Capitol building was ready for Congress; the president moved into the Executive Mansion. There was, however, no official place for the Court. Because the justices were expected to spend only about six weeks in the capital, Congress decided a small room in the basement of the Capitol would suffice.

THE COURT UNDER JOHN MARSHALL

What was to change the development of the federal government and the Court was John Marshall's appointment as chief justice. Marshall, who served from 1801 to 1835, strengthened and enhanced the powers of the federal government and the responsibilities and powers of the Court through a liberal interpretation of the Constitution and a series of incisive, far-reaching decisions.

In 1807 and 1808, disturbed by ongoing construction, the Court met in the former library of the House of Representatives. In 1809, because of the extreme cold, it met in Long's Tavern. In 1810 the Court was given new quarters under the recently constructed Senate chamber. The semidome-shaped space, measuring thirty-five by seventy-five feet, was still inadequate. It was humid because of its basement location and lacked a separate entrance and a robing room for the justices, forcing them to robe in public. The bench where they sat was only slightly elevated, and the whole area dimly lit and with poor acoustics. The room was likened to a "dark potato hole."

The justices had to evacuate their quarters when the British burned the Capitol in August, 1814, during the War of 1812. In 1815 and 1816 the Court met in a private house; in 1817 and 1818 it moved into a habitable part of the Capitol.

By 1819, their former quarters had been repaired. The justices returned to their quarters, where they remained until 1860, despite the growing inadequacy of the space. Marshall died in 1835, to be succeeded by chief justices who mainly followed his lead. Not only were the physical arrangements not in keeping with the dignity of the Court, but also the justices had no office space or a law library, which became increasingly necessary.

THE MOVE TO THE SENATE'S CHAMBER

During the 1850's, additions to the north and south wings of the Capitol provided larger chambers for the Senate and the House of Representatives. In 1860 the Court moved to the chamber vacated by the Senate and remained there until 1935. These quarters, too, became increasingly deficient as the work of the Court mounted. Although the justices had a robing room, it had to double as their dining room. They had no office space or conference room. Work space for the Court's personnel was small and crowded, and the acoustics were still bad. A law library installed in their former quarters was shared by other governmental departments.

After the Civil War, the duties of the Court increased considerably as their duties in the field decreased. In 1869 federal circuit judges were appointed; in 1891 Congress created the courts of appeals, which would handle many of the cases formerly heard by the Court; in 1925 the Court was given control of its own docket.

THE NEW BUILDING

By the end of the nineteenth century, the shift to an industrial economy placed an increased burden on the Court. Between 1870 and 1890 the number of cases the Court handled increased fivefold. Despite the power and prestige of the Court, it was still a tenant of Congress. To be coequal with the other branches of the government as the Constitution intended, the Court needed to be housed separately.

The driving force behind the new building was William H. Taft, president from 1908 to 1912 and chief justice from 1921 to 1930. As president he began promoting the idea of a separate building for the Court and enlisted the aid of Cass Gilbert, a distinguished architect also from Ohio. Working at first without a commission, Gilbert drew up plans for the building in the classical style favored by the Founders. Through personal influence and political pressure, Taft per-

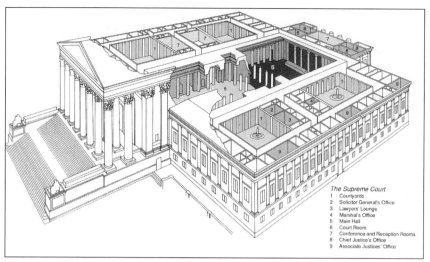

Interior of the Supreme Court building.

suaded Congress to appropriate $9.7 million for the building—at the time a large sum. The building was completed in 1935, and the Court met there for the first time on October 7.

Neither Taft nor Gilbert lived to see their work completed, but they had planned carefully. Every convenience was given the justices. They could enter and leave the building, their quarters, and the courtroom without contact with the public. They had suites of rooms for their personal use, a library, dining rooms, garage space, and a gymnasium. They were provided with adequate clerical assistance and electronic support. Built of the finest materials, the building is noted for the splendor of the courtroom. Eighty-two by ninety-one feet with a forty-four-foot ceiling, the chamber is lined with columns of the finest marble. The impressive mahogany bench of the justices helps make this an effective and awe-inspiring seat for what has become the world's most important and powerful court.

Nis Petersen

FURTHER READING
Baum, Lawrence. *The Supreme Court.* 8th ed. Washington, D.C.: CQ Press, 2004.

571

Jost, Kenneth, ed. *The Supreme Court, A to Z.* 2d ed. Washington, D.C.: Congressional Quarterly, 1998.

Maroon, Fred J., and Suzy Maroon. *The Supreme Court of the United States.* New York: Thomasson-Grant & Lickle, 1996.

Savage, David G., ed. *Guide to the United States Supreme Court.* 4th ed. Washington, D.C.: Congressional Quarterly, 2004.

Schwartz, Bernard. *A History of the Supreme Court.* New York: Oxford University Press, 1993.

SEE ALSO Chief justice; Marshall, John; Separation of powers; Taft, William H.; Workload.

Hudson v. Michigan

CITATION: 547 U.S. ___
DATE: June 15, 2006
ISSUES: Exclusionary rule; search warrants
SIGNIFICANCE: In a major departure from previous rulings on the exclusionary rule, the Supreme Court allowed the use of criminal evidence that was the fruit of a search conducted contrary to the "knock-and-announce" rule.

From colonial times, American courts have subscribed to the common law requirement that police, before using force to enter a private home, should knock and announce their identity and purpose. In *Wilson v. Arkansas* (1995), the Supreme Court explicitly affirmed that the Fourth Amendment incorporates this requirement, even though the ruling allowed exceptions for "exigent circumstances," leaving it to the states to decide the details. In *Richards v. Wisconsin* (1997), the Court explained that a no-knock entry is justified when the police have a "reasonable suspicion" that announcing their presence would be dangerous or "inhibit the effectiveness" of police efforts. If the police were to conduct no-knock entries without adequate justification, however, any evidence obtained by the search would be suppressed according to the exclusionary rule.

In 1998, Detroit police officers obtained a regular warrant (with no exemption from the knock-and-announce rule) to search for drugs and weapons in the home of Booker T. Hudson. Without knocking, the officers announced their presence and waited only three or four seconds before entering through an unlocked door. They found guns and cocaine. At trial, Hudson's lawyers argued that the evidence should be suppressed because the police had violated the knock-and-announce rule. Although agreeing that the rule had not been followed, the judge nevertheless allowed the evidence to be admitted, and Hudson was sentenced to eighteen months' probation.

The U.S. Supreme Court voted five to four to uphold the conviction. Speaking for the majority, Justice Antonin Scalia acknowledged that the "knock-and-announce" rule was an ancient common law principle, but he argued that the suppression of evidence should be a last resort because "it generates substantial social costs which sometimes include setting the guilty free and the dangerous at large." He further asserted that there was no causal connection between the constitutional violation (the failure to knock) and the discovery of evidence. The "increasing professionalism of the police," moreover, minimized the need to deter misconduct. In a concurring opinion, Justice Anthony M. Kennedy wrote that the *Hudson* ruling should be viewed narrowly, for it was not meant to diminish either the knock-and-announce principle or the exclusionary rule.

Speaking for the four-member minority, Justice Stephen Breyer wrote a heated dissent, charging that the majority had departed from the Court's "basic principles" and had destroyed the major legal incentive of the police to comply with the knock-and-announce requirement. He took particular exception to Scalia's causality argument for disregarding the exclusionary rule, which he wrote could make the Fourth Amendment unenforceable.

Thomas Tandy Lewis

SEE ALSO Breyer, Stephen G.; Common law; Kennedy, Anthony M.; Police powers; Scalia, Antonin; search warrant requirement.

Charles Evans Hughes

IDENTIFICATION: Associate justice (October 10, 1910-June 10, 1916),
   chief justice (February 24, 1930-July 1, 1941)
NOMINATED BY: William H. Taft (associate justice); Herbert Hoover
   (chief justice)
BORN: April 11, 1862, Glen Falls, New York
DIED: August 27, 1948, Osterville, Massachusetts
SIGNIFICANCE: Having resigned as an associate justice in 1916 to run
   for the presidency of the United States, Hughes returned to the
   Supreme Court in 1930 as chief justice. In that capacity, he led the
   Court through the critical days of the Great Depression and the
   New Deal.

Charles Evans Hughes attended Madison University (later Colgate)
and was graduated from Brown University in 1881, the youngest
member of his graduating class. Lacking funds to attend law school,
he taught school for a year. In 1882 he entered Columbia University
Law School, graduating with honors in 1884. He entered the private
practice of law, taking time out from 1891 to 1893 to teach at Cornell
University's Law School. He gained considerable recognition for his
investigations of gas lighting and insurance companies for the New
York State legislature.

LAUNCHING A POLITICAL CAREER

Hughes's success in his investigatory activities in New York resulted in his being elected Republican governor of New York in 1906.
Running on a reform platform, he soundly defeated his opponent,
William Randolph Hearst. He won a second term in 1908. As governor, he imposed controls on race-horse gambling, set up public service commissions, and initiated many reforms in state government.

When Hughes's second term as governor ended, President William H. Taft nominated him as an associate justice on the Supreme
Court. Hughes served in this position until 1916 when he received
the Republican nomination for the presidency. He lost the election
to the incumbent, Woodrow Wilson, by twenty-three electoral votes.

Resuming his law practice, Hughes often argued cases before the

574

Court. After the United States entered World War I (1917-1918), he served as chair of the draft appeals board of New York City. In 1921 President Warren G. Harding appointed Hughes secretary of state, placing him in the delicate position of negotiating his country's separate peace with Germany after the U.S. Senate rejected the Versailles Treaty. He organized the Washington Disarmament Conference (1921) and worked to foster productive relations with foreign countries, excluding only the Soviet Union. Although he supported the League of Nations, he failed to promote it because of Harding's resolute opposition to the League. He worked diligently to gain Harding's support for the World Court.

Returning in 1925 to his law practice, which grew increasingly lucrative as it became international in scope, Hughes again entered public service when he agreed to serve as judge of the Permanent Court of International Justice from 1928 to 1930. His frequently returning to the practice of law helped Hughes develop an encyclopedic knowledge of law and of complex legal questions.

APPOINTMENT AS CHIEF JUSTICE

On February 3, 1930, the day William H. Taft resigned as chief justice of the United States, President Herbert Hoover nominated Hughes to take his place. The enthusiasm that had marked Hughes's nomination as an associate justice in 1910 was notably absent when his nomination for chief justice was announced two decades later. The debate over his confirmation focused largely on Hughes's personal wealth and on his close association with powerful business leaders. Many senators feared that Hughes could not distance himself sufficiently from his associates to make fair decisions in cases that involved labor disputes and ordinary citizens. The Senate voted fifty-two to twenty-six for Hughes's confirmation.

During Hughes's term as an associate justice, the Court made few far-reaching decisions, but such was not the case during his eleven years as chief justice. Social change was rampant. The burgeoning New Deal presented challenges unlike any the court had previously faced. Conservatives feared the nation was moving toward socialism. Under Hughes's leadership, the Court declared unconstitutional the establishment of New Deal agencies such as the National Recovery

Charles Evans Hughes.
(Harris and Ewing/
Collection of the
Supreme Court of
the United States)

Administration and the Agricultural Adjustment Board.

Franklin D. Roosevelt, his New Deal hobbled by the Court's conservatism, proposed increasing the number of justices by six if the justices over age seventy did not retire. He hoped that such an increase might enable him to appoint more liberal justices, thereby achieving a balance on the Court. Congress rejected this proposal, but the fact it was suggested indicated the strains that existed between the executive and judiciary.

HUGHES'S CONTRIBUTIONS

During his six years as associate justice, Hughes served well on a Court focused on matters involving the United States' transformation from an agrarian to an industrial society. Hughes wrote 151 opinions as associate justice and dissented in only 32 instances. Other justices dissented from 12 of his decisions.

During his term as chief justice, Hughes assumed a heavier work-load than was typical of people in his position, often preferring to write opinions himself rather than to delegate. As chief justice, he wrote 283 majority opinions and 23 dissents. He surprised some skeptics by up-holding a great deal of legislation favorable to labor and voting against legislation designed to curtail labor's organizing activities.

R. Baird Shuman

FURTHER READING

Bader, William H., and Roy M. Mersky, eds. *The First One Hundred Eight Justices.* Buffalo, N.Y.: William S. Hein, 2004.

Danelski, David, and Joseph S. Tulchin, eds. *The Autobiographical Notes of Charles Evans Hughes.* Cambridge, Mass.: Harvard University Press, 1973.

Friedman, Leon, and Fred L. Israel, eds. *The Justices of the United States Supreme Court: Their Lives and Major Opinions.* 5 vols. New York: Chelsea House, 1997.

Glad, Betty. *Charles Evans Hughes and the Illusions of Innocence: A Study in American Diplomacy.* Urbana: University of Illinois Press, 1966.

Hendel, Samuel. *Charles Evans Hughes and the Supreme Court.* New York: King's Crown Press of Columbia University, 1951.

Parrish, Michael E. *The Hughes Court: Justices, Rulings, and Legacy.* Santa Barbara, Calif.: ABC-Clio, 2002.

Perkins, Dexter. *Charles Evans Hughes and American Democratic States-manship.* Boston: Little, Brown, 1956.

Pusey, Merlo. *Charles Evans Hughes.* New York: Macmillan, 1951.

Shoemaker, Rebecca S. *The White Court: Justices, Rulings, and Legacy.* Santa Barbara, Calif.: ABC-Clio, 2004.

SEE ALSO Chief justice; Clerks of the justices; Court-packing plan; Dissents; New Deal; Resignation and retirement; Taft, William H.

Ward Hunt

IDENTIFICATION: Associate justice (January 9, 1873-January 27, 1882)
NOMINATED BY: Ulysses S. Grant
BORN: June 14, 1810, Utica, New York
DIED: March 24, 1886, Washington, D.C.
SIGNIFICANCE: Hunt was one of the last Supreme Court justices of the Reconstruction era to adhere stubbornly to the principles of emancipation and full equality. His vigorous dissent in an 1876 case was an attempt to secure Fifteenth Amendment voting rights for African Americans.

Born in Utica, New York, Ward Hunt was the son of a bank cashier. He received his education at Oxford and Geneva Academies. He later attended Hamilton and also Union College, where he received his LL.D. in 1828. He subsequently completed his legal education at the Litchfield Law School in Connecticut, where he studied under Judge Hiram Denie. Admitted to the bar in 1831, Hunt spent some time recuperating from poor health in the South before entering into a legal partnership with Denie. He soon established a flourishing practice and entered politics. Beginning his career as a Jacksonian Democrat, Hunt won election to a term in the New York assembly in 1838. He was later elected mayor of Utica in 1844. His real ambition, however, lay with the judiciary, and he aspired to a seat on the state supreme court.

His first effort to be elected to a judiciary post failed. His defeat at the polls was largely attributed to widescale opposition from the Irish community. Hunt had earlier incurred the community's anger by successfully defending a police officer who had been accused of murdering an Irishman. Hunt became part of the Free-Soil movement in 1848, thereby incurring the enmity of the proslavery "Hunker" faction of New York's Democratic Party. In 1854 he joined the newly formed Republican Party and helped organize the party in New York. He again attempted to win election to a judicial post, but lost, largely because of his conversion to the Republican Party. In 1865 he was elected to the New York Court of Appeals. After gaining the patronage of such powerful Republicans as Roscoe Conkling, Hunt was

Ward Hunt.
(Library of Congress)

nominated to the Supreme Court by Ulysses S. Grant in 1872 and confirmed by the Senate just one week later. As a justice, his most notable opinion was his dissent in the 1876 voting rights case of *United States v. Reese*, in which Hunt argued that the Fifteenth Amendment guaranteed the right of African Americans to vote in state as well as federal elections.

Although *Reese* involved the denial of voting rights by state officials, Hunt later acquiesced to the majority when the Court ruled that the Fifteenth Amendment did not apply in cases where blacks were denied their right to vote by private individuals. Moreover, in 1873, Hunt refused to recognize arguments advanced by Susan B. Anthony that the Fourteenth Amendment extended similar voting rights to women.

Joining with the Court majority in *Munn v. Illinois* (1877), Hunt proved sympathetic to the use of state police power to regulate private business. His overall influence on the Court was nevertheless minimal.

Harvey Gresham Hudspeth

FURTHER READING

Bader, William H., and Roy M. Mersky, eds. *The First One Hundred Eight Justices.* Buffalo, N.Y.: William S. Hein, 2004.

Fairman, Charles. *Reconstruction and Reunion, 1864-1888.* Vol. 6 in *Oliver Wendell Holmes' Decisive History of the Supreme Court of the United States.* New York: Macmillan, 1971.

Friedman, Leon, and Fred Israel, eds. *The Justices of the Supreme Court: Their Lives and Major Opinions.* 5 vols. New York: Chelsea House, 1997.

Lurie, Jonathan. *The Chase Court: Justices, Rulings, and Legacy.* Santa Barbara, Calif.: ABC-Clio, 2004.

Magrath, C. Peter. *Morrison Waite: The Triumph of Character.* New York: Macmillan Press, 1963.

Stephenson, Donald Grier, Jr. *The Waite Court: Justices, Rulings, and Legacy.* Santa Barbara, Calif.: ABC-Clio, 2003.

SEE ALSO Equal protection clause; Fifteenth Amendment; Reconstruction; Waite, Morrison R.

Hustler Magazine v. Falwell

CITATION: 485 U.S. 46
DATE: February 24, 1988
ISSUE: Libel
SIGNIFICANCE: The Supreme Court ruled against a religious leader's libel claim, providing a right of parody for the press.

Publisher Larry Flynt's *Hustler* magazine printed an issue containing a parody of Jerry Falwell, in which the conservative religious leader was depicted having sex with his mother in an outhouse. A Virginia federal district court jury rejected Falwell's libel claim because it believed that no reasonable person would believe the parody was truthful but awarded Falwell $200,000 for "intentional infliction of emotional distress"—a ruling that did not require that a false statement was made. By an 8-0 vote, the Supreme Court overturned the lower court's decision. In the opinion for the Court, Chief Justice William H. Rehnquist wrote that a public figure could not recover for intentional infliction of emotional harm absent a statement made with actual malice. Public figures such as Falwell must expect robust criticism because the press protection under the First Amendment takes precedence over their emotional loss from nonlibelous statements.

Richard L. Wilson

SEE ALSO First Amendment; Libel; *New York Times Co. v. Sullivan*; *New York v. Ferber*; Obscenity and pornography; Rehnquist, William H.

Illegitimacy

DESCRIPTION: Status accorded a person whose biological parents are not legally married to each other.

SIGNIFICANCE: The Supreme Court first applied the equal protection clause of the Fourteenth Amendment in 1968 to statutory classifications based on marital status. The Court used this clause to proscribe all substantive discrimination while permitting certain procedural discrimination.

Because of the traditional moral and, by consequence, legal stigmatization of illegitimate births, children born outside of marriage had only limited rights before 1968. With regard to support or maintenance and inheritance rights, illegitimate children generally were in a far less advantageous situation than children born to married parents.

In 1968 the validity of a statutory classification based on marital status under the equal protection clause was challenged before the Supreme Court in *Levy v. Louisiana* (1968). In its landmark decision, the Court struck down a Louisiana statute that denied illegitimate children a right to recover for the wrongful death of their mother. Justice William O. Douglas's opinion for the majority rejected the statute for discriminating on a basis that was completely irrelevant to its purpose and subject matter. The Court held that it was "invidious to discriminate against [the children] when no action, conduct, or demeanor of theirs is possibly relevant to the harm that was done the mother."

In a companion case, *Glona v. American Guarantee and Liability Insurance Co.* (1968), the Court declared unconstitutional a state law that prevented parents from suing for the wrongful death of their illegitimate children. The Court concluded that "where the claimant is plainly the mother, the State denies equal protection of the laws to withhold relief merely because the child, wrongfully killed, was born to her out of wedlock." *Levy* and *Glona* were fundamental decisions that had significance for later decisions.

In its next illegitimacy case, *Labine v. Vincent* (1971), the Court departed from *Levy* and *Glona*. The Court examined Louisiana's intestate succession laws, which barred illegitimate children from sharing equally with legitimate children in their father's estate. The Court under Warren E. Burger upheld the Louisiana succession statute. According to Justice Hugo L. Black, *Levy* did not mean that a state can never treat illegitimate children differently from those born within marriage. The Court reasoned that the Louisiana succession laws did not create an "insurmountable barrier" for the child, who could have inherited under a will or if the parents married. The Court also rejected claims that illegitimacy was a suspect classification. Black supported the states' right to use inheritance penalties on illegitimate children to promote birth of children within legally recognized marriages.

EQUAL PROTECTION

In *Jiminez v. Weinberger* (1974), the Court invalidated a provision of the Social Security Act that allowed intestate inheritance of disability benefits by all legitimate children and by illegitimate children who had been "legitimated." Other illegitimate children could inherit benefits only if they proved that they were living with or being supported by the father at the time the disability began. In other words, illegitimate children who were neither living with the father nor being supported by him when the disability arose could not get benefits. The Court ruled the act's provision unconstitutional. The Court reasoned that, assuming the illegitimate children were actually dependent on the father, the purposes of the Social Security Act would not be served by conclusively denying them benefits. The provision would also discriminate between two classes of illegitimate children, although the "potential for spurious claims" would be the same between both groups.

At issue in *Trimble v. Gordon* (1977) was the constitutionality of an Illinois probate statute that refused intestate succession to illegitimate children. Justice Lewis F. Powell, Jr., writing for a bare majority of five justices, struck down the law on the ground that the law was not "substantially related to permissible state interests." He also rejected the state's argument that the discrimination was justified by the promotion of traditional, legal family relationships. He criticized *Labine* because it had accepted similar reasoning without sufficient analysis or scrutiny.

Trimble's small majority demonstrated the Court's ambivalence regarding illegitimate children, which became clear in *Lalli v. Lalli* (1978), decided just one year later. *Lalli* presented the Court with a challenge to the constitutionality of New York's Estates, Powers, and Trusts Laws, which required illegitimate children to submit a court order declaring paternity in order to inherit from their fathers by intestate succession. The Court upheld this law, reasoning that the state had an important interest in preventing fraud and that requiring paternity to be established during the father's lifetime was substantially related to that objective.

Similarly, in *Mathews v. Lucas* (1976), the Court sustained a provision of the Social Security Act that allowed children to receive survivors' benefits only if they could establish both paternity and that the father was providing financial support. The law created a presumption of dependency for all legitimate children and all illegitimate children who were entitled to inherit under state law. The law allowed other illegitimate children to inherit only if they could prove financial dependency on their fathers. The Court found that the distinction among illegitimate children was constitutional because it allowed the government to reduce its administrative burdens. Requiring every child to prove dependency would have been a substantial additional burden on the government; allowing all children to inherit without having to prove dependency would have been a greater cost on the government, one which it was not constitutionally required to absorb.

Although in a number of cases the Court stated that illegitimate children must not be given a lesser status because of their illegitimacy, it also made clear that their illegitimacy can justify certain qualifications of their rights in order to satisfy legitimate state interests. In examining questions regarding the status of illegitimate children, the Court must weigh the rights of the individual children born out of wedlock against society's larger interests in protecting the family unit.

Susan L. Thomas

FURTHER READING

Ball, Howard. *The Supreme Court in the Intimate Lives of Americans: Birth, Sex, Marriage, Childbearing, and Death.* New York: New York University Press, 2002.

Hoover, Sonja. *Welfare Reform and States' Efforts to Prevent Births Outside of Marriage.* Denver, Colo.: National Conference of State Legislatures, 1998.

Langerin-Falcon, Catherine. "Second Class Citizens?" *The Humanist* 58, no. 6 (November/December, 1991): 11-15.

Nechyba, Thomas J. *Social Approval, Values, and AFDC: A Re-examination of the Illegitimacy Debate.* Cambridge, Mass.: National Bureau of Economic Research, 1999.

Reekie, Gail. *Measuring Immorality: Social Inquiry and the Problem of Illegitimacy.* Cambridge, England: Cambridge University Press, 1998.

Zingo, Martha. *Nameless People: Legal Discrimination Against Non-Marital Children in the United States.* Westport, Conn.: Praeger, 1994.

SEE ALSO Birth control and contraception; Equal protection clause; Fourteenth Amendment; Judicial scrutiny; Stevens, John Paul.

Immigration Law

DESCRIPTION: Statutes that regulate the entry of non-U.S. citizens into the United States.

SIGNIFICANCE: The Supreme Court recognized the right of Congress to regulate immigration and restricted the regulation of immigration to the federal government. The Court, however, placed some constitutional limitations on the enforcement of immigration laws within the territorial boundaries of the United States.

The Supreme Court has less control over immigration law than over almost any other area of the legal system because congressional power over the immigration of aliens into the country is considered part of the nation's sovereignty. During the first hundred years of U.S. history, there were few immigration laws to concern the Court. With the exception of the short-lived and controversial Alien and Sedition Acts of 1798, which gave the president power to deport immigrants judged to be dangerous, the federal government made little effort to regulate immigration. Congress did not even create a federal bureau to deal with questions of immigration until 1864, when it appropriated funds for a commissioner of immigration and a staff of five officials to assist immigrants with transportation and settlement problems.

Despite its relative lack of involvement in questions of immigration, though, the Court did help lay the groundwork for federal control of the entry of aliens into the United States. As numbers of immigrants increased, states with large ports that served as points of entry began issuing their own regulations. New York, Pennsylvania, Maryland, and Massachusetts set health standards for new arrivals and taxed shipmasters. In 1876 the issue of state control of immigrants came before the Court in the case of *Henderson v. Mayor of New York*. The Court ruled that state regulatory statutes covering immigration violated Congress's power in interstate commerce. This judicial decision encouraged those interested in regulating immigration to seek federal laws that would replace the state statutes struck down by the Court. The Immigration Act of 1875 was a modest piece of legislation concerned with Asian laborers, but it did mark a historic turn because it signaled the end of the period of unrestricted migration to the United States.

CONGRESSIONAL POWER

Congress replaced older state regulations by imposing a duty of fifty cents per foreign passenger on ships bringing in passengers from foreign countries. In the *Head Money Cases* (1885), the Court held that this was a valid exercise of the right of Congress to regulate commerce.

One of the earliest pieces of major immigration legislation was the Chinese Exclusion Act of 1882. Chinese laborers had been arriving in the United States since 1849, when people in China received word of the California gold rush. Although Chinese workers had helped build the nation's railroads, as the numbers of immigrants from China grew, hostility toward them also grew. The Exclusion Act banned most new migration from China. The Court upheld the right of Congress to exclude entire groups of people from entering the country in *Chae Chan Ping v. United States* (1889) and *Fong Yue Ting v. United States* (1893), citing the jurisdiction of the United States over its own territory as justification.

The right of Congress to act as a sovereign government has enabled Congress to bar the entry of certain groups of people, including convicts, prostitutes, and people who hold objectionable political beliefs. The Court has repeatedly upheld these exclusions. Although U.S. immigration law no longer discriminates on the basis of race, this has not been a result of any action of the Court but because of laws passed by Congress.

Immigration law is largely the province of Congress, not the Supreme Court. In this 1924 photo, officers of the U.S. Public Health Service inspect passengers who have arrived from Asia. (National Archives)

IMMIGRANTS ON U.S. SOIL

Deportation is the act of sending a noncitizen who has entered the United States, either legally or illegally, then been denied the right to remain, back to his or her country of origin. The Court officially recognized the right of Congress to enact deportation laws in the 1892 case *Nishimura Ekiu v. United States.* The 1952 Immigration and Nationality Act, also known as the McCarran-Walter Act, made immigrants subject to exclusion and deportation for political activities, including membership in the Communist Party or Nazi Party. In *Galvan v. Press* (1954), the Court upheld the deportation of resident alien Juan Galvan for having been a member of the Communist Party, even though it was a legal party when Galvan belonged.

Although the Court has recognized the right of Congress to establish and enforce immigration policy, it has sometimes restricted the immigration activities of the government when the immigrants are actually inside U.S. territory. In *Wong Yang Sung v. McGrath* (1950), *Carlson v. Landon* (1952), *Marcello v. Bonds* (1955), *Abel v. United States* (1960), and *Kimm v. Rosenberg* (1960), the Court found that legal and illegal immigrants facing deportation do enjoy some constitutional rights, such as Fourteenth Amendment guarantees of equal protection under the law and Fourth Amendment freedom from unreasonable searches and seizures.

The principle of freedom from unreasonable searches and seizures has involved the Court in the enforcement of immigration law against illegal immigrants. In the case of *Almeida-Sanchez v. United States* (1973), the Court ruled that officers of the Immigration and Naturalization Service could not use roving patrols far from the border to stop vehicles without a warrant or probable cause.

Carl L. Bankston III

FURTHER READING

Baldwin, Carl R. *Immigration: Questions and Answers.* New York: Allworth Press, 1995.
Daniels, Roger. *Guarding the Golden Door: American Immigration Policy and Immigrants Since 1882.* New York: Hill & Wang, 2004.
Helewitz, Jeffrey A. *U.S. Immigration Law.* Dallas: Pearson Publications, 1998.

Hing, Bill Ong. *Defining America Through Immigration Policy*. Philadelphia: Temple University Press, 2004.

Jacoby, Tamar, ed. *Reinventing the Melting Pot: The New Immigrants and What It Means to Be American*. New York: Basic Books, 2004.

Neuman, Gerald L. *Strangers to the Constitution: Immigrants, Borders, and Fundamental Law*. Princeton, N.J.: Princeton University Press, 1996.

Williams, Mary E., ed. *Immigration: Opposing Viewpoints*. San Diego: Greenhaven Press, 2004.

SEE ALSO *Chinese Exclusion Cases*; Citizenship; Commerce, regulation of; Japanese American relocation; Separation of powers.

Income Tax

DESCRIPTION: A tax levied directly on the income earned by individuals or corporations.

SIGNIFICANCE: In 1895 the Supreme Court ruled that an income tax was a direct tax and therefore prohibited by the Constitution. Income taxes remained unconstitutional until the ratification of the Sixteenth Amendment in 1913, which expressly permitted such a tax.

In the Constitutional Convention of 1787, the Framers included two clauses relating to taxation: "all duties, imposts, and excises shall be uniform throughout the United States" and "no capitation, or other direct, tax shall be laid, unless in proportion to the census or enumeration herein before directed to be taken." The latter clause has led to disputes because the word "direct" was not defined in the Constitution or in the debates at the convention. It is clear, however, that this category of tax was to be apportioned among the states according to their population. Taxes that are not direct are presumably categorized as "duties, imposts, and excises," which need not be apportioned; rather, they need only be uniform. There is no explicit mention of an income tax.

The word "direct" was added almost as an afterthought in the midst of a heated debate regarding how the enumeration of slaves was to affect the apportionment of representation and taxes. In the course of this debate, Governeur Morris moved that "taxation shall be in proportion to representation." Then, realizing that the rule would be inapplicable with regard to indirect taxes on exports, imports, and consumption, he inserted the word "direct," and the motion passed.

At the time of the convention, there was only one possible source for the distinction between direct and indirect taxes: Adam Smith's *The Wealth of Nations* (1776). Smith asserted that the income of individuals ultimately arises from three different sources: rent, profit, and wages, and that every tax must be paid ultimately from one of these three. He goes on to state that on occasion, "the state not knowing how to tax, directly and proportionably, the revenue of its subjects, endeavors to tax it indirectly . . . by taxing the consumable commodities upon which it is laid out."

Alexander Hamilton, in *The Federalist* (1788) No. 21, discussing duties on articles of consumption, describes them as falling "under the denomination of indirect taxes," while "those of the direct kind, which principally relate to land and buildings, may admit of a rule of apportionment." His use of the word "principally" rather than "solely" implies the possibility of other taxes in this category. Such taxes as a general tax upon income did not exist in his time.

The Supreme Court narrowed Hamilton's demarcation in *Hylton v. United States* (1796), when it limited direct taxes to taxes on earnings from land. In addition, it ruled that if the tax could not be apportioned, it was not a direct tax of the kind referred to by the Constitution. In *Springer v. United States* (1881), the Court unanimously upheld the first income tax, established by an 1864 act of Congress as a means of financing the Civil War, ruling that it was an indirect tax, which could therefore be levied without apportionment. Direct taxes, it continued, were only taxes on real estate.

POLLOCK AND ITS AFTERMATH

In 1894 Congress levied an income tax that provided for a tax of 2 percent on all income above $4,000, a tax that would affect only the richest 1 percent of the population. The tax was challenged in *Pollock v. Farmers' Loan and Trust Co.* (1895). The Court ruled that the tax was a direct tax and thus prohibited by the Constitution. The tax was judged to be a direct tax only because income for the purposes of the tax included earnings from the lease of real estate, but this inclusion caused the Court to declare the entire tax unconstitutional. There was a popular outcry against this decision.

When President William H. Taft assumed office in 1909, he urged the passage of a constitutional amendment to allow the government to levy an income tax. In the interim, he proposed a tax on corporate income, carefully described as an excise tax. The Court approved this tax in *Flint v. Stone* (1911). The Sixteenth Amendment was ratified in 1913, ending the debate over the constitutionality of an income tax. The amendment granted Congress the power to "lay and collect taxes on incomes, from whatever source derived, without apportionment among the several States, and without regard to any census or enumeration." Subsequent Court cases dealt with details such as the definition of income.

John Andrulis

FURTHER READING

Berson, Susan A. *Federal Tax Litigation*. New York: Law Journal Press, 2004.

Biskupic, Joan, and Elder Witt. *The Supreme Court and the Powers of the American Government*. Washington, D.C.: Congressional Quarterly, 1997.

Hamilton, Alexander, James Madison, and John Jay. *The Federalist Papers*. Reprint. New York: New American Library of World Literature, 1961.

Madison, James. *Notes of Debates in the Federal Convention of 1787*. New York: W. W. Norton, 1966.

Schwartz, Bernard. *Federal and State Powers*. Vol. 1 in *The Powers of Government*. New York: Macmillan, 1963.

Smith, Adam. *An Inquiry into the Nature and Causes of the Wealth of Nations*. Reprint. New York: Random House, 1937.

Swindler, William. *Court and Constitution in the Twentieth Century: The Modern Interpretation*. New York: Bobbs-Merrill, 1974.

Yancey, Richard. *Confessions of a Tax Collector: One Man's Tour of Duty Inside the IRS*. New York: HarperCollins, 2004.

SEE ALSO Bankruptcy law; General welfare clause; Jackson, Howell E.; Native American sovereignty; Poll taxes.

Inverse Incorporation

DESCRIPTION: Supreme Court's gradually arrived-at conclusion that the equal protection requirement of the Fourteenth Amendment is binding on the federal government through the due process clause of the Fifth Amendment.

SIGNIFICANCE: Since the landmark case of *Bolling v. Sharpe* (1954), the Supreme Court has examined equal protection claims against the federal government with the same standards of scrutiny that it uses when examining similar claims against the states.

In contrast to the Declaration of Independence of 1776, neither the original Constitution nor the Bill of Rights explicitly mentioned a right to equality. The wording of the Fifth Amendment, however, implied a degree of legal equality: "no person" was to be deprived of "life, liberty, or property, without due process of law," nor was any person to be denied the privileges against self-incrimination or double jeopardy. The words "person" and "persons" apparently denoted human beings, and both words were used to refer to slaves in Articles I and IV of the Constitution. The same year that Congress approved the Bill of Rights, it expressed an egalitarian spirit in the Judiciary Act of 1789, requiring judges to "solemnly swear or affirm [to] administer law without respect to persons, and do equal right to the poor and to the rich."

Despite those foundation documents, many federal laws mandated racial discrimination. The Naturalization Act of 1790, for example, restricted naturalized citizenship to "any alien being a free white person." Despite the due process clause, the Fugitive Slave law of 1850 did not allow alleged fugitives in northern states to testify in trials or hearings that determined their freedom or enslavement, and the law was found to be constitutional in *Ableman v. Booth* (1859). In the Dred Scott case, *Scott v. Sandford* (1857), moreover, the Court asserted that persons of African ancestry possessed "no rights which the white man was bound to respect."

The Fourteenth Amendment, which was ratified after the Civil War, prohibited the states from denying any person the "equal protection of the laws." This important clause was not applicable to the federal government, apparently because the framers of the amendment were focusing on racial discrimination in the southern states, and the states controlled most public policies applicable to race. When debating the amendment, nevertheless, its framers often made moral allusions to the Declaration of Independence and expressed a belief that all governments were obligated to respect a natural right to equality. Nevertheless, over the ensuing century, the Supreme Court interpreted the equal protection clause so narrowly that the question of a possible federal application seemed of little consequence.

Gibson v. Mississippi (1896) was probably the first case in which a Supreme Court justice unequivocally declared that the Fifth Amendment's due process clause prohibited the federal government from practicing racial discrimination. Justice John Marshall Harlan, a former slave owner, explained that the clause protected the life, liberty, and property of "all persons within the jurisdiction of the United States." Likewise, Justice Harlan Fiske Stone's famous footnote four in *United States v. Carolene Products Co.* (1938) did not make any distinction between the federal and state governments when suggesting that the Court should use heightened scrutiny in the evaluation of legislation that discriminated against "discrete and insular minorities."

During World War II, the Court had to decide whether discriminatory policies toward persons of Japanese ancestry violated constitutional rights. Approving a curfew in *Hirabayashi v. United States* (1943), Chief Justice Stone wrote for the Court that racial distinctions were "by their very nature odious to a free people whose institutions are founded upon the doctrine of equality," and he also observed that precedents based on the equal protection clause would be "controlling" except for the dangers of espionage and sabotage. Although a 6-3 majority of the Court upheld the federal government's displacement program in *Korematsu v. United States* (1944), all the justices implicitly agreed that principles of due process prohibited the federal government from depriving persons of liberty simply because of their race or ethnicity. Justice Hugo L. Black's majority opinion asserted that "all legal restrictions which curtail the civil rights of a single racial group are immediately suspect," demanding "the most rigid scrutiny."

One member of the Court, Justice Frank Murphy, wrote a dissent that explicitly articulated the concept of inverse incorporation: "Being an obvious racial discrimination, the [displacement] order deprives all those within its scope of the equal protection of the laws as guaranteed by the Fifth Amendment."

A decade later, in *Brown v. Board of Education* (1954), the Court ruled that segregated schools in the southern states were incompatible with the equal protection clause of the Fourteenth Amendment. In a companion case, *Bolling v. Sharpe*, the justices ruled that segregated schools operated by the federal government in the nation's capital were also unconstitutional. However, because they were unable to base the *Bolling* decision directly on the Fourteenth Amendment, they relied instead on a substantive due process interpretation of the Fifth Amendment. As historical precedents, Chief Justice Earl Warren referred to the earlier *dicta* (or statements) of justices Harlan, Stone, Black, and Murphy. In his argument, Warren utilized a broad definition of liberty, which was said to include "the full range of conduct which the individual is free to enjoy." Finding evidence that the policy of racial segregation denied African American children of basic life opportunities, he logically concluded that the policy constituted "an arbitrary deprivation of their liberty in violation of the due process clause."

Since its landmark *Bolling* ruling, the Court has not recognized any distinctions between federal and state cases insofar as they relate to the standards of scrutiny for evaluating equal protection claims. In *Rostker v. Goldberg* (1981), for example, the Court evaluated a gender classification of the federal government with an approach called "intermediate scrutiny," the same approach used in considering gender classifications by the state governments. In *Adarand Constructors v. Peña* (1995), moreover, the Court utilized the strictest level of judicial scrutiny in striking down a racial preference mandated by the federal government, just as it had earlier done in a case involving a racial preference by a city government.

Federal cases dealing with equal protection under the Fifth Amendment are relatively rare in comparison with state cases relating to alleged violations under the Fourteenth Amendment.

Thomas Tandy Lewis

SEE ALSO *Adarand Constructors v. Peña; Bolling v. Sharpe; Brown v. Board of Education;* Equal protection clause; Fifth Amendment; Incorporation doctrine; Race and discrimination.

Incorporation Doctrine

DESCRIPTION: Process by which the Supreme Court has gradually nationalized, or "incorporated," the Bill of Rights, requiring state governments to extend to residents much the same rights as the federal government must.

SIGNIFICANCE: The Court held that some of the rights protected by the first eight amendments to the Constitution are also safeguarded by the due process clause of the Fourteenth Amendment and thus applied to the states as well as the federal government.

In *Barron v. Baltimore* (1833), the Supreme Court ruled that rights enumerated in the Bill of Rights restrained the actions of the United States government, not the actions of the state governments. Specifically, the Court held that the eminent domain clause of the Fifth Amendment did not apply to a dispute over whether the city of Baltimore had taken Barron's property for public use without just compensation.

After the passage of the Fourteenth Amendment in 1868, lawyers began to seek ways to use its provisions to undermine *Barron.* The two provisions that lent themselves to this effort were the privileges or immunities clause and the due process clause. These two clauses appear next to one another in the amendment: "No State shall make or enforce any law which shall abridge the privileges or immunities of citizens of the United States; nor shall any State deprive any person of life, liberty or property, without due process of law."

In the *Slaughterhouse Cases* (1873), the attorney for the petitioners argued that engaging in a lawful and useful occupation was a privilege or immunity of U.S. citizenship and an aspect of liberty or property that could not be taken away without due process of law. At issue was an act of the Louisiana legislature creating a corporation and bestowing on that corporation a monopoly over the New Orleans slaughterhouse

---

BILL OF RIGHTS PROTECTIONS NOT EXTENDED TO THE STATES

- Second Amendment right to keep and bear arms
- Third Amendment limit on quartering of soldiers in private homes
- Fifth Amendment right to indictment by grand juries
- Seventh Amendment right to jury trials in civil cases
- Eighth Amendment right against excessive fines (scholars disagree about the status of the right against excessive bail)

---

industry. Butchers disadvantaged by the law asked the courts to declare it unconstitutional. Failing to get a favorable result in the state courts, they appealed to the U.S. Supreme Court.

Justice Samuel F. Miller wrote an opinion that differentiated between privileges or immunities of U.S. citizenship and privileges or immunities of state citizenship. Only the former were protected by the Fourteenth Amendment, and engaging in a lawful and useful occupation was not among them; it was an aspect of state, not national, citizenship. In a similar vein, Justice Miller argued that due process protected persons against takings of life, liberty, or property by improper procedures but did not place limitations on the substance of laws themselves.

THE DUE PROCESS CLAUSE

The Court continued its narrow interpretation of the privileges or immunities clause in subsequent cases, but its view of the due process clause gradually changed. In *Hurtado v. California* (1884), the Court rejected the contention that the Fifth Amendment right to indictment by a grand jury in serious criminal cases was part of Fourteenth Amendment due process. However, in *Chicago, Burlington, and Quincy Railroad Co. v. Chicago* (1897), the Court held that the Fifth Amendment right to just compensation when private property is taken for public use is part of the Fourteenth Amendment protection against property being taken without due process. The Court continued to view criminal procedure rights as less important in *Maxwell v. Dow* (1900) and *Twining v. New Jersey* (1908). In *Maxwell*, the Court found trial by jury not to be incorporated into Fourteenth Amendment due process, and in *Twining*, the justices reached a similar conclusion with respect to the immunity against compulsory self-incrimination. In the latter case, the Court did recognize that it was possible that some of the rights safeguarded by the first eight amendments might be part of the concept of due process and therefore be protected against state action.

ADDITIONAL INCORPORATIONS

It was some time after *Twining*, however, before the Court identified additional provisions of the first eight amendments to be incorporated into Fourteenth Amendment due process. In *Gitlow v. New York* (1925), the Court stated that it assumed that freedom of speech and of the press were among the liberties protected by the Fourteenth Amendment's due process clause, but nevertheless upheld Benjamin Gitlow's conviction for violating the New York law prohibiting language that advocated overthrow of the government by unlawful means. The Court subsequently held unconstitutional a conviction under a similar law in *Fiske v. Kansas* (1927) and overturned a state restriction on the press in *Near v. Minnesota* (1931), thereby confirming what it had assumed in *Gitlow*.

In 1932 the Court appeared to incorporate the right to counsel when it decided *Powell v. Alabama*, but it later ruled in *Betts v. Brady* (1942) that the *Powell* decision was limited to capital offenses. In a case reminiscent of *Gitlow*, the Court said in *Hamilton v. Board of Regents of the University of California* (1934) that freedom of religion was part of the concept of due process, but that a religious pacifist was not entitled to an exemption from the military training required by the university. The Court did clearly hold in *DeJonge v. Oregon* (1937) that the right to assemble peacefully was implicit in due process. This right barred the state of Oregon from convicting Dirk DeJonge for attending a peaceful meeting sponsored by the Communist Party.

A few months after the *DeJonge* decision, the Court attempted to provide a rationale for its incorporation decisions. The case was *Palko v. Connecticut* (1937). Frank Palko had been retried and convicted of first-degree murder after his conviction for second-degree murder had been overturned by the state supreme court. Prosecutors argued, and the state high court agreed, that the trial court judge had erred in excluding Palko's confession to robbery and murder in the first trial. Palko's attorney argued that the two trials constituted double jeopardy in violation of the Fifth Amendment, as incorporated by the due process clause of the Fourteenth. Justice Benjamin N. Cardozo wrote for the Court that only those rights "implicit in the concept of ordered liberty" were part of the notion of due process. These rights were so important "that neither liberty nor justice would exist if they were sacrificed." Justice Cardozo did not find the sort of double jeopardy involved in the *Palko* case inconsistent with the nation's fundamental principles of justice, and double jeopardy was, accordingly, not incorporated.

After *Palko*, the Court once again incorporated rights at a deliberate pace. It absorbed freedom to petition for redress of grievances in *Hague v. Congress of Industrial Organizations* (1939). *Cantwell v. Connecticut* (1940) confirmed the *Hamilton* statement that freedom of religion had been incorporated. The Court assumed that establishment of religion and the prohibition of cruel and unusual punishment were incorporated in 1947, although neither case, *Everson v. Board of Education of Ewing Township* and *Louisiana ex rel. Francis v. Resweber,* respectively, resulted in state action being overturned. The Court confirmed its assumptions in these two cases in *Illinois ex rel. McCollum v. Board of Education* (1948), which struck down a religious education program conducted on school property as a violation of the establishment clause, and *Robinson v. California* (1962), which found a law that made being a drug addict a status crime, to be cruel and unusual punishment. In 1948 the Court incorporated the right to a public trial in the case of *In re Oliver* and the requirement of due notice of the charges against a criminal defendant in *Cole v. Arkansas.*

An Alternate View

In *Adamson v. California* (1947), the Court again confronted the matter of a rationale for its incorporation doctrine. In this case, the

Court once again held that the immunity against self-incrimination was not a part of due process of law. In a lengthy dissent, Justice Hugo L. Black argued that the framers of the Fourteenth Amendment had intended to incorporate all of the provisions of the first eight amendments into the Fourteenth. The Court rejected his views by a 5-4 vote. Justices Frank Murphy and Wiley B. Rutledge, Jr., agreed with Black, but contended that the Court should not restrict the meaning of due process to the rights contained in the first eight amendments. Black, a textualist, wanted to limit the meaning of due process in this way. Justice William O. Douglas agreed with Black in *Adamson*, but in later cases adopted the Murphy-Rutledge position.

Two years later, in *Wolf v. Colorado* (1949), Justice Felix Frankfurter put forward an alternative view of what incorporation meant. At issue was the Fourth Amendment concept of unreasonable search and seizure. Frankfurter conceded that this right was part of due process but argued that only the essential core of the right—not the specific meanings of that right worked out by the federal courts for use in cases involving the U.S. government—restrained state action. Therefore the exclusionary rule, which meant that federal judges could not admit criminal evidence seized in violation of the Fourth Amendment, did not apply to the states. Instead, the courts would have to determine on a case-by-case basis whether states had violated the essential core meaning of the Fourth Amendment. Justice Black referred to this doctrine as applying a "watered down version" of the Bill of Rights to the states. The Frankfurter position dominated the Court in the 1950's, especially in criminal procedure matters such as search and seizure cases. Use of the case-by-case approach was brought to an end by *Mapp v. Ohio* (1961), in which the Court held that states were obliged to follow the exclusionary rule.

After the *Mapp* decision, the Court incorporated an additional seven rights in seventeen years. The Court first acted on the right to counsel in felony cases in *Gideon v. Wainwright* (1963) and expanded this right to include misdemeanors where a jail term was possible in *Argersinger v. Hamlin* (1972). Next it incorporated the immunity against self-incrimination in *Malloy v. Hogan* (1964) and the right to confront and cross-examine adverse witnesses in *Pointer v. Texas* (1965). The Court incorporated the right to a speedy trial in *Klopfer v.*

North Carolina (1967) along with the right to compulsory process to obtain witnesses in *Washington v. Texas* (1968). It followed with the right to a jury trial in *Duncan v. Louisiana* (1968) and completed its incorporation jurisprudence with double jeopardy in *Benton v. Maryland* (1969). Only the Second Amendment right to keep and bear arms, the Third Amendment right against quartering soldiers, the Fifth Amendment right of grand jury indictment, the Seventh Amendment right to a jury trial in civil cases, and the Eighth Amendment protection against excessive bail and fines remain beyond the scope of due process.

The selective incorporation doctrine of *Palko* remains the majority view. However, Frankfurter's case-by-case approach continues to enjoy considerable support. Justice John Marshall Harlan II, Chief Justice Warren Burger, and Justice Lewis F. Powell, Jr., supported the doctrine when they were on the Court. Chief Justice William H. Rehnquist succeeded them as the strongest proponent of the case-by-case approach on the Court, and the doctrine seems to enjoy some favor among several other Court members as well. Justice Black's total incorporation approach and the total incorporation-plus doctrine of Murphy and Rutledge have had little support since such justices as Douglas and Arthur J. Goldberg left the Court.

Daryl R. Fair

FURTHER READING

Michael J. Perry's *We the People: The Fourteenth Amendment and the Supreme Court* (New York: Oxford University Press, 2001) examines the charge that the Supreme Court has usurped the political process and examines each major Fourteenth Amendment issue. An excellent basic source on incorporation doctrine is *Freedom and the Court: Civil Rights and Liberties in the United States* by Henry J. Abraham and Barbara A. Perry (8th ed. Lawrence: University Press of Kansas, 2003). Horace Flack made a case for total incorporation of the first eight amendments in *The Adoption of the Fourteenth Amendment* (Baltimore, Md.: Johns Hopkins University Press, 1908), as did Michael Curtis in the more recent *No State Shall Abridge: The Fourteenth Amendment and the Bill of Rights* (Durham, N.C.: Duke University Press, 1986).

Two scholars who agree in part with the total incorporation doctrine but reject some of the historical generalizations made by Justice Black and Professor Flack are Jacobus ten Broek, *The Antislavery Origins of the Fourteenth Amendment* (Berkeley: University of California Press, 1951) and J. B. James, *The Framing of the Fourteenth Amendment* (Urbana: University of Illinois Press, 1956).

Raoul Berger's *Government by Judiciary: The Transformation of the Fourteenth Amendment* (Cambridge, Mass.: Harvard University Press, 1977) forcefully rejects the total incorporation doctrine. Raold Y. Mykkeltvedt discusses the Frankfurter case-by-case approach in *Nationalization of the Bill of Rights: Fourteenth Amendment Due Process and the Procedural Rights* (Port Washington, N.Y.: National University Publications, 1983). In *The Supreme Court and the Second Bill of Rights* (Madison: University of Wisconsin Press, 1981), Richard C. Cortner tells the story of the cases in which the Court incorporated various rights into the Fourteenth Amendment. *The Bill of Rights*, a two-volume work edited by Thomas Tandy Lewis (Pasadena, Calif.: Salem Press, 2002), provides comprehensive coverage of the Bill of Rights, with articles on each of the amendments, the Constitution, the incorporation doctrine, and many other topics.

SEE ALSO *Adamson v. California*; *Barron v. Baltimore*; Bill of Rights; Black, Hugo L.; Cardozo, Benjamin N.; Double jeopardy; Due process, substantive; *Duncan v. Louisiana*; Fourteenth Amendment; Frankfurter, Felix; Fundamental rights; *Gideon v. Wainwright*; *Gitlow v. New York*; *Mapp v. Ohio*; *Palko v. Connecticut*; Privileges and immunities; *Slaughterhouse Cases*.

James Iredell

IDENTIFICATION: Associate justice (May 12, 1790-October 20, 1799)
NOMINATED BY: George Washington
BORN: October 5, 1751, Lewes, England
DIED: October 20, 1799, Edenton, North Carolina
SIGNIFICANCE: Serving on the Supreme Court for nearly a decade, Iredell was a supporter of judicial restraint, a strict constructionist, and defender of the original design of the Constitution.

Born in Lewes, England, James Iredell spent his childhood in Bristol. The eldest of five sons born to Francis and Margaret McCulloh Iredell, he was forced to leave school after his father suffered a debilitating stroke in 1766. With the assistance of relatives, Iredell came to America in 1768 to accept an appointment as comptroller of the customs in Port Roanoke in Edenton, North Carolina. The young man's salary was sent directly to his parents. A gregarious person, Iredell quickly made friends, including many of the most talented citizens of Edenton. He began legal studies under the tutelage of Samuel Johnston, who would later serve as governor of North Carolina. Iredell also married Johnston's sister, Hannah, in 1773.

In 1770 Iredell was licensed to practice law in the lower courts of the colony, and in 1774 he was allowed to practice law in the superior courts. In 1774 he was also promoted to collector of the port at Edenton. During this period, Iredell published various tracts urging a healing of relations between England and America, while expressing concern about the violation of the colonists' chartered rights as Englishmen. With great precision and restraint, Iredell presented a series of thoughtful commentaries that served as a defense of the American position. The central problem of the English system, according to Iredell, was a weak judiciary, unable to defend the constitution against the usurpations of Parliament and the Crown.

Iredell was appointed to serve on a committee to revise the statues of North Carolina in 1776 and elected by the general assembly to serve as a superior court judge, the equivalent of a state supreme court judicial post, in 1777. He served in this capacity for six months. After serving as North Carolina's attorney general, Iredell returned to his law practice and continued to defend colonists' positions in his speeches and writings. By the time of the Constitutional Convention, Iredell was a highly respected jurist and legal theorist.

Iredell was elected as a delegate to North Carolina's first ratifying convention. Under the pseudonym "Marcus," Iredell had already published an essay entitled "Answers to Mr. Mason's Objections to the New Constitution," defending the Constitution as a moderate document that would correct the weaknesses of the Articles of Confederation. He was one of the most articulate and influential of the Federalist advocates of the Constitution; however, as Iredell had anticipated, the initial attempt at ratification failed. A second convention was held in November, 1789, and the Constitution was ratified. In defense of the Constitution, Iredell stated that "no power can be exercised but what is expressly given." For Iredell, the adoption of the Constitution was an improvement because it provided for a separation of powers and af-

James Iredell.
(Albert Rosenthal/
Collection of the
Supreme Court of
the United States)

firmed state sovereignty. His thoughtful defense of the need for ratification attracted many admirers, including President George Washington, who appointed Iredell to the Supreme Court in 1790.

As an associate justice, Iredell was an original thinker and representative of southern federalism. In his decisions and legal analysis,
he differed substantially from his colleagues, including Chief Justice
John Jay and Justice James Wilson. In the case of *Chisholm v. Georgia*
(1793), the judiciary's first reevaluation of the federal arrangement
after ratification, Iredell provided the lone dissent, arguing that a citizen of one state could not sue another state in federal court. The
other justices claimed the plaintiff had a right to be heard. Iredell
suggested that "each state in the Union is sovereign as to all powers
reserved." In 1798 the states ratified the Eleventh Amendment,
which overturned the *Chisholm* decision and affirmed Iredell's criticism of implied power and defense of state authority. As the first justice to articulate a strict constructionist view of the Constitution,
Iredell was a representative of a school of interpretation that continues to influence judicial decision making.

H. Lee Cheek, Jr.

FURTHER READING

Bader, William H., and Roy M. Mersky, eds. *The First One Hundred
Eight Justices.* Buffalo, N.Y.: William S. Hein, 2004.

Bradford, M. E. "James Iredell: An Old Whig in Edenton." In *Against
the Barbarians.* Columbia: University of Missouri Press, 1992.

Graebe, Christopher. "The Federalism of James Iredell in Historical
Context." *North Carolina Historical Review* 69 (1990).

Harrington, Matthew P. *Jay and Ellsworth, The First Courts: Justices, Rulings, and Legacy.* Santa Barbara, Calif.: ABC-Clio, 2007.

Higginbotham, R. Don, ed. *The Papers of James Iredell.* 2 vols. Raleigh:
North Carolina Division of Archives and History, 1976.

Wexler, Natalie. "James Iredell." In *American National Biography.* New
York: Oxford, 1999.

SEE ALSO *Calder v. Bull*; *Chisholm v. Georgia*; Eleventh Amendment;
Ellsworth, Oliver; Federalism; Jay, John; Judicial self-restraint; Rutledge, John.

Howell E. Jackson

IDENTIFICATION: Associate justice (March 4, 1893-August 8, 1895)
NOMINATED BY: Benjamin Harrison
BORN: April 8, 1832, Paris, Tennessee
DIED: August 8, 1895, Nashville, Tennessee
SIGNIFICANCE: A Southern Democrat who had served with the Confederacy, Jackson was the final Supreme Court appointee of outgoing Republican president Benjamin Harrison. In 1895 on his deathbed, Jackson wrote a dissent favoring a federal income tax.

Born in Paris, Tennessee, Howell E. Jackson soon moved with his family to Jackson where he attended Jackson Male Academy and West Tennessee College. After attending the University of Virginia and Cumberland School of Law, Jackson practiced law in Jackson and Memphis before accepting appointment as Confederate receiver of sequestered property for West Tennessee in 1861. Resuming his legal practice in 1865, Jackson served as special judge on Tennessee's post-Reconstruction court of arbitration before losing a bid in 1878 for a seat on the state supreme court. Jackson won election to the state legislature in 1880, and his leadership within the "State Debt" Democratic faction, which had opposed Tennessee's repudiation of its postwar debts, helped secure his election as the legislature's compromise candidate for the U.S. Senate in 1881.

Jackson served in the Senate for the next five years, supporting Stanley Matthews during his bitterly contested nomination for the Supreme Court in 1881 and opposing Roscoe Conkling's nomination to that body in 1882. A former Whig turned Democrat, Jackson voted to support both the Chinese Exclusion Act of 1882 and the Pendleton Civil Service Act of 1883. He was also a strong advocate of railroad regulation and federal aid to local education. Additionally, his strong opposition to the Tenure of Office Act (1867) helped position him to be Grover Cleveland's first major judicial appointee in 1886.

Jackson's colleagues during his seven years of service as Sixth Circuit Court judge included William H. Taft. One of his first recorded decisions proved instrumental in diffusing the Pan Electric Company's attempt to nullify the telephone patent then held by Alexan-

Howell E. Jackson.
(Landy, Cincinnati/
Collection of the
Supreme Court of the
United States)

der Graham Bell. His 1892 decision in the case of *In re Greene* later
served as the legal foundation for *United States v. E. C. Knight Co.*
(1895). Jackson's 1893 ruling in the case of *United States v. Patrick,* upholding the conviction of three Tennesseeans charged with violating
the Civil Rights Act of 1875, helped position Jackson as Republican
Benjamin Harrison's last appointee to the Supreme Court in 1893.

Jackson showed signs of tuberculosis shortly after his first term on
the Court. In the twenty-nine months he served on the Court, he rendered just forty-six decisions and four dissents. Although most of his
rulings pertained to matters involving patent law, he left a lasting record of opposition against both the right of the states to restrict federal authority and the right of both state and the national government to regulate private enterprise. He ultimately gained lasting
fame for his deathbed dissent favoring a federal income tax in the
1895 case of *Pollock v. Farmers' Loan and Trust Co.* He died exactly one
hundred days after delivering his dissent at his West Meade estate just
outside of Nashville.

Harvey Gresham Hudspeth

FURTHER READING

Bader, William H., and Roy M. Mersky, eds. *The First One Hundred Eight Justices.* Buffalo, N.Y.: William S. Hein, 2004.

Calvani, Terry. "The Early Legal Career of Howell E. Jackson." *Vanderbilt Law Review* 30 (1977): 39-73.

Ely, James W., Jr. *The Fuller Court: Justices, Rulings, and Legacy.* Santa Barbara, Calif.: ABC-Clio, 2003.

Hudspeth, Harvey G. "Howell Edmunds Jackson and the Making of Tennessee's First Native-Born Supreme Court Justice, 1893-1895." *Tennessee Historical Quarterly* (Summer, 1999): 56-76.

_____. "Seven Days in Nashville: Politics, The State Debt, and the Making of a United States Senator." *West Tennessee Society Papers* 52 (December, 1998): 81-94.

Schiffman, Irving. "Escaping the Shroud of Anonymity: Justice Howell Edmunds Jackson and the Income Tax Case." *Tennessee Law Review* 37 (1970): 334-348.

SEE ALSO Fuller, Melville W; Income tax; Matthews, Stanley.

Robert H. Jackson

IDENTIFICATION: Associate justice (July 11, 1941-October 9, 1954)

NOMINATED BY: Franklin D. Roosevelt

BORN: February 13, 1892, Spring Creek, Pennsylvania

DIED: October 9, 1954, Washington, D.C.

SIGNIFICANCE: During his thirteen years on the Supreme Court, Jackson wrote eloquent defenses of free expression in some cases, while in others he upheld state power to suppress speech and other freedoms. His opinions were individualistic, pragmatic, hard to predict, and middle-of-the-road.

The son of a hotel and livery stable owner, Robert H. Jackson grew up in Frewsburg, New York. After graduation from high school, he worked as a clerk in a law office in Jamestown, New York, a small upstate town, and became active in Democratic Party politics. After a year of study at Albany Law School, Jackson returned to his clerkship and passed the bar in 1913. He was the last justice to qualify for the bar as an apprentice rather than graduating from law school. Jackson established a successful and profitable general law practice in Jamestown and became active in the state bar association.

In a heavily Republican area, Jackson, at the age of twenty-one, was elected Democratic state committee member. In this role, he served as an adviser on federal patronage to Assistant Secretary of the Navy Franklin D. Roosevelt in the administration of President Woodrow Wilson. When Roosevelt was governor of New York from 1928 to 1932, Jackson again served as his informal adviser. During Roosevelt's 1932 presidential campaign, Jackson electioneered for him throughout the state. In 1934 Jackson went to Washington, D.C., as general counsel for the Bureau of Internal Revenue. He subsequently served as assistant attorney general for the tax and then the antitrust divisions in the Department of Justice. In 1938 Roosevelt appointed him solicitor general, and in 1940 Jackson became a member of Roosevelt's cabinet as attorney general. Jackson's extensive political and administrative experience gave him a deeper insight into the political process of the government than many of his colleagues.

APPOINTMENT TO THE COURT

In June, 1941, Roosevelt, who had discussed the possible appointment of Jackson to the chief justiceship before deciding to elevate Associate Justice Harlan Fiske Stone to that post, nominated Jackson as an associate justice. By the time of Jackson's appointment, the Supreme Court had virtually completed its transition in terms of constitutional doctrine. The social and economic changes championed by the New Deal were for the most part accomplished. The Court, with a new majority of Roosevelt appointees, went about determining how the dominant liberal view would be applied in deciding cases that increasingly raised questions of civil liberties. As associate justice, Jackson, for the most part, maintained an ideological middle ground between the libertarian judicial activists led by justices Hugo L. Black and William O. Douglas and the far right in the Court alignment. He frequently agreed with the moderate conservative views of Justice Felix Frankfurter, although they differed on such matters as judicial supremacy and the scope of interpreting the Bill of Rights.

Jackson was a man of solid and outstanding talents, but the contrasts and contrarieties of his character were great. From June, 1945, through October, 1946, Jackson, at the request of President Harry S. Truman, served as chief counsel for the United States in the Nuremberg war trials (which he described as the most satisfying and gratifying experience of his life) and did not sit with the Court. While Jackson was in Nuremberg, Chief Justice Stone died, and Truman considered Jackson and Black as possible successors.

In the untoward verbal battle that followed, both Jackson and Black threatened to resign from the Court if the president nominated the other. Jackson made public details of a feud with Black that originated in the Court's hearing of the *Jewel Ridge Coal Corp. v. Local No. 6167, United Mine Workers of America* (1945) and that called into question the Court's impartiality. This controversy embarrassed Jackson, Black, and the Court, and Truman nominated his loyal friend Fred M. Vinson to be chief justice. Black was conciliatory when Jackson returned to the

Robert H. Jackson.
(Harris and Ewing/
Collection of the
Supreme Court of
the United States)

Court for the October, 1946, term. In 1954 Jackson was hospitalized with a serious heart condition. Nevertheless, he continued his work on the Court and took part in the *Brown v. Board of Education* (1954) decision. A few days after the beginning of the 1954 term, Jackson died.

PARTICULAR RIGHTS

Jackson was accused of being erratic in his civil liberties opinions. He frequently espoused judicial self-restraint, but he was the author of memorable opinions about the values of the First Amendment. He wrote for the majority in striking down a compulsory flag salute in public schools in *West Virginia State Board of Education v. Barnette* (1943), noting that the purpose of the Bill of Rights was to withdraw certain subjects from the vicissitudes of political controversy. His opinion was in stark contrast to Frankfurter's dissenting plea for judicial self-restraint. In *Ballard v. United States* (1944), Jackson would have dismissed the indictment against an offbeat religious group in a mail fraud case and avoided judicially examining other people's faiths.

After his return from the Nuremberg trials, Jackson seemed more concerned with the need to balance freedom and public order. When the Court reversed a conviction for breach of peace in *Terminiello v. Chicago* (1949), Jackson, in dissent, worried that the majority's doctrinaire view might convert the Bill of Rights into a suicide pact. During the McCarthy era, Jackson concurred in upholding federal anticommunist measures in *Dennis v. United States* (1951) and *American Communications Association v. Douds* (1950). The pragmatic character of his free speech votes stemmed from his attentiveness to the circumstances of each case.

FEDERALISM

Several of Jackson's judicial-restraint values derived from his view of the federal system. Although he was willing to selectively incorporate Bill of Rights protections to apply to the states if they were fundamental to liberty and justice, Jackson's view of the federal system limited his willingness to see the states forced into a common mold by judicial action in criminal proceedings under the Fourteenth Amendment due process clause. On the other hand, Jackson was an activist in restricting state legislation when challenged as conflicting with an unexercised federal commerce power. He interpreted dormant commerce power in such a way as to restrict efforts under state taxing and police powers to deal with local matters affecting interstate commerce.

In *Edwards v. California* (1941), Jackson concurred in the Court's use of the federal commerce power to strike down the state's law against immigrants from Oklahoma and added that travel among states was a privilege of U.S. citizenship. In *Wickard v. Filburn* (1942), Jackson's opinion for the Court upheld the Agricultural Adjustment Act of 1938 and further extended the federal commerce power to regulate the production and consumption of wheat that was never marketed. In the review of administrative determinations, Jackson also was more of an activist than a majority of his colleagues.

In short, it is difficult to associate Jackson's views with any set of doctrines that neatly explain them all. He was willing to grant much validity to various judicial doctrines, but he was unwilling to follow any of them to the point where they obscured the practical effects. Jackson apparently was forced to the right of the Court by the sweeping views of his more libertarian colleagues—although he did not like it. Jackson possessed an acute mind and wrote with a pithy, brilliant style punctuated with pungent and memorable phrases. At his best, his prose has rarely been matched in sheer force and persuasiveness.

CONSTITUTIONAL PHILOSOPHY

In his history of the Court, *The Struggle for Judicial Supremacy* (1941), Jackson described the existence of a restraintist philosophy of the judiciary's place in government at the time of his appointment to the bench. He advocated narrowing the limits of the Court's jurisdiction in contrast to the activists' expansionist views. In the posthumously published *The Supreme Court in the American System of Government* (1955), Jackson wrote that the task of a justice was to maintain the system of balance upon which free government is based.

According to Jackson, the Court is the most detached, dispassionate, and trustworthy custodian that the U.S. system affords for the translation of abstract doctrines into concrete constitutional commands. Jackson viewed the judiciary as the branch of government most qualified to correct the inadequacies of the political process and the one least able to make needed adjustments among competing social claims.

Theodore M. Vestal

FURTHER READING

Bader, William H., and Roy M. Mersky, eds. *The First One Hundred Eight Justices.* Buffalo, N.Y.: William S. Hein, 2004.

Belknap, Michal R. *The Vinson Court: Justices, Rulings, and Legacy.* Santa Barbara, Calif.: ABC-Clio, 2004.

Gerhart, Eugene. *Robert H. Jackson: Country Lawyer, Supreme Court Justice, America's Advocate.* Buffalo, N. Y.: William S. Hein, 2003.

Hockett, Jeffrey D. *New Deal Justice: The Constitutional Jurisprudence of Hugo L. Black, Felix Frankfurter, and Robert H. Jackson.* Lanham, Md.: Rowman & Littlefield, 1996.

Jackson, Robert H. *The Supreme Court in the American System of Government.* Cambridge, Mass.: Harvard University Press, 1955.

Renstrom, Peter G. *The Stone Court: Justices, Rulings, and Legacy.* Santa Barbara, Calif.: ABC-Clio, 2001.

Schubert, Glendon, ed. *Dispassionate Justice: A Synthesis of the Judicial Opinions of Robert H. Jackson.* Indianapolis, Ind.: Bobbs-Merrill, 1969.

Urofsky, Melvin I. *The Warren Court: Justices, Rulings, and Legacy.* Santa Barbara, Calif.: ABC-Clio, 2001.

SEE ALSO Federalism; Judicial self-restraint; New Deal; Speech and press, freedom of; Stone, Harlan Fiske; Vinson, Fred M.

Japanese American Relocation

DATE: 1942

DESCRIPTION: The removal of more than 112,000 Japanese immigrants and their children, most of whom were U.S. citizens, to detention camps as a result of President Franklin D. Roosevelt's Executive Order 9066.

SIGNIFICANCE: The removal of tens of thousands of U.S. citizens to detention camps and the restrictions placed on the movement of thousands of others, purely on the basis of national origin, were found to be unconstitutional acts by the Supreme Court, though most of these wartime restrictions were not actually lifted until 1945.

In 1790 the Nationality Act established the standards to be used for U.S. citizenship and naturalization. The law stated that only free white persons were eligible to become U.S. citizens. The primary intent of this law was to create a legal distinction between people of African descent and European immigrants. Although the law did not specifically address Asian immigrants, whose numbers were insignificant, in practice those who entered were categorized as nonwhites and therefore denied citizenship.

After the Civil War, the Fourteenth Amendment (ratified in 1868) proclaimed that anyone born in, and subject to, the jurisdiction of the United States would be a U.S. citizen. The intent of this amendment was to grant citizenship to the black former slaves in the South. However, in 1870 Congress passed legislation to amend the naturalization law, effectively retaining the prohibition of citizenship for nonwhite immigrants. The result was that only white people or people of African descent already in the United States could become naturalized citizens. Neither Asian immigrants nor their U.S.-born children were granted these rights.

In 1898 the Supreme Court ruled in the *United States v. Wong Kim Ark* that anyone born in the United States could became a citizen. This decision was the result of a three-year lawsuit by an American-born Chinese man, Wong Kim Ark, who was detained and prevented from reentering the United States after returning from a trip to China. Although this decision upheld birthright citizenship for all U.S.-born

Asians, the Supreme Court still acknowledged the power of Congress to restrict naturalization. In *Ozawa v. United States* (1922), the Court rejected the application for citizenship of Takao Ozawa, who had been raised and educated in the United States but was born in Japan, judging him ineligible for naturalization because he was nonwhite.

Also in 1922, Congress passed the Cable Act. This law provided that "any woman citizen who marries an alien ineligible to citizenship shall cease to be a citizen of the United States." The justification for this act was that civil law generally recognized a husband's citizenship over the wife's. An Asian American or white woman with U.S. citizenship who married an Asian immigrant lost her citizenship. If the marriage terminated by divorce or death, the white woman was eligible to reapply for citizenship, but the Asian American woman could not. The law was amended in 1931 to permit Asian American women married to Asian immigrants to retain or regain their U.S. citizenship, but it was repealed in 1936.

THE SEEDS OF RELOCATION

After the first Japanese arrived in Hawaii in 1868, many workers immigrated to the island. Immigration to the U.S. mainland, however, largely remained limited to wealthier, more highly educated Japanese. After Hawaii became an American possession in 1898, the number of laborers who reached the mainland increased significantly. In 1899, 2,844 Japanese arrived on the mainland, but two years later, in 1900, 12,635 Japanese entered the continental United States. Many white Americans viewed the influx of Japanese and Chinese immigrants as an economic and cultural threat, and racial tensions grew, especially on the West Coast where most Asian immigrants had settled. Pressure from the western states forced the federal government to restrict Japanese immigration by means such as the Gentlemen's Agreement with Japan (1908).

The Gentlemen's Agreement prohibited immigration by Japanese men; however, it permitted the wives of immigrants already in the country to enter. Ironically, the agreement actually increased immigration because immigrant men believed that they must immediately send for their wives in Japan or risk permanent separation. Many single men hurriedly sent pictures of themselves to Japan to find wives or asked relatives and friends to send pictures of prospective brides willing to come to the United States. Thus, many Japanese women, while still in Japan, married Japanese men living in the United States without ever seeing more than a photo; these "picture brides" crossed the ocean by themselves with visas sent by their husbands in the United States. To stem this great influx, Congress passed the Immigration Exclusion Act of 1924, virtually barring any further Japanese immigration.

WORLD WAR II

Immediately after Japan bombed Pearl Harbor in 1941, Lieutenant General John L. DeWitt (military commander of the western defense zone) suggested removal of all persons of Japanese ancestry—citizens or aliens—from all West Coast states. Many Japanese Americans' homes were searched by Federal Bureau of Investigation agents, and within four days, 1,370 Japanese immigrants had been taken from their homes and places of business with no warning. Less than a month after Pearl Harbor, the Treasury Department froze the financial assets of Japanese nationals and bank accounts registered under Japanese-sounding names. Although the Treasury Department soon eased these restrictions, Japanese Americans were not allowed to withdraw more than one hundred dollars per month from the bank. The federal government also seized money from Japanese American clubs and organizations; for example, in 1942 the government took seventy thousand dollars from the Japanese Association of New York, returning fifty thousand of it in 1953.

In February, 1942, just one week after DeWitt submitted the final recommendation for relocation, President Franklin D. Roosevelt signed Executive Order 9066, which sent 112,350 people of Japanese descent to detention camps, describing them as either "enemy aliens" or "strangers from a distant shore." This order applied only to the mainland; in Hawaii, where one-third of the population was of Japanese ancestry, no restrictions were ever enacted. In March of 1942, the draft status of Japanese Americans was reclassified, and men of military age were exempted under a 4-F classification, which implied that being of Japanese ancestry was a physical defect, eliminating the possibility of military service. In 1943, however, the government changed this policy, making Japanese American men subject to the draft. By the end of the war in 1945, almost 40,000 Japanese Americans served in the U.S. armed services, several thousand of them coming from the detention camps.

SUPREME COURT DECISIONS

Japanese Americans soon questioned the legality of the executive order and other government policies. Some objected to the loss of property on the grounds of due process; some questioned the right of the government to restrict the liberty and movement of U.S. citizens; and others disputed the moral authority of the government to force men in detention centers to join the military. Most of these challenges were eventually heard by the Supreme Court, though the Court itself avoided acting on the constitutionality of exclusion and actual detention until near the war's end.

Min (Minoru) Yasui, a Japanese American lawyer and U.S. citizen, doubted the legality of the curfews for Japanese Americans that were

Japanese Americans in San Pedro, California, board a train to a relocation center in Manzanar in 1942. The Supreme Court upheld the constitutionality of their relocation. (National Japanese American Historical Society)

615

imposed soon after the start of the war. He deliberately violated a curfew in Portland in 1942 to force the courts to hear this issue. After he was arrested, his U.S. citizenship was taken away because he had studied in a Japanese language school and had worked for the Japanese consulate. Though a lower court found the curfew unconstitutional, the Supreme Court in *Yasui v. the United States* (1943) reversed this finding, claiming that the government possessed extraordinary powers in time of war, especially in the light of Japanese Americans' "continued attachment" to Japan. The same year, Gordon Hirabayashi, also a U.S. citizen of Japanese descent, was arrested for violating curfew. Hirabayashi turned himself in to the Seattle office of the Federal Bureau of Investigation for failing to report for imprisonment. After Hirabayashi had spent five months in jail, the Supreme Court, in *Hirabayashi v. United States* (1943), unanimously upheld the constitutionality of the curfew. He was ordered to serve another ninety days of work on a government road crew.

In October, 1944, in *Korematsu v. United States*, the Court upheld the constitutionality of the exclusion order by a 6-3 vote. Fred Korematsu, a U.S. citizen of Japanese descent, was arrested for trying to avoid incarceration in a detention camp. He had plastic surgery done on his nose and eyelids to look less Japanese and changed his name to Clyde Sarah, a Spanish-Hawaiian sounding name. Unlike Yasui and Hirabayashi, Korematsu did not wish to create a test case; he just wanted to stay with his fiancé, who was not of Japanese ancestry.

In July, 1942, attorney James Purcell filed a writ of habeas corpus with the federal court in San Francisco on behalf of Mitsuye Endo, an American-born civil service employee. Although the cases of Yasui, Hirabayashi, and Korematsu challenged the curfews and exclusion orders, Endo's case challenged the legality of the detention camps themselves. At first, lower courts found against Endo. However, after a two-year struggle, in December, 1944, in *Ex parte Endo*, the Supreme Court set her free, saying that because she had been found to be a loyal citizen, the War Relocation Authority could not detain her against her will. The Court, thus, ruled that detention of citizens was unconstitutional and loyal U.S. citizens of Japanese descent were free to move anywhere in the United States.

In spite of the federal government's discriminatory treatment of

Japanese Americans, the Court's decisions showed progress toward protecting this group's rights. For example, Fred Oyama, a U.S. citizen of Japanese descent, became the titleholder of land in California that his immigrant parents were prohibited from owning because of the California Alien Land Act of 1913. While the Oyama family was in the detention camps, the state government attempted to seize the land, and Fred Oyama sued under the equal protection clause. The Supreme Court's 6-3 decision in *Oyama v. California* (1948) supported Oyama, stating that "the rights of a citizen may not be subordinated merely because of his father's country of origin."

These various wartime Supreme Court decisions were instrumental in establishing equal rights for Japanese Americans. By the early 1950's most state and local alien land acts and other discriminatory ordinances against Japanese had been repealed. However, these decisions also represent a substantial cost to all Americans' constitutional liberties. As was evident in the Yasui, Hirabayashi, and Korematsu decisions, the guarantees of due process in the Constitution are not unambiguous. If the government can claim military necessity, the Court may uphold the restriction of individual liberties.

THE LEGACY OF EVACUATION

One-third of the people interned by the War Relocation Authority were not American citizens. This lack of citizenship does not necessarily indicate a lack of allegiance to or intent to remain in the United States, however, because Japan-born immigrants were not eligible to naturalize regardless of their wishes. Although Chinese immigrants were allowed to naturalize in 1943, and Indians and Filipinos in 1946, Japanese were not permitted to become naturalized citizens until the McCarran-Walter Act in 1952.

In the late 1960's, Japanese American groups in San Francisco, Southern California, and Seattle began to agitate for compensation for the detention and subsequent losses suffered during World War II. After much legal paperwork and protest, in 1988 Japanese Americans were recognized as being guilty of nothing but being of the wrong ancestry at the wrong time: Abe Fortas, who had overseen the War Relocation Authority while undersecretary of the interior, called the evacuation "a tragic error." By 1993 some sixty thousand surviving Japanese American former detainees received compensation in the amount of twenty thousand dollars per person.

Nobuko Adachi

FURTHER READING

Perhaps the best place to begin the study of the legal aspects of the Japanese American incarceration is Wendy L. Ng's *Japanese American Internment During World War II: A History and Reference Guide* (Westport, Conn.: Greenwood Press, 2002), a comprehensive reference source on the internment years. Another good source to begin with is Angelo N. Ancheta's *Race, Rights, and The Asian American Experience* (New Brunswick, N.J.: Rutgers University Press, 1998). Ancheta, a civil rights attorney, covers legal issues historically, looking at both Japanese Americans and other Asian Americans in the United States.

Masako Herman's *The Japanese in America, 1843-1973* (New York: Oceania Publications, 1974) is highly recommended for its chronology of Japanese American lawsuits and documentation on the various laws, acts, and orders. *Democracy on Trial: The Japanese American Evacuation and Relocation in World War II* (New York: Simon & Schuster, 1995), by Page Smith, helps link military, political, economic, racial, and personal motivations of the relocation. Peter Irons's *Justice at War: The Inside Story of the Japanese-American Internment* (Berkeley: University of California Press, 1993) presents the best narrative of the cases at trial and before the Supreme Court, with evidence that the government concealed evidence.

Advanced students may consult *Justice Delayed: The Record of the Japanese American Internment Case* (Middletown, Conn.: Wesleyan University Press, 1989). Jerry Kang explores the complex legal issues of the internment decisions in *Race, Rights, and Reparations: Law and the Japanese American Internment* (New York: Aspen, 2001). Susan Dudley Gold's *Korematsu v. United States: Japanese American Internment* (New York: Benchmark Books, 2005) is written specifically for younger readers.

SEE ALSO *Bolling v. Sharpe*; *Chinese Exclusion Cases*; Citizenship; Fourteenth Amendment; Immigration law; *Korematsu v. United States*; Murphy, Frank; Race and discrimination; War powers; World War II.

John Jay

IDENTIFICATION: Chief justice (October 19, 1789-June 29, 1795)
NOMINATED BY: George Washington
BORN: December 12, 1745, New York, New York
DIED: May 17, 1829, Bedford, New York
SIGNIFICANCE: As the first chief justice, Jay was responsible for establishing procedures, admitting practitioners, and organizing the Supreme Court's business. A strong nationalist in his constitutional views, he believed that the Court had judicial authority to hear cases against a state.

The son of a prominent New York City merchant, John Jay was a member of colonial New York's social elite. Educated at King's College, later Columbia University (A.B., 1764), he was apprenticed to lawyer Benjamin Kissam, and admitted to practice in 1768. He was clerk to the New York-New Jersey Boundary Commission from 1769 to 1774. A leader of the conservative faction of New York patriots, he served in the First and Second Continental Congresses (1774 and

John Jay.
(C. Gregory Stapko/ Collection of the Supreme Court of the United States)

```
                 FIRSTS AMONG JUSTICES
   1789    John Jay became the first justice.

   1836    Roger Taney became the first Roman
           Catholic justice.

   1916    Louis Brandeis became the first Jewish
           justice.

   1967    Thurgood Marshall became the first
           African American justice.

   1981    Sandra Day O'Connor became the first
           female justice.
```

1775). Following New York's declaration of independence on July 9, 1776, Jay helped draft the first state constitution and was elected the first chief justice of New York, serving from 1777 to 1778. Reelected to the Continental Congress, he became president (1778-1779) and then minister to Spain (1779-1783) and a member of the Peace Commission (1779-1783). Jay was secretary for foreign affairs (1784-1789), and a coauthor of *The Federalist* (1788).

An austere and dignified leader, Jay was particularly qualified to establish institutional forms and traditions that would well serve the Supreme Court. Admitting the first group of attorneys and counselors, he insisted upon the Court's making an independent judgment concerning their character and abilities. In *Hayburn's Case* (1792), the Court first enunciated principles of separation of powers and rejected requests that it issue advisory opinions; it repeated its objections to advisory opinions in the justices' letter to President George Washington, declining to give such an opinion on the Neutrality Proclamation of 1793.

In *Chisholm v. Georgia* (1793), the Court majority held that a state might be made a defendant in the Supreme Court in a contract claim brought by another state's citizen. Although Jay had modified the extreme nationalist position that he expressed in 1786—that states were mere administrative subdivisions of the national government—he held that the Constitution vested supreme authority in the federal government, including judicial authority to hear cases against a state. This arose from the constitutive act of the people of the United States, expressed in their various state ratifying conventions. Jay also questioned the doctrine of sovereign immunity as applied to republican governments where citizens were equal to each other. Public outcry against *Chisholm* caused its reversal by the Eleventh Amendment, ratified in 1795 and proclaimed in effect in 1798.

While on circuit in Richmond, Virginia, Jay held that the 1783 Peace Treaty with Great Britain (known as Jay's Treaty) guaranteed the collectibility of debts that Americans owed to British merchants when the American Revolution began. Under Jay's instruction to the jury, a verdict for the plaintiff upheld the terms of the treaty. After Jay's resignation, in *Ware v. Hylton* (1796), the Court sustained Jay's position that treaties were the supreme law of the land.

While serving as minister to Britain (1794-1795) but still retaining his commission as chief justice, Jay was elected governor of New York. He resigned from the Court, and served as governor from 1795 to 1801. Renominated to serve as chief justice in November, 1800, he declined the appointment on January 2, 1801, and lived in virtual retirement until his death.

Herbert A. Johnson

FURTHER READING

Bader, William H., and Roy M. Mersky, eds. *The First One Hundred Eight Justices.* Buffalo, N.Y.: William S. Hein, 2004.

Casto, William R. *The Supreme Court in the Early Republic: The Chief Justiceships of John Jay and Oliver Ellsworth.* Columbia: University of South Carolina Press, 1995.

Goebel, Julius, Jr. *Antecedents and Beginnings to 1801.* Vol. 1 in *History of the Supreme Court of the United States.* New York: Macmillan, 1971.

Harrington, Matthew P. *Jay and Ellsworth, The First Courts: Justices, Rulings, and Legacy.* Santa Barbara, Calif.: ABC-Clio, 2007.

Marcus, Maeva, et al., eds. *The Documentary History of the Supreme Court of the United States, 1789-1800.* 7 vols. New York: Columbia University Press, 1985-   .

Monaghan, Frank. *John Jay: Defender of Liberty Against Kings and Peoples.* New York: Bobbs-Merrill, 1935.

Morris, Richard B. *John Jay, the Nation, and the Court.* Boston: Boston University Press, 1967.

Van Santvoord, George. *George Van Santvoord's Sketch of John Jay: From Sketches of the Lives, Times and Judicial Services of the Chief Justices of the Supreme Court of the United States.* 3d ed. Washington, D.C.: Green Bag Press, 2001.

SEE ALSO *Chisholm v. Georgia*; Cushing, William; Eleventh Amendment; Ellsworth, Oliver; Rutledge, John; States' rights and state sovereignty.

Thomas Johnson

IDENTIFICATION: Associate justice (August 6, 1792-January 16, 1793)
NOMINATED BY: George Washington
BORN: November 4, 1732, Calvert County, Maryland
DIED: October 26, 1819, Rose Hill, Maryland
SIGNIFICANCE: Although he served only briefly on the Supreme Court, Johnson participated in an important case involving the power of federal officials.

Thomas Johnson practiced law and served on the Maryland provincial assembly before the American Revolution. He served as the first governor of Maryland from 1777 to 1779. During the 1780's, he worked to ratify the U.S. Constitution and to elect George Washington as president. In 1790 he was appointed chief judge of the Maryland general court.

On August 5, 1791, President Washington appointed Johnson as an associate justice on the Supreme Court. The Senate confirmed him on November 7 and he took office on August 6, 1792. During this period of history, each justice was required to travel throughout a particular region of the country and serve as a circuit judge when the Court as not in session. Ill health and the difficulties of travel caused Johnson to resign from the Court on January 16, 1793.

In *Hayburn's Case* (1792), Johnson held the opinion that the attorney general, without the specific permission of the president, had the power to require a federal court to hear a petition. Because the Court

Thomas Johnson.
(Vic Boswell/
Library of Congress)

was equally divided, however, this power was denied. This case had a major influence on later federal procedures. Johnson also participated in *Georgia v. Brailsford* (1792), the first case in which written opinions were filed.

Rose Secrest

SEE ALSO Circuit riding; Elastic clause; Jay, John.

William Johnson

IDENTIFICATION: Associate justice (May 8, 1804-August 4, 1834)
NOMINATED BY: Thomas Jefferson
BORN: December 27, 1771, Charleston, South Carolina
DIED: August 4, 1834, Brooklyn, New York
SIGNIFICANCE: The first Jeffersonian appointed to the Supreme
    Court, Johnson resisted Chief Justice John Marshall's desire for
    unanimous decisions by the Court. His example established the
    custom of justices reading individual dissenting or concurring
    opinions as a regular practice of the Court.

William Johnson graduated from Princeton with honors in 1790 and
returned to Charleston, South Carolina, to study law with Federalist
Charles Cotesworth Pinckney. He was admitted to the bar in 1793.
From 1794 to 1798 he served three consecutive terms in the state
House of Representatives as a Jeffersonian Republican. During his fi-
nal term Johnson was speaker of the House. In 1798 the legislature
elected Johnson to the court of common pleas, which was then South
Carolina's highest court.

A REPUBLICAN ON THE COURT

When Thomas Jefferson took office as president of the United
States in 1801, Federalist appointees opposed to his political principles staffed the entire federal judiciary. Jefferson was particularly dis-
pleased with the Court decisions written by Chief Justice John Marshall. Jefferson's first chance to appoint a Republican to the Court
came in 1804 when an elderly and ill Federalist judge resigned. Jefferson nominated Johnson, believing him to be a staunch Republican whom he could trust to stand up to Marshall.

In order to strengthen the Court's claim as the ultimate interpreter of the law and the Constitution, Marshall discouraged the justices from writing separate opinions. Marshall strove for unanimous
decisions and delivered the opinion of the Court himself in most
major cases. Johnson disliked this practice and produced his first
published dissent in the 1807 case of *Ex Parte Bollman and Swartwout*
when the majority granted a writ of habeas corpus to two accomplices

of Aaron Burr who were accused of treason. The following year Johnson demonstrated his independence from Jefferson's influence in a circuit court decision, *Gilchrist v. Collector of Charleston* (1808). Johnson rescinded a presidential executive order, issued under the Embargo Act of 1807, which prevented a ship from leaving Charleston harbor, by ruling that the act did not authorize Jefferson's edict.

A moderate Republican, Johnson agreed with Marshall on such fundamental constitutional questions as the need for a strong central government and an independent judiciary, but he hoped to achieve a more even balance between the federal and state governments. Although both men believed in the necessity of protecting property rights, Johnson was much less rigid regarding the preservation of the sanctity of private contracts and was more willing than Marshall to grant state legislatures leeway in areas of economic and social policy.

Johnson feared excessive deference on the part of the Court toward moneyed interests and denounced the Court's use of the Constitution's contract clause to support speculators rather than legislatures. In *Ogden v. Saunders* (1827), Johnson convinced a majority of the Court that states had the power to write bankruptcy laws applying to future contracts without violating the contract clause. Marshall vigorously protested this decision in his only written dissent on a constitutional issue.

OPINIONS AND DISAGREEMENTS

Even when he agreed with a decision, Johnson insisted on presenting his own views. During the thirty years he served on the Court, Johnson wrote an overwhelming majority of concurring opinions (twenty-one of thirty-five) and nearly half of all dissenting opinions (thirty-four of seventy-four). His dissenting opinion in *Osborn v. Bank of the United States* (1824) acknowledged that the bank needed special protection but rejected the enormous expansion of federal jurisdiction that Marshall's decision permitted. Johnson's powerful sense of American nationalism permeated his concurring opinion in *Gibbons v. Ogden* (1824), in which his interpretation of the power of Congress to act under the commerce clause of the Constitution was even broader than that of Marshall.

Johnson strongly opposed Justice Joseph Story's attempts to establish a federal common law dealing with criminal matters. In *United States v. Hudson and Goodwin* (1812), Johnson persuaded the Court to follow his view, to the great disgust of Story, who pointedly ignored the decision when sitting as a circuit court justice. Johnson was less successful in preventing Story from expanding the admiralty jurisdiction of the federal government.

As the years passed, Johnson found himself increasingly out of harmony with public opinion in his native state. Although himself a slaveholder and opposed to abolition, Johnson strongly supported black civil rights. When South Carolinians reacted hysterically, in 1823, to the discovery of a slave rebellion plotted by Denmark Vesey, Johnson publicly criticized the denial of due process to the slaves. In a circuit court decision that same year, Johnson invalidated South Carolina's Negro Seamen Act, which required that free black sailors be kept in prison while their ships were docked in the state. As defen-

William Johnson.
(Library of Congress)

siveness concerning slavery increased in the wake of the Vesey affair, South Carolina's intellectuals began to stress extreme states' rights. To the fury of his neighbors, Johnson, in an 1832 circuit court decision, denounced the doctrine that states could nullify acts of the federal government. In 1834 Johnson moved to Philadelphia.

Johnson's death in August, 1834, was unexpected. Having suffered for some time from an infection of his jaw, Johnson went to Brooklyn, New York, to undergo surgery. Anesthetics were not yet available. Half an hour after the completion of an extremely painful operation, he died; newspapers listed the cause as exhaustion.

Always an independent thinker, Johnson's defense of legislative power irritated colleagues insistent on judicial supremacy. His strong support of the Constitution and the national government infuriated states' rights theorists. He is best remembered for his insistence on the right to free expression that helped establish the Supreme Court tradition of publishing dissenting opinions.

Milton Berman

FURTHER READING

Bader, William H., and Roy M. Mersky, eds. *The First One Hundred Eight Justices.* Buffalo, N.Y.: William S. Hein, 2004.

Clinton, Robert, Christopher Budzisz, and Peter Renstrom, eds. *The Marshall Court: Justices, Rulings, and Legacy.* Santa Barbara, ABC-Clio, 2007.

Ellis, Richard P. *The Jeffersonian Crisis: Courts and Politics in the Young Republic.* New York: Oxford University Press, 1971.

Friedman, Leon, and Fred Israel, eds. *The Justices of the Supreme Court: Their Lives and Major Opinions.* 5 vols. New York: Chelsea House, 1997.

Morgan, Donald B. *Justice William Johnson, the First Dissenter: The Career and Constitutional Philosophy of a Jeffersonian Judge.* Columbia: University of South Carolina Press, 1954.

SEE ALSO Dissents; *Gibbons v. Ogden*; Marshall, John; Opinions, writing of.

Johnson and Graham's Lessee v. McIntosh

CITATION: 21 U.S. 543 (8 Wheat)
DATE: March 10, 1823
ISSUES: Native American land claims; natural law
SIGNIFICANCE: Going back to the rights of discovery and conquest, the
Supreme Court upheld the U.S. government's ultimate authority to
extinguish title of occupancy and to convey title in the soil.

In 1775 William Johnson purchased land in Illinois from the Pian-
keshaw tribe, but Virginia in 1783 conveyed the land to the federal
government for the public domain. In 1818 William McIntosh purchased part of this Illinois land from the federal government, but the
Johnson family claimed to be the legitimate owner. By a 7-2 vote, the
Supreme Court ruled in favor of McIntosh and held that the tribe
had not possessed an absolute right to sell its land.

Writing for the Court, Chief Justice John Marshall paid homage to
the idea of natural justice, while deciding on the basis of positive law
and actual practice. He found that the property rights of natives, although not entirely disregarded, were "to a considerable extent, impaired." The discovering European nations had exercised "ultimate
dominion" to decide questions of land ownership. Native Americans
had been mere "occupants" of the land. Conquest had given "a title
which the courts of the conqueror cannot deny," and it superseded
any consideration for "original justice." British authority over land title, moreover, had been transferred to the government of the United
States. Although the rhetoric changed, subsequent Court decisions
upheld Marshall's position on congressional authority over tribal
land claims.

Thomas Tandy Lewis

SEE ALSO Curtis, Benjamin R.; Marshall, John; Native American sovereignty.

Judicial Activism

DESCRIPTION: Term applied to court decisions seen as going beyond the usual canons of constitutional or statutory interpretation; it is the opposite of judicial self-restraint.

SIGNIFICANCE: When the Supreme Court engaged in judicial activism, it made important and often controversial public policy and was a major player in shaping national policies.

The term "judicial activism" can be applied to any decision in which the Court alters or nullifies the policy of another policymaker such as Congress or the president. Judicial activism occurs whenever the Court exercises judicial review or interprets a constitutional or statutory provision to mean something different than it was commonly thought to mean. Typically, however, the term is used negatively by critics of a Court decision or doctrine. Few justices or judges overtly champion judicial activism.

Sometimes the Court is criticized as being too countermajoritarian. As an unelected body, critics charge, the Court should be cautious about finding laws adopted by democratically elected bodies unconstitutional. The classic arguments on this issue are found in

Under Chief Justice Earl Warren, the Supreme Court took on somewhat of an activist role. Members of the Warren Court included (clockwise from upper left) Abe Fortas, Potter Stewart, Byron R. White, Thurgood Marshall, William J. Brennan, Jr., William O. Douglas, Warren, Hugo L. Black, and John Marshall Harlan II. (Harris and Ewing/Collection of the Supreme Court of the United States)

Justice Robert H. Jackson's opinion and Justice Felix Frankfurter's dissent in the compulsory flag salute case, *West Virginia State Board of Education v. Barnette* (1943). The preferred freedoms doctrine of the 1940's and its modern counterpart, the strict scrutiny level of review, also represent countermajoritarian activism because they consciously place minority rights ahead of majority preferences.

Critics also charge the Court with activism when it interprets a constitutional provision differently from its presumed original intent or the normal meaning of its text. *Roe v. Wade* (1973) is good example of the Court's giving a new meaning to the Fourteenth Amendment's due process clause. Another example of this type of activism is Justices William J. Brennan, Jr., and Thurgood Marshall's finding that capital punishment is unconstitutional. (The latter's dissent in *Gregg v. Georgia*, 1976, is a good illustration of an activist opinion.) Brennan generally defended judicial activism (although not by name) when he argued that the spirit of constitutional provisions must be interpreted to apply to the United States in the twentieth century. Occasionally the Court is charged with judicial activism when it overrules or severely modifies one of its own precedents (for example, when *Brown v. Board of Education*, 1954, overruled *Plessy v. Ferguson*, 1896).

Judicial activism can help both conservative and liberal causes. From 1890 to 1937 when the Court appeared to support business interests by developing the freedom of contract and dual federalism doctrines (as in *Lochner v. New York*, 1905, and *Hammer v. Dagenhart*, 1918), Progressives and later New Dealers protested loudly that the Court was engaged in excessive activism. Under Chief Justice Earl Warren (1953-1969), the shoe was on the other foot. Conservatives charged the Court with liberal activism for making controversial decisions that significantly reshaped the law in criminal justice, legislative apportionment, right of privacy, libel, and other areas. Although less activist following the Warren era, the Court still engaged in some activism such as bringing commercial speech under First Amendment protection. However, some 1990's decisions were activist in a conservative sense, for example *Printz v. United States* (1997), which struck down portions of the 1993 Brady Act controlling the sale of handguns.

Bradley C. Canon

FURTHER READING

Bork, Robert H., ed. *"A Country I Do Not Recognize": The Legal Assault on American Values.* Stanford, Calif.: Hoover Institution Press, Stanford University, 2005.

Keck, Thomas Moylan. *The Most Activist Supreme Court in History: The Road to Modern Judicial Conservatism.* Chicago: University of Chicago Press, 2004.

Powers, Stephen. *The Least Dangerous Branch? Consequences of Judicial Activism.* Westport, Conn.: Praeger, 2002.

Rosen, Jeffrey. *The Most Democratic Branch: How the Courts Serve America.* New York: Oxford University Press, 2006.

Schwartz, Herman, ed. *The Rehnquist Court: Judicial Activism on the Right.* New York: Hill & Wang, 2002.

Tushnet, Mark. *A Court Divided: The Rehnquist Court and the Future of Constitutional Law.* New York: W. W. Norton, 2005.

Wolfe, Christopher. *Judicial Activism: Bulwark of Freedom or Precarious Security?* Lanham, Md.: Rowman & Littlefield, 1997.

SEE ALSO Capital punishment; *Carolene Products Co., United States v.*; Constitutional interpretation; Contract, freedom of; *Hammer v. Dagenhart*; Judicial review; Judicial scrutiny; Judicial self-restraint; *Lochner v. New York*; *Roe v. Wade*.

Judicial Review

DESCRIPTION: The Supreme Court's power to declare lower court decisions, state constitutional provisions, state laws, federal legislation, and other actions to be contrary to the U.S. Constitution and therefore null and unenforceable.

SIGNIFICANCE: The Court's most important and controversial power is not mentioned explicitly in the U.S. Constitution but is implied by the notion of a written constitution and the rule of law.

The Supreme Court's power of judicial review is in one sense unexceptional, but in another, radically controversial. The Court's power derives from the principle of uniformity necessary to maintain a

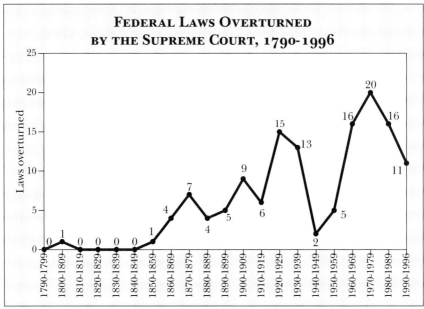

**FEDERAL LAWS OVERTURNED
BY THE SUPREME COURT, 1790-1996**

Source: Lawrence Baum, *The Supreme Court* (6th ed. Washington, D.C.: Congressional Quarterly, 1998), p. 201.

common-law court system of the kind that evolved out of the British experience. The word "common" in "common law" means "uniform across the country." This uniformity is achieved by having appellate courts resolve conflicts from lower courts. The Court departed from that experience by claiming in addition that laws passed by Congress and signed by the president could also be declared unconstitutional if they did not conform to the principles in a transcendent legal document: the U.S. Constitution. The British legal system does not use this idea because there is no authoritative document that can be used for purposes of comparison in declaring laws unconstitutional. Rather its view is that the authority of the "monarch in parliament" is absolute, and courts may not overturn its enactments. Although the British Law Lords occasionally set aside the impact of parliamentary enactments through interpretation, such results are comparatively minor and quite rare.

The Court's power of judicial review is important because it places the Court potentially and by elaboration in a position to govern the entire country unless the Court exercises self-restraint. In principle, judicial review could give the Court a nearly absolute veto over actions of any level of the government because of the difficulty of amending the Constitution. The rigidity of the amendment process leaves the Court generally as a sole interpreter of the Constitution.

The Court also claims that it can declare state constitutional provisions and state enactments unconstitutional. These powers of judicial review can be logically separated into actions declaring coordinate national branches unconstitutional and cases voiding actions of subordinate state governments. The power over state constitutions and state laws, although controversial at many times in history, can be justified by reference to Article VIII of the U.S. Constitution, which explicitly states that the Constitution and laws and treaties of the United States constitute the "supreme law of the land"—regardless of anything in state laws to the contrary. No such explicit words exist to allow the Court to declare coordinate national branch actions unconstitutional, but such declarations of unconstitutionality have been made repeatedly over the last two hundred years.

ORIGINS OF JUDICIAL REVIEW

If the power of judicial review is not explicit in the Constitution, it is reasonable to ask how the Court can claim it. It is generally accepted that the earliest authoritative legal assertion of the Court's power of judicial review occurred in the case of *Marbury v. Madison* (1803). In his opinion for the Court, Chief Justice John Marshall wrote that the Court's power of judicial review was unquestioned. There was, in fact, a considerable justification for Marshall's assertion. Most fundamentally, if the written Constitution were to have meaning, some authoritative way of interpreting it must have been intended by its Framers. Without some form of judicial review, there would be no way to police boundaries separating the branches of the national government or those separating the federal and state governments. Chaos might ensue if everyone interpreted the document individually. Judicial review is thus an element in enforcing the rule of law in the U.S. system of government.

Marshall could also point to several precedents (an extremely important feature in common law) as well. The old British privy council exercised judicial review in voiding acts of colonial legislatures, so the idea was not entirely alien to Anglo-Saxon law. Marshall himself would not have used such a controversial example because some of the reasons that led to American independence were concerns that the government in London had invalidated laws duly passed by the colonial legislatures.

More compelling were the eight instances before 1789 of state courts invalidating acts of their own state legislatures as having violated their own state's constitution. Such an exercise of judicial review is strongly analogous to the Supreme Court power to declare actions of coordinate branches of national government unconstitutional. Research by constitutional scholars and historians has established that at least twenty-five of forty delegates to the 1787 Constitutional Convention favored some form of judicial review. Moreover, eight of the state conventions that afterward ratified the Constitution discussed and accepted judicial review as one of the principles.

Before *Marbury v. Madison*, in *Hylton v. United States* (1796), both parties (and the Court itself) acted as if the Court had the authority to declare law unconstitutional, even though the Court upheld the law in this case. In *Calder v. Bull* (1798), individual justices asserted the right of judicial review, but the use of seriatim opinions in that case kept their rulings from being authoritative. Thus, *Marbury v. Madison* remained the authoritative case in which the Court declared a duly enacted national law unconstitutional. The lack of any effective opposition by the other branches reinforced the Court's assertion of judicial review.

THE SCOPE OF JUDICIAL REVIEW

If some form of judicial review was justified, the kind and scope of judicial review were still in doubt, and here the Supreme Court's power of judicial review has remained controversial. Notwithstanding the clear language of Article VI, even the Court's exercise of judicial review over state enactments and actions has been controversial. Early in U.S. history, Presidents Thomas Jefferson and James Madison and their supporters claimed state legislatures could interpose their own interpretation of the Constitution over the Court's interpretation. Throughout U.S. history in various forms, state authorities objected, particularly when state constitutional provisions were overturned.

Even in the late twentieth century, state authorities and their supporters objected when the Court invalidated state constitutional provisions on reapportionment or a wide range of segregation provisions in state constitutions, relating to public education and many other matters. However, despite political criticism, the Court's authority to use judicial review to invalidate states' laws withstood the test of time. The Court has been willing to declare thousands of such state provisions and enactments invalid.

The Court has exercised the greatest care in using judicial review in the highly controversial arena of invalidating national legislation or other actions of national government. Because of lack of explicit authority in the Constitution itself, the Court has maintained this part of judicial review only by exercising self-restraint. The lack of explicit authority has no doubt been among reasons why in more than two hundred years only about 150 national enactments and actions have been declared unconstitutional.

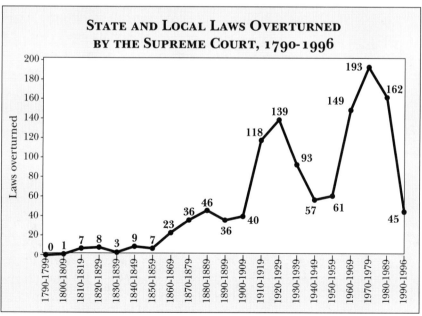

STATE AND LOCAL LAWS OVERTURNED
BY THE SUPREME COURT, 1790-1996

Source: Lawrence Baum, *The Supreme Court* (6th ed. Washington, D.C.:
Congressional Quarterly, 1998), p. 203.

635

Still the Court's restraint in striking down actions of coordinate branches of national government has not been sufficient to avoid controversy. Indeed, the entire controversy over judicial activism versus self-restraint has to do with the exercise of judicial review. If the Court had been completely self-restrained, it would never have declared any action of national government to be unconstitutional. Neither the controversy nor this significant form of judicial review would exist. This might well have led to criticism that the Court failed to do its job as guardian of the Constitution. Some controversy over action is inherent in any power of judicial review over other coordinate national branches.

SOME CONTROVERSIES

The issue of judicial activism versus restraint does not fall clearly along liberal and conservative lines. Political liberals tend to become more active on some subjects and more restrained on others. Conservatives who are normally expected to support judicial restraint have been activists on some issues at various points in U.S. history. Other controversies have flowed from the Court's exercise of judicial review. The debate over the extent to which due process should be considered either substantive or procedural bears directly on the issue of judicial review. This issue itself mixes with the question of judicial activism and self-restraint, but it also is a subject of judicial review.

After the Civil War, with the addition of the Thirteenth, Fourteenth, and Fifteenth Amendments, other controversies arose over the Court's exercise of judicial review. The Fourteenth Amendment's promise of "due process" and "equal protection" raised particularly important questions as to the degree to which other sections of the Constitution, such as the Bill of Rights, applied to the states as well as the federal government. The question of total or selective incorporation of the Bill of Rights and its application to the states turned partly on the question of judicial review.

Significant policy issues have fallen within the controversial purview of judicial review. For a long period, the question was whether the Court could exercise judicial review by striking down state and federal economic regulations. Using either the contract clause for the states or the commerce clause for the federal government, the

Court pushed its own power of judicial review to the point that some feared it might become a board of economists who determined the future of all economic regulations. Arguably the Court was expanding the scope of judicial review dramatically by these decisions. Although the Court substantially abandoned its interference with economic regulations by the 1930's, it expanded its judicial review of other areas, such as civil liberties and rights, creating extensive controversy over the last two-thirds of the twentieth century.

The Court's judicial review power is also inherent in the controversy over the scope of the federal government. When Congress and the president expanded the federal government's power into areas previously belonging to the states and individuals, that expansion fell within the purview of the Court's judicial review power. The Court's judicial review power generally parallels the growth of the power of the federal government.

More than simple enlargement, the form of the enlargement has also been controversial. The Court's judicial review power is fundamental to the rule of law in American society. One principle of the rule of law is that law should be knowable and predictable. From this, the Court has derived the principle that enactment should not be overbroad or vague and, therefore, unpredictable. Although the Court has exercised judicial review in declaring some laws void for vagueness, the Court's judicial restraint has kept it from striking a whole range of increasingly vague enactments.

Closely related and still more controversial is the issue of whether the Court should strike down Congress's vague delegations of lawmaking power to bureaucratic agencies. If the power of judicial review were said to be definitive, it would seem that the Court could easily declare that Congress improperly delegated the fundamental legislative power in violation of Article I of the U.S. Constitution. When the Court took this position in the 1930's by invalidating Congress's New Deal enactments, it provoked a strong controversy. President Franklin D. Roosevelt threatened to flood the Court with new members who would force it to abandon judicial review in this arena. The Roosevelt administration ultimately backed away from this constitutional exercise of its power for political reasons.

Faced with Roosevelt's Court-packing plan, the Court withdrew from the confrontation without ever overturning explicitly its decisions. The Court simply stopped exercising judicial review over vague delegations of power by Congress. As a result, the number of vague delegations of power to administrative agencies has increased dramatically. The absence of the Court's exercise of judicial review is thought by some to be a major weakness in the current system.

Another aspect of judicial review is the difference between the Court when it acts as a statutory as opposed to constitutional interpreter. When the Court interprets statutes said to be at variance with the Constitution, it is authoritative unless the Constitution is amended, which is not an easy task. The Court has generally, but not unanimously, agreed to exercise this power with great care. The 1973 *Roe v. Wade* abortion decision is a prime example of how controversial this power remains in U.S. society.

When the Court uses judicial review to interpret statutes passed by Congress, there is an easier check on its power because Congress may presumably amend the statute and repair an interpretation placed on the statutes by the Court. The Court has been freer to exercise judicial review in statutory interpretation, knowing that a relatively easy remedy to repair the result exists. Still this entire area is another example of the controversy that flows from the power of judicial review.

LIMITS ON POWER

In principle, the Court's power is not absolute. The Court can be overturned by amendment. Such amendments have occurred, but because of the difficult amending process, they are rare. At various times in its existence, the Court rendered decisions with which the vast majority of American people disagreed but were unable to pass a corrective constitutional amendment, through either Congress or the states.

Congress could exercise restraint on the Court by reducing its jurisdiction. However, the prestige of the Court and fears of political interference with the Court's power by Congress and the president have led to great restraint on the part of coordinate branches of the government. The jurisdiction of the Court has withstood attacks by Congress and the president in this area.

A still more dramatic restraint flows from Congress's authority to determine how many justices sit on the Court. Congress and the president have the power to determine the total number of justices by ordinary legislative enactment. This power could be significant because if the Court rendered a controversial decision by five to four, the addition of just two new justices could potentially reverse that decision, assuming there were no other changes of mind or members. Nonetheless, the experience of Roosevelt's administration in attempting to pack the Supreme Court by adding justices demonstrated that this is a politically difficult step to take.

AN INTERNATIONAL PERSPECTIVE

The Court's important and controversial power of judicial review is a significant contribution of the U.S. political system to the global system of governance. Particularly since World War II, concerns developed that democracy defined as pure majority rule has led to totalitarian governments. Because many European governments came to view the United States' protection of minority rights along with majority rule as cardinal principles of democracy, constitutions and authoritative courts to interpret them have become more popular. Starting with their immediate post-World War II constitutions, Germany, Japan, and Italy created constitutional courts with the power to declare ordinary laws unconstitutional. That is to say, these courts were given the power of judicial review. Subsequently France, Ireland, and Israel added analogous constitutional courts.

Following the American example, rather than that of Great Britain, Canada and South Africa adopted their own courts to interpret their governmental charters. The creation of a European union required a court to interpret the provisions of the charters or treaties founding that union, and therefore, the European Court of Justice was created. The European Convention on Human Rights led to the creation of the European Court of Human Rights.

In the wake of the collapse of the Soviet Union and the satellite countries in Europe, there was a call for the rule of law in those countries. In many respects the rule of law can be best protected by a written constitution and a court of last resort with the authority to declare ordinary enactments and actions of governments to be at variance with that constitution and therefore unconstitutional. Several of these countries wrote constitutions and adopted courts to interpret them. Although their success or failure cannot be determined yet, the Court's power of judicial review clearly had an effect on ideas of proper governance in many countries far from its shores.

In some senses, the power of judicial review may be said to be more important and a more important contribution to government than the creation of legislatures or other democratic institutions.

Richard L. Wilson

FURTHER READING

Two excellent works with which to begin a study of judicial review are Larry D. Kramer's *The People Themselves: Popular Constitutionalism and Judicial Review* (New York: Oxford University Press, 2005) and *Judicial Review and Judicial Power in the Supreme Court*, edited by Kermit L. Hall (New York: Garland, 2000). From among the voluminous literature on judicial review, readers might profitably begin with Henry J. Abraham's *The Judicial Process* (6th ed. New York: Oxford University Press, 1993).

Edward S. Corwin left two classic works that are still widely read: *The Higher Law Background of American Constitutional Law* (Ithaca, N.Y.: Cornell University Press, 1929) and *Court over Constitution: A Study of Judicial Review as an Instrument of Popular Government* (Princeton, N.J.: Princeton University Press, 1938). Alexander Hamilton made a strong case for giving the Court the power of judicial review in essay No. 78 in *The Federalist* (1788), which is available in many editions. Abraham Lincoln expressed his view on the relationship between judicial review and popular sovereignty in his first inaugural address, which is also available in many works.

James B. Stoner, Jr., offers an excellent recent history of the long and contentious history of judicial review in *Coke, Hobbes, and the Origins of American Constitutionalism* (Lawrence: University Press of Kansas, 1992). A popular liberal view of judicial review is available from John Hart Ely in his *Democracy and Distrust: A Theory of Judicial Review* (Cambridge, Mass.: Harvard University Press, 1980). For a more conservative view, see Christopher Wolfe's *The Rise of Modern Judicial Review: From Constitutional Interpretation to Judge-Made Law* (New York: Basic Books, 1986).

Sylvia Snowiss's *Judicial Review and the Law of the Constitution* (New Haven, Conn.: Yale University Press, 1990) shows how John Marshall redefined judicial review, while persuading his contemporaries that he was simply following precedent. Jesse Choper's *Judicial Review in the National Political Process* (Chicago: University of Chicago Press, 1980) argues that the case for judicial review is stronger when the Court is restrained than when it is active.

SEE ALSO Constitutional interpretation; Constitutional law; Due process, procedural; Due process, substantive; Judicial activism; Judicial self-restraint; Judiciary Act of 1789; *Marbury v. Madison*; Separation of powers.

Judicial Scrutiny

DESCRIPTION: Standard by which the Supreme Court evaluates the constitutionality of certain governmental actions. The three levels of judicial scrutiny are strict scrutiny, intermediate (or heightened) scrutiny, and ordinary (or minimum) scrutiny.

SIGNIFICANCE: These levels of judicial scrutiny and their consistent usage by the Court enable institutions and citizens alike to feel comfortable that similar cases will be adjudicated in similar ways.

The Supreme Court employs tests, or standards of review, with the aim of giving parties to a specific case some reasonable expectation as to the outcome of their particular constitutional claims. The use of standards permits each party to know, prior to the actual hearing, how the judiciary will probably approach the case and how the judiciary is likely to resolve any single issue. Variations in levels of review also signify the Court's willingness to provide (through more rigorous tests) increased judicial protection for "discreet and insular minorities," as it did in *United States v. Carolene Products Co.* (1938). These tests can take many forms and can be used in many different constitutional inquiries, but the most common tests are those that involve the Court's scrutinizing governmental activity.

THE COURT'S THREE LEVELS OF JUDICIAL SCRUTINY

Level	Application	Standard of review	Classifications/restraints
Strict	Suspect classifications and fundamental rights	Is there a compelling state interest in the classification or restraint? Is the classification or restraint narrowly tailored?	Race; aliens (those not performing essential government functions); fundamental rights (right to vote, right to interstate travel, reproductive rights)
Intermediate	Quasi-suspect classifications	Is there an important governmental objective and a substantial relationship between that objective and the classification or restraint?	Gender; illegitimacy
Minimal	Economic regulations and nonsuspect classifications	Is there a good reason to justify the classification or restraint?	Poverty; age discrimination; homosexuality; aliens (performing essential government functions); rights (education, housing, welfare)

THE THREE LEVELS

The Court uses three levels of judicial scrutiny. The lowest standard of review is defined as ordinary, or minimal, scrutiny. Here, the burden to demonstrate a violation of the Constitution falls on the individual, as the Court presumes the governmental action in question is constitutional. When applying an ordinary level of scrutiny, the Court employs the rational basis test, which asks the government to demonstrate that the action is reasonably related to a legitimate governmental objective. If the government can do so, then the Court will reject the argument of the petitioner and the action will be deemed constitutional. The Court regularly uses ordinary scrutiny in cases involving economic regulation, such as *Williamson v. Lee Optical Co.* (1955). The Court has also applied minimal scrutiny for equal protection cases alleging discrimination in four areas: age discrimination, as in *Massachusetts Board of Retirement v. Murgia* (1976); discrimination based on indigence, as in *San Antonio Independent School District v. Rodriguez* (1973); discrimination based on homosexuality, as in *Romer v. Evans* (1996); and alienage, which occurs when employment involves an essential government function, as in *Foley v. Connelie* (1978).

An intermediate, or heightened, level of scrutiny is applied by the Court when a government action potentially discriminates on the basis of gender or illegitimacy and therefore violates the equal protection clause of the Fourteenth Amendment. The impetus for applying a more rigorous test in the areas of gender and illegitimacy stems from the perception that these groups require additional—or heightened—judicial protection due to their status as (numerical or de facto) minorities. Because of the heightened nature of the review, the Court does not adopt the presumption of constitutionality standard found in the ordinary level of scrutiny but instead mandates that the government demonstrate more than simply a reasonable purpose for the law. Intermediate review requires that the government identify an important governmental objective that is substantially furthered by that particular action.

Craig v. Boren (1976) is the principal case that formally introduced an intermediate level of scrutiny. In *Craig*, the Court addressed the issue of gender discrimination by reviewing an Oklahoma statute that prohibited the sale of 3.2 percent beer to women under the age of eighteen and men under the age of twenty-one. In an opinion written by Justice William J. Brennan, Jr., the Court ruled that under the newly instituted intermediate standard of review, the Oklahoma legislature could not satisfy the requirements set up by the test. The law treating men differently than women, Brennan argued, "did not serve important governmental objectives and [was not] substantially related to [the] achievement of those objectives."

The third level of judicial scrutiny is the most difficult for the government to satisfy. Strict scrutiny refers to the standard used by the Court when assessing the constitutionality of governmental actions that may interfere with fundamental rights or potentially discriminate on racial grounds. In the area of racial discrimination, the Court, in *Korematsu v. United States* (1944), noted that "all legal restrictions which curtail the civil rights of a single racial group are immediately suspect. That is not to say that all such restrictions are unconstitutional. It is to say that courts must subject them to the most rigid scrutiny." As such, the Court adopts a presumption of unconstitutionality when applying this most rigorous test; it asks the government to articulate a compelling reason for discriminating based on race or impinging on a fundamental right. Additionally, the Court insists that the government action be closely related to the state's compelling objective. If the government is going to discriminate based on racial classifications or regulate one of the most fundamental freedoms, the Court demands that it have an extraordinarily important reason for doing so. Needless to say, very few governmental actions have ever satisfied the strict scrutiny test.

EVOLVING STANDARDS

Distinctions between differing levels of review—and the subsequent application of the actual tests—are not always easy to define. The difference between an important governmental objective and a legitimate one or between means that are closely related and ones that are merely substantially related are not always clear. However, the Court has provided some guidelines for the application of the various tests. A compelling governmental interest is one that is of paramount importance, and a close relationship is one in which the Court is satisfied that there is no alternative, that the government has no option but to interfere with a fundamental right or discriminate based on race.

Korematsu v. United States (1944) provides the most cited example. The case involved the Court's review of the constitutionality of President Franklin D. Roosevelt's executive order mandating that people of Japanesee ancestry on the West Coast adhere to certain restrictions on their freedom (including curfews, detentions, and relocations) during the early part of World War II. In upholding the order, the Court claimed that a "pressing public necessity" may justify the violation of certain freedoms and discrimination against certain groups. Although the Court applied the strict scrutiny test, the government cited national security as a compelling reason for detaining Japanese Americans. Additionally, the government claimed that in order to maintain national security during such a major conflict, it had no alternative but to restrict the extension of some basic freedoms to a group of Americans. Until 2003, *Korematsu* was the only case in which the majority of the justices unambiguously applied the strict scrutiny test to a racially based restriction and upheld the law.

Most scholars of constitutional law once said that the strict scrutiny test was "strict in theory, fatal in fact." Justice Sandra Day O'Connor, however, challenged this assumption in the case of *Adarand Constructors v. Peña* (1995), when the Court held that strict scrutiny would be the appropriate test any time that a governmental racial classification resulted in unequal treatment based on race. O'Connor suggested that the Court might someday apply strict scrutiny and still approve an affirmative action program as being narrowly tailored to promote a compelling government interest. Her prediction turned out to be true in the case of *Grutter v. Bollinger* (2003), in which a 5-4 majority on the Court upheld a policy of limited racial preferences for admission to the University of Michigan Law School. The Court's majority accepted the goal of diversity as a compelling interest and found that the school's policy of assessing students, using individualized evaluations of each student, was narrowly tailored to achieve that interest. Critics of the decision, including Justice Anthony M. Kennedy, accused the majority of departing from the rigorous standards that had previously been used in strict scrutiny analysis.

Because justices frequently disagree about the semantics and subjective values used in judicial scrutiny, the nature of the three levels of scrutiny change continually over time. Justice John Paul Stevens, in fact, has expressed disapproval of the entire practice of making distinctions based on specific legislative classifications. He has frequently said that there is "only one equal protection clause." Similarly, Justice Thurgood Marshall advocated replacing the three levels with a "sliding scale." In 1973, he wrote that the variations of scrutiny should be based "on the constitutional and societal importance of the interest adversely affected." Although the majority of the justices have never accepted Marshall's proposal, they have nevertheless tended to move in the direction that he proposed.

Beau Breslin
Updated by the Editor

FURTHER READING

Chemerinsky, Erwin. "Breakdown in the Levels of Scrutiny." *Trial* 33 (March, 1997): 70-71.

Coffin, Elizabeth Buroker. "Constitutional Law: Content-based Regulations on Speech, a Comparison of the Categorization and Balancing Approaches to Judicial Scrutiny." *University of Dayton Law Review* 18 (Winter, 1993): 593-633.

Devins, Neal, and Davison M. Douglas, eds. *A Year at the Supreme Court.* Durham, N.C.: Duke University Press, 2004.

Levinson, Sanford. "Tiers of Scrutiny—from Strict Through Rational Bases—and the Future of Interests: Commentary on Fiss and Linde." *Albany Law Review* 55 (1992): 745-761.

Mongkuo, Maurice Y. *Race Preference Programs and the United States Supreme Court Strict Scrutiny Standard of Review.* Lewiston, N.Y.: Edwin Mellen Press, 2005.

O'Brien, David. *Constitutional Law and Politics, Volume Two: Civil Rights and Liberties.* 6th ed. New York: W. W. Norton, 2005.

Wexler, Jay D. "Defending the Middle Way: Intermediate Scrutiny as Judicial Minimalism." *George Washington Law Review* 66 (January, 1998): 298-352.

SEE ALSO *Adarand Constructors v. Peña*; Black, Hugo L.; Brennan, William J., Jr.; *Carolene Products Co., United States v.*; Constitutional interpretation; Equal protection clause; Fundamental rights; Gender issues; *Gratz v. Bollinger/ Grutter v. Bollinger*; Illegitimacy; *Korematsu v. United States*; Stevens, John Paul.

Judicial Self-Restraint

DESCRIPTION: The view that unelected federal judges should generally be reluctant to interfere with the decisions of the democratically elected branches of government.

SIGNIFICANCE: The struggle between advocates of judicial activism
and judicial self-restraint poses the question of when, if ever, the
Supreme Court should strike down a democratically enacted statute. This question reveals the potential tension between judicial
power and democratic government.

Advocates of judicial self-restraint argue that the Supreme Court
should generally refrain from interfering with the exercise of authority by Congress, the president, and the state governments. This doctrine is rooted in concerns regarding legitimacy and capacity. Federal
courts are neither authorized to, nor institutionally capable of, resolving complex questions of social policy. Therefore, they should
defer to statutes adopted by democratically enacted legislatures and
refrain from usurping executive functions, particularly the administration of governmental institutions such as public schools, prisons,
and medical facilities. During the Earl Warren, Warren E. Burger,
and William H. Rehnquist eras, this doctrine was associated primarily
with constitutional conservatives, but this was not always the case.

ORIGINS

Following the New Deal constitutional revolution of 1937, a number of liberal justices and constitutional scholars concluded that the
Court had been illegitimately thwarting the democratic will and that,
in the future, it should exercise a much greater degree of restraint.
Justice Oliver Wendell Holmes had argued consistently that the
Court should defer to legislative judgments as long as they were not
wholly irrational or unreasonable. For example, he dissented in cases
such as *Lochner v. New York* (1905) and *Adkins v. Children's Hospital*
(1923), insisting that the Court was wrongly striking down democratically enacted regulatory statutes on the basis of the justices' own conservative laissez-faire economic philosophy.

As these constitutional struggles came to a head during the New

Deal, justices such as Harlan Fiske Stone sought to build on Holmes's restrained vision of the judicial role. Dissenting in *United States v. Butler* (1936), for example, Stone observed that "while unconstitutional exercise of power by the executive and legislative branches of the government is subject to judicial restraint, the only check upon our own exercise of power is our own sense of self-restraint. For the removal of unwise laws from the statute books appeal lies not to the courts but to the ballot and to the processes of democratic government." In response, the Court's conservatives, led by Justice George Sutherland, continued to defend their activist enforcement of constitutional limits on legislative power. In *West Coast Hotel Co. v. Parrish* (1937), however, the Court adopted the Holmesian approach in its famous "switch in time." From this point on, the Court upheld a wide range of New Deal legislation, abandoned its active enforcement of the constitutional limits on government regulatory authority, and generally deferred to the judgments of the legislative and executive branches on such questions.

Following this New Deal switch in time, Justice Stone led the Court in articulating a new set of modern constitutional foundations in support of the continued exercise of judicial power. In *United States v. Carolene Products Co.* (1938), Stone held that while the Court would generally defer to the political branches in the area of economic legislation, it would more closely scrutinize laws that infringed on a particular provision of the Bill of Rights, interfered with the fair operation of the democratic process, or discriminated against a relatively powerless minority group. Stone's Footnote Four in *Carolene* (1938) thus laid the foundation for much of modern judicial activism, in which the Court has actively protected constitutional rights and liberties.

In response, Justice Felix Frankfurter continued to build on the Holmesian concept of restraint, insisting that judicial activism was no more legitimate in the area of personal liberties than in the area of economic rights. In cases such as *Minersville School District v. Gobitis* (1940), *West Virginia State Board of Education v. Barnette* (1943), and *Dennis v. United States* (1951), Frankfurter insisted that the Court should almost always defer to the decisions of the elected branches, even when fundamental constitutional liberties were at stake. In *Dennis*, for example, the Court upheld the convictions of several members of the Communist Party under the Smith Act, a 1940 Cold War statute that outlawed the teaching of communist ideas. In his concurring opinion, Frankfurter urged his colleagues to remember that the Court's power of judicial review was not an "exercise of the powers of a super-legislature," and he insisted—in contrast to the Court's emerging fundamental rights doctrine—that direct policy making was not the province of the court and that free speech cases were not "an exception to the principle that we are not legislators."

THE WARREN COURT

Beginning with *Brown v. Board of Education* (1954), the Warren Court exercised extensive judicial activism in an effort to protect individual liberties and minority rights against infringement by the majority. Although the Court's decision in *Brown* was unanimous, many of these decisions provoked extensive controversy, and the Court's dissenting justices often emphasized the principle of judicial self-restraint. In a series of cases in the 1960's, for example, the Court held that to ensure equal representation of all voters, the Constitution required that legislative districts be of approximately equal size.

Under Chief Justice William H. Rehnquist, the Supreme Court became more conservative. Clockwise from upper left, members of the Rehnquist Court included Ruth Bader Ginsburg, David Souter, Clarence Thomas, Stephen Breyer, Anthony Kennedy, Sandra Day O'Connor, Rehnquist, John Paul Stevens, and Antonin Scalia. (Richard Strauss/Smithsonian Institution, Courtesy the Supreme Court of the United States)

The Court viewed these decisions as necessary to rectify the tremendous imbalances in representation that existed in many states. The state of Alabama, for example, had not redrawn its legislative districts since 1900, and because so many people had moved from rural to urban areas, the population of the districts was now dramatically skewed. In the state house, the districts ranged from 6,700 to 104,000 people, and in the senate, from 15,000 to 634,000. In *Reynolds v. Sims* (1964), the Court held that these malapportioned districts violated the constitutional principle of "one person, one vote."

In dissenting opinions in this and related cases, Frankfurter and Justice John M. Harlan II argued that the Court was violating the principle of self-restraint by inserting itself into the legislative districting process, which had always been considered a "political question." Frankfurter denounced the Court for entering this "political thicket," and Harlan emphasized that the Court's "elaboration of its new 'constitutional' doctrine indicates how far—and how unwisely— it has strayed from the appropriate bounds of its authority. . . . It is difficult to imagine a more intolerable and inappropriate interference by the judiciary with the independent legislatures of the States." Harlan concluded that "these decisions give support to a current mistaken view of the Constitution and the constitutional function of this Court. This view, in a nutshell, is that every major social ill in this country can find its cure in some constitutional 'principle,' and that this Court should 'take the lead' in promoting reform when other branches of government fail to act." In leading the Court's dissenters in these voting rights cases, Frankfurter and Harlan articulated the conservative conception of judicial restraint in its modern form, sharply stated as an attack on illegitimate judicial power and closely linked to an "originalist" conception of the Fourteenth Amendment.

THE BURGER COURT

Many of the Warren Court's decisions protecting civil rights and civil liberties were politically controversial, and in 1968, Republican Richard M. Nixon made the Court's liberal activism a key theme in his campaign for the presidency. Nixon promised that if elected, he would appoint justices who would exercise a much greater degree of self-restraint. During his first term in office, he appointed Warren E.

Burger, Harry A. Blackmun, Lewis F. Powell, Jr., and William H. Rehnquist, and in many areas of constitutional law, these justices lived up to Nixon's expectations. Justice Rehnquist was particularly faithful to this constitutional vision, and throughout the 1970's, he consistently dissented from the Court's decisions protecting constitutional rights and liberties. In 1973, for example, he dissented from the Court's landmark abortion decision, *Roe v. Wade*, insisting that the Court was wrongly striking down the abortion laws of more than half the states. Over the next twenty years, the Court's abortion decisions were one of the principal targets of conservative advocates of judicial self-restraint.

Although constitutional conservatives never succeeded in overturning *Roe*, they did have some influence on the Court in other areas of the law. In *Bowers v. Hardwick* (1986), for example, the Court held by a 5-4 vote that Georgia's statute criminalizing consensual sodomy did not violate the Constitution. Although Michael Hardwick, a gay man, had been arrested in his own bedroom for engaging in oral sex, Justice Byron R. White held that this statute did not violate the constitutional "right to privacy" because the Court should generally be reluctant to invalidate democratically enacted statutes on the basis of a right that is not explicitly mentioned in the constitutional text.

THE REHNQUIST COURT

Like Nixon, Presidents Ronald Reagan and George H. W. Bush were also sharp critics of liberal judicial activism, and they made an explicit effort to appoint justices who would exercise judicial self-restraint. Despite ten consecutive Republican appointments by the end of the Bush administration, however, the Court continued to exercise judicial activism in defense of individual liberties and minority rights in cases such as *Planned Parenthood of Southeastern Pennsylvania v. Casey* (1992), *Romer v. Evans* (1996), and *United States v. Virginia* (1996). Justice Antonin Scalia was the Court's sharpest critic of these decisions, frequently denouncing his colleagues for engaging in "act[s], not of judicial judgment, but of political will."

In a number of contexts, however, constitutional conservatives themselves abandoned the principle of judicial self-restraint. Beginning in the mid-1970's, a series of New Right political movements denounced the modern liberal political order, including its twin foundations in national government policy, the New Deal and the Great Society. These political conservatives denounced the welfare state in particular and government taxing and regulatory authority more generally. They also denounced what they perceived as the policies of a "liberal cultural elite" and were particularly critical of egalitarian policies such as affirmative action and gay and lesbian rights.

During the 1990's, these New Right political ideas worked their way into constitutional discourse, at times posing a conflict with the longstanding conservative principle of self-restraint. In the area of affirmative action, for example, the conservative justices of the Rehnquist Court struck down a number of state and federal affirmative action policies in an effort to enforce their "color-blind" vision of the Fourteenth Amendment. They even carried this principle so far as to enter the "political thicket" of legislative districting by holding that the states may not draw legislative districts on the basis of race, not even to improve the representation of relatively powerless racial minorities. In these cases, relatively liberal justices such as John Paul Stevens and David H. Souter denounced the Court for interfering with the majority will.

Thus, the constitutional decisions handed down by the Rehnquist Court reflected a complex mix of liberal activism and conservative self-restraint in some contexts and conservative activism and liberal self-restraint in others.

Thomas M. Keck

FURTHER READING

Two broad works on the Supreme Court that pay special attention to the issue of judicial restraint are Jeffrey Rosen's *The Most Democratic Branch: How the Courts Serve America* (New York: Oxford University Press, 2006) and Thomas M. Keck's *The Most Activist Supreme Court in History: The Road to Modern Judicial Conservatism* (Chicago: University of Chicago Press, 2004).

Although there are countless books and articles on the topic of judicial self-restraint, readers would do well to start with chapter 10 in Judge Richard Posner's *The Federal Courts: Challenge and Reform* (Cambridge, Mass.: Harvard University Press, 1996). Other helpful readings on the topic include Justice John Paul Stevens's "Judicial Restraint" in *San Diego Law Review* 22 (May-June, 1985): 437-452, and the essays collected in Stephen C. Halpern and Charles M. Lamb, eds., *Supreme Court Activism and Restraint* (Lexington, Mass.: Lexington Books, 1982).

For examples of conservative arguments for judicial self-restraint, see Robert H. Bork's *The Tempting of America: The Political Seduction of the Law* (New York: Free Press, 1990) and the essays collected in Mitchell S. Muncy's *The End of Democracy? The Judicial Usurpation of Politics* (Dallas: Spence, 1997).

For one of the most influential liberal critiques of such arguments, see Ronald Dworkin's *Freedom's Law: The Moral Reading of the American Constitution* (Cambridge, Mass.: Harvard University Press, 1996). For an argument by a liberal constitutional scholar in favor of an innovative conception of self-restraint, see Cass R. Sunstein's *One Case at a Time: Judicial Minimalism on the Supreme Court* (Cambridge, Mass.: Harvard University Press, 1999).

SEE ALSO *Carolene Products Co., United States v.*; Fourteenth Amendment; Frankfurter, Felix; Holmes, Oliver Wendell; Judicial activism; Judicial review; *Lochner v. New York*; *Reynolds v. Sims*; *Roe v. Wade*; Stone, Harlan Fiske; Sutherland, George.

Judiciary Act of 1789

DATE: 1789
DESCRIPTION: Bill passed by Congress establishing a three-tier system of federal courts.
SIGNIFICANCE: This act of the First Congress created the working structure of the federal judiciary, including the Supreme Court.

The Constitution, written during the summer of 1787 and ratified in 1788, established a new government that started working in April, 1789, when the newly formed Congress began meeting. President George Washington was sworn into office on April 30. At that point two of the three branches of the new government had been formed, but the judicial branch had yet to be created.

During the Constitutional Convention, most of the debate revolved around the executive and legislative branches. There was near complete agreement on the need for a federal judiciary, although there was considerable disagreement about what exactly the judiciary would do. That is, the supporters of both the Virginia and New Jersey plans during the Constitutional Convention favored the creation of a federal judiciary—something that did not exist under the previous governing document, the Articles of Confederation. The proposals for a federal judiciary were quite similar. Both supported the creation of a supreme court as well as the formation of inferior tribunals. The inferior courts would be trial courts, and the highest court would primarily be a court of appeals but would also hear some cases in the first instance. When the Committee on Detail, a small group formed by the men convened in Philadelphia, reported a draft to the full assembly on August 8, 1787, the section in the proposed Constitution regarding the judiciary was nearly identical to final product of the Convention, which was signed on September 17, 1787.

The new Constitution treated the judicial branch of government in Article III, which contains less detail than Articles I and II, which, respectively, lay out the structures and powers of Congress and the president. Article III, section 1, states that "the judicial Power of the United States, shall be vested in one supreme Court, and in such inferior Courts as the Congress may from time to time ordain and establish." The Framers of the Constitution did not believe it was prudent or even possible to determine the specifics of the structure of the federal judiciary. They left the exact structure to be determined by the legislative branch.

Moreover, Article III, section 2, states that "The judicial Power shall extend to all Cases . . . arising under this Constitution, [and] the laws of the United States" as well as matters specifically stated that were best suited for the federal judiciary.

THE CONTENT OF THE JUDICIARY ACT

Thus the Framers left it to Congress to determine the specifics, and Congress did so with the Judiciary Act of 1789. The Judiciary Act was the first bill introduced in the Senate and consumed much of the Senate's time during the summer of 1789. It had three principal authors: Oliver Ellsworth of Connecticut, a member of the Constitutional Convention and later a chief justice; William Paterson of New Jersey, previously the attorney general in New Jersey, a participant in the Constitutional Convention, and later an associate justice; and Caleb Strong of Massachusetts, who also attended the Constitutional Convention but was not an active participant.

The Judiciary Act, which was officially titled, "An Act to Establish the Federal Courts of the United States," was signed by President Washington on September 24, 1789. The most significant aspects of the act were its establishment of a three-tier system of courts, establishing district courts along state boundaries and legislating the jurisdictions, both original and appellate, of the various courts.

The highest tier of the newly formed judicial system was the Supreme Court, which, according to the act, would "consist of a chief justice and five associate justices." The act also indicated that four justices needed to be present for the Court to operate and that the Court would have two sessions each year in the seat of the government.

The lowest tier of the federal judiciary would be the district courts. The act set the precedent that jurisdiction for district courts would follow state boundaries. It established thirteen district courts, one for each of the eleven states that had ratified the Constitution at that point and for the districts of Maine and Kentucky, which were not yet regarded as states. The arrangement of the district courts was a compromise between Federalists and Antifederalists. Some Antifederalists wanted state courts to adjudicate violations of federal law, and some Federalists wanted the boundary lines for district courts to be distinct from state boundaries. The judges appointed to each district court would hear criminal cases involving admiralty and maritime crimes as well as other cases involving federal law. All criminal cases would go before a jury. The district courts would also hear minor civil cases involving the federal government. These courts were to meet four times each year.

The other tier created by the act was the circuit courts of appeals. The act created three circuits: eastern, middle, and southern. The most remarkable characteristic of these courts to the modern observer is that there were no separate corps of judges for these courts. The judges for the circuit courts of appeals would consist of two Supreme Court justices along with a district court judge from within the territory of each circuit court of appeals. These courts were to be both trial and appellate courts. These courts would hold trials in cases of diversity of citizenship in civil cases as well in cases involving major federal crimes. These courts also heard appeals from the district courts. The act prevented district court judges from hearing appeals in cases in which they had already participated. Supreme Court justices were not prevented from hearing cases in their capacities both as circuit court of appeals judges and as justices of the Supreme Court. However, most justices removed themselves from any cases in which they had previously participated. Those justices appointed during the early years of the Court often served mostly as circuit court judges because few cases made it to the high court.

After the establishment of the courts, the most significant aspect of the Judiciary Act is the assignation of original and appellate jurisdiction for the various courts. In section 13, the act restated the original jurisdiction for the Supreme Court as outlined in Article III of the Constitution. The act also dictated what kind of appellate jurisdiction the Court would have. Section 13 further stated that the Court could issue writs of *mandamus* "in cases warranted by the principle and usages of law, to any courts appointed, or persons holding office under the authority of the United States." Such a writ would in effect force a higher-level official to act in a particular manner.

Regarding the jurisdiction of the Court, section 25 of the act indicated that the Court could hear appeals from the highest court in each state on matters of law alone. This section truly established the Court as the highest judicial authority in the new United States.

CASES INVOLVING THE JUDICIARY ACT OF 1789

The most famous of the Court cases involving the Judiciary Act of 1789 was *Marbury v. Madison* (1803). This decision set the precedent for judicial review because the Court ruled on the constitutionality of a statute. William Marbury, who had been appointed by President John Adams to be a justice of the peace in the District of Columbia, asked the Court to deliver a writ of *mandamus* forcing Madison, who was Jefferson's secretary of state, to deliver his commission to him. Marbury asked for such an action by the Court because the Judiciary Act of 1789 gave the Court original jurisdiction regarding writs of *mandamus*. Chief Justice John Marshall declared in his decision that section 13 of the Judiciary Act of 1789 was unconstitutional because Article III of the Constitution indicated the specific kinds of cases in which the Court would have original jurisdiction, and issuing writs of *mandamus* was not one of those.

Another significant case involving the Judiciary Act of 1789 is *Martin v. Hunter's Lessee* (1816). In *Fairfax's Devisee v. Hunter's Lessee* (1813), the Court had overturned the decision of Virginia's highest court. The Virginia court of appeals refused to adhere to the Supreme Court's decision and declared that "the appellate power of the Supreme Court does not extend to this court." The Virginia court further stated that section 25 of the Judiciary Act of 1789 was not constitutional. The Supreme Court in *Martin* affirmed the constitutionality of this appellate jurisdiction. In the majority opinion, Justice Joseph Story affirmed the constitutionality of section 25, arguing that the Congress, except for specified cases, was given latitude in determining jurisdiction of the federal courts.

In *Cohen v. Virginia* (1821), the Court reaffirmed the constitutionality of section 25 of the Judiciary Act of 1789. This case is significant because Chief Justice John Marshall had not participated in *Fairfax's Devisee* or *Martin* because he and his brother had contracted to purchase some of the disputed land. In *Cohen*, Marshall was part of the majority in affirming the Court's jurisdiction in reviewing state supreme court decisions.

The Judiciary Act of 1789 established the federal judiciary, and, although portions of the act have been amended, many of the precedents it set have continued to this day.

Michael L. Coulter

FURTHER READING

As good a starting point as any are two comprehensive but concise histories of the Supreme Court: Robert Langran's *The Supreme Court: A Concise History* (New York: P. Lang, 2004) and Westel Woodbury

Willoughby's *The Supreme Court of the United States: Its History and Influence in Our Constitutional System* (Union, N.J.: Lawbook Exchange, 2001). From there, readers may wish to probe more deeply into the Court's history in *The Documentary History of the Supreme Court of the United States, 1789-1800* (New York: Columbia University Press, 1985), edited by James R. Perry et al., which contains the complete text of the Judiciary Act of 1789.

Any serious investigation of this topic should consult the only recent book devoted to the act, Wilfred Ritz's *Rewriting the History of the Judiciary Act of 1789: Exposing Myths, Challenging Premises, and Using New Evidence* (Norman: University of Oklahoma Press, 1990). Robert McCloskey's *The American Supreme Court*, revised by Sanford Levinson (4th ed. Chicago: University of Chicago Press, 2005), devotes a chapter to the early years of the Court.

Congressional Quarterly's *Guide to the United States Supreme Court*, edited by David G. Savage (4th ed. Washington, D.C.: Congressional Quarterly, 2004), includes essays on the formation of the federal judiciary.

SEE ALSO Circuit riding; Ellsworth, Oliver; *Marbury v. Madison*; Marshall, John; Paterson, William.

Trial by Jury

DESCRIPTION: Legal process in which a group of citizens sworn as jurors hears evidence presented at trial and then collectively decides on the accused's culpability for a crime or civil offense.

SIGNIFICANCE: Supreme Court rulings affirm the importance of trial by jury as a protection against government oppression of the accused and as an avenue for citizen participation in the democratic process.

Article III, section 2, of the U.S. Constitution provides the right to trial by jury for all crimes except impeachment, and the Seventh Amendment grants this right in civil cases involving twenty dollars or more. The Sixth Amendment provides the right to be tried by an impartial jury.

In *Palko v. Connecticut* (1937), the Supreme Court interpreted these constitutional provisions as applicable only in federal trials, reasoning that trial by jury was not a fundamental right and therefore was not applicable to the states through the Fourteenth Amendment's due process clause. This meant states were not required to provide jury trials but could choose to do so.

The Court reversed its position in *Duncan v. Louisiana* (1968), ruling that trial by jury in criminal cases is a fundamental right applicable to the states. The Court's reasoning in *Duncan* emphasized the importance of jury trials as part of due process and as a significant aspect of participatory democracy. In subsequent cases, the Court clarified the scope of the right to trial by jury, finding it applicable in any case involving a minimum possible sentence of six months of incarceration and in some cases with a shorter penalty. However, the Court did not extend the Seventh Amendment requirement of trial by jury in civil cases to the states, instead leaving state governments to decide this.

Despite the Court's recognition of the importance of trial by jury, minors in the juvenile justice system lack this right. The Court, in the case *In re Gault* (1967), reasoned that because juvenile court proceedings are not adversarial, jury trials are not necessary. However, juveniles tried in adult court gain the right to trial by jury.

Historically, jurors had the right to decide questions of both law and fact, but in *Sparf and Hansen v. United States* (1899), the Court restricted jurors to deciding issues of fact. In their capacity as fact finders, jurors in criminal trials decide whether the prosecution has proven beyond a reasonable doubt that the defendant is guilty as charged, a requirement the Court noted in *In re Winship* (1970) that is intended to protect against erroneous convictions. Jurors in most civil cases use the less stringent "preponderance of the evidence" standard. In *Witherspoon v. Illinois* (1968), the Court emphasized the role of jurors as the conscience of the community.

Diana R. Grant

FURTHER READING

Abramson, Jeffrey. *We, the Jury.* New York: Basic Books, 1994.
Del Carmen, Rolando V. *Criminal Procedure: Law and Practice.* 6th ed. Belmont, Calif.: Thomson/Wadsworth, 2004.

Finkel, Norman J. *Commonsense Justice: Jurors' Notions of the Law.* Cambridge, Mass.: Harvard University Press, 1995.

Jonakait, Randolph N. *The American Jury System.* New Haven, Conn.: Yale University Press, 2003.

Kalven, Harry, Jr., and Hans Zeisel. *The American Jury.* Chicago: University of Chicago Press, 1970.

Litan, Robert E., ed. *Verdict: Assessing the Civil Jury System.* Washington, D.C.: Brookings Institution, 1993.

Schwartz, Victor E. et al. *Safeguarding the Right to a Representative Jury: The Need for Improved Jury Service Laws.* Washington, D.C.: National Legal Center for the Public Interest, 2003.

SEE ALSO *Batson v. Kentucky*; Bill of Rights; *Duncan v. Louisiana*; Sixth Amendment.

Katz v. United States

CITATION: 389 U.S. 347

DATE: December 18, 1967

ISSUE: Search and seizure

SIGNIFICANCE: Overturning an important precedent that had endured for almost forty years, this Supreme Court ruling significantly expanded Fourth Amendment rights in ruling that police must obtain warrants before wiretapping private conversations, even inside public telephone booths.

In *Olmstead v. United States*, in a 5-4 decision in 1928, the Supreme Court held that conversations were not protected by the Fourth Amendment because they are not tangible objects that can be seized. The Court further ruled that if the tapping of a telephone conversation occurs without the police entering into a private home, there is no "search" of a constitutionally protected area. In dissent, Justice Louis D. Brandeis wanted to interpret the Fourth and Fifth Amendments to protect the privacy of individuals, not just material objects. However, the Court reaffirmed the *Olmstead* ruling in *Silverman v. United States* (1961), declaring that in order for a Fourth Amendment search to take place, the police must physically intrude into "a constitutionally protected area."

Around that same time, federal agents attached an electronic listening device to the outside of a public phone booth frequently used by bookmaker Charles Katz. The conversations overheard by the officers were used in his criminal trial. Katz argued that the listening devices violated his Fourth Amendment protection against illegal searches. The lower courts, referring to *Olmstead* and *Silverman*, concluded that no search had occurred, because no tangible object was involved and the wall of the booth had not been physically penetrated.

By a 7-1 margin, however, the Supreme Court ruled in Katz's favor. Delivering the opinion for the Court, Justice Potter Stewart argued that the agents had intruded into Katz's privacy, thereby conducting a search and seizure according to the Fourth Amendment, which required a warrant from a neutral magistrate. He further explained that "the Fourth Amendment protects people, not places," and that the information a person "seeks to preserve as private, even in an area accessible to the public, may be constitutionally protected." In an often quoted concurring opinion, Justice John Marshall Harlan wrote more broadly of a "reasonable expectation of privacy." He stated that this expectation was based on two things: that the person's actions indicate an expectation of privacy, and that the expectation is one judged by society to be reasonable.

The seminal *Katz* ruling, as interpreted in Harlan's concurrence, provided the standard for deciding countless later Fourth Amendment cases. The Court, however, has tended to take a relatively narrow interpretation of the concept "reasonable expectation of privacy." For example, it found that a person had no reasonable expectation of privacy in bank records in *United States v. Miller* (1976), because the information is voluntarily given to banks and is exposed to the banks' employees. In *California v. Ciraolo* (1986), the Court found that people have no reasonable expectation of privacy against warrantless police surveillance by a helicopter flying over a fenced backyard. Likewise, in *Minnesota v. Carter* (1998), the Court held that temporary visitors in a home, unlike the homeowner, did not have any reasonable expectation of privacy.

Richard L. Wilson
Revised and updated by the Editor

SEE ALSO Fourth Amendment; *Kyllo v. United States*; *Mapp v. Ohio*; Privacy, right to; Search warrant requirement; Stewart, Potter.

Kelo v. City of New London

CITATION: 545 U.S. 469
DATE: June 23, 2005
ISSUES: Takings clause of the Fifth Amendment; eminent domain
SIGNIFICANCE: The Supreme Court held that government may use its power of eminent domain to seize private property against an owner's will for the purpose of transferring the property to private developers to promote economic development and increase the tax base.

When the city government of New London, Connecticut, became alarmed that the tax base was continually decreasing, it authorized a private entity, the New London Development Corporation (NLDC), to devise plans for economic development. When the Pfizer Corporation built a plant near the Fort Trumbull neighborhood, which contained mostly older homes, the city approved an NLDC plan to acquire the neighborhood in order to encourage economic activity. Among the owners of 115 residential and commercial lots, fifteen property owners refused to sell their lots. The city chose to exercise its power of eminent domain and authorized the NLDC to seize the lots. The controversy attracted national attention because such seizures were becoming increasingly common.

Susette Kelo and the other property owners sued the city, arguing that the Fifth Amendment only authorized the taking of property for a "public use," not to sell the land to private developers. The city countered that the concept of public use was broad enough to include considerations of employment and the alleviation of the city's economic distress. The Connecticut Supreme Court agreed with the city's position.

The U.S. Supreme Court upheld the ruling by a 5-4 margin. Defending the decision, Justice John Paul Stevens argued that the taking of land in New London was not simply for the private benefit of a few private individuals, but rather it was part of a development plan to promote the public's interest in overcoming economic difficulties.

Rather than a narrow and "literal" reading of the takings clause, Stevens defended a "broader and more natural interpretation of public use as 'public purpose.'"

Justice Sandra Day O'Connor characterized the majority decision as a "reverse Robin Hood" action, taking from the poor to give to the rich. Justice Clarence Thomas wrote that the development plan appeared to give special consideration to the needs of the Pfizer Corporation. Throughout the country, property owners indicated strong agreement with the Court's minority. Minnesota and other states responded to the Court's ruling with legislation that significantly restricted applications of the eminent domain power.

Thomas Tandy Lewis

SEE ALSO *Barron v. Baltimore;* Contracts clause; Fifth Amendment; O'Connor, Sandra Day; Takings clause; Thomas, Clarence; Zoning.

Anthony M. Kennedy

IDENTIFICATION: Associate justice (February 18, 1988-   )
NOMINATED BY: Ronald Reagan
BORN: July 23, 1936, Sacramento, California
SIGNIFICANCE: A moderately conservative justice with distinct libertarian tendencies, Kennedy has often provided the swing vote on important issues before the Supreme Court.

The son of a prominent lawyer, Anthony M. Kennedy earned a bachelor's degree in political science from Stanford University and a law degree from Harvard Law School in 1961. After his graduation, he worked for a prestigious law firm in San Francisco but left in 1963 to take over his deceased father's law practice in Sacramento. In addition to being a successful lawyer, he actively worked with the Republican Party. In 1975, President Gerald Ford nominated him to the Court of Appeals for the Ninth Circuit, on which he wrote more than four hundred decisions over the next thirteen years. He also found the time to teach constitutional law at California's University of the Pacific from 1965 to 1988.

In late 1987, President Ronald Reagan nominated Kennedy as associate justice of the Supreme Court. Kennedy was Reagan's third nominee to replace the centrist Lewis F. Powell, Jr. After the contentious and unsuccessful nominations of Robert Bork and Douglas Ginsburg, Reagan was looking for a reliable conservative judge with a noncontroversial reputation for stability, competence, and moderation. Although both liberals and conservatives on the Senate Judiciary Committee expressed reservations about Kennedy's views, he made a favorable impression as a highly competent and openminded man of judicial temperament, and the Senate confirmed him with a 97-0 vote. He took his seat on February 18, 1988.

During his first few years on the Court, Kennedy had a strongly conservative record, most often voting with Chief Justice William H. Rehnquist and Justice Antonin Scalia. The chief justice assigned an unusually large number of opinions to Kennedy, and some commentators referred to him as "Rehnquist's lieutenant."

Justices Anthony Kennedy (left) and Clarence Thomas at a House Appropriations subcommittee hearing in April, 2006. (AP/Wide World Photos)

It was widely assumed that Kennedy, a practicing Roman Catholic, favored the reversal of *Roe v. Wade,* which had recognized the right of women to terminate unwanted pregnancies. This was particularly true after he joined a 5-4 majority in approving restrictions on abortions in *Webster v. Reproductive Health Services* (1989). However, in the highly publicized case, *Planned Parenthood of Southeastern Pennsylvania v. Casey* (1992), he surprised observers with his support for the 5-4 majority that reaffirmed *Roe,* joining the plurality opinion that the rejection of an established precedent required more than simply a belief that the case had been wrongly decided. Kennedy continued, nevertheless, to approve of restrictions on abortion. He dissented, for example, in *Stenberg v. Carhart* (2000), when the majority struck down Nebraska's law that criminalized partial-birth abortions.

On the issue of gay rights, Kennedy wrote the Court's opinion in *Romer v. Evans* (1996), invalidating a section in Colorado's constitution that forbade communities from passing antidiscrimination ordinances to protect gays and lesbians. Gays were disappointed when he voted with the majority in *Boy Scouts of America v. Dale* (2000), recognizing that the organization's rights of expression and association permitted it to ban gay scoutmasters. In *Lawrence v. Texas* (2003), however, he wrote the Court's opinion, holding that states may not prohibit homosexual relations between consenting adults. One of the most notable aspects of Kennedy's *Lawrence* opinion was its many references to European jurists and international law as references for interpreting the U.S. Constitution.

During the early twenty-first century, Kennedy joined the liberal wing of the Court in many high-profile cases. He authored the majority opinion in *Roper v. Simmons* (2005), prohibiting the executions of felons younger than eighteen when they commit their crimes. He also authored the official opinion in *Ashcroft v. Free Speech Coalition* (2002), declaring that government had no constitutional authority to prohibit computer-generated child pornography. In the highly controversial case, *Kelo v. City of New London* (2005), he joined the liberals in supporting local governments' use of eminent domain to take private property for economic development.

However, Kennedy also was frequently on the side of the more conservative justices, as when he dissented in *Rompilla v. Beard* (2005), arguing that the Court should be very cautious about making after-the-fact judgments about the strategies and qualifications of defense attorneys. He voted with the minority in *Grutter v. Bollinger* (2003), opposing the use of racial preferences for university admissions to promote diversity. In *Hudson v. Michigan* (2006), he supported the use of criminal evidence obtained in a search when the officers did not follow the procedure of "knock and announce," although he wrote a separate concurrence saying that the decision would not affect other applications of the exclusionary rule. Often he supported states' rights, although in the highly publicized case of *Bush v. Gore* (2000), he angered liberals when supporting the cessation of the recount of Florida ballots, ensuring the victory of President George W. Bush.

In early 2006, when Justice Sandra Day O'Connor, who had often provided the swing vote, was replaced by Samuel Alito, whose record was quite conservative, commentators noted that this change left Kennedy as the most centrist of the nine justices. For this reason, it was widely expected that his positions would have a disproportionate impact on the direction of the court through the next few years. During the second half of the Court's 2005-2006 term, he did indeed provide the swing vote in a number of 5-4 decisions. In the *Hudson* ruling, for example, he joined with the four more conservative justices to allow for an exception in the application of the exclusionary rule. In the case of *Rapanos v. United States*, in contrast, he joined with the four more liberal justices to prevent a significant weakening of the Clear Water Act (1972).

In addition to his work on the Court, Kennedy has not been timid about speaking out on public policy issues. In July, 2003, Attorney General John Ashcroft announced that the Department of Justice would monitor whether federal judges were imposing the federal mandatory minimum sentences. Kennedy responded in a speech to the American Bar Association on August 9, 2003. Calling the guidelines "unwise and unjust," he declared, "Our resources are misspent, our punishments too severe, our sentencing too long," and he urged ABA members to work toward reforming the criminal justice in a more humane way. Observing the social costs of giving long sentences for the possession of small amounts of marijuana, he concluded that "out of sight, out of mind is an unacceptable excuse for a prison system that incarcerates over two million human beings in the United States."

Thomas Tandy Lewis

FURTHER READING

Bader, William H., and Roy M. Mersky, eds. *The First One Hundred Eight Justices.* Buffalo, N.Y.: William S. Hein, 2004.

Deegan, Paul. *Anthony Kennedy.* New York: ABDO, 2001.

Eastland, Terry. "The Tempting of Justice Kennedy." *American Spectator* 26, no. 2 (1993): 32-38.

Hensley, Thomas R. *The Rehnquist Court: Justices, Rulings, and Legacy.* Santa Barbara, Calif.: ABC-Clio, 2006.

Keck, Thomas M. *The Most Activist Supreme Court in History: The Road to Modern Judicial Conservatism.* Chicago: University of Chicago Press, 2004.

Toobin, Jeffrey. "Swing Shift: How Anthony Kennedy's Passion for Foreign Law Could Change the Supreme Court." *The New Yorker,* September 12, 2005.

Tushnet, Mark. *A Court Divided: The Rehnquist Court and the Future of Constitutional Law.* New York: W. W. Norton, 2005.

Yarbrough, Tinsley. *The Rehnquist Court and the Constitution.* New York: Oxford University Press, 2000.

SEE ALSO Abortion; *Boerne v. Flores; Bush v. Gore; Church of Lukumi Babalu Aye v. Hialeah; Gratz v. Bollinger/ Grutter v. Bollinger; Hudson v. Michigan; Lawrence v. Texas; Lee v. Weisman;* Nominations to the Court; Rehnquist, William H.; Religion, freedom of; *Roper v. Simmons.*

Korematsu v. United States

CITATION: 323 U.S. 14

DATE: December 18, 1944

ISSUES: Due process, substantive; equal protection; war powers

SIGNIFICANCE: The Supreme Court upheld the exclusion of persons of Japanese ancestry from the West Coast and the requirement that they report to assembly centers, which almost always resulted in assignment to internment camps.

667

After the United States entered into a war with Japan, President Franklin D. Roosevelt issued executive orders authorizing a military program that removed persons of Japanese descent from the West Coast and resettled them in internment centers. Congress enacted a statute that implemented the executive orders. In *Hirabayashi v. United States* (1943), the Court unanimously upheld the military's curfew that applied almost exclusively to persons of Japanese ethnicity, but the Court refused to even consider the more fundamental issues of exclusion and resettlement.

Fred Korematsu was a Japanese American who tried to evade the evacuation program in order to live and work in California. When discovered, he was prosecuted for two crimes: remaining in the restricted area and not reporting to an assembly center for assignment under the program. He was sentenced to five years in prison but was paroled and sent to an internment camp in Utah. Korematsu claimed that his conviction violated the due process clause of the Fifth Amendment.

By a 6-3 vote, the Supreme Court rejected Korematsu's claim. Writing for the majority, Justice Hugo L. Black accepted the military's argument that the presence of Japanese Americans on the West Coast presented a danger to the national security, and he insisted that their "temporary exclusion" was based on military necessity rather than any racial hostility. Although Black accepted the exclusion program without any solid evidence of sabotage or espionage, he nevertheless wrote that "all legal restrictions that curtail the rights of a single racial group are immediately suspect" and must be given "the most rigid scrutiny." Ironically, this statement helped establish the Court's use of the strict scrutiny test in cases involving racial restrictions. Because Korematsu was not convicted under the internment portion of the program, Black avoided any consideration of internment, and he examined only the constitutionality of the exclusion and reporting requirements.

The three dissenters emphasized the issue of racial discrimination and worried about future applications of the *Korematsu* precedent. Justice Frank Murphy wrote an especially strong dissent challenging "this legalization of racism" and insisted that investigations of Japanese Americans should have been conducted "on an individual basis" as had been done in cases involving persons of German and Italian ancestry.

In *Ex parte Endo*, announced the same day as *Korematsu*, the Court narrowly ruled that the War Relocation Authority must release any person whose loyalty to the United States had been clearly established. Because of the difficult burden of proof requirements in the *Endo* decision, this did not help Korematsu and most other Japanese Americans. In the 1980's lawyer Peter Irons discovered that the military had concealed evidence about Korematsu and others from the courts, and their convictions were overturned.

Thomas Tandy Lewis

FURTHER READING

Irons, Peter. *Justice at War.* New York: Oxford University Press, 1988.
_____. *Justice Delayed.* Middletown, Conn.: Wesleyan University Press, 1989.
Ng, Wendy L. *Japanese American Internment During World War II: A History and Reference Guide.* Westport, Conn.: Greenwood Press, 2002.

SEE ALSO Black, Hugo L.; Due process, substantive; Equal protection clause; Jackson, Robert H.; Japanese American relocation; Judicial scrutiny; Race and discrimination; War and civil liberties; War powers; World War II.

Kyllo v. United States

CITATION: 533 U.S. 363
DATE: June 11, 2001
ISSUE: External searches of homes with high-tech equipment
SIGNIFICANCE: In a decision that limited the use of modern privacy-threatening technology, the Supreme Court held that police must have a search warrant in order to use a thermal imager to detect patterns of heat coming from a private home.

In 1992, federal agents aimed a sensitive heat detector, the Agema Thermovision 210, at Danny Kyllo's home in Florence, Oregon. The agents were acting on the basis of tips and utility bills suggesting the possibility that Kyllo might be growing marijuana indoors under high-intensity lamps. After the instrument registered suspicious-looking hot spots, the agents obtained a warrant to enter and search the home, where they discovered more than one hundred marijuana plants growing under lamps. Although Kyllo agreed to plead guilty of a misdemeanor requiring one month in jail, he contested the validity of the search.

The Supreme Court, by a 5-4 margin, agreed with Kyllo's contention that the warrantless use of the thermal imager had violated his "reasonable expectation of privacy." Writing the opinion for the Court, Justice Antonin Scalia argued that the most fundamental purpose of the Fourth Amendment was to keep private homes "safe from prying government eyes," and he emphasized the importance of not "leaving the homeowner at the mercy of advancing technology." In a surprising dissent, Justice John Paul Stevens, who was often called the Court's most liberal justice, wrote that the use of the device outside the home "did not invade any constitutionally protected interest in privacy."

The Kyllo ruling highlighted the unpredictable nature of the Court's line drawing when applying Fourth Amendment principles. The previous year, in *Bond v. United States*, a 7-2 majority of Court had found that the police had engaged in an unconstitutional search when they walked down the aisle of a bus and squeezed a passenger's luggage to look for contraband. In that case, Stevens had voted with the majority, while Scalia had dissented.

Thomas Tandy Lewis

SEE ALSO Fourth Amendment; Privacy, right to; Scalia, Antonin; Search warrant requirement; Stevens, John Paul.

Joseph R. Lamar

IDENTIFICATION: Associate justice (January 3, 1911-January 2, 1916)
NOMINATED BY: William H. Taft
BORN: October 14, 1857, Ruckersville, Georgia
DIED: January 2, 1916, Washington, D.C.
SIGNIFICANCE: An esteemed legal historian and jurist, Lamar believed that law must slowly adjust to changing times. The clear, logical style expressed in opinions he wrote while on the Supreme Court enhanced the ability of executive officials to provide the necessary details for implementing laws.

After studying law at Washington and Lee University, Joseph R. Lamar was admitted to the Georgia bar in 1878. He served two terms in the Georgia legislature (1886-1889) and on a commission that recodified the state's civil law. Establishing himself as one of the lead-

Joseph R. Lamar.
(Library of Congress)

671

ing members of the legal profession, he was appointed to the Georgia supreme court in 1904.

Lamar was appointed to the Supreme Court by President William H. Taft in 1911. Lamar typically voted with the majority, writing only eight dissents. He wrote clearly and tersely but without creativity. Lamar's best-known opinion was rendered in *Gompers v. Buck's Stove and Range Co.* (1911), which upheld the right of courts to punish violations of injunctions, but at the same time set aside Gompers's conviction on procedural grounds. Lamar's most far-reaching opinion came in the *United States v. Midwest Oil Co.* (1915), which upheld the president's right to withhold public oil lands from private exploitation. In 1914 Lamar represented President Woodrow Wilson at a conference involving sensitive negotiations to settle some differences with Mexico.

Alvin K. Benson

SEE ALSO Civil law; Progressivism; Taft, William H.; White, Edward D.

Lucius Q. C. Lamar

IDENTIFICATION: Associate justice (January 18, 1888-January 23, 1893)
NOMINATED BY: Grover Cleveland
BORN: September 17, 1825, Eatonton, Georgia
DIED: January 23, 1893, Vineville, Georgia
SIGNIFICANCE: Lamar was the first southerner appointed to the Supreme Court after the Civil War. As an associate justice, he championed the rights of business over government.

Lucius Q. C. Lamar was born into the landed southern aristocracy, in which public service was a tradition. A cousin, Joseph R. Lamar, also served on the Supreme Court. Lamar graduated from Emory College in 1845, read the law in Macon, Georgia, and passed the bar in 1847. For the next five years, he taught mathematics at the University of Mississippi in Oxford and practiced law. In 1852 he returned to Georgia and, with a friend, established a successful law practice in Covington.

Lucius Q. C. Lamar.
(Library of Congress)

During the Civil War, he served as colonel of the Eighteenth Mississippi Regiment and the Confederate ambassador to Russia. He ended the Civil War as a judge advocate for the Confederate Army. After the war, he resumed the practice of law in Mississippi.

After receiving a pardon, Lamar served in the U.S. Congress and was appointed secretary of the interior by President Grover Cleveland in 1885. On December 6, 1887, he was nominated to the U.S. Supreme Court by President Cleveland, a nomination that was the object of a bitterly fought battle, with attacks on his age and lack of judicial experience. Those senators leading the battle for confirmation feared his rejection would be a ban on all Confederate veterans. Lamar was confirmed on January 16, 1888, by a vote of 32-28, and sworn in two days later. He was the first Democrat appointed to the Court since Stephen Field in 1862.

The Interstate Commerce Commission (ICC) was created in 1887 with broad regulatory powers. These powers were challenged by an Iowa law forbidding manufacture of liquor for both intrastate and interstate sale. In the majority opinion in *Kidd v. Pearson* (1888), Lamar defined commerce as the transportation and sale of goods, which excluded manufacturing, the transformation of goods. The ICC could regulate commerce but could not regulate manufacturing, a severe limitation on its powers.

Although he served as an associate justice for only five years, much of Lamar's renown came as a result of his dissenting opinions in a number of cases. In *Chicago, Milwaukee, and St. Paul Railway Co. v. Minnesota* (1890), Lamar's dissent said legislators, not courts, should have the power to decide the reasonableness of railroad rates. In *In re Neagle* (1890), Lamar wrote a dissenting opinion upholding the conviction of a U.S. marshal for killing a judge's assailant, saying an act was not done in an official capacity unless there was an explicit statute to that effect. In *Field v. Clark* (1892), Lamar wrote that Congress's giving the president the right to impose discretionary tariffs by executive decision was an improper delegation of power.

Elizabeth Algren Shaw

FURTHER READING

Bader, William H., and Roy M. Mersky, eds. *The First One Hundred Eight Justices.* Buffalo, N.Y.: William S. Hein, 2004.

Ely, James W., Jr. *The Fuller Court: Justices, Rulings, and Legacy.* Santa Barbara, Calif.: ABC-Clio, 2003.

Wagman, Robert J. *The Supreme Court: A Citizen's Guide.* New York: Pharos Books, 1993.

Witt, Elder. *Congressional Quarterly's Guide to the U.S. Supreme Court.* Washington, D.C.: Congressional Quarterly, 1990.

SEE ALSO Civil War; Fuller, Melville W.; States' rights and state sovereignty.

Lawrence v. Texas

CITATION: 539 U.S. 558
DATE: June 26, 2003
ISSUE: Gay and lesbian rights
SIGNIFICANCE: In overturning a Texas statute that had outlawed
homosexual conduct, the Supreme Court extended the Constitu-
tion's protection of "liberty interests" to gays and lesbians.

After the watershed case of *Griswold v. Connecticut* (1965), the Court
emphasized that the due process clauses of the Fifth and Fourteenth
Amendments protected a substantive right of generic liberty (or privacy), especially in intimate sexual relationships. The justices, however, often disagreed about the contours of this protection, and in
Bowers v. Hardwick (1986), the Court held that Georgia's criminalization of homosexual sodomy did not violate the Constitution. The
majority of the justices accepted the theory that the due process
clauses protected only those liberties that had been recognized in the
history and traditions of the United States.

In 1998, a Texas police officer, responding to a report of a weapons disturbance, entered the private apartment of John Lawrence.
The officer observed Lawrence and another man in an act that was
forbidden by Texas's antisodomy statute. The two men were found
guilty and fined $125 each. The Texas Supreme Court upheld the
judgment, based primarily on the *Hardwick* precedent.

When the case reached the U.S. Supreme Court, however, the justices, in a 5-1-3 decision, ruled that the Texas antisodomy law was unconstitutional. Speaking for five of the justices, Anthony M. Kennedy
directly overturned *Hardwick* and recognized the liberty of consenting adults to make decisions about intimate relationships within the
privacy of their homes. He argued that the Court's precedents since
1986 had expanded the scope of constitutional protection for liberty
and that the decision of *Romer v. Evans* (1996) had weakened *Bowers*
as a precedent. Kennedy noted that only thirteen states retained
antisodomy statutes, with only four of these states actively enforcing
those laws. Observing that the Court in *Bowers* had referred to Western traditions, he wrote that most Western countries no longer

provided criminal penalties for homosexual practices. His opinion included expansive rhetoric about the need to respect gays and lesbians.

Although Justice Sandra Day O'Connor did not join Kennedy's opinion, she agreed that the law was unconstitutional. Her reasoning was that it violated the principle of equal protection because it punished only homosexual conduct, not heterosexual conduct. In a short dissent, Justice Clarence Thomas rejected the entire notion of a "general right of privacy." Justice Antonin Scalia's long dissent denounced the majority for supporting the "homosexual agenda." He warned that the logic of the decision might have broad consequences, such as forcing states to recognize same-sex marriages and requiring admission of openly gay persons into the military.

Thomas Tandy Lewis

SEE ALSO Equal protection clause; Fifth Amendment; Fourteenth Amendment; O'Connor, Sandra Day; Privacy, right to; Scalia, Antonin; Thomas, Clarence.

Lee v. Weisman

CITATION: 505 U.S. 577
DATE: June 24, 1992
ISSUE: Establishment of religion
SIGNIFICANCE: The Supreme Court declared that public schools could not conduct prayer exercises at graduation ceremonies.

Graduation ceremonies at a high school in Providence, Rhode Island, were voluntary. When inviting local clergy to offer nonsectarian invocations and benedictions, the principal would give them guidelines suggesting the use of "inclusiveness and sensitivity." The principal took care to invite a diversity of local clergy—Protestant, Roman Catholic, Jewish, and others if available. Daniel Weisman, the father of two students, asked for a court order prohibiting the practice. In response, a federal appellate court ruled that the ceremony constituted an "advancement of religion" without a secular purpose, which was contrary to *Lemon v. Kurtzman* (1971). When the case was appealed to the Supreme Court, the administration of President George H. W. Bush submitted a brief asking the Court to overturn the *Lemon* precedent.

By a 5-4 vote, the Court upheld the lower court's judgment. Justice Anthony M. Kennedy emphasized the element of government coercion to participate in the ceremony, with social pressures on students to attend, to stand, and to maintain respectful silence. In presenting clergy with guidelines for the prayers, moreover, the principal "directed and controlled the content of the prayer." Justice Antonin Scalia's dissent endorsed Kennedy's standard of coercion but found no coercion in this instance. The *Weisman* opinion did not limit the extent to which speakers at school events might discuss religious themes, and it did not address the question of whether students might organize prayer ceremonies without the involvement of public officials.

Thomas Tandy Lewis

SEE ALSO *Abington School District v. Schempp*; *Engel v. Vitale*; *Lemon v. Kurtzman*; Religion, establishment of; *Wallace v. Jaffree*.

Lemon v. Kurtzman

CITATION: 403 U.S. 602
DATE: June 28, 1971
ISSUE: Separation of church and state
SIGNIFICANCE: While vetoing state subsidies for teachers of parochial schools, the Supreme Court established a three-part *Lemon* test for evaluating whether governmental programs ran afoul of the establishment clause of the First Amendment.

In 1968, the Pennsylvania legislature enacted a statute which allowed direct salary supplements for teachers of secular subjects in private schools. Alton Lemon, supported by the American Civil Liberties Union, brought suit against David Kurtzman, state superintendent of schools. The Supreme Court consolidated this case with a similar one from Rhode Island, and it ruled, by a 7-0 vote, that both state laws were unconstitutional.

Chief Justice Warren E. Burger's opinion for the majority was of later importance because of its three-part test known as the *Lemon* test: First, a statute must have a secular legislative purpose; second, its primary effect must not be to either advance or inhibit religion; and third, it must not promote "an excessive government entanglement with religion." Burger noted that the teachers at religious schools, many of whom were nuns, would find it impossible to make a clear distinction between religious and nonreligious instruction. Government grants, moreover, would require surveillance and controls, which would involve a great deal of entanglement between state and religion.

The *Lemon* test, in its application, is susceptible to a great deal of interpretation, depending on whether the particular justice desires "accommodation" or a "high wall of separation" between church and state. Applying the test often split the justices into 5-4 votes. Although often criticized, the *Lemon* test has endured because a majority of the justices have been unable to coalesce behind an alternative standard. In *Agostini v. Felton* (1997), Justice Sandra Day O'Connor cited the *Lemon* test as good law, but she endorsed an accommodationist view of the first part of the test.

Thomas Tandy Lewis

SEE ALSO Evolution and creationism; First Amendment; *Lee v. Weisman*; Religion, establishment of; *Wallace v. Jaffree.*

Libel

DESCRIPTION: Printed or broadcast defamation, which entails false statements holding an individual up to ridicule, contempt, or hatred, or causing an individual to be avoided by others.

SIGNIFICANCE: Libel law is an attempt to balance individuals' interest in reputation against the media's freedom of the press. In 1964 the Supreme Court began to shift from favoring individuals to favoring the media in cases involving libel.

Victims of libel, or defamatory false statements, sue the media for damages. Courts award monetary compensation to victims for the injury they suffered and stipulate punitive measures to chastise the press and thereby deter it and media companies from libeling others. The Supreme Court long considered defamatory statements irrelevant to the First Amendment because the statements did not contribute to the exposition of ideas and search for truth envisioned by those who wrote the amendment. The limited value of the statements was outweighed by the need to protect individuals' reputation. Therefore, the Court allowed states to fashion libel law as they saw fit, and it rarely heard libel cases. One exception was *Beauharnais v. Illinois* (1952), which involved "group libel" (later called "hate speech"). The Court upheld the law.

ACTUAL MALICE

In *New York Times Co. v. Sullivan* (1964), the Court, under Chief Justice Earl Warren, began to shift the balance in libel doctrine toward the media. In the early 1960's, the police commissioner of Montgomery, Alabama, sued *The New York Times* for printing an ad, with minor inaccuracies, bought by black clergymen protesting the treatment of civil rights demonstrators in the city. Although the ad did not mention the police commissioner by name or title, he claimed that it attacked him implicitly. Although he did not claim that it caused him any injury, he did not have to under state law, and the jury awarded him half a million dollars. Another county commissioner sued *The New York Times* for the same ad and was also awarded half a million dollars. By the time the case reached the Court, eleven more libel suits had been brought by local or state officials in Alabama against *The New York Times* or the Columbia Broadcasting Service for seven million dollars. There was nothing unusual about Alabama's law, which resembled other states' laws. The justices, then, could see that libel laws could be used by public officials to punish the press for criticism—in this case, a northern newspaper for coverage of southern race relations—even if the inaccuracies were minor and the officials suffered no real injury.

The Court's ruling made it harder for plaintiffs who were public officials to win libel suits. It established the actual malice test, which requires plaintiffs to prove that the defamatory statements were made with knowledge of their falsity or with reckless disregard for their truth or falsity. This standard is somewhat ambiguous, but the Court made clear that recklessness is beyond carelessness, which is the usual basis for establishing negligence in lawsuits. Despite its name, the test does not revolve around the everyday meaning of the word "malice." The plaintiff does not have to show maliciousness; and even if the plaintiff does show maliciousness, this showing by itself does not meet the test. A reporter can be "out to get" an official, publish defamatory statements, and still not be found guilty of actual malice. Maliciousness is relevant only if it helps the official prove that the reporter knew the statements were false or published them with reckless disregard for their truth or falsity.

The Court recognized that this test would allow the press to publish more false statements but insisted that this result was necessary to allow breathing room so the press can enjoy its full rights under the First Amendment.

APPLICATION OF THE TEST

The Court solidified its ruling by applying the actual malice test to an array of public officials, including judges (*Garrison v. Louisiana*, 1964); county attorneys (*Henry v. Collins*, 1965), court clerks (*Beckley Newspapers v. Hanks*, 1967), and law-enforcement officers, including police on the beat (*St. Amant v. Thompson*, 1968, and *Time v. Pape*, 1971). In applying the test to the manager of a small county-owned and operated ski area, the Court showed how far down the ranks of public employees its definition of public officials would extend. The Court also solidified its ruling by indicating that reckless disregard meant having serious doubts about the truth of the statements in *St. Amant*. Even being extremely sloppy would not be considered reckless.

At the same time, the Warren Court extended its ruling by applying the actual malice test to public figures in 1967 in *Curtis Publishing Co. v. Butts* and *Associated Press v. Walker*. Public figures are people who are well known or who have sought public attention. The Court's justifications were that the distinction between the public and private sectors has blurred and that public figures, like public officials, often play an influential role in society and also have sufficient access to the media to rebut any false accusations against them. This ruling made it harder for public figures to win libel suits.

The Warren Court classified as public figures a university athletic director, who was not paid by the state and therefore not a public official (*Curtis*) and a retired air force general (*Associated Press*). The Court, under Chief Justice Warren E. Burger, classified as public figures a real estate developer who was engaged in a controversy with the local school board (*Greenbelt Cooperative Publishing v. Bresler*, 1970) and candidates for public office (*Monitor Patriot Co. v. Roy*, 1971, and *Ocala Star-Banner v. Damron*, 1971).

A plurality of the early Burger Court sought to extend *The New York Times* doctrine by applying the actual malice test to private persons embroiled in public issues (*Rosenbloom v. Metromedia*, 1971). They maintained that people are all public persons to some degree and that public officials and public figures are private persons in some ways. The key was whether public issues were involved. If so, the press should feel free to report on these issues for the public's benefit. The plurality's views, if adopted by a majority of the justices, would have made it harder for private persons to win libel suits.

As more holdovers from the Warren Court retired from the Burger Court, the new majority concluded that the balance had tipped too far toward the First Amendment and away from guarding the reputations of private persons. In 1974 a majority ruled that private persons, even if embroiled in public controversies, would not have to meet the actual malice test to win compensatory damages. (States could set the exact standard, but plaintiffs would have to show at least negligence by the press.) However, they would still have to prove actual malice to win punitive damages (*Gertz v. Robert Welch*, 1974). The justices sympathized with private persons' desires to be compensated for any injuries they suffered but not their efforts to be awarded additional, punitive damages, which often were sizable and unrelated to the severity of the injuries.

With this ruling, the Burger Court completed the process of nationalizing and constitutionalizing libel law—making the law conform to certain national constitutional standards, rather than allowing it to develop through the process of state common law—that the Warren Court began in *The New York Times*.

The Burger Court also began to define the public figure category narrowly. The Court held that plaintiffs could be considered public figures if they have general fame or notoriety to the people exposed to the defamatory statements. In *Gertz*, a lawyer who was well known in legal and civic circles in Chicago was not known by the general population of the city, so he was not deemed a public figure. A socialite in Palm Beach, Florida, who was so prominent that she subscribed to a local clipping service, was not known outside of her community, so she was not deemed a public figure in a lawsuit against a national publication (*Time v. Firestone*, 1976). Alternatively, the Court held that plaintiffs could be considered public figures if they thrust themselves into a public controversy. However, a lawyer who represented a family who sued a police officer in a controversial case (*Gertz*) and a scientist who applied for federal funds for research (*Hutchinson v. Proxmire*, 1979) were not classified as public figures. The Court ruled that they were doing their jobs rather than thrusting themselves into public controversies. Thus, these plaintiffs, as private persons, did not need to meet the actual malice test to win compensatory damages.

The Burger Court also clarified the point that public issues must be involved before the constitutional standards developed in libel cases could be invoked by the defendants in libel suits. Dun and Bradstreet, which had issued an inaccurate credit report, argued that as a widely known company, it should be considered a public figure (and, therefore, the plaintiff would be forced to prove actual malice). However, the Court insisted that this was a private dispute, rather than a public issue, and as such Dun and Bradstreet was not entitled to any First Amendment protection in *Dun and Bradstreet v. Greenmoss Builders* (1985).

THE REHNQUIST COURT

Under the guidance of Chief Justice William H. Rehnquist, the Court held that companies can be considered public figures if the dispute involves a public issue. Bose Corporation sued *Consumer Reports* for a magazine article critical of the sound of Bose speakers. The article addressed a subject of interest to the public, so it was considered a public issue and Bose Corporation was deemed a public figure (*Bose Corp. v. Consumers Union of the United States*, 1984).

Although the Rehnquist Court reversed or eroded many rulings made by the Warren and Burger Courts, it maintained protection for media defendants in decisions involving the burden of proof in libel suits in *Philadelphia Newspapers v. Hepps* (1986) and *Anderson v. Liberty Lobby* (1986) and the attempt to circumvent libel law by suing for torts that have easier standards for plaintiffs in *Hustler Magazine v. Falwell* (1988). In *Masson v. New Yorker Magazine* (1991) the Court gave leeway to reporters, when quoting individuals, to clarify or condense direct quotations as long as reporters do not materially alter the meaning of the statements.

For statements to be considered defamatory, they must be capable of being proven false. The Rehnquist Court found that they must have been asserted as facts, rather than mere opinions in *Milkovich v. Lorain Journal Co.* (1990). Accordingly, it found that parodies cannot be defamatory, even if they humiliate their subjects, in *Hustler Magazine v. Falwell.*

The Supreme Court's doctrinal changes beginning in 1964 reduced the total number of libel suits filed and also the success rate for plaintiffs who are public officials or figures. Only one out of ten of these plaintiffs wins his or her suit.

John Gruhl

FURTHER READING

Two comprehensive and up-to-date works on libel are Peter A. Downard's *Libel* (Dayton, Ohio: LexisNexis/Butterworths, 2003) and *Gatley on Libel and Slander,* edited by Patrick Milmo and others (10th ed. London: Sweet & Maxwell, 2004). Anthony Lewis's *Make No Law* (New York: Random House, 1991) is a readable case study of *New York Times Co. v. Sullivan.* Harry Kalven, one of the foremost First Amendment scholars at the time, analyzed the landmark case in "The *New York Times* Case: A Note on 'The Central Meaning of the First Amendment,'" *Supreme Court Review* (1964): 191.

James Kirby's *Fumble* (New York: Dell, 1986) is a fascinating case study of *Curtis Publishing Co. v. Butts.* Kirby, a lawyer hired by the Southeastern Conference to investigate the allegations that gave rise to the suit—that two college coaches conspired to fix a football game between their teams—reports his conclusions. Renata Adler's *Reckless*

Disregard (New York: Alfred A. Knopf, 1986) examines a pair of prominent cases that never reached the Supreme Court—the libel suits of U.S. general William Westmoreland against the Columbia Broadcasting System and Israeli general Ariel Sharon against *Time*.

The decisions of juries in these and other libel suits are examined in *Trial by Jury* (New York: Simon & Schuster, 1990), edited by Stephen Brill, which shows the difficulty jurors have when asked to apply the actual malice test. The impact of the Court's decisions involving public officials and figures is analyzed in Randall Bezanson, Gilbert Cranberg, and John Soloski's *Libel Law and the Press* (New York: Free Press, 1987). Proposed reforms in libel law are addressed in Lois Forer's *A Chilling Effect* (New York: W. W. Norton, 1988).

SEE ALSO Brennan, William J., Jr.; Burger, Warren E.; First Amendment; Hate speech; *Hustler Magazine v. Falwell*; *New York Times Co. v. Sullivan*; Seditious libel; Warren, Earl.

Brockholst Livingston

IDENTIFICATION: Associate justice (January 20, 1807-March 18, 1823)
NOMINATED BY: Thomas Jefferson
BORN: November 25, 1757, New York, New York
DIED: March 18, 1823, Washington, D.C.
SIGNIFICANCE: An expert in maritime and commercial law, Livingston wrote a number of Supreme Court majority opinions on these issues. His most notable decision stated that the disputed Embargo Act of 1807, which prohibited trade with Great Britain, was constitutional.

Brockholst Livingston graduated from the College of New Jersey (later Princeton) in 1774, where he was a classmate of James Madison's. He planned to study law, but after the outbreak of the Revolutionary War, he joined the Continental Army. Livingston served as a captain with General Philip Schuyler in the siege of Ticonderoga, participated as an aide to Benedict Arnold in the battle of Saratoga, and witnessed the surrender of British General John Burgoyne in 1777.

In 1779 Livingston traveled to Spain on a diplomatic mission, serving as the private secretary to John Jay, his brother-in-law. Although Livingston served the duration of the mission, he developed a lifelong animosity for Jay and was often a vocal critic of the future chief justice of the United States. In 1782 Livingston returned to the United States and pursued the study of law in Albany, New York. After being admitted to the bar in 1783, he settled in New York City, established a legal practice, and became a respected lawyer. In 1786 he was elected to the New York assembly and was reelected to two more terms.

In 1802 Livingston was appointed to the New York Supreme Court, where he developed a reputation as an independent and energetic judge. In only four years, he wrote 149 opinions. Because New York was a major port, he became increasingly involved in deciding commercial, maritime, and prize ship cases, areas of expertise that would be invaluable when he served on the Supreme Court.

In 1804 he was considered for the position on the Court that went

Brockholst Livingston. (Albert Rosenthal/ Collection of the Supreme Court of the United States)

685

to William Johnson. After the death of Associate Justice William Paterson in December, 1806, Livingston was nominated to the Court by President Thomas Jefferson and confirmed by the Senate five days later. He was sworn in on January 20, 1807. Although he showed occasional flares of temper, Livingston was generally a very congenial justice. Colleague Joseph Story described him as a very able, independent, solid-thinking judge and noted that Livingston's judgments on maritime and commercial law were invaluable to the Court.

Livingston's writing style was crisp and factual. In sixteen years on the Court, he wrote fifty-two opinions, with thirty-eight for the majority, six concurrences, and eight dissents. Because of Chief Justice John Marshall's persuasive personality and strong influence on the Court, Livingston did not display the independence that he did while serving on the New York court. Although Livingston participated in many of the landmark cases of the Marshall Court, Chief Justice Marshall wrote most of those opinions. Due to his previous experience, however, Livingston left his mark on the Court in eight opinions he wrote concerning prize ship cases.

Alvin K. Benson

SEE ALSO Brown, Henry B.; Jay, John; Judiciary Act of 1789; Marshall, John.

Lochner v. New York

CITATION: 198 U.S. 45
DATE: April 17, 1905
ISSUE: Maximum-hour laws
SIGNIFICANCE: *Lochner* is the most famous case in which the Supreme Court used the doctrine of substantive due process to overturn a statute regulating labor conditions.

Journeymen bakers in the late 1900's often worked more than one hundred hours per week, sometimes in squalid tenement cellars. There was good evidence that the combination of working long hours, breathing flour dust, and being subjected to extremes of hot and cold harmed the health of these workers. In New York, journalist Edward Marshall joined forces with the leader of the Bakers' Union, Henry Weismann, in a crusade for legislation to improve working conditions in bakeries. In 1895 the state legislature unanimously passed the Bakeshop Act, regulating standards of sanitation and setting maximum hours of work. However, the statute harmed owners of small bakeries that operated on small profit margins. In 1902 one such owner, Joseph Lochner of Utica, was fined fifty dollars when one of his employees worked sixty hours during a week. Appealing the conviction, Lochner's attorneys argued that the statute violated the substantive liberty protected by the due process clause of the Fourteenth Amendment.

After losing in New York courts, Lochner prevailed in the Supreme Court with a vote of five to four. Reaffirming the basic idea in *Allgeyer v. Louisiana* (1897), Justice Rufus W. Peckham's opinion for the majority argued that the due process clause protected an unenumerated freedom of contract, and that the legislation regulating hours of labor interfered with the right of employers and employees to agree on the terms of employment. Although the Court had upheld a maximum-hour law for mines and smelters in *Holden v. Hardy* (1898), the *Lochner* majority found that such a law in bakeries exceeded the legitimate police powers of the states. Emphasizing the liberty of employees to work as many hours as they wished, Peckham's opinion suggested that employers and employees possessed similar powers in negotiating conditions of work.

In dissent, John Marshall Harlan argued for a presumption in favor of the legislature's determination, so that the Court should overturn only laws that are "plainly and palpably beyond all question in violation of the fundamental law of Constitution [1789]." In addition, he quoted statistical evidence that indicated serious health hazards in bakeries. Likewise, Oliver Wendell Holmes criticized the majority's narrow view of police powers, and he charged that the decision was influenced by social Darwinism and laissez-faire theories.

The *Lochner* case firmly entrenched the freedom of contract doctrine into constitutional law. In subsequent cases, the Court followed the precedent in overturning numerous laws regulating businesses and working conditions. It was only in *West Coast Hotel Co. v.*

Parrish (1937) that the Court firmly rejected the *Lochner* rationale. Often the period from 1905 to 1937 is referred to as the *Lochner* era.

Thomas Tandy Lewis

SEE ALSO Capitalism; Contract, freedom of; Due process, substantive; Holmes, Oliver Wendell; Peckham, Rufus W.

United States v. Lopez

CITATION: 514 U.S. 549
DATE: April 26, 1995
ISSUES: Commerce clause; Tenth Amendment
SIGNIFICANCE: The Supreme Court held that a federal statute was unconstitutional because Congress had overstepped its authority to regulate interstate commerce.

In 1990 Congress passed the Gun-Free School Zones Act, making it a federal crime to possess a gun within one thousand feet of a school. After Alfonso Lopez, Jr., a high school student in Texas, was arrested for taking a handgun to school, he was tried under federal law because the federal penalties were greater than those under state law. A federal court of appeals found that the federal statute violated the Tenth Amendment. Most observers expected the Supreme Court to reverse the judgment because the Court in *Garcia v. San Antonio Metropolitan Transit Authority* (1985) had held that the scope of federal authority to regulate commerce was a political question to be decided by the political process rather than by the Courts.

By a 5-4 vote, however, the Court upheld the ruling. Chief Justice William H. Rehnquist's majority opinion reasoned that possession of guns near a school had nothing to do with interstate commerce and that such an issue is traditionally a concern of local police power. As a principle, he wrote that Congress could regulate only "those activities that have a substantial relationship to interstate commerce."

The *Lopez* decision appeared to mark a renaissance for the principle of dual sovereignty, which had largely been abandoned following *Carter v. Carter Coal Co.* (1936). It was not clear how far the trend would go, but the Court in *Printz v. United States* (1997) held that Congress had no power to force states to enforce federal regulations absent a particular constitutional authorization.

Thomas Tandy Lewis

SEE ALSO Commerce, regulation of; *Darby Lumber Co., United States v.*; Federalism; *Garcia v. San Antonio Metropolitan Transit Authority*; *Printz v. United States*; Rehnquist, William H.; Second Amendment; States' rights and state sovereignty; Tenth Amendment.

Loving v. Virginia

CITATION: 388 U.S. 1
DATE: June 12, 1967
ISSUES: Marriage; racial discrimination
SIGNIFICANCE: The Supreme Court, in striking down a Virginia antimiscegenation law, voided statutes preventing interracial marriage throughout the United States.

In *Pace v. Alabama* (1883), the Supreme Court upheld a law that punished interracial fornication more severely than fornication between members of the same race on grounds that both partners were punished equally. This created the equal application or, in reality, equal discrimination exception to the Fourteenth Amendment's equal protection clause. After *Shelley v. Kraemer* (1948) and *Brown v. Board of Education* (1954), this became an increasingly untenable distinction, but the Court was apparently unwilling to face such a sensitive issue. In the 1960's, Loving, a white man who had married a black woman, was convicted under a Virginia antimiscegenation law and subsequently challenged the law's constitutionality. Chief Justice Earl Warren, writing for a unanimous Court, declared the Virginia law unconstitutional both as a denial of the Fourteenth Amendment's equal protection law and as a denial of liberty. The decision invalidated all laws forbidding interracial marriage, including those in fifteen southern states.

Richard L. Wilson

SEE ALSO *Brown v. Board of Education*; Due process, procedural; Equal protection clause; Fourteenth Amendment; Race and discrimination; *Shelley v. Kraemer*; Warren, Earl.

Loyalty Oaths

DEFINITION: Formal pledges or affirmations to support and defend one's country or a particular regime.

SIGNIFICANCE: After the Civil War (1861-1865), the Supreme Court invalidated retroactive "test oaths" that deprived persons of civil privileges for having supported the cause of the Confederacy. Beginning in the late 1950's, the Court applied increasingly libertarian standards to requirements that public employees take oaths concerning proscribed associations and beliefs.

Throughout recorded history, governments and leaders have utilized loyalty oaths as a means of consolidating power and punishing nonconformists. In England, after the Reformation, such oaths had the effect of restricting the legal rights of Roman Catholics and other religious dissidents. In colonial America, citizens were typically required to take oaths to support and defend their commonwealths, and some oaths included the duty to report dissidents against the government. During the American Revolution, the Continental Congress and state legislatures mandated that citizens pledge allegiance to the U.S. government. Loyalists and Quakers refusing to make this pledge were sometimes punished with exile and confiscation of property.

Although the First Amendment suggests a significant degree of free expression, it has usually not been interpreted as prohibiting all mandatory oaths of loyalty to the United States. Only a small minority of citizens object to making nonreligious affirmations of general loyalty to their country. Nevertheless, there are law-abiding groups, including the Jehovah's Witnesses, who refuse on religious grounds to affirm allegiance to any secular government. In the modern period, the most controversial oaths have been those that require public employees to swear or affirm that they do not belong to associations that advocate the overthrow of the government through illegal means.

CONSTITUTIONALLY APPROVED MANDATES

Article VI of the U.S. Constitution requires the president, members of Congress and state legislatures, and all executive and judicial officers to pledge by oath or affirmation to support the Constitution. Following this model, Congress has mandated that members of the armed forces, naturalized citizens, and employees in sensitive governmental positions must pledge or affirm allegiance to the United States. Most jurists interpret these requirements to be consistent with the First Amendment's guarantees of freedom of religion, speech, and association.

In *Cole v. Richardson* (1972), the Supreme Court upheld legislation requiring positive oaths or affirmations of loyalty similar to the one found in Article VI, so long as they are not unduly vague and do not infringe on constitutional freedoms. The *Cole* decision allowed the oath to include a pledge to oppose the forceful overthrow of the government. A minority of the justices argued that requiring this pledge was unconstitutional because it might be interpreted in ways that restrict freedom of speech and association. The majority, however, found the pledge acceptable, because the Constitution does not guarantee any right to advocate or endorse the overthrow of the government by violence or other illegal means.

Although *Cole* upheld the constitutionality of requiring adults to pledge loyalty as a condition of public employment, a federal Court of Appeals in 1994 ruled that such a requirement violated the Religious Freedom Restoration Act (1993), because the government could not show that loyalty oaths served a compelling objective. However, the decision was based on a federal statute that is no longer enforceable, which means that courts in the future may not utilize the decision as a precedent.

UNCONSTITUTIONAL REQUIREMENTS

Jurists distinguish between positive oaths to support one's country and negative oaths to refrain from particular acts and associations. One variant of negative oaths, called "test oaths," makes reference to the past rather than the future. Test oaths became especially common during the Civil War and Reconstruction periods. In 1862, Congress passed the "ironclad test oath" act, which required oaths of past loyalty by public officials. Three years later, the oaths were extended to numerous persons, including lawyers practicing in federal courts. After the war, many of the military regimes of the South also required test oaths as a requirement for public employment.

In 1867, the Supreme Court challenged the constitutionality of these retrospective loyalty oaths in two decisions, *Cummings v. Missouri* and *Ex parte Garland*. The first case dealt with a Missouri policy requiring persons in various public positions to swear that they had not supported secession or the Confederacy. *Garland* examined the federal statute as it applied to lawyers. The Court struck down the test oaths in both cases by 5-4 votes. Writing for the majorities, Justice Stephen J. Field began by concluding that the measures were punitive measures because they prevented persons from practicing their profession. As such, the acts violated the Constitution's ban on bills of attainder because they punished a class of persons without trials. In addition, Field wrote that they were ex post facto laws because they punished acts that had not been defined as crimes when committed.

During World War I, many states had test oath requirements as parts of professional licensing procedures and criminal syndicalism laws. At the federal level, because of the fear of foreign radicals, test oaths were especially common for naturalization requirements for aliens. Such oaths were upheld in *United States v. Schwimmer* (1929), when a pacifist was refused citizenship after refusing to swear to take up arms in defense of the United States.

Because of fears of communism after World War II, Congress and most of the states required public employees to sign loyalty oaths that included pledges of nonassociation with the Communist Party or another subversive organization. In 1949, thirty-one professors of the University of California were fired for refusal to take one such oath. In *Adler v. Board of Education* (1952), the Court upheld New York's Feinberg law, which provided for the dismissal of any public employee who belonged to an organization that advocated overthrow of the government.

Federal courts began to support more libertarian positions during the 1950's. Examining an Oklahoma law requiring public employees to take an oath disavowing membership in a subversive organization in *Wieman v. Updegraff* (1952), the Court ruled that loyalty oath statutes may only punish employees who joined subversive organizations with knowledge of their illegal purposes. The case of *Pennsylvania v. Nelson* (1956) was particularly notable because when the Court reaffirmed federal primacy in matters of loyalty, it thereby invalidated the criminal statutes in more than forty states. In *United States v. Brown* (1965), the Court invalidated a federal law that had excluded former communists from holding positions of leadership in labor unions.

During the 1960's, the Supreme Court found that almost all forms of negative oaths were unconstitutional. In the most important such case, *Elfbrandt v. Russell* (1966), the issue was an Arizona statute that required employees to take an oath to support the federal and state constitutions, and the oath was accompanied by a legislative interpretation that prohibited employment of persons who knowingly belonged to the Communist Party or another organization advocating the violent overthrow of the government. Failure to take the oath meant discharge, and a person making an untrue oath could be prosecuted for perjury. The Supreme Court overturned the statute in a 5-4 decision, finding that individuals might join an organization because of its legal purposes without supporting its illegal goals. Justice William O. Douglas declared that this interfered with the constitutional right of association, and he also noted that persons not sharing the illegal goals of an organization posed no threat to the public. *Elfbrandt* meant that a loyalty oath could only be used to punish an employee who acknowledged a specific intent to support a violent revolution or another illegal purpose.

Loyalty statutes applicable to teachers have almost always been designed to prevent the expression of ideas considered dangerous, treasonable, or unorthodox. In *Sweezy v. New Hampshire* (1957), the Court supported a left-wing professor's refusal to answer questions about his political beliefs and teachings. Chief Justice Earl Warren emphasized the importance of freedom of expression to an academic institution. A decade later, in *Keyishian v. Board of Regents* (1967), the Court applied the doctrine of vagueness to invalidate a New York law that, among other things, had criminalized advocacy of violent revolution. Justice William Brennan, Jr., reasoned that the law unduly restricted teachers' speech in the classroom because the law made it imposible to know which statements about abstract doctrines might be considered treasonable or seditious. He further declared that academic freedom "is a special concern of the First Amendment, which does not tolerate laws that cast a pall of orthodoxy over the classroom." With *Sweezy* and *Keyishian* as precedents, it became almost impossible for public educational institutions to design restrictive loyalty oaths that would be found constitutional.

Thomas Tandy Lewis

FURTHER READING

Gardner, David. *The California Oath Controversy.* Berkeley: University of California Press, 1967.

Hyman, Harold. *To Try Men's Souls: Loyalty Tests in American History.* Westport, Conn.: Greenwood Press, 1982.

SEE ALSO Bill of attainder; Civil War; Constitutional interpretation; Douglas, William O.; Miller, Samuel F.; National security; Reconstruction; Swayne, Noah H.; Warren, Earl; World War II.

Horace H. Lurton

IDENTIFICATION: Associate justice (January 3, 1910-July 12, 1914)
NOMINATED BY: William H. Taft
BORN: February 26, 1844, Newport, Kentucky
DIED: July 12, 1914, Atlantic City, New Jersey
SIGNIFICANCE: The appointment of this former Confederate officer to the Supreme Court was a symbol of regional reconciliation.

The son of a medical doctor who became an Episcopalian minister, Horace H. Lurton was an avid backer of the South and expressed his support for the region even after the Civil War (1861-1865). He enlisted in the Confederate army at age seventeen and was twice captured by Union forces. After the war, Lurton attended Cumberland School of Law, then located in Lebanon, Tennessee. Following his graduation in 1867, Lurton became much more nationalistic in his political views, perhaps a result of exposure to the Cumberland faculty, which had always been nationalistic and had even resisted secession.

Horace H. Lurton.
(Harris and Ewing/
Collection of the
Supreme Court of
the United States)

After establishing a legal practice, Lurton became a chancery judge in 1883 and then won election to the Tennessee Supreme Court in 1886. He served there until 1893, when he received an appointment to the Circuit Court of Appeals for the Sixth Circuit, under the leadership of Presiding Judge William H. Taft. When Taft became president, he appointed Lurton to the Supreme Court.

As a justice, Lurton's most significant opinions interpreted the Sherman Antitrust Act (1890). He wrote for the majority of the Court in enforcing the statute but construing it narrowly so as to render the law effective only against smaller combinations and local monopolies.

A competent judge of a conservative, nationalistic bent, Lurton never played a leading role on the Court. He saw his appointment as somewhat symbolic, and following his appointment, he deliberately charted his train journey from his home in Clarksville, Tennessee, to

Washington, D.C., by a route that passed through as many southern states as possible.

David J. Langum

FURTHER READING

Bader, William H., and Roy M. Mersky, eds. *The First One Hundred Eight Justices.* Buffalo, N.Y.: William S. Hein, 2004.

Langum, David J., and Howard P. Walthall. *From Maverick to Mainstream: Cumberland School of Law, 1847-1997.* Athens: University of Georgia Press, 1997.

Shoemaker, Rebecca S. *The White Court: Justices, Rulings, and Legacy.* Santa Barbara, Calif.: ABC-Clio, 2004.

Tucker, David M. "Justice Horace Harmon Lurton: The Shaping of a National Progressive." *American Journal of Legal History* 13 (July, 1969): 223-232.

Watts, James F., Jr. "Horace H. Lurton." In *The Justices of the United States Supreme Court, 1789-1969: Their Lives and Major Opinions,* edited by Leon Friedman and Fred L. Israel. Vol. 3. New York: Chelsea House, 1969.

SEE ALSO Civil War; Progressivism; Reconstruction; Taft, William H.; White, Edward D.

McCleskey v. Kemp

CITATION: 481 U.S. 279
DATE: April 22, 1987
ISSUE: Capital punishment
SIGNIFICANCE: The Supreme Court ruled that Georgia's use of capital punishment was constitutional, despite statistical studies showing that killers of white victims were four times more likely to be executed than killers of black victims.

Warren McCleskey, an African American, was convicted and sentenced to die for killing a white police officer in an armed robbery in 1978. On appeal, his attorneys argued that the state's death penalty statute was implemented in a racially discriminatory manner, contrary to both the Eighth and Fourteenth Amendments. They emphasized the empirical studies of David Baldus, which demonstrated that the race of the victim was a significant factor in determining whether the defendant would receive the death sentence. Prosecutors had sought the death penalty in 70 percent of the cases involving black defendants and white victims but in only 15 percent of the cases involving black defendants and black victims. Because of the tendency of defendants and victims to belong to the same race, the study found that 4 percent of the black defendants received the death penalty, compared with 7 percent of the white defendants.

By a 5-4 margin, the Supreme Court rejected McCleskey's claim. Justice Lewis F. Powell, Jr.'s opinion for the majority began with the principle that a defendant alleging an equal protection violation had the burden of proving that decision makers in his case had acted "with discriminatory purpose." McCleskey had presented no evidence that the legislature had enacted or maintained the death penalty to further a racially discriminatory purpose, and the Court had earlier determined, in *Gregg v. Georgia* (1976), that Georgia's capital sentencing system "could operate in a fair and neutral manner." Powell expressed concern that if the Court were to invalidate the use of the death penalty on the basis of a statistical disparity that correlated with race, a logical inference would be to question all criminal punishments in which a similar statistical pattern might be found.

The four dissenters answered that the death penalty should be judged by standards more rigorous than those used in other sentences. They also found it unacceptable to accept the risk of racial considerations influencing whether a defendant would live or die.

Thomas Tandy Lewis

SEE ALSO Capital punishment; Eighth Amendment; Equal protection clause; *Furman v. Georgia; Gregg v. Georgia;* Race and discrimination.

McConnell v. Federal Election Commission

CITATION: 540 U.S. 93
DATE: December 10, 2003
ISSUES: Regulation of political contributions; free speech
SIGNIFICANCE: In what was a review of the Campaign Finance Reform
   Act of 2002, the Supreme Court upheld the constitutionality of
   the act's limits on contributions to political parties.

In 1974, Congress amended federal election campaign laws by limiting the amount that citizens could contribute to political candidates. In *Buckley v. Valeo* (1976), the Supreme Court upheld the amendment as only a minimal restriction on speech, but it also held on free speech grounds that government could not put a limit on expenditures in campaigns. The federal law did not put any limits on "soft money," which referred to donations to political parties for activities such as educating voters.

In 2002, Congress enacted the Bipartisan Campaign Reform Act (BCRA; also called the McCain-Feingold Act), which, among its provisions, restricted the amount that could be contributed to national political parties, and it also prohibited advertisements by special-interest groups sixty days before an election. That same year, the District of Columbia Court of Appeals ruled that the BCRA's limit on donations to political parties violated constitutional rights of free speech.

The Supreme Court voted five to four to uphold the two main provisions of the federal law: the control of soft money and the time regulation on issue ads. On the soft-money issue, Justices Sandra Day O'Connor and John Paul Stevens wrote that the restriction on free expression was minimal and that the limits furthered the government's legitimate interest in opposing both corruption and the appearance of corruption that resulted from large contributions.

The dissenters argued that the majority had erred in not applying a "strict scrutiny" standard to the law. Justice Antonin Scalia wrote that the majority's decision was based on the fallacy that money is not speech. Justice Clarence Thomas characterized the decision as the most significant abridgment of free speech since the Civil War.

Thomas Tandy Lewis

SEE ALSO First Amendment; O'Connor, Sandra Day; Political questions; Scalia, Antonin; Speech and press, freedom of; Stevens, John Paul; Thomas, Clarence.

McCulloch v. Maryland

CITATION: 17 U.S. 316
DATE: March 6, 1819
ISSUES: Federalism; elastic clause
SIGNIFICANCE: In this, one of its most significant decisions, the Supreme Court broadly interpreted the elastic clause to uphold Congress's authority in establishing the Bank of the United States, thereby providing a foundation for federal involvement in the economy.

Chief Justice John Marshall was at his most eloquent in writing the majority opinion for the Supreme Court in this case, which defined the essential relationship between the federal government and the states. The system developed by the Constitution's Framers is not quite as clear cut as it initially appears. In addition to listing the powers delegated to the federal government and specifying that other powers would be reserved to the states, the Framers inserted a phrase in the Constitution that provided the basis for implied powers. The phrase, which appears at the very end of the Article I, section 8, reads: "Congress shall have the power . . . to make all laws which shall be necessary and proper for carrying into execution all of the foregoing powers." Given its powers of judicial review, the Supreme Court would eventually be called on to interpret the meaning of the phrase "necessary and proper."

The state of Maryland disagreed with the national government over the creation of the Second National Bank of the United States and imposed a tax on the bank that its employee, McCulloch, refused to pay. Maryland maintained that "necessary and proper" was a very restrictive provision that meant the federal government could do only those things that are absolutely necessary to carry into effect the delegated or enumerated powers. The federal government, on the other hand, argued that "necessary and proper" meant, more broadly, that the Congress could pass legislation simply "appropriate" for carrying into effect its delegated powers, many of which related to banking, such as taxation, borrowing money, regulating the value of the money, and spending money for the general welfare and the common defense.

The Supreme Court endorsed this broader view, which affirmed the doctrine of implied powers, thereby upholding Congress's power to charter institutions such as a national bank. In addition, the Court held that Maryland had no constitutional authority to tax an "instrument" of the federal government. Marshall reasoned that the power to tax is the power to destroy, and pointing to the Constitution's supremacy clause, he insisted that state governments must not be allowed to interfere with congressional prerogatives.

The necessary and proper clause has come to be known as the elastic clause because it can be stretched to create new federal powers. It expands the prerogatives of Congress under Article I, section 8, of the Constitution, and laws passed under its authority are covered by the supremacy clause. Although the *McCulloch* decision promoted the growth of federal power in the early nineteenth century, only in the second half of the twentieth century has the federal government's sphere of activity really expanded, largely as the result of other interpretations and reinterpretations of the Constitution.

Richard L. Wilson
Revised and updated by the Editor

SEE ALSO Elastic clause; Federalism; First Amendment; Marshall, John; Ninth Amendment; States' rights and state sovereignty; Tenth Amendment.

Joseph McKenna

IDENTIFICATION: Associate justice (January 26, 1898-January 5, 1925)
NOMINATED BY: William McKinley
BORN: August 10, 1843, Philadelphia, Pennsylvania
DIED: November 21, 1926, Washington, D.C.
SIGNIFICANCE: The sole Court appointee of President William Mc-
    Kinley, McKenna was the last justice from the Gilded Age and is
    best remembered for a twenty-six-year record of ambivalence as to
    the question of government regulation of the economy.

Born into an immigrant Irish family in Philadelphia, Joseph McKenna
moved to Benecia, California, at the age of twelve. Raised as a Catholic, he attended parochial schools and at one point considered entering the priesthood. Ultimately deciding instead to pursue a career in
law, McKenna graduated from the law department of Benecia Colle-
giate Institute in 1865. Admitted to the bar that same year, he later
relocated to Fairfield in Solano County where he served as district
attorney from 1866 to 1870.

After serving as a California state representative in 1875 and 1876,
McKenna made two unsuccessful runs for Congress before securing
election in 1884. Becoming a political protégé of powerful Republican
senator and railroad magnate Leland Stanford, McKenna resigned
from Congress in March of 1892 when Stanford secured his appointment to the U.S. Circuit Court by President Benjamin Harrison.

Serving on the Ninth Judicial Circuit for the next five years,
McKenna resigned on March 7, 1897, to become attorney general in
the cabinet of President William McKinley. Shortly after the death of
Associate Justice Stephen J. Field, a Californian, in early 1898, McKinley appointed McKenna to the Supreme Court largely to maintain
representation of the West Coast. McKenna's tenure spanned the entire Progressive Era and continued into the 1920's. During this time,
the Court's primary focus was on the issue of government regulation
of the economy. Of his 633 written opinions, the two most notable
were the cases of *Hipolite Egg Co. v. United States* (1911) and *Hoke v.
United States* (1913).

In *Hipolite*, McKenna upheld the constitutionality of the Pure

Food and Drug Act (1906) and the government's authority to regulate food sanitation standards. Similarly, in *Hoke*, McKenna upheld the legality of the Mann Act (1910) and the government's power to prevent the transportation of women beyond state lines for immoral purposes. McKenna registered a dissent in *Hammer v. Dagenhart* (1918), in which the Court's five-person majority voted to negate a federal statue barring the interstate transportation of goods produced by child labor. McKenna also joined in the dissent in *Adair v. United States* (1908), in which the Court denied the power of the federal government to outlaw the imposition of antiunion "yellow dog" contracts in interstate commerce.

On the other hand, McKenna voted to deny the states similar powers of regulation. Similarly, in the cases of *Lochner v. New York* (1905) and *Adkins v. Children's Hospital* (1923), he voted to deny both state and federal government the power to enact minimum-wage or maximum-hour workday legislation.

At the time of *Adkins*, McKenna was suffering a steady decline in

Joseph McKenna.
(Library of Congress)

his mental resources. Gently eased off the bench two years later, he died at the age of eighty-three.

Harvey Gresham Hudspeth

FURTHER READING

Bader, William H., and Roy M. Mersky, eds. *The First One Hundred Eight Justices.* Buffalo, N.Y.: William S. Hein, 2004.

Ely, James W., Jr. *The Fuller Court: Justices, Rulings, and Legacy.* Santa Barbara, Calif.: ABC-Clio, 2003.

McDevitt, Brother Matthew. *Joseph McKenna: Associate Justice of the United States.* Washington, D.C.: Catholic University Press, 1946.

Renstrom, Peter G. *The Taft Court: Justices, Rulings, and Legacy.* Santa Barbara, Calif.: ABC-Clio, 2003.

Semanche, John E. *Charting the Future: The Supreme Court Responds to a Changing Society, 1890-1920.* Westport, Conn.: Greenwood Press, 1978.

Shoemaker, Rebecca S. *The White Court: Justices, Rulings, and Legacy.* Santa Barbara, Calif.: ABC-Clio, 2004.

SEE ALSO Capitalism; Commerce, regulation of; Contract, freedom of; Fuller, Melville W.; *Hammer v. Dagenhart*; Taft, William H.; White, Edward D.

John McKinley

IDENTIFICATION: Associate justice (January 9, 1838-July 19, 1852)
NOMINATED BY: Martin Van Buren
BORN: May 1, 1780, Culpepper County, Virginia
DIED: July 19, 1852, Louisville, Kentucky
SIGNIFICANCE: As a Supreme Court justice, McKinley supported states' rights over the authority of the federal government.

John McKinley began his long, diverse political career in 1820 with a seat in the Alabama state legislature. In November, 1826, he entered the U.S. Senate upon the death of Henry Chambers. While a senator, he advocated governmental assistance to individual settlers as opposed to large land speculators. McKinley also favored bankruptcy

McKinley, John

John McKinley.
(Library of Congress)

laws that favored the small, landowning farmer. By 1829 he was chairman of the Senate committee on public lands. In 1830, however, McKinley was not reelected, and he returned to the Alabama state legislature. After two years, McKinley returned to Congress as a representative, but after one term, he was back in the state legislature and running again for the Senate.

McKinley was reelected senator but never took office. Congress increased the number of Supreme Court justices from seven to nine in March, 1837. President Andrew Jackson first offered a seat to William Smith of Alabama. When he refused, Jackson then offered it to McKinley, who accepted. President Martin Van Buren nominated McKinley on April 22, 1837. The Senate confirmed his nomination on September 25, 1837, and McKinley took his seat on January 9, 1838. He was assigned to the newly created Ninth Circuit, which included Alabama, Mississippi, Louisiana, and Arkansas. McKinley claimed that his far-flung circuit, quite distant from Washington, D.C., was an overwhelming duty that required him to travel ten thousand miles a year, despite his relocation to Louisville, Kentucky, which placed him between the capital and his circuit.

In *Bank of Augusta v. Earle* (1838), McKinley was the sole dissenter, claiming that a Georgia bank, as a foreign corporation, had no business in the sovereign state of Alabama. The Court, however, held that while a state could exclude a foreign company from doing business, it must make its reasons or conditions clear, which Alabama had not, and ruled for the banks. In *Lane v. Vick* (1845), McKinley dissented, stating that the Court had no interest in determining whether the Mississippi Supreme Court had been in error in a case involving a will because it had nothing to do with federal law. In *Pollard v. Hagan* (1845), McKinley argued that, as territories became states, they should receive public lands from the federal government, which had granted them to the original thirteen states.

In the 1849 *Passenger Cases*, McKinley claimed that the federal government, not New York and Massachusetts, had authority over immigrants entering the two states from overseas until they became permanent residents of either state. Despite McKinley's strong support of states' rights, he was actually a moderate who acknowledged the necessity of occasional federal intervention.

Rose Secrest

FURTHER READING

Bader, William H., and Roy M. Mersky, eds. *The First One Hundred Eight Justices.* Buffalo, N.Y.: William S. Hein, 2004.

Huebner, Timothy S. *The Taney Court: Justices, Rulings, and Legacy.* Santa Barbara, Calif.: ABC-Clio, 2003.

Miller, F. Thornton. "John McKinley." In *The Supreme Court Justices: Illustrated Biographies, 1789-1993,* edited by Clare Cushman. Washington, D.C.: Congressional Quarterly, 1993.

Monroe, Elizabeth Brand. "John McKinley." In *The Supreme Court Justices: A Biographical Dictionary,* edited by Melvin I. Urofsky. New York: Garland, 1994.

SEE ALSO Circuit riding; Federalism; States' rights and state sovereignty; Taney, Roger Brooke.

John McLean

IDENTIFICATION: Associate justice (January 11, 1830-April 4, 1861)
NOMINATED BY: Andrew Jackson
BORN: March 11, 1785, Morris County, New Jersey
DIED: April 4, 1861, Cincinnati, Ohio
SIGNIFICANCE: As Supreme Court justice, McLean is remembered for his antislavery dissent in the 1857 case involving slave Dred Scott.

John McLean was reared on a farm in Ohio and apprenticed with a lawyer in Cincinnati. He was admitted to the bar in 1807. Along with his legal career, he pursued newspaper publishing for a time before entering politics. He was elected to the House of Representatives in 1812 on a prowar platform and reelected in 1814. A supporter of James Monroe, he served on the Ohio supreme court after his second term in Congress until Monroe, upon election to president, appointed him commissioner of the General Land Office and later postmaster general. When John Quincy Adams became president, McLean retained his post. A savvy player of the political game, McLean was able to lend his support to Andrew Jackson without losing his position as postmaster general. When Jackson gained the presidency, he appointed McLean to the Supreme Court on March 6, 1829. The appointment was confirmed the next day, although he was not sworn in until January of the following year. McLean replaced Robert Trimble, who had died the year before.

Appointment to the Supreme Court was not the end of McLean's political ambitions. While serving, he maneuvered for the presidency, courting political groups of all stripes. He also sought to be chief justice, but his opinions on cases, in particular his pro-Indian vote in the Cherokee Cases, alienated him from Jackson. A devout Methodist, he recused himself from *Smith v. Swormstedt* (1853), which concerned a division within the church, but upheld the right of a private school to ban members of the clergy.

McLean was a clear states' right advocate in such cases as *Briscoe v. Bank of the Commonwealth of Kentucky* (1837) and *Ex parte Dorr* (1845), but he saw more complexity in the states' rights issue as it applied to commerce, which caused Justice Benjamin R. Curtis to label him as

John McLean.
(Library of Congress)

one of the most federalist jurists on the bench. Nevertheless, McLean did not view copyright law as a federal prerogative in *Wheaton v. Peters* (1834), although today it is often considered that the wider intellectual property law jurisdiction is applied, the better.

McLean is most remembered for his role in the infamous *Scott v. Sandford* (1857) case. He had never made a secret of his opposition to slavery, and he let it be known that he was not planning to endorse a narrowly worded or otherwise evasive opinion in the highly politicized case. His statement, in turn, prompted the pro-Southern justices to address the case squarely and issue the majority opinion of Roger Brooke Taney. As promised, McLean's dissenting opinion on behalf of Dred Scott did not mince words, and it led to his consideration for the Republican presidential nomination of 1860 despite his age. McLean has sometimes been blamed for provoking the Scott decision, but it seems more fair to blame the decision on those justices who supported it.

Eric Howard

707

McReynolds, James C.

SEE ALSO Curtis, Benjamin R.; Marshall, John; *Scott v. Sandford*; States' rights and state sovereignty; Taney, Roger Brooke.

James C. McReynolds

IDENTIFICATION: Associate justice (September 5, 1914-February 1, 1941)
NOMINATED BY: Woodrow Wilson
BORN: February 3, 1862, Elkton, Kentucky
DIED: August 24, 1946, Washington, D.C.
SIGNIFICANCE: An isolated and irascible personality, McReynolds developed over the course of his twenty-six years of service into one of the most conservative justices of the twentieth century. As one of the Four Horsemen, he was notorious for his adamant opposition to President Franklin D. Roosevelt's New Deal measures.

James C. McReynolds has been characterized by his contemporaries and historians as arrogant, abrasive, nasty, bad-tempered, and thoroughly disagreeable. Chief Justice William H. Taft said McReynolds "seems to delight in making others uncomfortable." A lifelong bachelor, he was particularly unkind to women. He was also a virulent racist and an anti-Semite, openly offensive to the two Jews among his fellow justices, Louis D. Brandeis and Benjamin N. Cardozo. By the time he left the Court, he was an isolated and embittered old man.

McReynolds was born in rural Kentucky and schooled in private institutions. He graduated from Vanderbilt with honors in 1882 and received his legal training at the University of Virginia. He practiced in Nashville, Tennessee, and taught law for a few years at Vanderbilt. In 1896 he ran for Congress but was defeated. Although he was a Democrat, Republican Theodore Roosevelt appointed him assistant to the attorney general and from 1903 to 1907, McReynolds vigorously pursued the trusts.

After returning to law practice, this time in New York City, he was appointed attorney general of the United States by President Woodrow Wilson. Within a year, he had made numerous enemies as much because of his demeanor as because of his antitrust efforts. On Au-

James C. McReynolds.
(Library of Congress)

gust 19, 1914, Wilson nominated McReynolds to fill the vacant seat on the Court left by the deceased Horace H. Lurton.

In his 1920's opinions, McReynolds was hostile to government regulation of business, with the notable exception of antitrust cases. He championed the rights of private property and was not a friend to organized labor but had a curiously mixed record in the area of civil liberties. During the 1930's, McReynolds joined with justices Willis Van Devanter, George Sutherland, and Pierce Butler to form a solid conservative opposition to Franklin D. Roosevelt's New Deal innovations. These four justices, known as the Four Horsemen, succeeded in overturning critical parts of Roosevelt's attempt to combat the Great Depression through legislative experimentation. McReynolds thought Roosevelt was "a fool" and "an utter incompetent." The attitude of McReynolds and the others led Roosevelt to propose the famous court-packing scheme of 1937. When two of McReynolds's allies resigned and the third died, he became the lone dissenting voice of reactionary conservatism in a nation that had moved beyond his doctrinaire laissez-faire views. Between 1937 and 1941, he dissented from the majority 119 times. Upon his retirement, he complained that he had tried to protect the United States, but that "any country that elects Roosevelt three times deserves no protection."

David W. Levy

SEE ALSO Butler, Pierce; Cardozo, Benjamin N.; Court-packing plan; Hughes, Charles Evans; Lurton, Horace H.; New Deal; Sutherland, George; Taft, William H.; Van Devanter, Willis; White, Edward D.

Mapp v. Ohio

CITATION: 367 U.S. 643
DATE: June 19, 1961
ISSUES: Search and seizure; exclusionary rule
SIGNIFICANCE: In this landmark decision, the Supreme Court held that the exclusionary rule was binding on the states whenever evidence was obtained in an unreasonable search and seizure, thereby completing the "incorporation" of the Fourth Amendment into the due process clause of the Fourteenth Amendment.

In an earlier landmark case, *Weeks v. United States* (1914), the Supreme Court held that evidence obtained contrary to the principles of the Fourth Amendment would be inadmissible in federal criminal trials. The purpose of this controversial exclusionary rule was to protect people from police misconduct. Since the Fourth Amendment was not binding on the states at that time, the ruling had no impact on state trials, in which most criminal prosecutions took place.

In another landmark case, *Wolf v. Colorado* (1949), the Court unanimously required that the states must respect the "core" principle of the Fourth Amendment, which is freedom from unreasonable searches and seizures. By a 6-3 vote, however, the Court also held that the exclusionary rule was not binding on the states because it was not "an essential ingredient" of the amendment. The decision resulted in the so-called "silver platter doctrine," which permitted federal prosecutors to use evidence obtained illegally by the states, until 1960.

Seven police officers, claiming to have a warrant but never showing it, broke into the home of Dolly Mapp in Cleveland, Ohio. An informant had told them that they would find gambling paraphernalia and a fugitive wanted for a recent bombing. Although they found neither, they did find pornographic books and magazines. These items were used as evidence to convict Mapp of possessing illegal pornographic materials. Ohio's high court concluded that the incriminating evidence had been obtained illegally, but while referring to *Wolf*, it nevertheless allowed the evidence to be used. When the case was appealed to the U.S. Supreme Court, an *amicus* brief of the American Civil Liberties Union advocated that *Wolf* be overturned, although Mapp's attorney argued the case entirely on the issue of obscenity.

The majority of the justices decided to ignore the less important obscenity question. Five justices agreed that the exclusionary rule should be applied to the states. Speaking for the five, Justice Tom C. Clark referred to the rule as a "deterrent safeguard," without which the right might exist in theory, but not in reality. Observing that half of the states already had adopted the exclusionary rule, he wrote that there were no other practical means to prevent the police from conducting unreasonable searches. Concerning an earlier justice's complaint, "the criminal is to go free because the constable has blundered," he answered, "The criminal goes free if he must, but it is the law that sets him free." Justice Potter Stewart refused to join the majority because he wanted to base the decision on the First Amendment. The three dissenters rejected the incorporation doctrine, which in their view intruded upon the states' sovereignty.

Thomas Tandy Lewis

SEE ALSO Clark, Tom C.; Douglas, William O.; Due process, procedural; Exclusionary rule; *Ferguson v. City of Charleston*; Fourteenth Amendment; Fourth Amendment; *Hudson v. Michigan*; Incorporation doctrine; Search warrant requirement.

Marbury v. Madison

CITATION: 5 U.S. 137
DATE: February 24, 1803
ISSUE: Judicial review
SIGNIFICANCE: For the first time, the Supreme Court declared that a
    congressional statute was unconstitutional and therefore invalid.

Before 1803, there was a great deal of debate about whether the Supreme Court possessed the authority to make binding decisions in regard to the constitutionality of statutes, especially those of the federal
government. Many jurists argued that this prerogative, now called judicial review, was implied in the Constitution, and the majority of the delegates at the Constitutional Convention accepted the prerogative—
narrowly conceived—as legitimate. Alexander Hamilton, in *The Federalist* (1788) No. 78, emphasized the importance of judicial review
within a system of limited government. The Court, in *Ware v. Hylton*
(1796), did not hesitate to strike down a state statute that contradicted
the "supreme law of the land," a national treaty in this particular case.
Likewise, in upholding the constitutionality of a federal tax in *Hylton v.
United States* (1796), the Court clearly assumed that it had the power to
exercise judicial review over the statutes enacted by Congress.

Nevertheless, critics of the judiciary, including Thomas Jefferson,
argued that each of the three coordinate branches of the national
government had an equal right to decide on questions of constitutionality for itself.

The seminal *Marbury* decision evolved out of a bitter political
conflict between the Federalist Party, which had held power since
1789, and the emerging Republican Party (Democratic-Republicans),
headed by Thomas Jefferson. In the election of 1800, Jefferson defeated President John Adams, and Republicans gained firm control
of both houses of Congress. The lame-duck president and Congress, horrified at the prospects of a Republican government, attempted to expand Federalist dominance over the national judiciary before Jefferson's inauguration. The strategy included three
elements: the installation of John Marshall as chief justice, the Judiciary Act of 1801, which created new circuit court judgeships, and

James Madison.
(Library of Congress)

an organic act, which authorized Adams to appoint forty-one justices of the peace for the District of Columbia.

UNDELIVERED COMMISSIONS

As late as March 3, 1801, the day before Jefferson became president, the Senate was still confirming the last of the so-called "midnight judges." President Adams had to sign the commissions, which he then sent to Secretary of State Marshall, who had the duties of attaching the Great Seal of the United States and of dispatching the completed commissions to the appointees. Because of the confusion associated with a change of administrations, a number of the commissions never left the executive office building. Once Jefferson was installed as president, he was so infuriated by the stacking of the judiciary that he instructed his secretary of state, James Madison, to withhold the undelivered commissions from the appointees. Somewhat later, the Republican Congress repealed the Judiciary Act of 1801 and postponed the Supreme Court's next meeting until 1803.

Although William Marbury, a well-connected Federalist, had been appointed to a five-year term as justice of the peace, he was among the appointees who never received a commission. Marbury and three associates decided to seek a court order, called a writ of *mandamus*, directing the secretary of state to turn over their commissions as required by law. They based their suit on section 13 of the Judiciary Act of 1789, which authorized the Supreme Court to issue writs of *mandamus* to federal officeholders. The *Marbury* case created a dilemma for Chief Justice Marshall and his fellow justices. If the Court ordered the secretary of state to deliver the commissions, it would give Jefferson an occasion to refuse, exercising his theory about the Court's lack of authority over a coordinate branch. On the other hand, if the Court declined to issue a writ without providing a good rationale, the Court would then implicitly appear to give confirmation to Jefferson's theory. Marshall was able to find a satisfactory solution.

THE COURT'S RESPONSE

For a unanimous Court, Marshall declared that the Court had no authority to issue the requested writ of *mandamus* because of a constitutional principle of jurisdiction. He explained that Article III of the Constitution limited the Court's original jurisdiction to cases involving a state or a foreign diplomat. Marshall's most important point was that section 13 of the 1789 statute, which authorized the writs, contradicted the Constitution and was void. Referring to both constitutional principles and the constitutional text, Marshall insisted that it "is emphatically the province and duty of the judicial department to say what the law is." In a lengthy *obiter dictum* (an opinion not essential to the ruling), Marshall declared that Marbury and his associates were legally entitled to their commissions, and that the secretary of state, in withholding them, was "in plain violation" of the law. Because Marshall did not order Madison to do anything, however, it was impossible for him to disobey a Court ruling.

Modern commentators are often critical of two aspects of Marshall's interpretations in *Marbury*. In reference to the constitutional issue of original jurisdiction, Marshall could have concluded that the "exceptions" clause of Article III provided Congress with discretion for dealing with both original and appellate jurisdiction. This interpretation, however, was unacceptable to Marshall, because it would have forced the Court to exercise jurisdiction in the case. In regard to section 13 in the 1789 statute, Marshall could have interpreted the language to mean that the Court was authorized to issue only those writs that were proper according to the accepted principles of the law. Such an interpretation was not attractive to Marshall, because it would have prevented him from establishing a precedent of judicial review. In deciding the way he did, the chief justice was taking advantage of an opportunity to refute Jefferson's theory of "tripartite balance."

From the perspective of later history, the *Marbury* decision established the principle that the Court's interpretations of the law are binding on the other two coordinate branches of the national government. At the time, however, not many people recognized the significance of the case. After *Marbury*, with Congress threatening impeachment, the Marshall Court used considerable restraint when ruling on federal statutes. In *Stuart v. Laird* (1803), announced just six days later, the Court upheld the Republicans' constitutionally suspect law that displaced judges of the circuit courts. It was not until the infamous *Scott v. Sandford* decision of 1857 that a future Court would exercise the power of "coordinate branch" judicial review for the second time. In contrast, when scrutinizing the constitutionality of state laws, nineteenth century justices tended to be much more aggressive.

Thomas Tandy Lewis

FURTHER READING

Ackerman, Bruce A. *The Failure of the Founding Fathers: Jefferson, Marshall, and the Rise of Presidential Democracy.* Cambridge, Mass.: Belknap Press of Harvard University Press, 2005.

Clinton, Robert. *"Marbury v. Madison" and Judicial Review.* Lawrence: University Press of Kansas, 1989.

Clinton, Robert, Christopher Budzisz, and Peter Renstrom, eds. *The Marshall Court: Justices, Rulings, and Legacy.* Santa Barbara, Calif.: ABC-Clio, 2007.

Garraty, John. *"Marbury v. Madison."* In *Quarrels That Have Shaped the Constitution.* New York: Harper & Row, 1987.

Graber, Mark. *Marbury v. Madison: Documents and Commentary.* Washington, D.C.: CQ Press, 2002.

Hall, Kermit L., ed. *Judicial Review and Judicial Power in the Supreme Court.* New York: Garland, 2000.

Kramer, Larry D. *The People Themselves: Popular Constitutionalism and Judicial Review.* New York: Oxford University Press, 2005.

Robarge, David Scott. *A Chief Justice's Progress: John Marshall from Revolutionary Virginia to the Supreme Court.* Westport, Conn.: Greenwood Press, 2000.

Tushnet, Mark, ed. *Arguing Marbury v. Madison.* Stanford, Calif.: Stanford University Press, 2006.

SEE ALSO Chief justice; Common law; Judicial review; Judiciary Act of 1789; Marshall, John; Moore, Alfred; Presidential powers; *Scott v. Sandford*; Separation of powers.

John Marshall

IDENTIFICATION: Chief justice (February 4, 1801-July 6, 1835)
NOMINATED BY: John Adams
BORN: September 24, 1755, Germantown (Midland), Virginia
DIED: July 6, 1835, Philadelphia, Pennsylvania
SIGNIFICANCE: During his long tenure as chief justice, Marshall elevated the Supreme Court to a coequal branch of government through landmark decisions supporting judicial review and federal supremacy over the states. Legal scholars consistently rank him the United States' greatest justice.

Born on the frontier and the oldest of fifteen children, John Marshall had a father who instilled in him a love of English literature. Through his mother, a member of the prominent Randolph family, he was distantly related to Thomas Jefferson. Marshall fought in several battles during the Revolutionary War, served as the deputy judge advocate, and endured Valley Forge. Marshall's dislike of provincialism and weak national government grew out of his military experience. His lifelong admiration of George Washington, his father's boyhood friend, led to Marshall's eventual publication of the first biography of Washington.

After military service, Marshall briefly studied law with professor George Wythe at the College of William and Mary. He was admitted to Phi Beta Kappa and entered the practice of law in 1780. Married in 1783, Marshall relied on his legal work to support his wife, Mary Willis "Polly" Ambler, and their ten children. From 1785 to 1788, Marshall served as the recorder of the Richmond hustings court, his only judicial position before the Supreme Court.

POLITICAL CAREER

Expanding family financial responsibilities kept Marshall busy practicing law, but like his father, he found time to engage in state and local politics. Marshall served episodically in the Virginia House of Delegates between 1782 and 1795 and as a member of the governor's Council of State from 1782 to 1784. His legislative experience reinforced his disdain for parochial state government. He was a delegate to the Virginia convention to ratify the U.S. Constitution in 1788.

Marshall rejected several offers of positions in the administrations of George Washington and John Adams, finally accepting Adams's request that he become part of a three-man diplomatic team sent to France in 1797-1798 to negotiate a treaty. The team refused France's demand that the United States pay a financial tribute before the negotiations, making Marshall a national hero. The subsequent publication of the correspondence between the American diplomats and the French agents (designated Messrs. X, Y, and Z) provoked partisan debate between the Jeffersonians and anti-Jeffersonians. At the urging of Washington, Marshall ran for the congressional seat from Richmond to the U.S. House of Representatives. As the only Federalist congressman from Virginia (1798-1800), he became the spokesperson for the moderate Federalists, as exemplified by Adams. In May, 1800, he was nominated and confirmed as secretary of state. During the waning months of the Adams administration, Marshall also served as a de facto president because of Adams's frequent out-of-town trips.

APPOINTMENT TO THE COURT

Marshall was Adams's second choice for chief justice after the resignation of Oliver Ellsworth. John Jay declined the offer, and on January 20, 1801, the president appointed his loyal secretary of state to become the fourth chief justice. The U.S. Senate confirmed the nomination on January 27, and Marshall was sworn in on February 4. Marshall served as chief justice for thirty-four years, through the administrations of five presidents: Thomas Jefferson, James Madison, James Monroe, John Quincy Adams, and Andrew Jackson. He remained active on the Court until his death on July 6, 1835, from a liver ailment. As his funeral cortege made its way through Philadelphia two days later, the Liberty Bell in Independence Hall tolled on the same day as it had first rung in 1776 to celebrate U.S. independence, developing a crack that silenced it forever.

As chief justice, Marshall is credited with making the Court a co-equal branch of U.S. government. He persuaded his colleagues to stop issuing seriatim opinions and adopt a single opinion format to

John Marshall.
(Rembrandt Peale/
Collection of the
Supreme Court of
the United States)

give the Court a collective, authoritative voice. Marshall delivered 519 of the 1,215 opinions of the Court during his long tenure. In addition to his unusual energy, Marshall possessed political skills developed from his legislative and executive experience, and he combined this political astuteness with social skills and a sense of humor. His essential moderation in ideological and personal terms allowed him to educate others. Marshall maintained friendships even with those who opposed his nationalist policies with the single exception of his distant relative Thomas Jefferson. Still, Marshall followed in the footsteps of his political hero, George Washington, by demonstrating a classical magnanimity toward Jefferson. Marshall pledged financial support for Jefferson during his final years.

A COEQUAL BRANCH

Relying on knowledge gained in writing *The Federalist* (1788) and colonial and confederal experience, Marshall used the poorly written "case of the midnight justices," *Marbury v. Madison* (1803), to uphold the benchmark principle of judicial review of legislative and executive acts. For a unanimous Court, he ruled that section 13 of the Judiciary Act of 1789 was unconstitutional. In the process of making William Marbury, a fellow Federalist, the most famous loser in Supreme Court history and his rival Thomas Jefferson a shallow winner, Marshall figuratively rang a radical independence bell that reverberated through the late nineteenth century. Recognizing the activist potential of their decision, the Marshall Court did not strike down another act of Congress. In fact, the Court would not do that again until *Scott v. Sandford* (1857). Marshall's even-handed handling of the 1805 impeachment trial of Justice Samuel Chase contributed to his acquittal and promoted a spirit of moderation. In his longest judicial decision—the one that he considered the most disagreeable of his career, *United States v. Burr* (1807)—Marshall used a narrow definition of treason to acquit Aaron Burr, Jefferson's first-term vice president.

NATIONAL SUPREMACY

Marshall's identification with the national values of his political hero Washington are reflected in his greatest decisions. In the so-called Yazoo land case, *Fletcher v. Peck* (1810), not only did the Court hold a state law contrary to the U.S. Constitution but also used the contracts clause (Article I, section 10) to restrict state authority. The opinion was unpopular with states' righters, but it asserted judicial nationalization and encouraged the nation's economic development. Those twin values reflected those of Washington and his favorite nephew, Bushrod Washington, who served for twenty-nine years with Marshall on the Court and was his closest associate.

In Marshall's touchstone case, *McCulloch v. Maryland* (1819), he resolved the meaning of the necessary and proper clause (Article I, section 8, clause 18) and determined the distribution of powers between the federal government and the states. Using a broad interpretation, federal supremacy was proclaimed in this pivotal case involving whether Maryland had the right to tax a branch of the U.S. Bank. The doctrine of implied national powers provided the constitutional basis for the federal government's broad involvement in public policy. Marshall understood "the power to tax involves the power to destroy" and in the heart of the opinion stated, "Let the end be legitimate, let it be within the scope of the Constitution, and all means which are appropriate which are plainly adapted to that end, which are not prohibited, but consistent with the letter and spirit of the Constitution, are constitutional." Marshall's final classic statement of nationalism came in the so-called "steamboat case," *Gibbons v. Ogden* (1824), in which he emancipated national commerce through a broad view of the commerce clause (Article I, section 8, clause 3), removing the obstructions to free trade that the states had created.

CONSTITUTIONAL PHILOSOPHY

In his classic decisions, Marshall's jurisprudence was neither consistently activist nor restraintist. Although he established judicial review, Marshall upheld the Jeffersonian Congress's judiciary legislation. In one of his last decisions, *Barron v. Baltimore* (1833), he limited application of the Bill of Rights to the federal government, exempting state governments. He aimed for the middle path, consistent with his moderate Federalist views that promoted the broader cosmopolitan views of a developing nation over unenlightened and proprietary state and local interests. In short, he adapted George Washington's classical prudence and moderation to the judicial setting. Marshall's outgoing personality, industriousness, and balanced approach, when applied to a developing republic, shaped his leadership of his fellow justices during his tenure as chief justice of the United States. Though he was not the first chief justice, he set precedents for the Court that echoed those that his political hero, the first chief executive, set for the presidency, standards that still resonate throughout American jurisprudence.

William D. Pederson

FURTHER READING

As the most outstanding figure in the early history of the Supreme Court, John Marshall is well served by biographers. In *A Chief Justice's Progress: John Marshall from Revolutionary Virginia to the Supreme Court* (Westport, Conn.: Greenwood Press, 2000), David Scott Robarge covers Marshall's life up to the moment he joined the Supreme Court. R. Kent Newmyer's *John Marshall and the Heroic Age of the Supreme Court* (Baton Rouge: Louisiana State University Press, 2001) continues the story through Marshall's years on the Court. Among other biographies, among the best is Jean E. Smith's *John Marshall: Definer of a Nation* (New York: Henry Holt, 1996).

Marshall's work on the Court is treated exceptionally well in Charles F. Hobson's *The Great Chief Justice: John Marshall and the Rule of Law* (Lawrence: University Press of Kansas, 1996), which contains an outstanding biographical essay. A similarly exceptional volume employing comparative quantitative analysis is Herbert A. Johnson's *The Chief Justiceship of John Marshall, 1801-1835* (Columbia: University of South Carolina Press, 1997). A classic work putting the judicial process within a political context is Henry J. Abraham's *Justices and Presidents: A Political History of Appointments to the Supreme Court* (New York: Oxford University Press, 1974), and Robert J. Steamer's *Chief Justice: Leadership and the Supreme Court* (Columbia: University of South Carolina Press, 1986) offers a thoughtful comparative analysis of chief justices.

The first ranking of justices by means of a poll of experts is Albert P. Blaustein and Roy M. Mersky's *The First Hundred Justices* (Hamden, Conn.: Archon, 1978). The political context of rankings may be found in William D. Pederson and Ann McLaurin, editors,

The Rating Game in American Politics: An Interdisciplinary Approach (Rev. ed. New York: Irvington, 1987). The first volume with an updated poll and case studies is William D. Pederson and Norman W. Provizer, editors, *Great Justices of the U.S. Supreme Court* (New York: Lang, 1994).

SEE ALSO *Barron v. Baltimore*; Chief justice; *Gibbons v. Ogden*; Johnson, William; Judicial review; Judiciary Act of 1789; *McCulloch v. Maryland*; *Marbury v. Madison*; Native American treaties; States' rights and state sovereignty; Washington, Bushrod.

Thurgood Marshall

IDENTIFICATION: Associate justice (October 2, 1967-June 27, 1991)
NOMINATED BY: Lyndon B. Johnson
BORN: July 2, 1908, Baltimore, Maryland
DIED: January 24, 1993, Washington, D.C.
SIGNIFICANCE: Marshall was the first African American to serve on the Supreme Court. As a justice, he established a record for supporting the voiceless American, developing a profound sensitivity to injustice. He promoted affirmative action and is often remembered for his dissents in areas such as the guarantee in the Constitution of equal protection.

Thurgood Marshall was named for his paternal grandfather, a former slave who changed his name to Thoroughgood when he joined the U.S. Army during the Civil War. Marshall's mother, Norma Arica Marshall, was one of the first African Americans to graduate from Columbia Teachers College in New York City. His father, William Marshall, instilled in him from youth an appreciation for the Constitution and the rule of law. His father was also the first African American to serve on a grand jury in Baltimore in the twentieth century.

After completing high school in 1925, Thurgood followed his brother, William Aubrey Marshall, in attending the historically black Lincoln University in Chester, Pennsylvania. While in college Marshall participated in a successful sit-in at a local movie theater. Protesters occupied whites-only seats to force the theater to cease making black patrons sit in a segregated balcony section.

In 1930 Marshall applied to the University of Maryland Law School but was denied admission because he was black. He then sought admission and was accepted at the Howard University Law School in Washington, D.C., that same year. At Howard, Marshall came under the influence of the new dean, Charles Hamilton Houston, who instilled in all his students the desire to apply the tenets of the Constitution to all Americans. Foremost in Houston's outlook was the need to overturn the Supreme Court ruling, *Plessy v. Ferguson* (1896), which established the legal doctrine of separate but equal, which formed the legal basis for segregation. Marshall graduated first in his class in 1933, and his first major case came in that same year when he successfully sued the University of Maryland to admit a young African American Amherst University graduate named Donald Gaines Murray. Marshall practiced law for three years in Baltimore and in 1936 moved to New York City, where he became a staff lawyer of the National Association for the Advancement of Colored People (NAACP).

EARLY SUCCESSES

At the NAACP, Marshall helped develop and implement a strategy to fight racial segregation throughout the United States. Marshall won almost all the cases he argued before the Court on behalf of the NAACP. In *Chambers v. Florida* (1940), he persuaded the Court to overturn a criminal conviction based on a coerced confession. In *Smith v. Allwright* (1944), Marshall persuaded the Court to strike down a Texas practice, known as the white primary, which excluded African Americans from participating in primary elections. In *Shelley v. Kraemer* (1948), the Court agreed with Marshall that courts could not enforce restrictive covenants, private agreements not to sell land to blacks.

In *Sipuel v. Board of Regents of the University of Oklahoma* (1948) and *Sweatt v. Painter* (1950), Marshall won unanimous decisions forcing the universities of Oklahoma and Texas to integrate their law schools. Marshall's greatest courtroom victory came in *Brown v. Board of Education* (1954), a case that involved racial segregation in public schools. He argued that the equal protection clause of the Fourteenth Amendment to the Constitution requires that states treat all citizens alike, regardless of race. When Justice Felix Frankfurter asked Marshall to define "equal," Marshall answered, "Equal means getting the same thing, at the same time, and in the same place." Before Martin Luther King, Jr., came onto the national scene in 1955, Marshall was commonly referred to as "Mr. Civil Rights," and was probably the country's most prominent champion of African American advancement.

In 1961 President John F. Kennedy appointed Marshall to the Second U.S. Circuit Court of Appeals. However, a group of southern senators held up Marshall's confirmation for months, and he served initially under a special appointment made during a congressional recess. While serving on the Second Circuit, Marshall wrote 112 decisions on immigrant rights, limitation of government intrusion in cases involving illegal search and seizure, double jeopardy, and right to privacy issues. The Supreme Court did not reverse any of Marshall's ninety-eight majority decisions. In fact, several of his dissenting opinions, written while serving on the Second Circuit, were eventually adopted as majority opinions by the Court. Marshall served on the Second Circuit until 1965 when President Lyndon B. Johnson appointed him solicitor general of the United States. Before his subsequent nomination to the Court in 1967, Marshall won nineteen of the twenty-one cases he argued before the Court on behalf of the government.

As Supreme Court Justice

After Justice Tom C. Clark retired in 1967, President Johnson nominated Marshall to the Supreme Court. On August 30, 1967, the Senate confirmed Marshall's nomination. Marshall served on the Court until advanced age and failing health caused him to resign on June 28, 1991.

Marshall strongly believed that a judge's central function is to act as a neutral arbiter of disputes that arise under the law. He further believed that judges were bound through their code of ethics to avoid even the appearance of impropriety or partiality. Yet as he once said, he did not think the wisdom, foresight, and sense of justice demonstrated by the Framers of the Constitution to be profound. He found the government created by the Constitution to be "defective from the start, requiring several amendments, a civil war, and momentous social transformation to attain the system of constitutional government, and its respect for the individual freedoms and human rights,

Thurgood Marshall.
(Joseph Lavenburg,
National Geographic,
courtesy the
Supreme Court of
the United States)

we hold as fundamental today." He said the credit for a good government belonged to "those who refused to acquiesce in outdated notions of 'liberty,' 'justice,' and 'equality,' and who strived to better them." He believed that an African American child born in Mississippi had the same rights as any white child in the United States.

FROM MAJORITY TO MINORITY

During his early years on the Court, Marshall was a member of the Court's majority, led by Chief Justice Earl Warren and later by Justice William J. Brennan, Jr. For twenty-four years, in a few notable opinions for the Court and many dissents, Marshall continually supported organized labor, racial minorities, the advancement of women, the broadening of rights to freedom of expression, and the narrowing of police authority. He declared in *Police Department of Chicago v. Mosley* (1972), in language that has become a standard citation for constitutional lawyers, that

725

above all else, the First Amendment means that government has no power to restrict expression because of its message, its ideas, its subject matter, or its content. To permit the continued building of our politics and culture, and to assure self-fulfillment for each individual, our people are guaranteed the right to express any thought free from government censorship.

Marshall also wrote the majority opinion in *Stanley v. Georgia* (1969), overturning a Georgia ordinance that made private possession of obscene material a crime. He spoke once again for the Court in *Grayned v. Rockford* (1972), striking down an antipicketing ordinance that had been used against civil rights demonstrators.

Marshall spent, however, twenty-two of his twenty-four years, and especially his last ten years on the Court, in the minority. Therefore most of his opinions were dissenting, on such issues as abortion, affirmative action, and zoning. Surprisingly, Marshall wrote few opinions on civil rights cases. He had to recuse himself from many of the civil rights cases because he had worked on them before coming to the Court. Marshall dissented in *Florida v. Bostick* (1991) from the Court's decision that police could make random sweeps and searches of passengers in buses and trains. Marshall wrote, "A passenger unadvised of his rights and otherwise unversed in constitutional law has no reason to know that the police cannot hold his refusal to cooperate against him."

One of Marshall's best-known dissents is a sixty-three page opinion in *San Antonio Independent School District v. Rodriguez* (1973). The Court held, five to four, that the Constitution's guarantee of equal protection was not violated by the property tax system used in Texas and most other states to finance public education. Marshall accused the majority of "unsupportable acquiescence in a system which deprives children in their earliest years of the chance to reach their full potential as citizens."

In his role as a dissenter, Marshall tried to educate others, to alter their worldviews. When someone once remarked to Marshall about his writing mostly dissents while on the Court, he responded that Justice Louis D. Brandeis did the same thing during his tenure on the Court and later Justice Brandeis's dissents became the law.

Dana P. McDermott

FURTHER READING

As good a starting point as any is a collection of Marshall's own speeches and writings: *Thurgood Marshall: His Speeches, Writings, Arguments, Opinions, and Reminiscences* (Chicago: Lawrence Hill Books, 2001). Among the many good biographies of Marshall are Randall Walton Bland's *Justice Thurgood Marshall: Crusader for Liberalism: His Judicial Biography, 1908-1993* (Bethesda, Md.: Academica Press, 2001) and Juan Williams's *Thurgood Marshall: American Revolutionary* (New York: Random House, 1998). The latter is a careful and engrossing account of Thurgood Marshall's life that emphasizes his work as counsel for the NAACP.

Michael D. Davis and Hunter R. Clark's *Thurgood Marshall: Warrior at the Bar, Rebel on the Bench* (Secaucus, N.J.: Carol Publishing, 1994) examines Marshall's views on some of the most sensitive and politically charged social issues—abortion, capital punishment, women's rights, and affirmative action—and provides intriguing details on his relationships with John F. Kennedy, Martin Luther King, Jr., and others. James S. Haskins's *Thurgood Marshall: A Life for Justice* (New York: Henry Holt, 1991) emphasizes Marshall's enormous contributions to the Civil Rights movement and his unending commitment to the achievement of racial and social justice. Carl T. Rowan presents a riveting and absorbing portrait of Marshall's career from the early Jim Crow years in Baltimore to Marshall's twenty-four-year tenure on the Court in *Dream Makers, Dream Breakers: The World of Justice Thurgood Marshall* (New York: Welcome Rain, 2002).

Roger Goldman and David Galien have compiled a collection of fifteen opinions and dissents of this national defender of individual liberties and civil rights, as well as personal recollections of Marshall's closest associates in *Thurgood Marshall: Justice for All* (New York: Carroll and Graf, 1992). Other recommended works include Howard Ball's *A Defiant Life: Thurgood Marshall and the Persistence of Racism in America* (New York: Crown Publishing, 1998); Rae Bains's *Thurgood Marshall: Fight for Justice* (Mahwah, N.J.: Troll Communications, 1993); Seamus Cavan's *Thurgood Marshall and Equal Rights* (Brookfield, Conn.: Millbrook Press, 1994); and James T. Patterson's *"Brown v. Board of Education": A Civil Rights Milestone and Its Troubled Legacy* (New York: Oxford University Press, 2002).

Stanley Matthews

IDENTIFICATION: Associate justice (May 17, 1881-March 22, 1889)
NOMINATED BY: James Garfield
BORN: July 21, 1824, Cincinnati, Ohio
DIED: March 22, 1889, Washington, D.C.
SIGNIFICANCE: An abolitionist who was criticized for his reluctant enforcement of the Fugitive Slave Act (1850), Matthews narrowly won confirmation to become one of the most enlightened members of the Gilded Age Court.

Born in Cincinnati, Stanley Matthews graduated from Kenyon College in 1840 and spent the next two years studying law before gaining admission to the bar in Tennessee. It was not long after that, however, that he returned to Cincinnati to take an active role in the abolitionist movement.

Between 1846 and 1849, Matthews served as assistant editor with the antislavery publication, *Cincinnati Herald*. He remained active in the practice of law and was appointed common pleas court judge in 1851. Four years later, he won election to the Ohio state senate. Appointed U.S. attorney for southern Ohio in 1858, Matthews was obligated to enforce the Fugitive Slave Act (1850). He would later be accused of selling out his principles for political gain.

Matthews enlisted in the Union army in 1861 and became a lieutenant colonel under former Kenyon college classmate, Rutherford B. Hayes. He resigned his commission in 1863 to accept a seat on the superior court of Cincinnati. He left the bench one year later and returned to private practice. Republican Matthews was defeated in a run for Congress in 1876. Early in 1877, however, Matthews was named Republican counsel before the Electoral Commission appointed to determine the legitimate winner of the presidential elec-

Stanley Matthews.
(Handy Studios/
Collection of the
Supreme Court of
the United States)

tion between Hayes and Democrat Samuel Tilden. Successfully arguing on behalf of Hayes, Matthews was soon rewarded when the Ohio legislature elected him U.S. senator.

Matthews served in the Senate from 1877 to 1879 and is best remembered for successfully sponsoring a bill calling for the reestablishment of silver currency as legal tender. When outgoing President Hayes nominated Matthews to the Supreme Court on January 26, 1881, the Senate refused to act. Matthews's nomination met with the strong opposition of New York Republican Senator Roscoe Conkling and was further criticized as "very unbecoming" in view of the nominee's role in the electoral dispute. Nevertheless, on March 14, Matthews's name was resubmitted by the new president, James Garfield. After several weeks of debate, the Senate narrowly confirmed Matthews by a vote of twenty-four to twenty-three.

As a justice, Matthews's two most notable rulings were *Hurtado v.*

California (1884) and *Yick Wo v. Hopkins* (1886). In *Hurtado*, Matthews rejected claims that the due process provisions of the Fifth and Fourteenth Amendments required states to procure grand jury indictments before they could prosecute felonies. Instead, as long as criminal defendants were given fair notice of the charges against them and adequate time in which to prepare a legal defense, Matthews maintained that due process protection requirements of the Constitution were satisfied.

Having earlier determined that the Fourteenth Amendment did not apply to acts of private discrimination, in *Yick Wo* Matthews was subsequently able to guide a unanimous Court into declaring a seemingly race-neutral ordinance unconstitutional for its "evil eye . . . unequal hand" discrimination against Chinese laundry operators. In 1886 he also joined the majority in denying states the power to regulate railroads operating in interstate commerce.

Serving on the bench for seven years and ten months, Matthews authored 232 opinions and 5 dissents before his death at the age of sixty-four.

Harvey Gresham Hudspeth

FURTHER READING

Bader, William H., and Roy M. Mersky, eds. *The First One Hundred Eight Justices.* Buffalo, N.Y.: William S. Hein, 2004.

Ely, James W., Jr. *The Fuller Court: Justices, Rulings, and Legacy.* Santa Barbara, Calif.: ABC-Clio, 2003.

Friedman, Leon, and Fred Israel, eds. *The Justices of the Supreme Court: Their Lives and Major Opinions.* 5 vols. New York: Chelsea House, 1997.

Greve, Charles T. "Stanley Matthews." In *Great American Lawyers: A History of the Legal Profession in America*, edited by William Draper Lewis. Vol. 7. 1907-1909. Reprint. South Hackensack, N.J.: Rothman Reprints, 1971.

Magrath, C. Peter. *Morrison Waite: The Triumph of Character.* New York: Macmillan Press, 1963.

Stephenson, Donald Grier, Jr. *The Waite Court: Justices, Rulings, and Legacy.* Santa Barbara, Calif.: ABC-Clio, 2003.

SEE ALSO Fourteenth Amendment; Slavery; Waite, Morrison R.

Meyer v. Nebraska

CITATION: 262 U.S. 390
DATE: June 4, 1923
ISSUE: Parental rights
SIGNIFICANCE: The Supreme Court first applied the doctrine of substantive due process to strike down a law for infringing upon a noneconomic liberty.

Shortly after World War I, the Nebraska legislature passed a statute that prohibited schools from teaching any modern non-English language to children before the eighth grade. Meyer, who taught German in a Lutheran school, was convicted of disobeying the law. By a 7-2 vote, the Supreme Court ruled that the law violated the due process clause of the Fourteenth Amendment. Writing for the majority, Justice James C. McReynolds explained that the amendment protected long-recognized liberties such as the right to marry, to acquire knowledge, and to raise children. The law was "arbitrary" and "without reasonable relation" to a legitimate governmental purpose. In dissent, Justice Oliver Wendell Holmes, having often criticized the use of substantive due process to protect a freedom of contract, argued that the state had a reasonable interest in promoting a common language. *Meyer* was never overturned, and forty years later, it became an important precedent in the development of a constitutional right of privacy.

Thomas Tandy Lewis

SEE ALSO Due process, substantive; Holmes, Oliver Wendell; *Pierce v. Society of Sisters*; Privacy, right to.

Michigan Department of State Police v. Sitz

CITATION: 496 U.S. 444
DATE: February 27, 1990
ISSUE: Search and seizure
SIGNIFICANCE: The Supreme Court upheld the use of drunken driving checkpoints under certain conditions.

A group of licensed drivers sued Michigan, challenging the constitutionality of a state law and program that set up drunken driving checkpoints designed to catch people driving under the influence. They argued that the checkpoints constituted an illegal search and seizure under the Fourth Amendment. Lower courts ruled against the program, but by a 6-3 vote, the Supreme Court upheld the Michigan statute and program. The Court maintained that the lower courts had misread the relevant cases, *United States v. Martinez-Fuerte* (1976) and *Brown v. Texas* (1979). In the opinion for the Court, Chief Justice William H. Rehnquist agreed that Michigan had a legitimate interest in trying to curb drunken driving. Justice Harry A. Blackmun concurred, and Justices William J. Brennan, Jr., Thurgood Marshall, and John Paul Stevens dissented.

Richard L. Wilson

SEE ALSO Automobile searches; Due process, procedural; Exclusionary rule; Fourth Amendment; *Mapp v. Ohio*; Rehnquist, William H.; Search warrant requirement.

Military and the Court

DESCRIPTION: Armed forces of the United States, which have their own courts to enforce the Uniform Code of Military Justice, the foundation of American military law since created by Congress in 1950.

SIGNIFICANCE: The Supreme Court has limited power of review over the military, which is guided primarily by Congress and the executive branch.

When the Supreme Court defined the relationship between the military and the Court in the mid-nineteenth century, it recognized the military as a legally separate sphere that looks primarily to the Congress and the president for protection and governance rather than to the courts and the Constitution. In *Dynes v. Hoover* (1858), the Court recognized that the power to provide for a system of military justice arose from Article I, clause 14, of the Constitution, which permits

Congress to make rules to govern and regulate the armed forces, and not Article III, which gives Congress the authority to create a system of federal courts.

In *Burns v. Wilson* (1953), the Court determined that the military justice system exists separate and apart from the federal judicial system. In *Parker v. Levy* (1974), the Court characterized the military as "a specialized society separate from civilian society." The historical and contemporary relationships of the Supreme Court to the military are, therefore, highly deferential. Under this approach, the Court accords both Congress and the president substantial discretion with regard to the structuring and operation of the military. In *Orloff v. Willoughby* (1953), it found that judges were not suited to running the military. The Court therefore exercises a limited scope of review of the military.

The Court tends to defer to the determination of Congress. In *Weiss v. United States* (1994), the Court considered whether a special, additional appointment was required under the Constitution for military legal officers (judge advocate generals or JAGs) to serve as military judges. The Court held that Congress could determine the structure of the military justice system within its discretion and determine judicial appointments as it saw fit.

The Court has generally adhered to a deferential standard of review with few notable exceptions. One exception is *Frontiero v. Richardson* (1973), an equal protection challenge to a law that provided spouses of male members of the armed services quarters allowances and medical and dental benefits without a dependency test while requiring that spouses of female members show that they were in fact dependent for more than one-half of their support to qualify for allowances and benefits.

The Court held that such different treatment of spouses of men and women service members violated equal protection. A plurality of the Court applied strict scrutiny, which would require that the classification be narrowly tailored to meet a compelling governmental interest. Four other justices reached the same conclusion applying a less searching middle-tier scrutiny under which the classification must be closely related to the fulfillment of an important governmental interest. Justice William H. Rehnquist dissented, contending that the

Court should defer to Congress's policy choices in the area of military rules and regulations. *Frontiero* clearly departs from the judicial deference evident in *Weiss.*

THE BILL OF RIGHTS

Although the degree to which the Bill of Rights applies to members of the armed services has remained controversial, there are a number of areas in which those protections are either expressly or by necessary implication inapplicable. Indeed, a number of rights that Americans take for granted are either denied to members of the armed services or offered only in a limited way. In *United States ex rel. French v. Weeks* (1922), the Court found that a member of the armed services is "subject to military law, and the principles of that law, as provided by Congress, [constitute] for him due process of law in a constitutional sense."

Aside from due process rights, members of the armed services have fewer rights with respect to free speech and political participation. For example, Article 88 of the Uniform Code of Military Justice proscribes the use of "contemptuous words" against the president and other high political officials, and Articles 133 (proscribing conduct unbecoming) and 134 (the general article, proscribing service-discrediting conduct) may be used to prosecute disloyal statements. Rights to demonstrate and affiliate with advocacy groups, especially extremist groups or hate groups, which would be protected for civilians, are denied to those in the military. Similar First Amendment restrictions that would be unthinkable in a civilian context have been held constitutional. For example, the Military Honor and Decency Act, which prohibits the sale or rental of sexually explicit materials at military exchanges, was held constitutional in a lower court in *General Media Communications v. Cohen* in 1997. The Court also found that religious practices or beliefs cannot excuse compliance with military regulations such as those governing uniform standards. For example, in *Goldman v. Weinberger* (1986), the Court upheld a ban on wearing headgear indoors as applied to a Jewish officer who wanted to wear a yarmulke.

EQUAL PROTECTION

Even though racial classifications are subject to the "most rigid scrutiny" under the equal protection clause, the Court found that wartime necessities allow a military commander to issue a racially based curfew in *Hirabayashi v. United States* (1943). In addition to restrictions based on race, the Court allowed sex-based discrimination by upholding male-only draft registration in *Rostker v. Goldberg* (1981) and a naval officer promotion program that provided advantages to women over men in *Schlesinger v. Ballard* (1975). Likewise, privacy rights in the military enjoy a more limited scope than under the Court's civilian precedents. For example, a court of military appeals in 1990 upheld the issuance of "safe sex" orders to military personnel infected with the human immunodeficiency virus (HIV).

Some provisions of the Bill of Rights such as the Fifth Amendment expressly exempt members of the military from their scope. The Fifth Amendment excepts from its coverage "cases arising in the land or naval forces, or in the Militia, when in actual service in time of War or public danger." The Sixth Amendment's right to trial by jury has been treated similarly by implication in *Ex parte Milligan* (1866).

In *Woods v. Cloyd W. Miller Co.* (1948), the Court found that Congress and the president, but not the Court, decide on when and how to go to war and determine when war and its consequences are over. Case law, as well as the text of the Constitution, confirms Justice Harold H. Burton's observation that "we have a fighting constitution" in the opinion for *Lichter v. United States* (1948). The war powers of the national government embrace not only the power to fight but also "the power to wage war successfully," according to Chief Justice Charles Evans Hughes in *Hirabayashi*. Consequently, in the *Selective Draft Law Cases* (1918), the Court upheld conscription, involuntary military service, and the use of state militias to fight against foreign enemies abroad and rejected the notion that military service is "involuntary servitude" prohibited by the Thirteenth Amendment.

THE CIVIL WAR

A major period of conflict between the Court and the military occurred during the Civil War. Several cases taxed the independence and agility of the judiciary by implicitly or explicitly questioning the constitutionality of congressional Reconstruction and pitting the Court against the Radical Republican Congress. The stage was set by the Court's ruling in *Ex parte Milligan* that civilians could not be tried by military courts or commissions in peacetime when civilian courts were open and functioning. The much later case of *Ex parte Quirin* (1942) differs in that one of the defendants, Herbert Hans Haupt, who claimed U.S. citizenship, had entered the country as a spy and thus could be tried in wartime under military jurisdiction.

Like Milligan's case, the cases of *Ex parte McCardle* (1868) and *Ex parte Yerger* (1869) both involved trials before military commissions. Their trials had occurred long after the cessation of hostilities and during the period of congressional Reconstruction. McCardle was a Mississippi newspaper editor who vituperatively attacked Reconstruction, and Yerger was an accused murderer. Both sought review in the Court by writ of habeas corpus. Resolution of the merits of their attacks on the validity of military jurisdiction and Reconstruction were avoided by a ruling in McCardle's case that the particular habeas statute on which his petition was grounded had been repealed by Congress before a decision in his case, thus revoking the Court's appellate jurisdiction over his case, and by Yerger's release from custody to stand trial before a civilian court.

In addition, two other attempts to bring the matter of congressional Reconstruction before the Court directly failed on justiciability grounds. The resolution of these cases prevented a major contest between the Court and the military. Two other cases, *Mississippi v. Johnson* (1867), in which the Court held that it lacked the power to enjoin a president, and *Georgia v. Stanton* (1868), which held that a suit by a state raised a political question, concluded the post-Civil War power struggle. In the end, the Court never ruled on the validity of military rule during Reconstruction.

L. Lynn Hogue

FURTHER READING

Bishop, Joseph W., Jr. *Justice Under Fire: A Study of Military Law.* New York: Charterhouse, 1974.

Borch, Frederick L. *Judge Advocates in Combat: Army Lawyers in Military*

Operations from Vietnam to Haiti. Washington, D.C.: Office of the Judge Advocate General and Center of Military History, United States Army, 2001.

Fairman, Charles. *Reconstruction and Reunion, 1864-1888.* New York: Macmillan, 1971.

Lurie, Jonathan. *Arming Military Justice: Origins of the United States Court of Military Appeals, 1775-1950.* Princeton, N.J.: Princeton University Press, 1992.

_____. *Pursuing Military Justice: The History of the United States Court of Appeals for the Armed Forces, 1951-1980.* Princeton, N.J.: Princeton University Press, 1998.

Shanor, Charles A., and L. Lynn Hogue. *Military Law in a Nutshell.* 2d ed. St. Paul, Minn.: West Publishing, 1996.

SEE ALSO Bill of Rights; Burton, Harold H.; Civil War; *Milligan, Ex parte*; Vietnam War; *Virginia, United States v.*; War and civil liberties; War powers; World War II.

Samuel F. Miller

IDENTIFICATION: Associate justice (July 21, 1862-October 13, 1890)
NOMINATED BY: Abraham Lincoln
BORN: April 5, 1816, Richmond, Kentucky
DIED: October 13, 1890, Washington, D.C.
SIGNIFICANCE: Miller was one of the intellectual forces of the Supreme Court during the post-Civil War period. He wrote the first Court decision interpreting the breadth of the newly ratified Fourteenth Amendment.

Born in Kentucky, the oldest of eight children, Samuel F. Miller first practiced medicine. Dissatisfied with his life, he earned his law degree and moved to Iowa. Within a short time, he gained prominence and moved up through the Republican Party hierarchy. With the election of Abraham Lincoln to the presidency in 1860, Miller became a leading candidate to fill one of three Supreme Court vacancies. Lincoln appointed Miller associate justice in 1862.

Samuel F. Miller.
(Library of Congress)

Almost immediately, Miller exhibited his support for the Civil War by voting in the *Prize Cases* (1863) to uphold the Union navy's block-ade of Southern ports. After the war, he also favored loyalty oaths for former Confederate officials in *Ex parte Garland* (1867). He voted in the *Legal Tender Cases* (1870) to support the government's decision to issue paper money to finance the war. Yet his most important opinion came in the *Slaughterhouse Cases* (1873). In these cases, Louisiana butchers claimed a state monopoly violated their constitutional rights to pursue the occupation of their choice. In his opinion, Miller explained that the Fourteenth Amendment was intended to protect the newly freed slaves. He disparaged the argument that the privi-leges and immunities clause extended federal constitutional pro-tections to state citizens or that the due process clause protected an individual's liberty to work at the occupation of his or her choice.

Miller warned against using the Fourteenth Amendment to expand the federal courts' powers over state legislatures, noting that such a decision would radically alter the relationship between the state and federal governments.

Miller continued to assert this narrow interpretation of the amendment throughout his career. His main opponent was Justice Stephen J. Field, who argued that the Fourteenth Amendment prohibited most state regulation of business. Miller was able to best Field in this argument in the *Slaughterhouse Cases* and *Munn v. Illinois* (1877), where the Court upheld state regulation of grain elevators. However, because of changes in Court personnel and Field's dogged determination, Miller soon found himself outvoted. By the end of Miller's career on the Court, his colleagues had rejected his narrow view of the Fourteenth Amendment.

In addition to his legal opinions, Miller was a frequent letter writer. The single thread running through Miller's correspondence is his disgust with aging justices who were disabled but tenaciously hung onto office for fear of losing their salaries. Miller criticized his doddering colleagues and promised to retire upon reaching seventy. It was a promise he did not keep, remaining on the Court until 1890 when he died at the age of seventy-four.

Douglas Clouatre

FURTHER READING

Bader, William H., and Roy M. Mersky, eds. *The First One Hundred Eight Justices.* Buffalo, N.Y.: William S. Hein, 2004.

Ely, James W., Jr. *The Fuller Court: Justices, Rulings, and Legacy.* Santa Barbara, Calif.: ABC-Clio, 2003.

Fairman, Charles. *Mr. Justice Miller and the Supreme Court.* New York: Russell & Russell, 1939.

Friedman, Leon, and Fred Israel, eds. *The Justices of the United States Supreme Court:Their Lives and Major Opinions.* 5 vols. New York: Chelsea House, 1997.

Huebner, Timothy S. *The Taney Court: Justices, Rulings, and Legacy.* Santa Barbara, Calif.: ABC-Clio, 2003.

Lurie, Jonathan. *The Chase Court: Justices, Rulings, and Legacy.* Santa Barbara, Calif.: ABC-Clio, 2004.

Ross, Michael. *Justice of Shattered Dreams: Samuel Freeman Miller and the Supreme Court During the Civil War Era.* Baton Rouge: Louisiana State University Press, 2003.

Silver, David. *Lincoln's Supreme Court.* Urbana: University of Illinois Press, 1956.

Stephenson, Donald Grier, Jr. *The Waite Court: Justices, Rulings, and Legacy.* Santa Barbara, Calif.: ABC-Clio, 2003.

SEE ALSO Chase, Salmon P.; Fourteenth Amendment; *Munn v. Illinois*; Reconstruction; *Slaughterhouse Cases*; Taney, Roger Brooke; Waite, Morrison R.

Ex parte Milligan

CITATION: 71 U.S. 2
DATE: April 3, 1866 (opinions released December 17, 1866)
ISSUES: War and civil liberties; Military justice
SIGNIFICANCE: This decision, in which the Supreme Court determined that military courts did not have jurisdiction over civilians if civil courts were operating, is regarded as a constitutional landmark by many but has also been criticized and not always followed by the Court.

During the Civil War, numerous persons in Indiana and other midwestern states sympathized with the Confederate cause. In 1864, the Union Army arrested Lambdin Milligan and other antiwar Democrats, charging them with a conspiracy to steal weapons from the Army and to liberate Confederate prisoners held in Northern camps. Doubting the reliability of Indiana juries, Army officials decided to try the prisoners in military courts. After Milligan and two others were convicted and sentenced to be hanged, they argued on appeal that the military trial had violated their constitutional rights.

The U.S. Supreme Court unanimously voted to overturn their convictions and ordered the three men released. Howver, the justices strongly disagreed among themselves about the rationale for their decision. Justice David Davis wrote the opinion for the majority, while

The Supreme Court ruled that Lambdin Milligan, pictured here, should not have been tried by a military court, but by a civil court. (Indiana Historical Court)

Chief Justice Salmon P. Chase's concurrence was joined by three other justices.

Davis held that the Constitution was not suspended in wartime and not even the president or Congress could give military courts jurisdiction over civilians if the civil courts were open (as they were in the area in which Milligan was arrested). Chase's concurrence held that the statutes in this case suggested that the government had not even followed the 1863 Habeas Corpus Act, and thus it was not necessary for the Court to raise the constitutional question that Chase would have resolved by holding that Congress could have authorized military courts in extreme wartime conditions. During World War II, the Court ignored the *Milligan* ruling when allowing the forced relocation of Japanese Americans without court proceedings, and it used congressional legislation, rather than constitutional principle, as a basis for overturning the imposition of martial law in Hawaii.

Richard L. Wilson

SEE ALSO Civil War; Davis, David; *Korematsu v. United States*; Military and the Court; National security; Presidential powers; Swayne, Noah H.; War and civil liberties.

Sherman Minton

IDENTIFICATION: Associate justice (October 12, 1949-October 15, 1956)

NOMINATED BY: Harry S. Truman

BORN: October 20, 1890, Georgetown, Indiana

DIED: April 9, 1965, New Albany, Indiana

SIGNIFICANCE: Minton was the last justice to have political experience before his appointment to the Supreme Court, serving in the U.S. Senate from 1934 to 1940. As a result of his political experience, Minton believed in judicial restraint and deference to executive and legislative action in judicial decision making.

From hardscrabble origins in southern Indiana, Sherman Minton excelled through hard work, tenacity of purpose, and political friendships. Minton attended the University of Indiana as an undergraduate, where he did well in his classes and excelled in sports. He then attended the Indiana Law School, where he graduated at the top of his class in 1915. For this achievement, Minton won a scholarship for a year's graduate education at the Yale Law School where he studied under former president William H. Taft, who encouraged Minton's interest in politics.

After serving in the U.S. Army during World War I, Minton returned to southern Indiana and ran for Congress in 1920; he lost in the Democratic primary. To support himself and his family, Minton practiced law. In 1930 Minton again entered the Democratic primary and again lost. In the early 1930's he renewed a friendship with the future governor of Indiana, Paul V. McNutt, who appointed Minton to his first public position in 1933, public counselor to the Indiana Public Service Commission. Having kept his name before the public in this high-profile position, Minton decided to run for the U.S. Senate in 1934. An adamant supporter of President Franklin D. Roosevelt and the New Deal, Minton defeated incumbent Republican Senator Arthur Robinson and took his seat in March, 1935. Throughout his single term in the Senate, Minton unquestioningly supported the New Deal, and he proved himself to be a cagey political fighter. He became friends with the junior senator from Missouri who would later appoint him to the Court, Harry S. Truman. Minton led the attack on the Supreme Court when it appeared that the New Deal might be overturned in 1935-1936 and supported Roosevelt's Court-packing plan of 1937 before its failure. Minton ran for a second term in the Senate in 1940 but lost when Republican presidential nominee, Wendell Wilkie of Indiana, swept the state.

In 1941 Minton's friends secured for him a position as one of President Roosevelt's special assistants coordinating military agencies. In late 1941 when a judgeship became available on the Seventh Federal Circuit Court of Appeals, Roosevelt appointed Minton to the seat as payment for his service to the New Deal.

APPOINTMENT TO THE COURT

Minton served on the Seventh Circuit until September 15, 1949, when President Harry S. Truman appointed him to replace Wiley B. Rutledge, Jr., on the Court. His appointment was not without controversy. Republicans raised questions regarding whether Minton, known as a fierce Democrat, possessed the proper judicial temperament for the Court and questioned why he would want to serve on a Court he once bitterly attacked. Although he declined to testify before the Senate Judiciary Committee, saying that it would be improper for a sitting judge to testify, the committee advanced his nomination with a 9-2 vote. The Senate approved his appointment on October 4, 1949, by a 48-16 vote, and he was sworn in eight days later.

On the Court, Minton proved himself to be a competent justice. His most sympathetic biographers describe his effect on the Court as "minimal," while one biographer concludes that Minton "left no judicial legacy." As a justice, Minton's opinions reflected his years as a senator and the Cold War environment of the 1950's. He believed that the executive and legislative branches of the federal government should be granted wide discretion for action in a dangerous world,

Sherman Minton.
(Harris and Ewing/
Collection of the
Supreme Court of
the United States)

and judicial restraint should guide the judiciary. Three cases demonstrate these values. First, in *United States ex rel. Knauff v. Shaughnessy* (1950), Minton upheld the executive's power under a 1941 statute to bar from entering the country aliens who might be a security risk and to do so without granting them a hearing. The German bride of an American soldier sued when she was denied entry; she claimed that the War Brides Act of 1945 permitted her both a hearing and admission to the country. In his majority opinion for the Court, Minton wrote that the president could exclude Knauff and that the War Brides Act did not apply.

Two years later, in *Adler v. Board of Education* (1952), Minton demonstrated his deference to executive power when he wrote the majority opinion upholding New York's Feinberg Law, which permitted school boards to fire teachers who belonged to subversive organizations. Lastly, Minton joined the dissenters in *Youngstown Sheet and Tube Co. v. Sawyer* (1952), who would have upheld President Truman's seizure of the steel industry in a national crisis. Minton had always opposed state-sponsored discrimination based on race, so it is not surprising that he considered his participation in *Brown v. Board of Education* (1954) as the most important case heard by the Court during his term of service. His chronic pernicious anemia and circulatory problems persuaded him to leave the Court in 1956; President Dwight D. Eisenhower appointed New Jersey Supreme Court Judge William J. Brennan, Jr., in his place.

Thomas C. Mackey

FURTHER READING

Atkinson, David N. "Justice Sherman Minton and the Protection of Minority Rights." *Washington and Lee Law Review* 34 (Winter, 1977): 97-117.

Bader, William H., and Roy M. Mersky, eds. *The First One Hundred Eight Justices.* Buffalo, N.Y.: William S. Hein, 2004.

Belknap, Michal R. *The Vinson Court: Justices, Rulings, and Legacy.* Santa Barbara, Calif.: ABC-Clio, 2004.

Gugin, Linda C., and James E. St. Clair. *Sherman Minton: New Deal Senator, Cold War Justice.* Indianapolis, Ind.: Indiana Historical Society, 1997.

Urofsky, Melvin I., ed. *The Supreme Court Justices: A Biographical Dictionary.* New York: Garland, 1994.

_____. *The Warren Court: Justices, Rulings, and Legacy.* Santa Barbara, Calif.: ABC-Clio, 2001.

Wallace, Harry L. "Mr. Justice Minton—Hoosier Justice on the Supreme Court." *Indiana Law Review* 34 (Winter, 1959): 145-205; (Spring, 1959): 377-424.

SEE ALSO Brennan, William J., Jr.; *Brown v. Board of Education*; Court-packing plan; Judicial self-restraint; New Deal; Rutledge, Wiley B., Jr.; Vinson, Fred M.; *Youngstown Sheet and Tube Co. v. Sawyer.*

Miranda Rights

DESCRIPTION: A requirement that the police inform suspects of their right against self-incrimination and their right to counsel during custodial interrogation.

SIGNIFICANCE: A 1966 Supreme Court ruling created the Miranda rights. In a number of cases after its initial ruling, the Court clarified and refined its decision.

The Miranda rights were created by the Supreme Court's 5-4 decision in *Miranda v. Arizona* (1966). Miranda, a suspect in a kidnaping and rape case, confessed after being interrogated for two hours. The confession was admitted in trial, and Miranda was convicted. The Court overturned his conviction, ruling that the confession was inadmissible because the police failed to inform Miranda of his constitutional right to avoid self-incrimination and to obtain counsel before questioning him during a custodial investigation. The Court established guidelines, known as the Miranda rights, for informing suspects of their Fifth Amendment rights.

The *Miranda* ruling has been continually reexamined since its inclusion in the U.S. justice system. It left a number of unanswered questions, including how to determine whether the accused was in fact in custody (and therefore needed to be read his or her rights), whether the suspect's statements were spontaneous or the product of an investigation (and needed to be preceded by the reading of rights), and whether the individual effectively waived his or her rights. Subsequent cases helped answer these questions and define when the practice of reading suspects their rights can be suspended, which is usually if the questioning is being conducted in certain contexts and if larger issues—notably public safety—are concerned.

A QUESTION OF TIME AND PLACE

In *Orozco v. Texas* (1969), the Court upheld a lower court's ruling that four police officers should have read the Miranda rights to a suspect before questioning began in the suspect's bedroom at four o'clock in the morning. However, in *Beckwith v. United States* (1976), the Court held that statements received by Internal Revenue Service agents during a noncoercive and noncustodial interview of a tax-payer under a criminal tax investigation conducted in a private residence did not require a reading of the Miranda rights, provided that the taxpayer was informed that he was free to leave the interview at any time.

In its 1966 ruling, the Court stated that the reading of the rights is necessary only if the suspect is in custody or deprived of freedom in a significant way. In the case of *Oregon v. Mathiason* (1977), the suspect entered the police station after an officer told him that he would "like to discuss something with him." It was made clear to the suspect that he was not under arrest. During his visit to the police station, the suspect confessed, and his confession was ruled admissible, despite the suspect not having been read his Miranda rights. The Court, in *North Carolina v. Butler* (1979), stated that "the trial court must look at all the

---

MIRANDA WARNINGS

Minimal warning, as outlined in the *Miranda v Arizona* case:

> You have the right to remain silent. Anything you say can and will be used against you in a court of law. You have the right to speak to an attorney, and to have an attorney present during any questioning. If you cannot afford a lawyer, one will be provided for you at government expense.

Full warning:

> You have the right to remain silent and refuse to answer questions. Do you understand?
> Anything you do or say may be used against you in a court of law. Do you understand?
> You have the right to consult an attorney before speaking to the police and to have an attorney present during questioning now or in the future. Do you understand?
> If you cannot afford an attorney, one will be appointed for you before any questioning if you wish. Do you understand?
> If you decide to answer questions now without an attorney present you will still have the right to stop answering at any time until you talk to an attorney. Do you understand?
> Knowing and understanding your rights as I have explained them to you, are you willing to answer my questions without an attorney present?

circumstances to determine if a valid waiver has been made. Although an express waiver is easier to establish, it is not a requirement."

Still many questions remained unanswered, and further interpretations of *Miranda* followed. In *Smith v. Illinois* (1984), the Court declared that suspects taken into custody could invoke their Miranda rights very early in the process, even during the interrogator's reading of their rights, effectively ending their questioning before it starts. In *Berkemer v. McCarty* (1984), the Court determined that the Miranda rights must be read any time "in-custody" interrogation regarding a felony, misdemeanor, or minor offense takes place. However, it stated that routine questioning during traffic stops did not place enough pressure on detained people to necessitate officers' warning them of their constitutional rights.

SOME EXCEPTIONS

In *New York v. Quarles* (1984), the Court ruled six to three that there is a "public safety" exception to the requirement that Miranda rights be read. In *Quarles*, police officers arrested a man they believed had just committed a rape. They asked the man where he had discarded a gun. The arrest took place in a supermarket, and the suspect was thought to have concealed the gun somewhere inside the supermarket. The gun was found and used as evidence. In such circumstances, the Court declared, "The need for answers to questions in a situation posing a threat to the public safety outweighs the need for the prophylactic rule protecting the Fifth Amendment's privilege against self-incrimination." *Quarles* was a significant ruling, eroding *Miranda*'s influence.

Subsequent cases challenged the Court's interpretation of *Miranda*. In *Oregon v. Elstead* (1985), police officers received a voluntary admission of guilt from a suspect who had not yet been informed of his constitutional rights. The suspect made a second confession after he had been read his Miranda rights and had signed a waiver. Regarding the second confession, the Court ruled that "the self-incrimination clause of the Fifth Amendment does not require it to be suppressed solely because of the earlier voluntary but unwarned admission." Furthermore, in *Pennsylvania v. Muniz* (1990), the Court decided that the routine questioning and videotaping of drivers suspected of driving under the influence was permissible even if the Miranda rights had not been recited.

In addition, the Court held that reciting the Miranda rights is not required when the suspect gives a voluntary statement and is unaware that he or she is speaking to a law-enforcement officer. In *Illinois v. Perkins* (1990), an undercover government agent was placed in a cell with Perkins, who was incarcerated on charges unrelated to the subject of the agent's investigation. Perkins made statements that implicated him in the crime that the agent sought to solve, but he later claimed that the statements should have been inadmissable because he was not read his Miranda rights. However, even though Perkins was unaware that his cell mate was a government agent, his statements—which led to his arrest—were deemed admissible.

During the 1990's, as the Rehnquist Court became more conservative on criminal justice issues, it appeared that the requirement of Miranda warnings might be eliminated altogether. However, in a 7-2 opinion delivered by Chief Justice William H. Rehnquist himself in *Dickerson v. United States* (2000), the Court disallowed use of a voluntary confession in which the police acknowledged their failure to issue Miranda warnings. Rehnquist observed that the requirement that the police give the warnings has "become part of our national culture."

While upholding the *Miranda* precedent, the majority of the justices have often appeared to look for additional rationales that might allow noncoerced confessions whenever possible. The case of *Yarborough v. Alvarado* (2004), dealt with the admissibility at trial of a two-hour interview between police officers and a seventeen-year-old man who was implicated in a case of robbery and murder. The police claimed that since the young man was not being held in custody, he could have simply left without answering questions. Despite the youth and inexperience of the defendant, the trial court admitted the interview as evidence, arguing that a Miranda warning had not been required because the defendant was not being held in custody. Endorsing the lower court's custody test, the Supreme Court upheld the conviction, which was achieved with the help of the interview.

When a defendant's confession was ruled inadmissible at trial because of coercive tactics by the police, the justices in *Chavez v. Martinez* (2002) voted six to three that his constitutional rights had not been violated, so that he had no basis to bring a lawsuit against the police. Then, in *United States v. Patane* (2003), the Court approved the prosecutors' use of physical evidence (a gun) that was found as a result of a voluntary confession without Miranda warnings, even though the confession itself was inadmissible.

Dean Van Bibber
Updated by the Editor

FURTHER READING

Axtman, Kris. "The Tale Behind Cops' Most Famous Words." *Christian Science Monitor*, April 14, 2000.

Cassell, P. G., and R. Fowles. "Handcuffing the Cops? A Thirty-Year Perspective on Miranda's Harmful Effects on Law Enforcement." *Stanford Law Review* 50 (1998).

Del Carmen, Rolando V. *Criminal Procedure.* 6th ed. Belmont, Calif.: Thomson/Wadsworth, 2003.

Freidell, Ron. *Miranda Law: The Right to Remain Silent.* New York: Benchmark Books, 2005.

Hall, Kermit L. *The Rights of the Accused: The Justices and Criminal Justice.* New York: Garland, 2000.

National Research Council. *Fairness and Effectiveness in Policing: The Evidence.* Washington, D.C.: National Academies Press, 2003.

Savage, David G. "Speaking Up About Silence." *ABA Journal* (November, 2003).

Weinreb, Lloyd L. *Leading Constitutional Cases on Criminal Justice.* Rev. ed. New York: Foundation Press, 2001.

White, Welsh S. *Miranda's Waning Protections: Police Interrogation Practices After Dickerson.* Ann Arbor: University of Michigan Press, 2003.

SEE ALSO *Brown v. Mississippi*; Counsel, right to; Fifth Amendment; First Amendment; Self-incrimination, immunity against; *Terry v. Ohio*; Warren, Earl.

William H. Moody

IDENTIFICATION: Associate justice (December 17, 1906-November 20, 1910)

NOMINATED BY: Theodore Roosevelt

BORN: December 22, 1853, Newbury, Massachusetts

DIED: July 2, 1917, Haverhill, Massachusetts

SIGNIFICANCE: During Moody's relatively brief tenure on the Supreme Court, he was a voice for Progressive reform and a dissenter against conservative interpretations of the regulatory power of the federal government.

William H. Moody came from an old New England family and was educated at Phillips Academy, Andover, and Harvard College, from which he graduated in 1876. He attended Harvard Law School briefly and then read law with Richard Henry Dana, Jr., until he was admitted to the bar in 1878. Moody practiced in Essex County. He became district attorney for the Eastern District of the state in 1890 and was recruited as part of the prosecution in the murder trial of Lizzie

William H. Moody.
(Library of Congress)

751

Borden. Moody was elected to Congress in 1895 and was reelected three times.

By 1902 Moody had become a leading member of the House of Representatives, and President Theodore Roosevelt appointed him as secretary of the navy that same year. The two men worked well together, and Moody was named attorney general when Philander C. Knox resigned in 1904. Moody argued the case of *Swift and Co. v. United States* (1905), in which he advanced an expansive view of the government's power over interstate commerce. Moody was also deeply involved in the negotiations that led to the passage of the Hepburn Act to regulate railroads in 1906.

When Justice Henry B. Brown retired in 1906, Roosevelt wanted a progressive successor on the Supreme Court, and he nominated Moody with the expectation that the new justice would advance the president's antitrust policies and commitment to regulation. Moody received prompt Senate confirmation and was sworn in on December 17, 1906.

Moody lived up to Roosevelt's expectations, but his stay on the Court was all too brief. When the Court struck down the Employer's Liability Act in 1908 because it allegedly involved the regulation of intrastate as well as interstate commerce, Moody contended that the power of Congress to oversee interstate commerce extended to the relationship between employers and employees. Before Moody could make an indelible mark on the Court's deliberations, however, he was stricken with rheumatism and could not continue his work. By October, 1910, it was evident that he would have to leave the bench. Congress passed a special law to allow him the retirement privileges of justices who had served at least ten years. His previous service in the House made enactment of this law much easier. He resigned on November 20, 1910, and President William H. Taft named his successor. Moody, who never married, died in Haverhill, Massachusetts, on July 2, 1917. Because of his disability, Moody became one of the great might-have-beens of Supreme Court history. His nationalism, sympathy with reform, and tolerance for regulatory power might have helped take the Court in a more progressive direction had illness not tragically limited his years of influence and service.

Lewis L. Gould

FURTHER READING

Bader, William H., and Roy M. Mersky, eds. *The First One Hundred Eight Justices.* Buffalo, N.Y.: William S. Hein, 2004.

Bickel, Alexander M., and Benno C. Schmidt, Jr. *The Judiciary and Responsible Government, 1910-1921.* New York: Macmillan, 1984.

Ely, James W., Jr. *The Fuller Court: Justices, Rulings, and Legacy.* Santa Barbara, Calif.: ABC-Clio, 2003.

Friedman, Leon, and Fred Israel, eds. *The Justices of the United States Supreme Court: Their Lives and Major Opinions.* 5 vols. New York: Chelsea House, 1997.

SEE ALSO Antitrust law; Brown, Henry B.; Fuller, Melville W.; Progressivism; Taft, William H.

Alfred Moore

IDENTIFICATION: Associate justice (April 21, 1800-January 26, 1804)
NOMINATED BY: John Adams
BORN: May 21, 1755, Brunswick, North Carolina
DIED: October 15, 1810, Bladen County, North Carolina
SIGNIFICANCE: During his brief time on the Supreme Court, Moore issued a single opinion that was politically controversial.

Alfred Moore was educated in Boston and began practicing law in 1755. After serving as a military officer in the American Revolution, he was appointed state attorney general for North Carolina in 1782. He participated in *Bayard v. Singleton* (1787), a North Carolina case that was the first in which a court declared a law unconstitutional. This case provided a precedent for the Supreme Court case *Marbury v. Madison* (1803), which established the doctrine of judicial review.

After resigning his position in 1791, Moore returned to law practice, and served as a judge in the state superior court in 1798. President John Adams nominated him to the Supreme Court on December 4, 1799. He was confirmed by the Senate on December 10, and took office on April 21, 1800. Ill health caused him to retire from the Supreme Court on January 26, 1804.

Alfred Moore.
(Library of Congress)

Moore's only written opinion while on the Court was issued in *Bas v. Tingy* (1800), a case involving a U.S. ship captured by the French. Moore held that a "limited partial war" existed with France, a decision that was welcomed by the Federalist Party but denounced by the Democratic-Republican Party. A delay in traveling prevented him from participating in *Marbury*.

Rose Secrest

SEE ALSO Judicial review; *Marbury v. Madison*; Marshall, John.

Moore v. City of East Cleveland

CITATION: 431 U.S. 494
DATE: May 31, 1977
ISSUES: Right of privacy; substantive due process
SIGNIFICANCE: The Supreme Court used the doctrine of substantive due process to strike down a local zoning ordinance that prohibited extended families from living together in a single-unit residence.

A residential suburb of Cleveland, Ohio, wanting to maintain its character as a single-family neighborhood, enacted a zoning ordinance that restricted each dwelling to a single family. The ordinance defined a family so narrowly that it did not allow Inex Moore, a grandmother, to live with her two grandsons. When Moore refused to comply with the ordinance, she was sentenced to five days in jail and fined twenty-five dollars.

By a 5-4 vote, the Supreme Court held that the ordinance violated the due process clause of the Fourteenth Amendment. In a plurality opinion, Justice Lewis F. Powell, Jr., emphasized the importance of "personal choice in matters of marriage and the family," and he argued that the Fourteenth Amendment protects those liberties that are "deeply rooted in our history and tradition." He concluded that this tradition was broad enough to encompass various forms of extended families. Powell's opinion significantly extended the scope of the substantive due process approach, and his history and tradition standard has often served as a rationale for subsequent decisions.

Thomas Tandy Lewis

SEE ALSO Due process, substantive; Fourteenth Amendment; *Griswold v. Connecticut*; Powell, Lewis F., Jr.; Privacy, right to.

Munn v. Illinois

CITATION: 94 U.S. 113
DATE: March 1, 1877
ISSUE: Regulation of businesses
SIGNIFICANCE: This historic ruling recognized that a state might exercise its police power to regulate private businesses.

In the 1870's the Illinois legislature, responding to demands of the Patrons of Husbandry (the Grange), passed a statute limiting the maximum charges for the storage of grain in warehouses located in cities of 100,000 or more. The operators of several Chicago warehouses argued that the law violated two provisions in the Constitution: the commerce clause and the due process clause of the Fourteenth Amendment. By a 7-2 vote, however, the Supreme Court upheld the legislation. Justice Morrison R. Waite's majority opinion concluded that the law's effect on interstate commerce was only incidental, and it rejected the doctrine of substantive due process. Recognizing that the states possessed an inherent police power to protect the safety, welfare, and morality of the public, Waite concluded that this authority extended to the regulation of private property that is "affected with a public interest." Ironically, the concept of "affected with a public interest" was later used to prohibit regulation of businesses that were small and of limited influence—a practice finally abandoned in *Nebbia v. New York* (1934).

Munn is remembered not only for the majority opinion but also for Justice Stephen J. Field's vigorous dissent, which defended almost a laissez-faire position on private property. Field charged that the majority opinion was dangerous to liberty because it implied that "all property and all business in the state are held at the mercy of the legislature." Field's dissent included a coherent argument in favor of a substantive reading of the due process clause—an interpretation later accepted by the Court in *Allgeyer v. Louisiana* (1897).

Thomas Tandy Lewis

SEE ALSO *Allgeyer v. Louisiana*; Capitalism; Commerce, regulation of; Due process, substantive; Field, Stephen J.; Police powers; Waite, Morrison R.

Frank Murphy

IDENTIFICATION: Associate justice (January 18, 1940-July 19, 1949)

NOMINATED BY: Franklin D. Roosevelt

BORN: April 13, 1890, Sand Beach (later Harbor Beach), Michigan

DIED: July 19, 1949, Detroit, Michigan

SIGNIFICANCE: Murphy was the most consistent voice for basic fairness and tolerance on the socially conscious New Deal-era Supreme Court. He voted continually with the Court majority when it expanded civil liberties and wrote ringing dissents when it denied a claimed right.

Frank Murphy earned undergraduate and law degrees from the University of Michigan. After serving in Europe during World War I (1917-1918), he served as an assistant U.S. attorney and then as

Frank Murphy.
(Library of Congress)

a judge in Detroit's principal criminal court. In 1930 pro-labor Democrat Murphy was elected mayor of Detroit. In 1933 President Franklin D. Roosevelt appointed him governor general of the Philippines, where he served successfully until he returned to Michigan to run for governor in 1936. After he was elected, Murphy's refusal to use force to end sit-in strikes cost him reelection in 1938, whereupon Roosevelt appointed him U.S. attorney general. His one-year stint as attorney general long influenced future litigation before the Supreme Court because he created the Justice Department's first civil rights unit, which aggressively protected the civil liberties of racial, political, and religious minorities.

Upon the death of Justice Pierce Butler, a Roman Catholic Democrat from Minnesota, Roosevelt appointed Murphy, also a Catholic, to the vacant seat. After a year on the Court, Murphy joined with Justices Hugo L. Black, William O. Douglas, and later Wiley B. Rutledge, Jr., to form the Court's liberal core throughout the 1940's. Murphy decided cases independently, but he was not a great legal technician; when writing opinions, he relied extensively on his clerks. Chief Justice Harlan Fiske Stone usually assigned him cases that provided limited opportunity for memorable opinions.

Murphy described the court as a "great pulpit," and from it he supported society's underdogs. His moralizing *obiter dicta* (incidental remarks) gave rise to the phrase "justice tempered with Murphy." A devout Catholic, Murphy had faith that manifested itself in his compulsion to pursue justice. On the socially liberal New Deal-era Court, his was the most consistent voice for basic fairness and tolerance. He supported the religious rights of the anti-Catholic Jehovah's Witnesses, defending their claims to conscientious objector status and freedom to proselytize door to door.

In more than nine years on the Court, Murphy wrote 131 opinions for the Court majority or concurring with it and 68 dissents; his most outstanding opinions advocated protection for civil liberties. His first opinion, *Thornhill v. Alabama* (1940), extended constitutional protection for speech to peaceful picketing. In *Korematsu v. United States* (1944), he dissented from "this legalization of racism" (referring to the relocation of Japanese Americans). His dissent in *In re Yamashita* (1946) criticized the lack of due process in a Japanese general's war crime conviction. Writing the opinion for the Court in *United States v. United Mine Workers* (1947), he found no legal basis for a government injunction barring a coal miners' strike. His dissent in *Wolf v. Colorado* (1949) castigated the Court for applying Fourth Amendment search and seizure requirements to the states while not requiring the adoption of the exclusionary rule. Murphy's strengths as a justice were his independence, integrity, and his uncompromising advocacy for the protection of broad civil liberties

Chuck Smith

SEE ALSO Butler, Pierce; Exclusionary rule; Incorporation doctrine; Japanese American relocation; Religion, freedom of; Rutledge, Wiley B., Jr.

National Association for the Advancement of Colored People v. Alabama

CITATION: 357 U.S. 357
DATE: June 30, 1958
ISSUE: Freedom of association
SIGNIFICANCE: The Supreme Court explicitly recognized that a freedom of association was implied in the First Amendment's guarantee of free expression and free assembly and was an "inseparable aspect" of the liberty guaranteed by the due process clause of the Fourteenth Amendment.

As the Civil Rights movement started in the 1950's, several southern states tried to limit the activities of groups like the National Association for the Advancement of Colored People (NAACP). Alabama had a law that required out-of-state businesses to register with the state and disclose their membership list in order to do business in the state. A state court concluded that the NAACP was a business rather than a nonprofit organization and ordered the group to turn over the names of its members to the state attorney general. The NAACP refused and argued that the disclosure of rank-and-file members would lead to reprisals and public hostility, placing unacceptable burdens on the right of members to belong to the association and to support its goals.

The Supreme Court unanimously upheld the NAACP's position. Writing for the Court, Justice John M. Harlan II declared that the Constitution prohibited the states from limiting the ability of the members of a legal and nonsubversive organization "to pursue their collective efforts to foster beliefs which they admittedly have a right to advocate." Because the freedom to participate in an association is a fundamental right, Harlan instructed courts to use the closest scrutiny when examining state actions that have the effect of curtailing this freedom. In numerous cases since 1958, the Court upheld restrictions on the freedom of association whenever a group is engaged in criminal activities or invidious discrimination.

Thomas Tandy Lewis

SEE ALSO Assembly and association, freedom of; Civil Rights movement; *DeJonge v. Oregon*; Due process, substantive; Fundamental rights; Race and discrimination.

National Security

DESCRIPTION: Foreign and domestic policy designed to protect the independence and political and economic integrity of the United States. The constitutional and legal powers granted to government that provide both domestic and global security.

SIGNIFICANCE: When litigation involving the protection of individual rights reached the Supreme Court, it often sought to balance the claims of Bill of Rights guarantees versus national security needs. In the twentieth century, the Court consistently sided with governmental restriction of individual actions when confronted with claims of national security.

It has been said that the laws are no more and no less than what the courts will enforce. The Supreme Court has often avoided deciding a case on any ground that touches constitutional issues. Though vested with the power to interpret the law and the U.S. Constitution, the federal courts confront issues of national security under significant procedural restraints. Some of these are described in the Constitution itself, while others have developed out of political and administrative necessity. Taken together, they contributed to the lack of precise boundaries between the executive and legislative branches in the distribution of foreign policy powers.

Article III, section 2, of the Constitution limits the jurisdiction of federal courts to cases and controversies. The courts are thus prohibited from providing advisory opinions that are, in reality, hypothetical in nature. In the 1979 Taiwan treaty case, members of Congress challenged the constitutionality of President Jimmy Carter's decision to repeal a security treaty with Taiwan to establish diplomatic relations with the People's Republic of China. *Goldwater v. Carter* (1979) was dismissed, but the Court could not agree upon the proper grounds for its decision. Justice Lewis F. Powell, Jr., argued that the case should be dismissed because the level of conflict between the branches had not reached the level of "controversy." He stated that a dispute between Congress and the president is not ready for judicial review until each branch has taken action asserting its constitutional authority. Also, the majority of the differences between the two branches turn on political rather than legal considerations. Therefore, the judicial branch should not decide issues affecting the allocation of power between the president and Congress until the political branches reach a constitutional impasse. A Court receptive to such challenges would encourage small groups or even individual members of Congress to seek judicial resolution of issues before the normal political process resolves the conflict.

The two principal writers of *The Federalist* (1788), Alexander Hamilton and James Madison, agreed that the national government gains significant power in times of war and emergency. When national defense was at issue, Hamilton declared that the grant of power should exist without limitation because it was impossible to foresee or to define the extent to which such powers might be needed. Madison concurred, stating that it was futile to oppose constitutional barriers to the impulse of self-preservation. In *Schenck v. United States* (1919), Justice Oliver Wendell Holmes affirmed these priorities when applying them to questions of First Amendment speech protections. "When a nation is at war many things that might be said in times of peace are such a hindrance to its effort that their utterance will not be endured so long as men fight and that no Court could regard them as protected by any constitutional right."

CONGRESS AND THE PRESIDENCY

The federal courts have historically exercised restraint when deciding issues touching on national security. Yet one legal question has been consistently appealed to the judicial branch: the extent of presidential power absent congressional authorization when faced with threats to national security. During the Civil War, President Abraham Lincoln ordered the blockade of southern ports without prior approval from Congress. The Court's 5-4 ruling in the *Prize Cases* (1863) sustained the president's action on the ground that he was legally empowered to recognize hostile acts of rebels or from a foreign nation as acts of war and could respond without a congressional declaration.

Presidential primacy in national security policy was further enhanced in the years preceding World War II (1941-1945). In *United States v. Curtiss-Wright Export Corp.* (1936), the Court determined that foreign affairs, with their "important, complicated, delicate, and manifold problems," are best left to the president alone. "Into this field of negotiation the Senate cannot intrude; and Congress itself is powerless to invade it." The president is to be afforded a "degree of discretion" by Congress in foreign policy that would not be admissible if domestic affairs alone were at issue. A year later in *Belmont v. United States*, the Court held that the conduct of foreign relations, including the recognition of foreign governments, is exclusively an executive function.

However, when a conflict touches domestic issues and there is a strong assertion of power by Congress, the Court has given the president less latitude. During the Korean conflict, President Harry S. Truman claimed the power to seize the nation's steel mills based on his powers as commander in chief and through his inherent powers as chief executive. In *Youngstown Sheet and Tube Co. v. Sawyer* (1952), the Court disagreed, handing Truman an embarrassing defeat and invalidating his claim to emergency powers. However, only Justices Hugo L. Black and William O. Douglas held that the president had no such inherent powers in protecting the national interest, and only Black took the position that the president's power must stem either from an act of Congress or from the Constitution itself. The lack of a clear majority opinion left open the question of the scope and limits of presidential prerogative in times of war and crisis.

The aftermath of World War II saw dramatic shifts in international relations that had a profound impact on U.S. national security. The United Nations charter, ratified and put into effect in 1945, created a system of collective security that brought all member nations together to seek diplomatic, economic, and military solutions to solve crises and conflicts. In 1949 the United States joined the North Atlantic Treaty Organization to provide a single unified defense force for the North Atlantic region. These legal commitments, coupled with the presence of permanent standing armies stationed on foreign soil, changed the balance of war power between the president and Congress. The Soviet Union's demonstration of nuclear capability and the expanded U.S. role overseas enhanced the president's role as commander in chief and his constitutional power to "repel sudden attacks." The qualities of an effective president championed by Alexander Hamilton—energy, unity, secrecy, and dispatch—became necessary components of presidential power in the nuclear age.

As the undeclared war in Vietnam became both lengthy and unpopular in the late 1960's, the delegation of power from Congress to President Lyndon B. Johnson (through the passage of the Gulf of Tonkin Resolution) came into question. Members of Congress brought suit against the president, challenging his ability to conduct a war without a formal congressional declaration (*Holtzman v. Schlesinger,* 1973). The Court predictably declined to intervene and encouraged Congress to exert its ample constitutional powers to confront presidential policies and actions.

One of the ways in which Congress followed the advice of the Court was through passage of the War Powers Act in 1973 over the veto of President Richard M. Nixon. Its procedural mechanisms calling for consultation with Congress prior to placing military forces into hostilities and regular reports thereafter have been uniformly denounced by presidents as unconstitutional. When members of Congress have brought suit seeking enforcement of the War Powers

Act (*Crockett v. Reagan*, 1982), the federal courts have rejected their claims. Again, the courts determined that such controversies are best left to Congress acting through the passage of statutes. In 1990 fifty-four members of Congress sought an injunction against President George H. W. Bush using military force against Iraq. The decision of the Washington, D.C., district court stated that the case lacked ripeness, as the plaintiffs represented only 10 percent of the members of Congress. This left open the possibility that if a majority of Congress had joined in the suit, it might have been granted. The 1999 conflict in Bosnia saw the House of Representatives debating a motion to issue a formal declaration of war. Though the proposal was rejected, it highlighted the ongoing struggle within Congress to define war and to confront presidential initiative abroad.

CIVIL RIGHTS AND LIBERTIES

When personal rights and liberties have come into conflict with national security claims, the federal courts have usually sided with the government. Despite the clear wording of the First Amendment ("Congress shall make no law . . ."), the Court has never held to a literal interpretation of the expression's guarantees of speech, press, assembly, and petition. Instead, it has sought to determine the legal boundaries of where the government's right to restrict expression begins and constitutional protections end. Historically, these questions reached the Court during or immediately following times of war or national crisis and presented some of the greatest challenges to the constitutional framework of government.

The first major challenge to civil rights and liberties based on security concerns occurred seven years after ratification of the Bill of Rights by the states when Congress passed one of the most restrictive laws ever written, the Sedition Act of 1798. The law forbade any person from writing, printing, or uttering anything "false, scandalous, or malicious" against the government, its officials, Congress, or the president. The passage of the act coincided with an undeclared war with France (1798-1800) that saw Congress debate the possibility of war and pass a number of laws to place the country on a war footing.

Sixty years later, the Court openly challenged the power of President Lincoln to suspend the writ of habeas corpus (a court order directing an official who has a person in custody to bring the prisoner to court and to show cause for his or her detention). When Lincoln refused to accept the writ, the Court did not force a confrontation with the president (*Ex parte Merryman*, 1861). When the Court sought to clarify the role of military courts and strengthen the constitutional guarantees of a fair trial after the Civil War (1861-1865) in *Ex parte Milligan* (1866), Congress passed legislation limiting the Court's jurisdiction to hear cases involving military trials.

As World War I (1917-1918) began in Europe, Congress passed the Espionage Act of 1917, prohibiting interference or obstruction with military operations and activities. One year later, Congress passed the Sedition Act, prohibiting "the uttering of, writing, or publishing of anything disloyal to the government, flag, or military forces of the United States." Close to one thousand citizens were arrested and convicted under these statutes. In *Schenck v. United States* (1919), the Court upheld these convictions while pronouncing the "clear and present danger" doctrine. In the decade that followed, the Court upheld state convictions based on laws designed to suppress socialist and subversive organizations (*Gitlow v. New York*, 1925; *Whitney v. California*, 1927). Using a less restrictive "bad tendency test," the Court declared that freedom of speech does not confer an absolute right to speak and that a state may take steps to prevent its government's "overthrow by unlawful means."

Following the Japanese attack on Pearl Harbor in 1941, President Franklin D. Roosevelt issued an executive order authorizing "military zones" in which curfews and restrictions of movement could prevent espionage and sabotage. Congress followed with legislation affirming Roosevelt's orders and providing criminal penalties for their violation. Legal challenges to these laws relocating and interning Japanese Americans did not prevail. The Court, by wide margins, affirmed laws concerning curfews (*Hirabayashi v. United States*, 1943) and internment (*Korematsu v. United States*, 1944).

National security concerns did not cease with the close of World War II. In rapid succession, the fall of mainland China to communism, the detonation of an atomic weapon by the Soviet Union, and the war in Korea brought about concerns about communist influence in U.S. government and life. Congress, claiming broad powers to investigate, commissioned the House Committee on Un-American Activities to determine if Communist Party sympathizers had infiltrated the upper echelon of government. The Cold War era saw the Court uphold both convictions against free speech claims (*Dennis v. United States*, 1951) and speech, association, and self-incrimination protections (*Barenblatt v. United States*, 1959). Though the Constitution did not explicitly grant Congress the power to investigate, the Court consistently held that it was an implied power incident to lawmaking. Congress, the Court concluded, cannot legislate wisely or effectively without sufficient information pertaining to the subject or issue the legislation is intended to affect or change (*McGrain v. Daugherty*, 1927).

During the Vietnam War (1965-1973), cases based on rights of symbolic expression came before the Court. In *United States v. O'Brien* (1968), the Court ruled that a legitimate governmental activity (the issuance of draft cards to raise and support armies) superseded O'Brien's First Amendment right to symbolic speech and political protest (burning the draft card). The most controversial form of symbolic expression has been flag burning. Rooted in the Vietnam antiwar protests, flag burning touches on issues of freedom, patriotism, national interest, and political rights. Many states had laws outlawing flag desecration during the 1960's, but the question remained whether such laws were constitutional. In *Street v. New York* (1969), the justices divided four to four on whether states could prohibit flag burning and desecration. The landmark case of *Texas v. Johnson* (1989) upheld the right to such symbolic expression. Congress reacted that same year with a federal law prohibiting flag burning. The Court, using the same reasoning articulated in *Texas v. Johnson*, invalidated the law in *United States v. Eichman* (1990).

OTHER ISSUES

The Court on occasion ruled against broad claims of presidential power and prerogative based on national security claims. In the 1970's, as the Vietnam War was winding down, *The New York Times* was sued by the government to prevent the publication of the Pentagon Papers, which documented U.S. military strategy in Southeast Asia. In *New York Times Co. v. United States* (1971), the Court refused to enjoin publication, claiming that such actions would amount to prior restraint. However, the hastily delivered ruling was decided *per curiam* (by the court), and nine separate opinions (six in favor of *The New York Times*) were written. The variety of constitutional reasoning and argument within the opinions left no clear direction or precedent. The Court did not see a significant challenge to press freedoms based on national security after this case.

In early 1991 during the war in Iraq, military authorities placed significant restrictions on both television and print media. Most reports from the field had to be cleared by military personnel. However, in late 1992 U.S. military forces took part in a United Nations operation to protect humanitarian assistance to Somalia. Throughout the conduct of the operation, the news media had nearly complete freedom of movement and reporting.

Timothy S. Boylan

FURTHER READING

For a comprehensive survey of Court cases and a discussion of the political and social contexts in which they were decided, see Lee Epstein and Thomas G. Walker's *Constitutional Law for a Changing America: Rights, Liberties, and Justice* (5th ed. Washington, D.C.: CQ Press, 2004). *The United States and the International Criminal Court: National Security and International Law* (Lanham, Md.: Rowman & Littlefield, 2000), edited by Sarah B. Sewall and Carl Kaysen, is a collection of articles examining the relationship between national security and international crime. Norris Smith and Lynn M. Messina's *Homeland Security* (New York: H. W. Wilson, 2004) contains twenty-eight articles reprinted from newspapers and magazines about aspects of national security, terrorism, and civil liberties.

Important to any study of legislative/executive relations is the first commentary on the Constitution, *The Federalist,* which is contained in *The Federalist Papers* (New York: New American Library of World Literature, 1961), edited by Clinton Rossiter. Note especially Hamilton's treatment of the presidency and executive power in Nos. 70 to 78. Abraham Sofaer's *War, Foreign Affairs, and Constitutional Power* (2 vols. Cambridge, Mass.: Ballinger, 1984) discusses the complexities of squaring foreign policy with constitutional dictates.

Harold Koh's *The National Security Constitution* (New Haven, Conn.: Yale University Press, 1990) argues that many national security issues—especially the definition of "war"—are not political questions and should be reviewed by the Court. For a comprehensive discussion of all aspects of international and constitutional law, see John Norton Moore, Frederick Tipson, and Robert Turner's *National Security Law* (Durham, N.C.: Carolina Academic Press, 1990). See chapter 17, "The Constitutional Framework for the Division of National Security Powers," in *The Constitution and the Conduct of American Foreign Policy*, edited by David Gray Adler and Larry George (Lawrence: University Press of Kansas, 1996), which brings together fourteen essays on law and policy.

John Hart Ely's *War and Responsibility* (Princeton, N.J.: Princeton University Press, 1993) includes a treatment of policy making, public opinion, and the role of Congress during the Vietnam War. An assessment of Ely's work that provides an examination of constitutional interpretation can be found in "War Powers: An Essay on John Hart Ely's *War and Responsibility*" by Philip Bobbitt, *Michigan Law Review* 92 (May, 1994). For an in-depth treatment of the *Youngstown* case and a study of presidential power and constitutional constraints, see Maeva Marcus's *Truman and the Steel Seizure Case* (Durham, N.C.: Duke University Press, 1994).

SEE ALSO Civil War; *Curtiss-Wright Export Corp., United States v.*; *Schenck v. United States*; Vietnam War; War and civil liberties; War powers; World War II; *Youngstown Sheet and Tube Co. v. Sawyer.*

National Treasury Employees Union v. Von Raab

CITATION: 489 U.S. 656
DATE: March 21, 1989
ISSUE: Search and seizure
SIGNIFICANCE: The Supreme Court upheld a drug-testing program in the U.S. Customs Service that required urinalysis tests for employees who sought promotions to positions that involve drug interdiction, the carrying of firearms, or the handling of classified information.

A union of federal employees challenged the program as a violation of the Fourth Amendment because urine samples were taken without individualized suspicion, probable cause, or a search warrant. Writing for a narrow 5-4 majority, Justice Anthony M. Kennedy applied a balancing test to conclude that the government's compelling interests in public safety justified the program's restrictions on the privacy expectations of law-enforcement personnel who enforced drug statutes or carried weapons. Kennedy's opinion, however, remanded the question of tests for those handling classified information to the lower court for additional consideration. In a dissenting opinion, Justice Thurgood Marshall wrote that there was "no drug enforcement exception to the Constitution." In a less controversial companion case, *Skinner v. Railway Labor Executives Association* (1989), the justices voted seven to two to uphold federal regulations that required drug testing of all crew members of trains involved in serious accidents.

Thomas Tandy Lewis

SEE ALSO Fourth Amendment; Kennedy, Anthony M.; Marshall, Thurgood; Privacy, right to; Search warrant requirement.

Native American Sovereignty

DESCRIPTION: Within the context of the American constitutional system, Native American sovereignty constitutes the retained rights of Native American nations to self-determination not extinguished by treaty or by congressional statute.

SIGNIFICANCE: Native American tribes and the U.S. government maintain a complex and unique legal relationship. Like the fifty states, the tribes exercise sovereignty within their recognized spheres of control. Although tribal sovereignty is almost total in regard to the states, it is limited in regard to Congress, which has the final authority to determine issues such as tribal status and the continuation of treaty rights. The ambiguities and tensions relating to this limited sovereignty have elicited numerous decisions by the Supreme Court.

The U.S. Constitution does not specifically mention Native American sovereignty, and it offers relatively little guidance regarding the relationships among the tribal governments, the federal government, and the state governments. The Constitution expressly refers to Native Americans in only three places. Both Article I and the Fourteenth Amendment indicate that the "Indians not taxed" are not to be counted as part of the population for purposes of congressional representation. Article I, section 8, stipulates that Congress has the authority to "regulate commerce . . . with the Indian tribes."

In addition to the legislative powers expressly mentioned, the Constitution provides the federal government with several implicit powers to deal with Native Americans. The property clause in Article IV allows Congress to dispose of and make all rules regarding federal property and tribal lands. The necessary and proper clause in Article I, section 8, authorizes Congress to enforce its enumerated powers. The war powers clause in the same article gave the federal government authority to conduct military operations against hostile tribes. Article VI recognizes that both federal statutes and treaties, when consistent with the United States Constitution, are equally part of the "supreme law of the land"; therefore they take precedence over laws of the states. The Bill of Rights and other constitutional restrictions are not directly binding on Native American governments, although in 1968 Congress codified the Indian Bill of Rights, which theoretically requires the tribal courts to follow most of the provisions in the first eight amendments.

REMOVAL AND SEGREGATION, 1800-1879

Although the Constitution offered a rough outline of the federal government's authority over Native American affairs, the Supreme Court, in dialogue with Congress and the executive branch, clarified the parameters of these powers. Of particular significance was the so-called Marshall Trilogy: *Johnson and Graham's Lessee v. McIntosh* (1823), *Cherokee Nation v. Georgia* (1831), and *Worcester v. Georgia* (1832). In the first two of these decisions, Chief Justice John Marshall emphasized that the tribes "were under the sovereignty and dominion of the United States." Referring to their status as "domestic dependent nations," he wrote that "their rights to complete sovereignty, as independent nations, are necessarily diminished." More specifically, the tribes were not allowed to make agreements with other countries or to sell their land to any party other than the United States government.

Although Marshall never repudiated his statements in these two opinions, he used his *Worcester* opinion to emphasize nationhood more than dependency, recognizing that the tribes remained "distinct independent political communities," possessing their own territory and substantial elements of sovereignty. In addition, his Court ruled that the state governments had no authority to regulate tribal affairs. Future generations of Supreme Court justices would time and again refer to the alternative perspectives within the Marshall Trilogy.

Over the next four decades, few Native American cases came before the Supreme Court. With its acknowledgment of Congress's authority over Indian affairs, the Court had no occasion to become involved in the Indian Removal Act of 1830 or the hardships that Indians endured in the Trail of Tears. The justices generally viewed the coercive movement of Indians westward as a question of legislative prerogative, not susceptible to judicial review. Moreover, the justices appeared to assume that they had no jurisdiction to supervise the laws and legal processes conducted by the tribes.

Following the Civil War, the Court expanded on the key principles enunciated in Marshall's *McIntosh* and *Cherokee Nation* opinions, re-affirming the nearly absolute power of the federal government to regulate tribal affairs. In *United States v. Holliday* (1865) and *United States v. Forty-three Gallons of Whiskey* (1876), for example, the Court held that Congress had the authority to regulate the sale and consumption of alcohol on reservations through its commerce powers, thus allowing Congress to exercise expansive police powers involving the health, safety, and morality of Native Americans. In the words of the Court in *Forty-three Gallons of Whiskey,* the federal government had the authority, "to secure Indian communities against the debasing influence of spirituous liquors" and also "to promote the welfare of the Indians, as well as our political interests." At the same time, the Court consistently held that the state governments' supervisory powers over Native American affairs were severely limited. In the case of *In re Kansas Indians* (1866), for example, the Court ruled that because Native Americans were a "distinct" people not under the jurisdiction of the states, Kansas had no power to tax their incomes.

An important development during the late nineteenth century was the Indians' loss of symbolic negotiating power with the United States as a result of congressional enactment of the Appropriations Act of 1871. That statute effectively terminated the practice of treaty making between the federal government and the tribes. Most commentators agree that the central reason for this termination was the desire of the House of Representatives to play a more instrumental role in deciding Native American policies, especially policies involving expenditures of public funds. The statute recognized the continued validity of the treaties already concluded. Since agreements with the tribes had to be approved by Congress, the end of treaty making had little practical impact on issues of congressional prerogatives and tribal sovereignty.

AGE OF ASSIMILATION, 1880-1933

During the 1880's, the federal government switched from a policy of removal and separation to one of attempted assimilation. The central goal of assimilation was to dismantle tribal culture and absorb Native Americans into mainstream society. The movement was encouraged by the public's angry reaction to the Supreme Court's decision in *Ex parte Crow Dog* (1883). After Crow Dog murdered Sioux chief Spotted Tail on a Dakota Territory reservation, the aggrieved family agreed to forgive the offense with a payment of six hundred dollars and eight horses. Federal officials, believing the agreement to be unjust, tried and convicted Crow Dog in federal court. The Supreme Court, however, overturned the court's verdict and held that crimes committed "by Indians against each other were to be dealt with by each tribe for itself, according to its local customs." The decision recognized that their status as sovereign nations encompassed an inherent right to be governed by their own laws.

In 1885, outraged by the Court's decision, Congress passed the Major Crimes Act, which made it a federal offense for Native Americans to commit murder and other serious crimes on the reservations. In *United States v. Kagama* (1886), the Court upheld the constitutionality of the statute and articulated the "plenary power doctrine" of Congress's authority over Indian affairs. In a further attempt to promote greater assimilation two years later, Congress passed the Dawes General Allotment Act (1887), which was designed to end communal ownership by tribes and encourage private ownership. Sometimes Indian children were taken from their homes to be educated at boarding schools in the East.

Despite the Dawes Act, the Court continued to recognize the limited sovereignty of the tribes. The important case of *Talton v. Mayes* (1896) arose when a member of the Cherokee nation protested that his criminal trial in tribal court had not incorporated the grand jury requirement of the Fifth Amendment. In rejecting his appeal, the Supreme Court held that the provisions of the Bill of Rights did not apply to Native American governments, just as they did not apply at that time to the states. The Court recognized that the tribes retained the power to make their own laws, limited only by the provisions of federal legislation that were specifically applicable to the tribal governments.

Most of the justices apparently did not see any major contradiction between the tribes' retained sovereignty and Congress's plenary powers to determine their rights and organization. They unanimously emphasized the latter idea in *Lone Wolf v. Hitchcock* (1903), which has been called the Indians' *Dred Scott* decision. While upholding the forced sale of Indian land and the allotment process, the Court also recognized the power of Congress to terminate Indian treaties. Almost two decades later in *Winton v. Amos* (1921), the Court reaffirmed this perspective even more explicitly: "It is thoroughly established that Congress has plenary power over the Indians and their tribal relations, and full power to legislate concerning their tribal property."

An ongoing controversy was whether Native Americans were citizens according to the literal words of the Fourteenth Amendment. In *Elk v. Wilkins* (1884), the Court determined that they were not automatically citizens because as tribal members they were not subject to the federal government's jurisdiction. In 1924, however, Congress reversed the Court's decision by extending citizenship and voting rights to Native Indians. The tribes viewed this development with great skepticism, for they feared that citizenship status could lead to a renewal of assimilationist policies and further dilute tribal sovereignty.

TERMINATION VS. AUTONOMY, 1934-1967

During the period of the so-called Indian New Deal of the mid-1930's, there was a new enthusiasm for Native American autonomy and a departure from earlier assimilationist policies. The Indian Reorganization Act (1934), in particular, repealed the Dawes General Allotment Act, and it encouraged a return to community ownership of land and tribal culture. In addition, the statute gave Native Americans preferential treatment for government positions in Indian service.

Federal support for tribal autonomy, however, turned out to be short-lived. In the late 1940's and 1950's, Congress adopted a termination policy that the Eisenhower administration enthusiastically endorsed. The goal of the policy was to end the trust relationship between Native Americans and the federal government, thereby eliminating the reservations, tribal government, and most federal subsidies. The states naturally supported the termination policy because it promised to increase their own prerogatives. Most tribes resisted entering into termination agreements, and only a few agreements were ever concluded. The termination movement hit full stride when Congress passed Public Law 280 in 1953. That legislation allowed five states—and encouraged others—to maintain criminal and civil jurisdiction over Native Americans.

During the 1950's, the Warren Court's decisions sometimes appeared to encourage the termination policy. Reaffirming that the federal government's plenary power over Native American interests in *Tee-Hit-Ton Indians v. United States* (1955), the Court ruled that the Tlingit nation did not have aboriginal land rights over southeastern Alaska, even though its members had occupied the land for many centuries. Critics of the decision said that it harkened back to the age of forced assimilation and the *Lone Wolf* ruling.

During the termination period, however, the Warren Court initiated a "new federalism" policy in U.S.-Indian relations. The Court was especially strong in defending tribal sovereignty against the attempted encroachments by the states. In *Williams v. Lee* (1959), the Court quoted the *Worcester* precedent when ruling that the state courts were not the proper venue for the collection of debts when both parties lived on Indian land, even if one party was not an Indian. The Court held that the tribal courts had exclusive jurisdiction over such disputes. The *Williams* decision provided a precedent for several rulings that further recognized elements of Indian sovereignty, especially the right to tax, to regulate businesses, to police, and to exercise local self-government.

SOVEREIGNTY ISSUES AFTER 1968

By the late 1960's, the idea of termination had few supporters, and Congress was again ready to increase the self-determination of the tribes. The Civil Rights Act of 1968 contained provisions that prohibited the states from assuming most forms of jurisdiction on tribal lands (amending but not repealing Public Law 280). The statute also established the Indian Bill of Rights (IBR), which stipulated that most provisions in the Bill of Rights and the Fourteenth Amendment's equal protection clause were binding on tribal governments. Tribal lawyers were happy that IBR excluded the religious establishment clause, for religion was an integral part of many Native American cultures. They nevertheless were opposed to enforcement of the IBR in federal courts, for they feared that non-Indian judges would disrespect principles of tribal law that had been handed down from generations immemorial.

Tribal lawyers, therefore, were generally pleased with the Court's decision in the gender-discrimination suit *Santa Clara Pueblo v. Martinez* (1978), which held that the IBR did not authorize individuals to sue the tribes in federal courts because the Congress had not explicitly authorized such suits. The Court reasoned that the tribes, as "semi-sovereign nations," retained their rights to sovereign immunity unless "unequivocally" removed by federal legislation. The decision strengthened tribal self-determination, but at the cost of allowing tribal courts, if so inclined, to ignore the individual rights enumerated in the IBR. As a result of the decision, the power of the federal courts to enforce the IBR has been limited to habeas corpus relief for persons held in tribal custody. Advocates of women's rights have frequently expressed discontent with the outcome of the *Martinez* ruling.

Rather than following general doctrines, the Supreme Court has tended to opt for a case-by-case approach when deciding issues of Native American sovereignty. In *White Mountain Apache v. Bracker* (1980), the Court struck down state motor license and fuel-use taxes on a non-Indian corporation operating Indian country. Writing for the Court, Justice Thurgood Marshall acknowledged that federal Indian law "is not dependent upon mechanical or absolute conceptions of state or tribal sovereignty, but has called for a particularized inquiry into the nature of the state, federal, and tribal interests at stake."

This case-by-case approach in federal Indian law sometimes has led to apparent inconsistencies and provided little guidance for lower courts. In *United States v. Wheeler* (1978), the Court reaffirmed that the criminal trial of an Indian in federal court, after he had been convicted in a tribal court, did not amount to double jeopardy, because the tribes, like the states, were separate sovereign entities. The majority opinion noted that the tribes "still possess those aspects of sovereignty not withdrawn by treaty or statute." However, in *Washington v. Confederated Tribes* (1980), the Court upheld the right of the states to collect sales taxes on cigarettes and other products sold to non-Indians on reservations. In *Rice v. Rehner* (1983), the Court further dealt tribal sovereignty a stunning blow when it upheld concurrent tribal and state regulations of alcoholic beverages. However, in *Ramah Navajo School Board v. Board of Revenue* (1982), the Court struck down a state tax on non-Indian corporation buildings located on tribal lands.

Native American lawyers tended to view Chief Justice William H. Rehnquist, a transplanted Arizonan, as a proponent of a western anti-Indian jurisprudence. They were particularly critical of his opinion in *Oliphant v. Suquamish* (1981), a case that involved a white man convicted of disorderly conduct by a tribal court. Overturning his conviction, the Rehnquist Court utilized a "balancing test" and held that the Indian nations, despite their sovereignty, had no criminal jurisdiction over non-Indians. The *Oliphant* ruling, which recognized the doctrine of "dependent sovereignty," was extended to regulations of hunting and fishing in *Montana v. United States* (1981), and it was subsequently applied to cases involving other sovereignty-related issues, such as taxation and commerce.

The Rehnquist Court's decision in *Cabazon Band of Mission Indians v. California* (1987), however, was largely responsible for bringing about Indian gaming casinos on a massive scale. In this case, a majority of the justices agreed that the doctrine of tribal sovereignty implied that the states could not prohibit high-stakes bingo games on the reservations. The decision was accompanied by an expansive opinion recognizing the right of the tribes to control their own economies within a national framework, so long as federal interests were not impaired. Responding to this seminal decision, Congress enacted the Indian Gaming Regulatory Act of 1988, which stipulates that the tribes have the right to offer any form of gambling permitted anywhere within the state where the tribal land is located. The statute has had tremendous financial consequences. By the beginning of the twenty-first century, the tribes were operating more than 150 casinos in half the states, generating an estimated six to eight billion dollars of business a year. A few tribes located near large cities, most notably in Minneapolis, became quite wealthy, although the casinos were of little benefit to those tribes that were located in isolated parts of the country.

The 1988 statute required the states to negotiate with the tribes in "good faith" in order to establish "tribal-state compacts" for the creation and regulation of gambling casinos. When the governor of Florida refused to negotiate such a compact, the Seminole tribe brought suit in federal court. In the resulting case of *Seminole Tribe of Florida v. Florida* (1996), the Court ruled five to four that the tribes were unable to sue a state without its consent. The five-member majority based its decision on the sovereign immunity of the states under the Eleventh Amendment, a decision that demonstrated the inherent conflict between tribal sovereignty and the sovereignty of the fifty states. Clearly the majority of justices in the Rehnquist Court showed more concern for the latter than the former. In spite of this ruling, however, Native Americans often had the option of seeking permission from the Department of the Interior to open casinos.

The justices entered into an interesting debate about ambiguity of Native American sovereignty in the case of *United States v. Lara* (2004), when the Supreme Court ruled that the tribal courts could render a criminal penalty against a visiting Indian belonging to another tribe. Writing the opinion for the majority, Justice Stephen G. Breyer based the ruling on both a federal statute and the inherent sovereignty of the tribes. "The Constitution," he declared, "grants Congress broad general powers to legislate in respect to Indian tribes, powers that we have consistently described as 'plenary and exclusive.'" Dissenting, Justice Clarence Thomas complained that the jurisprudence on Indian sovereignty was "schizophrenic," insisting that the concepts of inherent tribal sovereignty and plenary congressional power were contradictory with each other. David H. Souter, on the other hand, emphasized the role of judicial precedents rather than abstract logic in Indian jurisprudence, and he commented that "conceptualizations of sovereignty and dependent sovereignty are largely rhetorical."

John R. Hermann
Revised and updated by the Editor

FURTHER READING

For a basic understanding of Native American law and sovereignty, readers should consult Stephen Pevar's *The Rights of Indians and Tribes* (3d ed. Carbondale: Southern Illinois University Press, 2002) and Vine Deloria, Jr., and Clifford M. Lytle's *American Indians, American*

Justice (Austin: University of Texas Press, 1983). A detailed pro-Indian analysis of the sovereignty issue can be found in David Wilkins and K. Tsianina Lomawaima's *Uneven Ground: American Indian Sovereignty and Federal Law* (Norman: University of Oklahoma Press, 2001). For a provocative pro-Indian account of the relationship between the tribes and constitutional rights, visit John R. Wunder's *"Retained by the People": A History of American Indians and the Bill of Rights* (New York: Oxford University Press, 1994).

Sidney Harring has written a fascinating book that combines cultural and legal materials: *Crow Dog's Case* (New York: Cambridge University Press, 1994). For an extensive evaluation of the fifteen Court cases that had the most adverse influence on Native American sovereignty, consult David Eugene Wilkins's *American Indian Sovereignty and the United States Supreme Court: The Masking of Justice* (Austin: University of Texas Press, 1997). Robert Williams, Jr., has written a somewhat extreme but interesting analysis: *Like a Loaded Weapon: The Rehnquist Court, Indian Rights and the Legal History of Racism in America* (Minneapolis: University of Minnesota Press, 2005).

SEE ALSO *Johnson and Graham's Lessee v. McIntosh*; Marshall, John; Native American treaties; *Worcester v. Georgia*.

Native American Treaties

DESCRIPTION: Native Americans' rights under U.S. law are primarily defined by treaties, which are, in turn, usually defined in international law as formal contracts between nations.

SIGNIFICANCE: Treaties signed between the United States and various Native American nations (372 of which were ratified by the Senate through 1871) have been a major source of litigation before the Supreme Court since the 1830's.

Article III of the U.S. Constitution specifies that the judicial power of the Supreme Court extends to all cases involving the Constitution, federal laws, and treaties. Article VI declares that the "supreme law of the land" includes the Constitution as well as valid congressional statutes and valid treaties, the latter two having equal weight and authority. Whenever a statute and a treaty come in conflict, as sometimes happens, the courts will apply the one that was most recently enacted. Contrary to what is sometimes said, the treaties did not promise to continue "as long as the water will flow and the grass will grow." If treaties were not necessarily meant to endure in perpetuity, however, the courts assume that they continue to be enforceable until such time as Congress clearly and explicitly declares their termination. The Court has insisted that treaties cannot be abrogated in "a backhanded way."

U.S. laws regarding Native Americans provide one of the major taproots of American jurisprudence. According to one legal scholar, between 1970 and 1981, the Supreme Court interpreted twenty-two laws written before 1800, and eight of those laws involved Native Americans. Of the twenty-nine Court interpretations of laws written between 1800 and 1850 that the Court ruled on between 1970 and 1981, fourteen involved Native Americans. Between 1970 and 1981, the Court ruled on a total of 182 laws passed between 1850 and 1875; thirty-two of those laws involved Native Americans. Overall, roughly one-quarter of the legal interpretations from the first century of U.S. law involved Native Americans. Among subject areas of law, only the civil rights statutes of the Reconstruction era have been referenced more often by the Court.

THE MARSHALL TRILOGY

Chief Justice John Marshall's rulings occupy a special place in the development of Native American law. They provided the foundations for later arguments about sovereignty as well as justifications for the harsh approaches to the survivors of the "westward movement." The term "Marshall Trilogy" refers to the principles in his three major opinions on Native American issues: *Johnson and Graham's Lessee v. McIntosh* (1823), *Cherokee Nation v. Georgia* (1831), and *Worcester v. Georgia* (1832). Through these decisions, Marshall conceived a model that can be broadly described as recognition for generally autonomous tribal governments that are subject to an overriding federal authority but essentially free of control by the state governments. Key concepts of the Marshall Trilogy have been interpreted by lawyers,

Native Americans began making treaties with European settlers during the colonial era. Here William Penn, the founder of Pennsylvania, is shown meeting with representatives of an unnamed Indian society during the late seventeenth century. (Library of Congress)

judges, legal scholars, and government officials in many different ways through more than a century and a half.

The 1823 *McIntosh* decision, which dealt with a dispute over land ownership, was the first case in which the Supreme Court defined the relationship between Native Americans and the United States. The Court unanimously held that Indians could not legally transfer land to individuals or to any foreign country, but only to the United States government. In discussing the issue, Marshall explained that the United States acquired absolute title to North American lands as a result of Great Britain's discovery and conquest of the area. Native Americans, on the other hand, had only a lesser right of occupancy, which could be abolished by either conquest or treaty.

In *Cherokee Nation v. Georgia* (1831), the Court held that the Cherokee nation, since it was not an independent country, had no standing in federal court to challenge the state of Georgia's seizure of its lands. Defining the "peculiar" status of the tribes, Marshall wrote that they were "under the sovereignty and dominion of the United States," and referred to them as "dependent domestic nations."

A year later, in *Worcester v. Georgia*, the Court overturned the imprisonment of Samuel Worcester, a missionary who had worked with the Cherokee without obtaining the license required by a state law. Marshall wrote that the state had violated three legal principles: the commerce clause of the Constitution, the treaties between the Cherokee and the federal government, and the residual sovereignty of the Cherokee nation. In contrast to his earlier opinion, he emphasized the word "nation" more than the word "dependent." He observed, moreover, that Americans of European ancestry had long applied the words "treaty" and "nation" to Indian relationships just as the words had been applied "to the other nations of the earth; they are applied to all in the same sense." The *Worcester* ruling would later provide a theoretical precedent to claim that treaties were contracts between two sovereign governments.

There were considerable differences and tensions between Marshall's *Johnson* and *Cherokee Nation* opinions and his *Worcester* opinion. The first two opinions emphasized congressional power and Native American dependency, while the third opinion focused primarily on Native American sovereign and treaty rights. Since the time that Marshall issued the trilogy, the Supreme Court has sometimes endorsed the one viewpoint, sometimes the other.

INDIAN TREATIES SINCE 1871

The practice of treaty making between the Indian tribes and the federal government ended with the Appropriations Act of 1871. The major reason for the statute was that the House of Representatives, which had no role in the treaty process, wanted to exercise more control over the expenditures of moneys on Native American concerns. The statute meant that subsequent dealings with Indians would be through agreements, and it specified that no treaty rights would be abrogated as a result of the statute. Whatever the intent of the law, it later turned out that there would be little difference between ratified treaties and agreements that had to be approved by Congress, since they were equally part of the supreme law of the land. In the case of *Antoine v. Washington* (1975), the Court explicitly declared that the change from treaties to agreements "in no way affected Congress's plenary power."

One of the most widely quoted of the treaty decisions is *Lone Wolf v. Hitchcock* (1903). One of the principal chiefs of the Kiowa people, Lone Wolf had sought an injunction to block congressional ratification of an agreement allotting tribal lands. He argued that the agreement violated the Treaty of Medicine Lodge of 1867, which required the approval of three-fourths of the adult men of the tribe for any cession of tribal land. The Supreme Court unanimously rejected Lone Wolf's argument. Justice Edward D. White's opinion stated that Congress had exercised total jurisdiction over tribal affairs "from the beginning" and that the Court must presume the "perfect good faith" of the Congress. He declared that Congress possessed plenary power over Indian property "by reason of its exercise of guardianship over their interests." Since treaties dealt with political questions, an Indian tribe would have no right to judicial review if Congress should decide to unilaterally modify or even abrogate a treaty. Congress was even empowered to take tribal property reserved in treaties without respecting the just compensation clause of the Fifth Amendment. Although *Lone Wolf* has sometimes been called "the Indians' *Dred Scott*," it has never been overturned.

Some of the most contested treaty cases that have come before the Supreme Court involve natural resources, including rights to water and rights to hunt and fish. In *Winters v. United States* (1908), the Court held that the creation of a reservation implies sufficient access to water to support the purpose of the reservation. In the West, where water supplies are in short supply, *Winters* means that every Native American tribe holds extensive rights to water, with priority based on the date the reservation was established. In dealing with resources, the Supreme Court has not always taken the side of Native Americans. In the case of *United States v. Dion* (1986), for example, the Court held that Indian treaty rights to hunt bald eagles had been abrogated by both the Bald Eagle Protection and Endangered Species Acts. Although the two statutes did not explicitly state that Congress had intended to abrogate such treaty provisions, the Court found that the statutes clearly and unambiguously indicated that the prohibition on hunting eagles would apply to everyone without exception.

Many of the early nineteenth century treaties reserved the right of Native Americans to fish and hunt in lands off the reservations, commonly using the phrase "usual and accustomed grounds." At the time, these provisions rarely attracted much notice because reservations tended to be located in sparsely populated regions. In the twentieth century, however, as the country became more densely populated, the issue of fishing and hunting rights has sometimes produced heated controversy. As early as *United States v. Winans* (1905) the Court ruled that the state governments had no authority to regulate the fishing rights found in treaties.

Conflict between Indians and non-Indians in the salmon fisheries of Washington State became particularly bitter and sometimes violent. In 1968, the Supreme Court upheld rulings in the federal district court recognizing that members of the Puyallup tribe had the right to fish in "usual and accustomed grounds." However, a few years later the Court upheld a ruling that allowed the state to prohibit net fishing for the purpose of conservation. The Court noted that a treaty provision could not be allowed to result in the depletion of a scarce resource. The relevant treaty of 1855 had stipulated that Indians had the "right of taking fish . . . in common with citizens." In 1974, district judge George Boldt interpreted these ambiguous words to mean that Native Americans had the right to take 50 percent of the allowable catch of their fishing regions. Throughout the Pacific Northwest non-Indians were infuriated by Boldt's ruling, especially after the Supreme Court upheld the ruling in the controversial case of *Washington v. Washington State Commercial Passenger Fishing Vessel Association* (1979).

Angry controversies about treaty fishing rights also occurred in the northern Midwest. In 1987, district judge Barbara Crabb of Wisconsin ruled that the Ojibwas' off-reservations fishing rights in northern Wisconsin had never been explicitly abrogated, despite the fact that the more recent treaties had not mentioned anything about fishing. In a subsequent ruling Crabb followed the Boldt precedent in allowing the Ojibwa to take 50 percent of the allowable catch of their fishing region. The Supreme Court upheld the rulings. During the so-called Walleye War of 1988-1991, angry white protestors hurled insults at Ojibwa fishermen. Signs appeared, "Save a walleye, spear an Ojibwa." The conflict eventually diminished after the governor and the Ojibwa reached an agreement that neither side could appeal. Another bitter controversy occurred in Minnesota after the Supreme Court upheld a lower court's judgment in *Minnesota v. Mille Lacs Band of Chippewa Indians* (1999), which recognized that the hunting and fishing rights under an 1837 treaty had not been explicitly abrogated by a later treaty.

Over the years the Supreme Court has developed a number of principles for interpreting treaties, often called "canons of construction," that tend to favor the Indian perspective. In the case of *Carpenter v. Shaw* (1930), for example, the Court's majority declared that "doubtful expressions are to be resolved in favor of the weak and defenseless people who are wards of the nation, dependent upon its protection and good faith." Another rule is that treaties should be interpreted as Native Americans understood them at the time of their negotiations. Not all justices on the Supreme Court, however, have accepted the validity of these canons of construction.

Bruce E. Johansen
Revised and updated by the Editor

FURTHER READING

A good starting point is general reference works on treaties, such as Charles Phillips and Alan Axelrod's *Encyclopedia of Historical Treaties and Alliances* (2d ed. New York: Facts On File, 2005) and *U.S. Laws, Acts, and Treaties* (3 vols. Pasadena, Calif.: Salem Press, 2003), edited by Timothy L. Hall. The most reliable and comprehensive historical account of the subject is in Frances Paul Prucha's *American Indian Treaties: The History of a Political Anomaly* (Berkeley: University of California Press, 1994). For the historical and philosophical context of treaty issues, see Charles F. Wilkinson's *American Indians, Time, and the Law: Native Societies in a Modern Constitutional Democracy* (New Haven, Conn.: Yale University Press, 1987).

The most detailed analysis of Marshall's rulings is in Jill Norgen's *The Cherokee Cases* (Norman: University of Oklahoma Press, 2004). Fay Cohen has written a fascinating account of a recent conflict in *Treaties on Trial: The Continuing Controversy over Northwest Indian Fishing Rights* (Seattle: University of Washington Press, 1988). For current treaty issues, see Bruce Johansen's *Enduring Legacies: Native American Treaties and Contemporary Controversies* (Westport, Conn.: Greenwood Press, 2004). Many important articles on treaties have appeared in the *American Indian Law Review*, published by the law school of the University of Oklahoma.

See also *Johnson and Graham's Lessee v. McIntosh*; Marshall, John; Native American sovereignty; Treaties; *Worcester v. Georgia*.

Natural Law

DESCRIPTION: A "higher law" that, according to some political philosophers, applies to all human beings everywhere, is discoverable by reason alone, and is a standard by which to evaluate the laws made by human beings.
SIGNIFICANCE: Considerable debate continues regarding whether a "higher law" exists and whether the Supreme Court should rely on it in interpreting the U.S. Constitution.

Natural law is best understood in contrast to positive law and to divine law. Positive law is that made by human beings; it may differ widely from one society to the next. Divine law is that set down in religious teachings; it often strongly influences the laws made by human beings and is said to be knowable only through revelation.

According to philosophers, natural law, unlike divine law, is knowable through the use of reason alone, via the human ability to reflect on the nature of the world and on other people. Because nature is universal, natural law is universal. It therefore stands as a body of "higher law" in relation to the laws made by human beings. According to the doctrine of natural law, positive law is just or morally right to the extent that it reflects the natural law.

Locke and Hobbes
Although the idea of natural law was first elaborated by the ancient Greeks and Romans and given its fullest premodern expression in the philosophy of the medieval philosopher Saint Thomas Aquinas,

the concept of natural law that most affected U.S. jurisprudence derives primarily from the political philosophy of John Locke. Together with other Enlightenment philosophers such as Thomas Hobbes, Samuel von Pufendorf, and Hugo Grotius, Locke transformed the classical and medieval understandings of natural law. This transformation was made possible on the basis of a fundamentally new conception of nature and its relationship to the human world of politics.

Ancient and medieval political philosophy shared the view that human beings are by nature political animals. Modern political philosophy, beginning with Niccolò Machiavelli and Hobbes, broke with this view, arguing that human beings are not naturally political. According to Hobbes, for example, life in the state of nature is "solitary, poor, nasty, brutish, and short." In the state of nature, no sovereign exists; each person must compete against all others. Competition, scarcity, the desire for glory, and fear for one's life make existence in the natural state terrifying. Although people are free in the state of nature to do what they desire, they cannot possibly enjoy this unlimited freedom. They have rights—natural rights—in the state of nature, but they cannot enjoy them. Therefore, they consent to form a "social compact"; they give up their unlimited freedom to be ruled in civil society so that they might enjoy a prosperous peace and comfortable self-preservation. People's natural desire to preserve themselves is thus fulfilled in the most rational manner possible by following what Locke termed the "first and fundamental natural law." This law commands the preservation of the society and everyone in it. Even the sovereign power that makes human laws is governed by this natural law.

NATURAL LAW AND U.S. LAW

The concept of natural law finds expression in the opening sentence of the Declaration of Independence (1776), which justifies the American Revolution in terms of an appeal to "the laws of nature and of nature's God." Following the philosophy of Locke, the laws of nature are transformed into natural rights: All human beings are endowed with the inalienable rights to life, liberty, property, and the pursuit of happiness, and all are equal insofar as they possess these inalienable rights. The purpose of government is to protect people's rights, and all legitimate government is based on the consent of the governed.

The idea of a body of "higher law," whether it takes the form of natural laws or natural rights, has been powerfully influential in U.S. jurisprudence, particularly in the context of interpreting the vague due process and equal protection clauses of the Fourteenth Amendment. In a number of famous cases, particularly *Calder v. Bull* (1798) and *Adamson v. California* (1947), the Supreme Court debated whether there is any "higher law" or are any "principles of natural justice" that should determine how the Constitution is to be interpreted. The issue was also hotly debated in the 1991 Senate hearings to confirm Court nominee Clarence Thomas. The issue of the existence of a "higher law" raises the question of how much latitude the Court has

The concept of natural law that has most influenced American law was developed by political philosopher John Locke, pictured here. (Library of Congress)

to read substantive moral values into the Constitution. Critics of the idea of a "higher law" interpretation of the Constitution fear that such a doctrine would allow justices to read their own moral values into the Constitution and would make the judiciary too powerful in its ability to override the will of the people as expressed by their national and state governments.

Patrick Malcolmson

FURTHER READING

Abadinsky, Howard. *Law and Justice: An Introduction to the American Legal System.* 5th ed. Chicago: Nelson-Hall, 2003.

Arkes, Hadley. *Beyond the Constitution.* Princeton, N.J.: Princeton University Press, 1990.

Berns, Walter. "Judicial Review and the Rights and Laws of Nature." In *The Supreme Court Review 1982*, edited by Phillip Kurland, Gerhard Casper, and Dennis Hutchinson. Chicago: University of Chicago Press, 1983.

Corwin, Edward S. *The "Higher Law" Background of American Constitutional Law.* Ithaca, N.Y.: Cornell University Press, 1955.

Fried, Charles. *Saying What the Law Is: The Constitution in the Supreme Court.* Cambridge, Mass.: Harvard University Press, 2004.

Gerber, Scott. *To Secure These Rights: The Declaration of Independence and Constitutional Interpretation.* New York: New York University Press, 1995.

Grey, Thomas. "Do We Have an Unwritten Constitution?" *Stanford Law Review* 27 (1975): 703.

Locke, John. *Essays on the Law of Nature.* Oxford, England: Clarendon Press, 1954.

Ritchie, Donald A., and JusticeLearning.org. *Our Constitution.* New York: Oxford University Press, 2006.

Willoughby, Westel Woodbury. *The Supreme Court of the United States: Its History and Influence in Our Constitutional System.* Union, N.J.: Lawbook Exchange, 2001.

SEE ALSO *Adamson v. California; Calder v. Bull;* Fourteenth Amendment; Judicial activism; Thomas, Clarence.

Near v. Minnesota

CITATION: 283 U.S. 697
DATE: January 30, 1931
ISSUES: Freedom of the press; prior restraint
SIGNIFICANCE: The Supreme Court for the first time applied the First Amendment guarantee of freedom of the press to state governments under the incorporation doctrine under the Fourteenth Amendment.

J. M. Near published a newspaper in Minneapolis and St. Paul, Minnesota, which denounced local government officials—particularly Jews—for graft and corruption. In the absence of applicable federal statutes, Minnesota authorities sought to use state statutes to prevent Near from publishing his newspaper. When the case reached the Supreme Court, there were two major issues involved. The first was whether the Bill of Rights applied to state laws. The second was whether prior restraint was justified. Despite the despicable character of Near's views, the Court rejected any prior restraint on newspapers and applied the freedom of press portion of the First Amendment to state governments under the incorporation doctrine under the Fourteenth Amendment. Near did not have a strong personal reputation, but his cause was taken up by Robert McCormick, owner of the *Chicago Tribune,* as an important case involving freedom of the press. With McCormick's financial help, the case reached the Court, where freedom of the press prevailed. *Near* remains the landmark case regarding prior restraint.

Richard L. Wilson

SEE ALSO First Amendment; Fourteenth Amendment; *Hustler Magazine v. Falwell;* Incorporation doctrine; *New York Times Co. v. Sullivan; New York Times Co. v. United States;* Speech and press, freedom of.

Nelson Samuel

IDENTIFICATION: Associate justice (February 27, 1845-November 28, 1872)

NOMINATED BY: John Tyler

BORN: November 10, 1792, Hebron, New York

DIED: December 13, 1873, Cooperstown, New York

SIGNIFICANCE: Associate Justice Nelson participated in important Supreme Court cases dealing with slavery and the Civil War.

Samuel Nelson began practicing law in 1817. He served as a state judge in New York from 1823 to 1831, when he was appointed to the state supreme court. He was nominated to the Supreme Court by President John Tyler in 1845 and quickly approved by the Senate.

Nelson was an authority on international law, maritime law, and patent law. He wrote hundreds of opinions for the Court, often dealing with technical aspects. His opinion in *Scott v. Sandford* (1857)

Samuel Nelson. (Handy Studios/ Collection of the Supreme Court of the United States)

avoided the controversial issue of whether the federal government could forbid slavery in new territories. This opinion, originally intended to be the majority opinion of the Court, was replaced by a stronger opinion written by Chief Justice Roger Brooke Taney that denied the federal government this power.

In the *Prize Cases* (1863), involving a blockade of Confederate ports ordered by President Abraham Lincoln during the Civil War (1861-1865), Nelson dissented from the majority by declaring that only Congress, not the president, could declare war. In *Ex parte Milligan* (1866), Nelson agreed with the majority in reversing a military commission's decision to hang a civilian convicted of treason, declaring that a jury trial was necessary.

Rose Secrest

SEE ALSO Chase, Salmon P.; Civil War; *Milligan, Ex parte*; *Scott v. Sandford*; Slavery; Taney, Roger Brooke.

New Deal

DATE: 1933-1938

DESCRIPTION: President Franklin D. Roosevelt's Depression-era legislative program to boost the economy, initially assaulted as unconstitutional but later upheld after Roosevelt threatened to pack the Supreme Court.

SIGNIFICANCE: Roosevelt's New Deal and challenge to the Court's authority increased the power of the executive branch of the government, expanded overall federal power, and replaced constitutional formalism with reform jurisprudence.

In the mid-1930's, Franklin D. Roosevelt's New Deal, a combination of emergency legislation and a liberal reform agenda designed to end the Great Depression, encountered a conservative Supreme Court led by Chief Justice Charles Evans Hughes. Much of early New Deal legislation contained emergency clauses designed to get around the Court's formalism and strict constructionism and to justify socioeconomic engineering. In 1934 the Roosevelt administration seemed relieved when the Court upheld two state regulatory laws.

However, in January, 1935, the Court invalidated the "hot oil" provision (section 9c) of the 1933 National Industrial Recovery Act (NIRA), arguing that the law wrongly gave legislative authority to the executive branch. After a reprieve in the *Gold Clause Cases* (March, 1935), the New Deal received a further blow in May, when the Court invalidated the Railway Retirement Act of 1934. Then on May 27, 1935, known as Black Monday, three separate 9-0 decisions declared unconstitutional the NIRA (*Schechter Poultry Corp. v. United States*) and the Frazier-Lemke Farm Bankruptcy Act of 1934 (*Louisville Joint Stock Land Bank v. Radford*) and voided presidential removal of regulatory commission members (*Humphrey's Executor v. United States*). Even the liberal justices—Louis D. Brandeis, Benjamin N. Cardozo, and Harlan Fiske Stone—voted with the majority in holding that the NIRA violated intrastate commerce laws and delegated legislative power to the executive.

The Court and President Roosevelt had different parameters concerning the permissible degree of government regulation. The president attacked the Court's decisions as "horse-and-buggy" thinking, rewrote legislation to circumvent the Court's objections, and in 1935 expanded his social reform agenda with the Social Security Act, National Labor Relations Act (Wagner Act), and Guffy Coal Act. The Supreme Court refused to capitulate and, in 1936, overturned the Agricultural Adjustment Act (1933) and the Guffy Coal Act and struck down a New York State minimum-wage law. This time, however, the Court's three liberals dissented strongly, with Justice Stone proclaiming the entire session disastrous.

Following his landslide reelection in 1936, aware that no justice was planning to retire and sure that the Wagner and Social Security Acts were threatened, Roosevelt declared war on the Court. After numerous verbal assaults, including charges that the Court imperiled American democracy, and after considering numerous options, he decided to reform the Court by statute. Charging the Court with old age and inefficiency, Roosevelt in February, 1937, announced his plan to add six new justices.

Despite the hugely divisive effect of the Court-packing plan on the public, Congress, and the Democratic Party, Roosevelt stood firm.

President Franklin D. Roosevelt addressing a joint session of Congress, along with members of the Supreme Court, cabinet members, and the diplomat corps, on the 150th anniversary of the founding of Congress. By this time, he had won most of his battles with the Court over the constitutionality of his New Deal programs. (Library of Congress)

Within months of his announcement, the Court reversed itself on a minimum-wage law and then upheld the Wagner and Social Security Acts, with Owen J. Roberts and Hughes joining the liberals. These decisions, plus Justice Willis Van Devanter's announcement of his retirement, defused the Court-packing crisis. Roosevelt claimed a victory, and the Court preserved its independence.

By 1940 the Court's turbulent New Deal era had ended. Departures from the Court would enable Roosevelt to appoint eight new justices, and the so-called "Roosevelt Court" upheld all later New Deal legislation.

Ken Millen-Penn

FURTHER READING

Leuchtenburg, William E. *The Supreme Court Reborn: The Constitutional Revolution in the Age of Roosevelt.* New York: Oxford University Press, 1995.

Hockett, Jeffrey. *New Deal Justice: The Constitutional Jurisprudence of Hugo L. Black, Felix Frankfurter, and Robert H. Jackson.* New York: Rowman & Littlefield, 1996.

McKenna, Marian C. *Franklin Roosevelt and the Great Constitutional War: The Court-Packing Crisis of 1937.* New York: Fordham University Press, 2002.

Pusey, Merlo John. *The Supreme Court Crisis.* New York: Da Capo Press, 1973.

Shaw, Stephen K., ed. *Franklin D. Roosevelt and the Transformation of the Supreme Court.* Armonk, N.Y.: M. E. Sharpe, 2004.

SEE ALSO Court-packing plan; Hughes, Charles Evans; Separation of powers; Stone, Harlan Fiske; *West Coast Hotel Co. v. Parrish.*

New York Times Co. v. Sullivan

CITATION: 376 U.S. 254
DATE: March 9, 1964
ISSUE: Libel
SIGNIFICANCE: The Supreme Court redefined freedom of the press by requiring that someone wishing to recover damages from a newspaper for a false story had to show that the newspaper had actual malice or a reckless disregard for the truth.

The New York Times printed an advertisement appealing for funds for civil rights organizations that included technically false statements about Montgomery, Alabama, police commissioner Sullivan. The Supreme Court was asked to rule on a half-million dollar civil damage award to Sullivan. There was no showing that the *Times* had any actual malice or reckless disregard for the truth in printing the statements. The most that could be alleged was that the *Times* was negligent.

The Court's unanimous decision in favor of the newspaper gave vastly greater protection to the news media from libel suits resulting from the publication of factual errors. In his opinion for the Court, Justice William J. Brennan, Jr., pointed out that allowing the damage award from the Alabama courts would provoke greater fear than criminal prosecution. Sullivan could show no monetary loss, but the newspaper would face a loss one thousand times greater than the maximum fine under Alabama criminal statutes. Because double jeopardy protection does not exist in civil litigation, other awards could be levied against the newspaper for the same advertisement. Fear of successive monetary losses would stifle the press, Brennan argued. The Court prohibited public officials from recovering damages for a defamatory falsehood relating to their official conduct unless they proved that the statement was made with actual malice—that is, with knowledge it was false or with a reckless disregard for whether it was false or not.

As a result, it became extraordinarily difficult for public officials to ever win a damage suit against a newspaper or television station, no matter how false or defamatory the statements against them were. The same situation also confronts those people who are defined as "public figures." A public figure, for purposes of defamation law, is a person who "thrusts himself into a public controversy in order to affect its outcome." An otherwise little-known person unwillingly caught up in a matter of public interest is not a public official and thus need prove only negligence (not actual malice) to prevail against a defamer, according to *Wolston v. Reader's Digest Association* (1979). "Public figure" is a more vague term than "public official," and for that reason, the Court has had to deal with a large number of libel suits involving people who believe they are ordinary citizens but whom the newspapers claim are public figures. Generally speaking, a public figure would be a movie star, a sports hero, or some other well-known person who had been mentioned in the press before a controversy arose. Presumably, the laws of libel apply to any ordinary citizen who is libeled or defamed by a newspaper, and private people are able to recover damages from newspapers or magazines.

Richard L. Wilson

SEE ALSO Brennan, William J., Jr.; Censorship; Double jeopardy; First Amendment; Libel; Seditious libel; Speech and press, freedom of; White, Byron R.

New York Times Co. v. United States

CITATION: 403 U.S. 713
DATE: June 30, 1971
ISSUES: Prior restraint; freedom of speech
SIGNIFICANCE: In this case, also known as the Pentagon Papers case,
the Supreme Court upheld the principle of no prior restraint, dis-
agreeing only on its application to the facts.

The Pentagon Papers case was only the second federal court case involving attempted prior restraint on the press—the first after *Near v.
Minnesota* (1931). The Pentagon Papers were several hundred pages
of top-secret documents prepared by the U.S. Defense Department at
the insistence of former secretary of defense Robert McNamara, who
wanted a study of all the documents that led to U.S. involvement in
the war in Vietnam. The documents revealed that McNamara and
other national leaders had misrepresented to Congress and the public many crucial facts involving the U.S. entrance into the war. They
also disclosed that the United States had arguably violated international law, then compounded the original violation by "punishing"
North Vietnam for what amounted to its legal response to U.S. actions in the Tonkin Bay incident.

Included among the documents were top-secret communications
between foreign governments and the United States, communications normally given exceptionally secret treatment because foreign
governments might retaliate for their disclosure by refusing to communicate their true position to U.S. leaders. The government had vi-
tal reasons for wanting to avoid publication, and the newspapers ob-
viously had important reasons to publish them as the scoop of the
decade.

All the Pentagon Papers were properly classified secret documents
and clearly stolen government property. The person who photocopied
the documents was Daniel Ellsberg, a semigovernmental think tank
employee required not to violate security clearances as a condition of
employment. Despite the criminal penalties for disclosing national se-
crets, Ellsberg believed that the public had a right to know what was in
these documents. After photocopying the papers, he gave them to *The

New York Times, the most prestigious daily newspaper in the United States. The *Times*, without any notice to the government, printed some of them in what it said would be a series of installments. Because the editors at the *Times* possessed the documents for a long time, did not return them to their proper governmental owners, and clandestinely prepared and precipitously published them, they clearly knew their actions might be considered as illegal as Ellsberg's had been.

In separate litigation, Ellsberg was prosecuted for stealing the documents, but the case was thrown out of court when it was discovered that President Richard M. Nixon had ordered a special team of burglars (the same ones who later caused the Watergate scandal) to break into the office of Ellsberg's psychiatrist, hoping to gain information to discredit him. Acting properly under the law that prohibits the government from pressing a prosecution when the government itself has violated the law, the judge dismissed the case. Failing to convict Ellsberg, the Justice Department decided it would be futile to proceed against the *Times*.

The government did not just want to convict Ellsberg, it also wanted to stop the damaging information before it got into the hands of the public by imposing a prior restraint on the publication of the Pentagon Papers. Despite the government's argument that national security would be compromised, it did not succeed in imposing a permanent prior restraint on newspapers. Almost immediately after the documents first appeared, government lawyers obtained an injunction blocking further publication, and the *Times* stopped publishing. Anticipating such events, someone had taken the precaution of distributing the Pentagon Papers to several other U.S. newspapers that were not so enjoined, and other newspapers started publishing the papers the next day. After much legal maneuvering, the cases were consolidated and prepared for immediate appeal to the Supreme Court.

When the Court ruled on the case, the vote went against the Nixon administration by a vote of six to three. All nine justices upheld the concept of no prior restraint, but they disagreed as to whether the restraint was justified by the extraordinary issues in this case. There was no majority opinion, and each justice wrote a separate opinion. Generally, three major groups of opinions can be distinguished, with four justices in one group, two justices in another, and three justices in a third group. The first group (Justices Hugo L. Black, William O. Douglas, William J. Brennan, Jr., and Thurgood Marshall) essentially maintained that the U.S. government had no right to impose prior restraints on newspapers. Marshall pointed out that the Nixon administration's case was further weakened because it could not rely on any duly passed congressional enactment and could only assert a vague presidential power. Some of the four maintained that it was wrong for a lower court to have given even a temporary restraining order, common as they are. Justices Potter Stewart and Byron R. White, who voted with the first four justices to allow publication of the Pentagon Papers to go forward, held that the presumption against prior restraint was too strong in this case but held open the option that someday the government might face such a grave danger that prior restraint might be justified. Chief Justices Warren E. Burger and Justices Harry A. Blackmun and John M. Harlan II maintained that they were opposed to prior restraint but requested more time to look at the documents before making a final judgment as to whether a permanent restraining order should be issued.

Richard L. Wilson

SEE ALSO Brennan, William J., Jr.; Censorship; First Amendment; *Near v. Minnesota*; Presidential powers; Speech and press, freedom of; Vietnam War; War and civil liberties.

New York v. Ferber

CITATION: 458 U.S. 747
DATE: July 2, 1982
ISSUE: Child pornography
SIGNIFICANCE: In this case, the Supreme Court held that erotic and sexually explicit depictions of children, whether obscene or indecent, have no protection under the First Amendment.

The state of New York, like nineteen other states, had a statute that criminalized the dissemination of materials depicting the sexual conduct of children under the age of sixteen, regardless of whether the material satisfied the legal definition of obscenity established by the Supreme Court in *Miller v. California* (1973). The owner of a Manhattan adult bookstore, Paul Ferber, was prosecuted and convicted for selling films that depicted young boys masturbating. However, the New York Court of Appeals reversed his conviction, holding that the state statute violated the First Amendment because it criminalized materials that were simply indecent, not obscene. The state then appealed the case to the Supreme Court.

The Court unanimously upheld Ferber's conviction in the lower New York court. Justice Byron R. White, writing for the Court, proclaimed that child pornography is "a category of material outside the protection of the First Amendment." He emphasized five points. First, the state has a compelling interest in safeguarding minor children from sexual abuse and exploitation. Second, the distribution of child pornography is intrinsically related to this abuse and exploitation. Third, the sexual abuse and exploitation of children is illegal everywhere in the United States. Fourth, child pornography has very modest literary, artistic, scientific, or educational value. Finally, the recognition that a category of material is outside of First Amendment protection is compatible with previous decisions of the Court.

Concluding that government has more discretion to prosecute child pornography than is true of adult pornography, White concluded that the standards may be less rigorous than the three-pronged test of the earlier *Miller* decision. He insisted, nevertheless, that state laws must clearly and explicitly define which kinds of photographs, films, and conduct are illegal. In a brief concurrence, Justice William J. Brennan, Jr., joined by Justice Thurgood Marshall, agreed that most child pornography did not merit First Amendment protection, but he nevertheless asserted that it would be unconstitutional to prosecute depictions of children that are of artistic or scientific value.

Thomas Tandy Lewis

SEE ALSO *Ashcroft v. Free Speech Coalition;* Censorship; First Amendment; Obscenity and pornography; *Roth v. United States/Alberts v. California.*

Ninth Amendment

DATE: 1791

DESCRIPTION: Amendment to the U.S. Constitution stating that the enumeration of certain rights in that document does not mean other, unenumerated rights should be denied.

SIGNIFICANCE: Relying on the Ninth Amendment, the Supreme Court did not confine itself to rights directly stated in the Constitution but also enforced unenumerated rights, including the right of privacy.

The Ninth Amendment is among the most enigmatic parts of the Bill of Rights. At one level, the thrust of the amendment is relatively clear. The Bill of Rights and other parts of the constitutional text do not contain an exhaustive listing of the people's rights. However, the questions of what other rights the Constitution protects and from whom, as well as who may enforce such rights and how they relate to delegated and reserved governmental powers, raise complex interpretive problems.

HISTORICAL ORIGINS AND EARLY INVOCATIONS

Federalist James Madison apparently drafted the amendment to address concerns that adding a bill of rights to the constitutional text might imply that the people held only the rights listed in that document. Claims that the people held other rights were often linked to a premise that the Constitution delegated limited powers to the federal government. Accordingly, the Ninth Amendment was viewed as a companion to the Tenth Amendment, which reserved for the states or the people all powers "not delegated to the United States by the

---

TEXT OF THE NINTH AMENDMENT

The enumeration in the Constitution, of certain rights, shall not be construed to deny or disparage others retained by the people.

Constitution, nor prohibited by it to the States."

Even before the Bill of Rights was ratified by three-fourths of the states, Madison relied on the terms of these two amendments to support arguments that Congress had no authority to establish a national bank. In debates within the House of Representatives on February 2, 1791, Madison claimed the Ninth Amendment "guard[ed] against a latitude of interpretation" and the Tenth Amendment "exclude[ed] every source of power not within the Constitution itself."

The Supreme Court's decision in *McCulloch v. Maryland* (1819) had implications for interpreting the Ninth and Tenth Amendments. In arguing that Congress had authority to establish a national bank, Chief Justice John Marshall rejected a narrow rule of construction for interpreting the Constitution's delegations of power. He argued instead that the Constitution gave Congress "vast powers," on whose execution "the happiness and prosperity of the nation so vitally depends."

Variations of this reasoning would eventually support expansive conceptions of federal power and correspondingly narrow conceptions of residuals—including reserved powers and retained rights. In *Fletcher v. Peck* (1810), however, Chief Justice Marshall suggested that judges might enforce unenumerated rights as limits on the states. In subsequent cases, the justices linked the idea of unenumerated rights to principles of limited federal power.

THE NINTH AMENDMENT AND SLAVERY

In *Scott v. Sandford* (1857), Chief Justice Roger Brooke Taney argued in his majority opinion that the Missouri Compromise Act of 1850 was invalid because it exceeded constitutional delegations, encroached on reserved powers, and abridged retained rights. Referring to rights of slave ownership, Taney wrote, "The powers over person and property of which we speak are not only not granted to Congress, but are in express terms denied, and they are forbidden to exercise them." More specifically, he argued that Congress "has no power over the person or property of a citizen but what the citizens of the United States have granted."

Reinforcing Taney's arguments, Justice John A. Campbell quoted statements made by the authors of the Constitution intended to assure Antifederalists that the federal government would be limited to certain enumerated powers. Despite these assurances, the Constitution's critics demanded an "explicit declaration" that the federal government would not assume powers not specifically delegated to it. As a result, Campbell said, the Ninth and Tenth Amendments were "designed to include the reserved rights of the States, and the people . . . and to bind the authorities, State and Federal . . . to their recognition and observance." Claiming faithfulness to these interpretive premises, Campbell denied that Congress had power to prohibit slavery in the territories.

The Civil War Amendments (especially the Thirteenth and Fourteenth) overturned the central holdings of *Scott* and formalized the results of the Civil War by invalidating slavery and making all native-born people, including African Americans, citizens. However, these changes, along with others, did not end controversy over the scope of delegated powers or their relationship to reserved and retained prerogatives. Accordingly, the justices continued to deal with the problems of constitutional construction that were at the heart of the Ninth Amendment.

TWENTIETH CENTURY PRECEDENTS

These problems came to a head again during the New Deal era. The mid-1930's inaugurated an increasingly deferential approach to assertions of national power and had corresponding implications for interpreting limitations on those powers. In this context, the Ninth Amendment made its first substantial appearance in a majority opinion for the Court.

In *Ashwander v. Tennessee Valley Authority* (1936), the justices upheld the operation of the Wilson Dam by the Tennessee Valley Authority, an agency of the U.S. government. Among other things, the plaintiffs argued that the sale of electric energy generated by the dam exceeded constitutional delegations of power and abridged rights protected by the Ninth Amendment. Chief Justice Charles Evans Hughes, writing the majority opinion, dismissed both arguments. Referring to the Ninth Amendment, he claimed that "the maintenance of rights retained by the people does not withdraw the rights which are expressly granted to the Federal Government. The question is as to the scope of the grant and whether there are inherent limitations which render invalid the disposition of property with which we are now concerned."

In this passage, Chief Justice Hughes relied on normative premises similar to those implicit in debates by the creators of the Constitution on matters of structure. Following Madison's example, the chief justice treated delegated powers and retained rights as mutually exclusive and reciprocally limiting prerogatives. However, Hughes suggested that a finding of delegated power precluded opposing claims of retained rights. He characterized the latter, like reserved powers, as residuals beyond the legitimate reach of federal delegations.

Eleven years later, Justice Stanley F. Reed commented further on the Ninth Amendment in his opinion for the majority in *United Public Workers v. Mitchell* (1947). In that case, the justices upheld a section of the Hatch Act (1939) that prohibited employees of the federal government from active participation in political campaigns. Reed accepted the employees' stance that "the nature of political rights reserved to the people by the Ninth and Tenth Amendments are involved. The rights claimed as inviolate may be stated as the right of a citizen to act as a party official or worker to further his own political views." The justice claimed, however, that "these fundamental human rights are not absolutes" and thus were subject to reasonable governmental restriction.

By this time, the Court had already enforced many of the guarantees of the Bill of Rights against the states through the Fourteenth Amendment's due process clause. In such cases, the Court repeatedly treated popular rights as "trumps" capable of preempting otherwise legitimate assertions of governmental power. The Court had also repeatedly interpreted enumerated rights as similar limitations on federal powers. In *Mitchell*, however, Justice Reed did not explore the possibility of judges' enforcing unenumerated rights as such limitations. Absent such a reconceptualization, the Ninth Amendment—along with the Tenth—would have diminished practical significance. Claims of unenumerated rights would be preempted by increasingly expansive conceptions of delegated powers.

THE RIGHT OF PRIVACY

In the 1960's, the Court first relied on the Ninth Amendment to enforce unenumerated rights as limits on state powers. The Court made this move in the landmark case of *Griswold v. Connecticut* (1965). The majority opinion, written by Justice William O. Douglas, invoked the Ninth along with the First, Third, Fourth, Fifth, and Fourteenth Amendments, to support the Court's invalidation of a state law prohibiting the use of contraceptives by married couples. According to Douglas, the state law abridged a right of privacy that was "older than the Bill of Rights." He presumed that the government's purpose was valid but suggested that the means chosen "swe[pt] unnecessarily broadly and thereby invade[d] the area of protected freedoms."

Justice Arthur J. Goldberg in his concurrence offered his view of the Ninth Amendment's relevance in this context. In the most extensive explicit analysis of the Ninth Amendment in a Court opinion to date, Goldberg reviewed commentary on the amendment by Madison and Joseph Story, along with judicial precedents enforcing fundamental liberties in addition to enumerated rights. His central claim was that the Ninth Amendment supported interpreting the Fourteenth Amendment as embracing unenumerated along with enumerated liberties.

Justice Hugo L. Black in his dissent criticized both the majority opinion and Justice Goldberg's concurrence. He denied that the Constitution protected a right of privacy and claimed that relying on the Ninth Amendment to enforce such a right against the states turned somersaults with history. He stated that the Ninth Amendment was added to constitutional text "to assure the people that the Constitution in all its provisions was intended to limit the Federal Government to the powers granted expressly or by necessary implication."

In *Roe v. Wade* (1973), the Court extended its holding in *Griswold*. Justice Harry A. Blackmun, in the majority opinion, wrote, "The right of privacy, whether it be founded in the Fourteenth Amendment's concept of personal liberty and restrictions upon state action, as we feel it is, or, as the District Court determined, in the Ninth Amendment's reservation of rights to the people, is broad enough to encompass a woman's decision whether or not to terminate her pregnancy."

Blackmun hesitated to rely squarely on the Ninth Amendment to strike down the challenged state law. Following Douglas and Goldberg's opinions in *Griswold*, however, he suggested connections between the Ninth and Fourteenth Amendments.

A SAVING CLAUSE

In *Richmond Newspapers v. Virginia* (1980), Chief Justice Warren E. Burger announced the Court's ruling that the First and Fourteenth Amendments guaranteed a right of the public and press to attend criminal trials. Burger relied on the Ninth Amendment to rebut arguments that such a right was not protected simply because it was nowhere spelled out in the Constitution. In his view, the Ninth Amendment was significant as a saving clause designed to allay fears that the explicit listing of certain guarantees could be interpreted as excluding others. The amendment prevented people from claiming that "the affirmation of particular rights implies a negation of those not expressly defined." Burger pointed out, moreover, that the Court repeatedly enforced fundamental rights going beyond those explicitly defined in the Constitution, including the rights of association, of privacy, to be presumed innocent, to travel freely, and to be judged by a standard of proof beyond a reasonable doubt in criminal trial.

It is impossible to ascertain with confidence the extent to which justices have relied on the Ninth Amendment as an interpretive guide but not cited it in their opinions. However, Chief Justice Burger's opinion in *Richmond Newspapers* is a reminder that justices have not confined themselves to protecting enumerated rights. They have also protected unenumerated rights and taken positions on what rights the people hold in connection with interpreting the character and scope of federal and state governmental powers.

Wayne D. Moore

FURTHER READING

The most comprehensive collection of materials on the Ninth Amendment is *The Rights Retained by the People: The History and Meaning of the Ninth Amendment* (2 vols. Fairfax, Va.: George Mason University Press, 1989-1993), edited by Randy E. Barnett. These two volumes include documentary sources, selections from books, reprints of law review articles, and a bibliography of writings on the amendment through 1992. Much of volume 2 reprints essays from a symposium on the amendment that were originally published in volume 64 of the *Chicago-Kent Law Review* (1988).

More recent works analyzing the Ninth Amendment include Calvin R. Massey's *Silent Rights: The Ninth Amendment and the Constitution's Unenumerated Rights* (Philadelphia: Temple University Press, 1995) and Wayne D. Moore's *Constitutional Rights and Powers of the People* (Princeton, N.J.: Princeton University Press, 1996). The latter explores premises of popular sovereignty and conceptions of constitutional structure, including how they inform interpretation of the Ninth Amendment. For a more current exploration of the same subject, see Larry D. Kramer's *The People Themselves: Popular Constitutionalism and Judicial Review* (New York: Oxford University Press, 2005).

SEE ALSO Abortion; Bill of Rights; Birth control and contraception; Campbell, John A.; Due process, substantive; Fourteenth Amendment; *Griswold v. Connecticut*; *McCulloch v. Maryland*; Privacy, right to; *Roe v. Wade*; Tenth Amendment.

Nominations to the Court

DESCRIPTION: Selection of candidates for an associate justice or chief justice position on the Supreme Court by the president. In each case, selection must be followed by confirmation (approval by a majority of the Senate).

SIGNIFICANCE: This process of nomination and confirmation is authorized by Article II, section 2, of the U.S. Constitution as the sole means by which any individual can become a member of the Court. Once on the Court, members have life tenure, although they can resign or be removed by impeachment.

This path to Court membership is essentially an American practice. It stems from historical precedent established in colonial times, when appointments by some governors required approval by their councils. Several state constitutions enacted under the Articles of Confederation provided for legislative endorsement of gubernatorial appointees.

Senate confirmation was adopted as a result of a compromise in the Constitutional Convention of 1787, and it applies to those nominated for positions in the executive branch and the lower federal courts, as well as all Supreme Court justices. Some delegates favored appointment by the president alone, others by the Senate alone, and still others by the president acting with an executive council chosen by the legislature. Arguing for compromise in *The Federalist* (1788) No. 76, Alexander Hamilton predicted the role of the Senate would be largely reactive and passive and that there would be "no difference between nominating and appointing." Although approval has been the norm, Hamilton's prediction has not always been accurate when applied to the process in practice.

Edward A. Bradford (1814-1872) was one of many nominees to the Court whose appointments failed for political reasons. Bradford was the first of three men whom President Millard Fillmore nominated to fill John McKinley's seat in 1852. Franklin Pierce eventually filled the seat after he became president in 1853. (Library of Congress)

The Constitution does not dictate the size of the Court, which is set by law. Membership fluctuated between five and ten justices from the founding of the republic in 1789 to 1869; in that year, the current number of nine was firmly established.

After 1789 the Senate has considered, on average, one Court nomination every two years, comparatively fewer than the other offices subject to Senate confirmation. However, these few nominations have been carefully considered in the Senate and highly publicized in the media, particularly in recent times, because of the underlying policy and political significance of the position and the long-term influence justices have.

PROCESS

Political parties have always played a central role in the confirmation process, as have members of the Senate Judiciary Committee and their staffs. In the early years of the Senate, unless a nominee was unknown or serious questions were raised about him, it was customary to act on nominations without sending them to committee for consideration. In 1868 the Senate amended its rules to require referral of each nomination to the Judiciary Committee, which held hearings (public since 1929), opening the process to interested groups and the media. Although the testimony of nominees, supporters, and opponents was once considered in subcommittees, nominations later began to be considered by the full committee. This reflects and intensifies the impact of the proceedings on committee members' opinion poll ratings in their home states and their chances for reelection or elevation to higher office.

Following a committee vote, the nomination is sent to the full Senate for consideration. After debate and action by the Senate, successful nominees assume office. At any step along the way, a nomination may be withdrawn by the president or challenged, blocked, postponed, or defeated by roll-call vote in the Senate.

DISCORD

Conflict has been a part of the process almost from the outset because of the perceived importance of nominations to the Court. Of all offices subject to Senate confirmation, Court positions are clearly the most controversial, as befits the justices' life tenure and their long-term impact on public policy. When a roll-call vote is taken, the more controversial nominees are those with ten or more senators recorded in opposition, and the most controversial of all are the small handful of those who are rejected.

Battles over nominations are the result of the impact of such developments as the direct election of senators, the growth of interest groups, the institutionalization of the confirmation process in the Senate, and the increasing openness of, and media attention to, Court nominees. In the twentieth century these battles came to be accompanied by circumstances that historically intensified controversy, such as divided governments and polarizing issues such as crime, race, and abortion.

Although more than 80 percent of those nominated to the Court were confirmed, of all offices subject to Senate approval, justices historically rank first in the proportion of nominations rejected. As the Constitution does not spell out what the Framers considered legitimate causes for rejection of Court candidates, the Senate created its own definition through the process of considering the qualifications of individual candidates.

During the eighteenth and nineteenth centuries, partisanship, patronage, and personality clashes played a central role in conflict over nominations, while ideology became a predominant factor in the twentieth century. However, relatively few controversies and no rejections occurred for long periods, such as from 1895 to 1929 and from 1931 to 1967. The record of controversy and rejection, while notable, has not been a consistent feature of Senate consideration.

From the outset, all rejected nominations to the Court were decided by roll-call vote, but beginning in 1967 every nomination to the Court was resolved in this manner, even when no recorded opposition existed. Most roll-call votes result in approval, but twenty-seven nominations have failed since 1789. Almost half of these were rejected outright by a Senate vote, and the balance were simply not acted on by that body. In addition, six people confirmed by the Senate in the nineteenth century declined to serve.

PRESIDENTIAL PERSPECTIVES

Presidents unpopular with the voters, interest groups, and members of Congress are more likely than others to have nominations challenged, as are lame duck presidents and presidents not of the same party as the Senate majority. This lack of popularity is indicated by low ratings in opinion polls or negative press.

Challenge to nominations may arise because of questions about a nominee's qualifications, competence, or ethical record; alternatively, they may be caused by personal, political, or policy-related opposition to the nominee or the president. The confirmation process involves more than an individual nomination; it also provides an arena for the ongoing struggle between the executive and legislative branches over public policy.

When a nomination faces powerful challenge and possible rejection, even the strongest president must decide if the battle is politically worthwhile, given his or her other priorities. Strategic considerations become critical in determining if it is possible to win the marginal votes of uncommitted senators or if the nomination should be withdrawn. When opponents diversify their appeal and address a

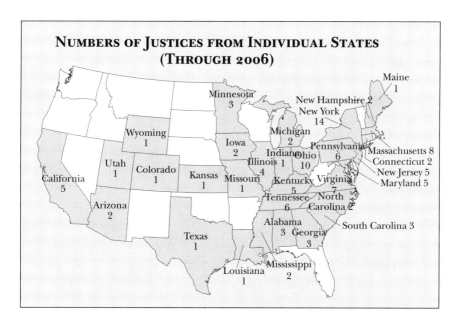

NUMBERS OF JUSTICES FROM INDIVIDUAL STATES (THROUGH 2006)

bipartisan audience and are united by a leadership armed with a powerful counterstrategy to that of the supporters of the nomination, the opposition will probably gain the marginal votes needed to turn challenge into rejection.

NOTABLE REJECTIONS

President George Washington's first eight nominations to the Court were confirmed, but the Senate rejected the 1795 nomination of John Rutledge as chief justice of the United States. Rutledge's nomination failed because of his criticism of Jay's Treaty of 1794, an effort to settle some differences between the United States and Great Britain, which was supported by a majority of senators.

The nineteenth century saw an escalation of contention over nominations. President Andrew Jackson's attorney general, Roger Brooke Taney, had earlier failed confirmation as secretary of the treasury because of the fight over the Bank of the United States. Consequently, he was at first rejected when nominated for a seat on the Court, but he finally secured confirmation as chief justice in 1836. President John Tyler was the first person to become president without being elected to that office, and he broke with his party soon after assuming office. He had four Court appointees rejected during his brief single term. President Andrew Johnson, who was impeached by the House of Representatives but narrowly acquitted in the Senate, was unable to secure appointment to the Court of his impeachment trial counsel, Henry Stanbery.

Increasing involvement in the nominations process by interest groups during the twentieth century resulted in the interjection of ideology. This factor played a central part in the rejection of several nominees. President Herbert Hoover's nomination of John J. Parker to the Court in 1930 was the first defeat of a nominee to the Court since 1894, brought about largely by the opposition of labor and civil rights groups.

President Lyndon B. Johnson had little difficulty with appointments until the last year of his presidency (1968), when his nomination of Abe Fortas to become chief justice was withdrawn in the face of likely defeat in the Senate. President Richard M. Nixon had two Court nominees rejected, as did President Ronald Reagan. The rejection of Reagan's nomination of Robert H. Bork, the result of a highly visible ideological struggle, marked the largest negative Senate vote on a Court nomination in history.

Reacting to such well-publicized ideological battles and to the careful scrutiny of nominees that followed, one critic of the confirmation process, Stephen L. Carter, titled his 1994 book *The Confirmation Mess*. Placed in perspective, however, at least as far as the Court is concerned, the "mess" may well have improved over time; in terms of sheer numbers, the number of rejections in the twentieth century was one-third the number in the previous century.

Donald G. Tannenbaum

FURTHER READING

Three twenty-first century assessments of the nomination process are Michael Comiskey's *Seeking Justices: The Judging of Supreme Court Nominees* (Lawrence: University Press of Kansas, 2004), Richard Davis's *Electing Justice: Fixing the Supreme Court Nomination Process* (New York: Oxford University Press, 2005), and Joyce A. Baugh's *Supreme Court Justices in the Post-Bork Era: Confirmation Politics and Judicial Performance* (New York: P. Lang, 2002). Henry J. Abraham's *Justices and Presidents: A Political History of Appointments to the Supreme Court* (3d ed. New York: Oxford University Press, 1992) is recommended for its comprehensiveness and because it is perhaps the most objective and up-to-date source available.

Two earlier works that place Court nominations in the perspective of the larger confirmation process are Joseph P. Harris's *The Advice and Consent of the Senate* (Berkeley: University of California Press, 1953), which covers the process from the founding of the republic through the administration of President Harry S. Truman, and G. Calvin Mackenzie's *The Politics of Presidential Appointments* (New York: Free Press, 1981), which picks up the story with the Truman presidency and carries it to the beginning of the administration of President Jimmy Carter.

Three works that take a critical look at the situation in the latter part of the twentieth century are John Anthony Maltese's *The Selling of Supreme Court Nominees* (Baltimore, Md.: Johns Hopkins University Press, 1995), Stephen L. Carter's *The Confirmation Mess: Cleaning up the Federal Appointments Process* (New York: Basic Books, 1994), and

Mark Silverstein's *Judicious Choices: The New Politics of Supreme Court Nominations* (New York: W. W. Norton, 1994).

Case studies can provide valuable insight into multiple aspects of a single Court confirmation battle. Donald G. Tannenbaum's "Explaining Controversial Nominations: The Fortas Case Revisited," *Presidential Studies Quarterly* 17 (1987): 573-586, is a briefer study that places the 1968 nomination of Abe Fortas as chief justice of the United States in the larger context of the confirmation process. William J. Burris's *The Senate Rejects a Judge: A Study of the John J. Parker Case* (Chapel Hill: University of North Carolina Press, 1962) examines that 1930 rebuff. An appreciation of the process as a whole will be greatly enhanced by the insights found in the classic work on understanding the presidency, Richard E. Neustadt's *Presidential Power and Modern Presidents: The Politics of Leadership from Roosevelt to Reagan* (New York: Free Press, 1990).

SEE ALSO Chief justice; Fortas, Abe; Senate Judiciary Committee; Thomas, Clarence; Thomas-Hill hearings.

Obscenity and Pornography

DESCRIPTION: An obscenity is an utterance or act that is morally or ethically offensive; pornography is the depiction of erotic behavior intended to arouse sexual excitement.

SIGNIFICANCE: The Supreme Court held obscenity to be a category of speech not protected by the First Amendment. The justices had difficulty agreeing on a definition of obscenity, not forming a standard until a 1973 ruling.

Obscenity is one of several categories of speech deemed unprotected by the First Amendment in *Chaplinsky v. New Hampshire* (1942). In this case, the Supreme Court argued that obscenity and lewdness are analogous to libel (knowingly false speech that injures a person's reputation) and fighting words (speech that may incite the individual to whom the speech is addressed to attack the speaker). The Court reasoned that such speech is not essential to the rational exchange of ideas cherished by the First Amendment and is of little value to society. Any harm arising from suppression is outweighed by society's interest in maintaining order and morality.

DEFINING OBSCENITY

The Court did not directly address the question of obscenity's constitutional status until *Roth v. United States* and *Alberts v. California* (1957). Writing for a 6-3 majority, Justice William Joseph Brennan, Jr., held that obscenity is unprotected by the First Amendment because it is "utterly without redeeming social importance." Brennan stressed that "sex and obscenity are not synonymous" and distinguished between them by explaining that obscene material deals with sex in a manner appealing to "the prurient interest." Brennan defined prurient as "having a tendency to excite lustful thoughts" or appealing to a "shameful and morbid interest in sex." What became known as the Roth-Alberts test for obscenity was formulated by Brennan in this way: Material was obscene if "to the average person, applying contemporary community standards, the dominant theme of the material taken as a whole appeals to the prurient interest."

In subsequent years, the Court found it difficult to define more precisely each element of the Roth-Alberts test. In *Jacobellis v. Ohio* (1964), Justice Potter Stewart questioned whether he could "intelligibly" define obscene material, though he averred that "I know it when I see it" and went on to find that the material involved was not obscene. Three years later, in *Redrup v. New York* (1967), the Court overturned an obscenity conviction in a *per curiam* decision (an opinion "by the court" that briefly expresses the decision but identifies no author), and for the next six years in more than thirty obscenity cases, the Court decided each *per curiam*, the individual justices applying their own understanding of the definition of obscenity. (Justice Hugo L. Black, true to his absolutist approach to First Amendment interpretation, refused to view any of the movies or publications involved in these cases.)

These Warren Court decisions were criticized for failing to provide clear guidelines to law-enforcement officials charged with applying federal, state, and local antiobscenity statutes. There was also concern that nonobscene sexually explicit speech might be stifled if

815

speakers feared that speech they thought protected might later be found punishable. However, others found the Warren Court's standards too permissive, and these decisions, among others, were issues in the 1968 presidential election.

In *Miller v. California* and *Paris Adult Theatre v. Slaton* (1973), the Burger Court reaffirmed *Roth*'s finding that obscenity is not protected by the First Amendment and expounded the current test for obscenity. Writing for a 5-4 majority, Chief Justice Warren E. Burger held that three requirements must be met to find material obscene. First, the average person, applying contemporary community standards, must find the material appealing to his or her prurient interest. Second, the material must depict sexual conduct in a patently offensive way ("patently offensive representations . . . of ultimate sexual acts" and "patently offensive representations . . . of masturbation, excretory functions, and lewd exhibition of the genitals"). Third, material is obscene if, taken as a whole—not simply focusing on isolated passages or pictures in, for example, a book or magazine—it "lacks serious literary, artistic, political, or scientific value." In short, obscenity is "hard core" pornography.

In *Paris Adult Theatre v. Slaton*, decided the same day as *Miller*, Justice Brennan, who authored the majority opinion in *Roth*, questioned whether this new approach would bring stability to the law of obscenity and suggested that fundamental First Amendment values were jeopardized. He argued that government's interest in regulating sexually explicit materials was confined to distribution to minors or unwilling adults and that regulation of the distribution of such materials to consenting adults was inconsistent with the First Amendment. Obscenity opponents praised the Court for achieving a majority opinion defining obscenity and rejecting an earlier approach—used by the Court in the 1966 Fanny Hill case (*A Book Named "John Cleland's Memoirs of a Woman of Pleasure" v. Attorney General of Massachusetts*)— that a work is obscene if it is "utterly without redeeming social value." This minimal social value test placed a heavy burden on prosecutors, in essence requiring them to prove a negative. Under *Miller*, prosecutors merely have to show that a work lacks "serious" literary, artistic, political, or scientific value.

In *New York v. Ferber* (1982), the Court created an important exception to the principle that nonobscene sexually explicit material is entitled to First Amendment protection. The *Ferber* case involved a New York State law prohibiting the knowing production, exhibition, or distribution of any material depicting a "sexual performance" by a child under sixteen. Ferber was convicted for selling two films showing young boys masturbating. The Court upheld the conviction, even though this material did not meet the Miller test for obscenity. The Court reasoned that the state had a "compelling interest" in protecting the physiological, emotional, and mental health of children, citing the close relationship between child pornography and child abuse.

In *Osborne v. Ohio* (1990), the Court held that the government may regulate private possession of child pornography. The Court reasoned that an earlier case, *Stanley v. Georgia* (1969), was not applicable here. In *Stanley*, the Court overturned a conviction for possession of obscenity. Justice Thurgood Marshall's opinion for the Court stressed the freedom of individuals to read or watch what they choose in the privacy of their own home. (*Stanley* has never been overruled but neither has it been extended. In *United States v. Reidel* [1971], for example, the justices rejected the argument that a right to possess obscene materials entails a right to receive them despite a governmental ban on shipment of such materials.) In *Osborne*, over a dissent by Justice Brennan in which he argued that the controlling precedent was *Stanley*, the Court reasoned that the privacy interest was outweighed by the state's need to protect children by attacking the "market for the exploitative use of children."

SEXUALLY ORIENTED NONOBSCENE SPEECH

Some types of sexual speech, while not meeting the definition of obscenity, are treated by the Court as low value speech. The government has more room to regulate such speech than it would if it were targeting a political speech or a newspaper editorial. The Court has used the metaphor of a ladder. Obscenity, libel, or fighting words are at the bottom of the ladder, while a speech at a political rally or a newspaper editorial are at the top. Sexually oriented nonobscene speech is somewhere in between and, in the eyes of some justices, closer to the bottom.

The Court has never given a detailed definition of this category, but it is clear that sexually explicit nonobscene material is included. One example involves movie theaters specializing in "adult" entertainment—material involving "specified sexual activities" or "specified anatomical areas." In *Young v. American Mini Theatres* (1976), the Court said cities could limit how many adult theaters could be on any block and exclude them from residential neighborhoods. The Court stressed that attempts to place complete bans on such establishments would raise First Amendment problems. Subsequently in *City of Renton v. Playtime Theatres* (1986), the Court approved a zoning ordinance that banned adult theaters located within one thousand feet of any residential zone, church, park, or school. The practical effect of Renton's law was to exclude such establishments from 95 percent of the land in the city. The remaining 5 percent was unsuitable for such establishments, but the Court, relying on *Young*, upheld the ordinance.

Also near the bottom of the ladder is nude dancing. In *Barnes v. Glen Theatre* (1991), the Court held that the government may completely ban nude dancing. At issue in *Barnes* was an Indiana statute prohibiting public nudity. The Court split five to four, and there was no majority opinion. The plurality opinion by Chief Justice William H. Rehnquist described nude dancing as "within the outer perimeters of the First Amendment, though . . . only marginally so." Rehnquist argued that the ban on nude dancing was needed to protect "societal order and morality." In the chief justice's view, Indiana was not proscribing erotic dancing but rather targeting public nudity. Justice Byron R. White's dissenting opinion argued that nudity is an expressive component of the dance rather than "merely incidental 'conduct.'"

Whatever the exact definition of sexually oriented nonobscene speech, the Court has indicated that nudity per se is not enough to place the communication near the bottom of the ladder. In *Erznoznik v. Jacksonville* (1975), the Court overturned a Jacksonville, Florida, ordinance prohibiting a drive-in movie theater from showing films including nude scenes if the screen was visible from a public street or any other public place. The Court stressed that nudity alone is not obscene and not enough to curtail First Amendment protections.

PROFANE AND INDECENT LANGUAGE

Profane and indecent language, the familiar Anglo-Saxon four-letter word being the prototypical example, does not meet the *Miller* definition of obscenity, and the Court has found such language protected by the First Amendment. The notion that the government may not punish speech simply because some find it offensive, a bedrock principle of First Amendment interpretation, found classic expression in *Cohen v. California* (1971). In *Cohen*, the Court overturned the conviction of an anti-Vietnam War protester charged with disturbing the peace by wearing in the corridor of a courthouse a jacket with the words "Fuck the Draft" emblazoned on its back. Justice John M. Harlan II's majority opinion rejected the notion that the state can prohibit offensive language. Harlan was concerned that, under the guise of prohibiting particular words, the government might seek to ban the expression of unpopular views. Additionally, Harlan endorsed Cohen's argument that words are often used as much for their emotive as their cognitive impact. Cohen could not have conveyed the intensity of his feeling if the jacket said "I Don't Like the Draft." In *Sable Communications v. Federal Communications Commission* (1989), the Court reiterated that government may prohibit obscene but not indecent speech.

However, the Court has also recognized situations in which the government can ban profane or indecent language. One such situation is broadcasting. In *Federal Communications Commission v. Pacifica Foundation* (1978), the Court allowed the Federal Communications Commission (FCC) to punish indecent language broadcast over an FM radio station. The station aired a portion of a monologue on "seven dirty words" by comedian George Carlin. Chief Justice Burger's opinion emphasized that broadcast media are unique in their pervasiveness and in their ability to intrude into the home. Burger also expressed concern about the accessibility of such broadcasts to children.

Applying *Pacifica* to another pervasive and intrusive medium, cable television, in 1996, the Court considered several provisions of a federal law regulating the broadcast of "patently offensive" sexually oriented material on cable. The Court held in *Denver Area Educational Consortium v. Federal Communications Commission* that cable operators could refuse to carry sexually explicit broadcasting. The Court again stressed the need to protect children. At the same time, the Court found unconstitutional a requirement that sexually oriented programs be confined to a single channel that could not be viewed unless the cable subscriber requested access in writing. Although concerned about the availability of such material to children, the Court believed that the law could have chosen less restrictive alternatives, such as facilitating parental blockage of such channels.

In *Reno v. American Civil Liberties Union* (1996), the Court overturned a 1996 federal law, the Communications Decency Act, which attempted to protect minors by criminalizing "indecency" on the Internet. Justice John Paul Stevens's 7-2 majority opinion found that the act placed too heavy a burden on protected speech and threatened "to torch a large segment of the Internet community." The Court said the Internet is analogous to the print rather than broadcast medium and therefore entitled to full First Amendment protections. The Court voiced concern that the law would threaten legitimate discussion of sexual topics posted online by the plaintiffs, for example, groups such as Stop Prisoner Rape or Critical Path AIDS Project.

Another exception to the Court's protection of profane and indecent language arises in the context of schools. The Court upheld the right of public school officials to punish a student for indecent speech. In *Bethel School District No. 403 v. Fraser* (1986), the Court found that Fraser's school assembly speech, containing no profanity but numerous sexual innuendoes, was "wholly inconsistent with the 'fundamental value' of public school education." *Bethel* exemplifies the Court's tendency to defer to school authorities and to emphasize an orderly educational process over student free speech rights.

Philip A. Dynia

FURTHER READING

A good place to begin a study of the legal aspects of pornography is Thomas C. Mackey's *Pornography on Trial: A Handbook with Cases, Laws, and Documents* (Santa Barbara, Calif.: ABC-Clio, 2002). For a comprehensive overview of the Supreme Court's approach to civil rights and liberties issues, consult Henry J. Abraham and Barbara A.

Perry's *Freedom and the Court: Civil Rights and Liberties in the United States* (8th ed. Lawrence: University Press of Kansas, 2003). Chapter 5, "The Precious Freedom of Expression," is an excellent introduction to the Court's First Amendment jurisprudence and includes a thorough and balanced discussion of pornography and obscenity.

For a collection of scholarly essays on this subject, see *Obscenity and Pornography Decisions of the United States Supreme Court* (Carlsbad, Calif.: Excellent Books, 2000), edited by Maureen Harrison and Steve Gilbert. *Obscene Profits: The Entrepreneurs of Pornography in the Cyber Age* (New York: Routledge, 2000), by Frederick S. Lane III, looks at changes in public and legal views of pornography brought by the spread of the Internet. Joan Mason-Grant's *Pornography Embodied: From Speech to Sexual Practice* (Lanham, Md.: Rowman & Littlefield, 2004) looks at the relationship between pornography and the modern women's movement.

In general, the literature on freedom of expression is voluminous. Readers might start with two classics by a towering figure, Alexander Meiklejohn: *Free Speech and Its Relation to Self-Government* (Port Washington, N.Y.: Kennikat Press, 1972) and *Political Freedom: The Constitutional Powers of the People* (New York: Oxford University Press, 1965). More recent studies that are also valuable include Lee Bollinger's *The Tolerant Society* (New York: Oxford University Press, 1986), Rodney A. Smolla's *Free Speech in an Open Society* (New York: Alfred A. Knopf, 1992), Nat Hentoff's *Free Speech for Me—But Not for Thee* (New York: Harper Perennial, 1993), and Kent Greenwalt's *Fighting Words* (Princeton, N.J.: Princeton University Press, 1995).

A variety of works deal specifically with obscenity or pornography. For a conservative approach, see Harry M. Clor's *Obscenity and Public Morality* (Chicago: University of Chicago Press, 1969) or Walter Berns's *The First Amendment and the Future of American Democracy* (New York: Basic Books, 1976). For a radical feminist approach to pornography, see two works by Catharine MacKinnon: *Only Words* (Cambridge, Mass.: Harvard University Press, 1993) and *Feminism Unmodified* (Cambridge, Mass.: Harvard University Press, 1987). For a response to MacKinnon and Clor, see Nadine Strossen's *Defending Pornography* (New York: New York University Press, 2000). A balanced overview of these and other positions can be found in a collection of essays edited by Robert M.

Baird and Stuart E. Rosenbaum, *Pornography: Private Right or Public Menace?* (Buffalo, N.Y.: Prometheus Books, 1991).

SEE ALSO *Ashcroft v. Free Speech Coalition*; *Barnes v. Glen Theatre*; Black, Hugo L.; Brennan, William J., Jr.; Burger, Warren E.; Censorship; Harlan, John M., II; *Mapp v. Ohio*; *New York v. Ferber*; *Roth v. United States/Alberts v. California*; Stewart, Potter; Zoning.

Sandra Day O'Connor

IDENTIFICATION: Associate justice (September 25, 1981-January 31, 2006)
NOMINATED BY: Ronald Reagan
BORN: March 26, 1930, El Paso, Texas
SIGNIFICANCE: The first woman to serve on the Supreme Court, O'Connor was a moderate justice who sometimes sided with the more conservative and sometimes with the more liberal justices, depending on specific issues.

Born Sandra Day, O'Connor grew up on a cattle ranch in southeastern Arizona. She described her early experiences of living in a desert environment and having contacts with cowboys in a popular book, *Lazy B: Growing Up on a Cattle Ranch in the American Southwest* (2003). At the age of sixteen she gained admission to Stanford University, where she earned both her undergraduate and law degrees. While at Stanford's law school, she had a few dates with future chief justice William H. Rehnquist, who graduated as valedictorian of the class. While a student, she also met her future husband, John O'Connor.

Although O'Connor graduated third in her law school class of 102, she was unable to find a position in a law firm because of discrimination against women in the legal professions. She soon realized that private law firms at that time did not hire women lawyers, so she began to work for the government, which did not discriminate overtly against women. She first served as a prosecutor in San Mateo County, California, just north of Stanford University, and then moved with her husband, John O'Connor, to Frankfurt, Germany, where he served as a lawyer in the U.S. Army. While in Frankfurt, O'Connor herself served as a civilian lawyer for the U.S. Army. After her husband completed his military service, the couple moved to Phoenix, Arizona. While he worked for a Phoenix law firm, she created a new law firm with another woman lawyer.

O'Connor became active in Republican politics and was appointed as an assistant attorney general in Arizona in 1965. She was the first woman to serve in that post. In 1969, she was appointed to a vacancy in the Arizona state senate, and in 1973 and 1974 she was the first woman to serve as a majority leader in that legislative body. In November, 1974, she was elected to the Maricopa County superior court.

Sandra Day O'Connor.
(Library of Congress)

Four years later, a Democratic governor appointed O'Connor to the Arizona court of appeals. Although she was a Republican, she was well respected by Republicans and Democrats alike. During the 1980 presidential campaign, Ronald Reagan promised to choose a woman as his first nominee to the Supreme Court. After the retirement of Justice Potter Stewart in 1981, newly elected president Reagan appointed O'Connor as his replacement. O'Connor was approved unanimously by the Senate and took her oath of office on September 25, 1981. Her appointment created a tremendous wave of enthusiasm, which was reflected in the sixty thousand letters that she received from private citizens.

JURISPRUDENCE AND DECISIONS

Although appointed by a president seeking to advance a conservative agenda, Justice O'Connor never favored a rigidly conservative interpretation of the Constitution. Sometimes she sided with more liberal justices, such as Thurgood Marshall and Ruth Bader Ginsburg, and sometimes she sided with more conservative justices, such as Rehnquist and Antonin Scalia. Her positions depended on the specific cases before the Court. Rather than voting on the basis of an overall ideology, she attempted to make decisions based on pragmatic case-by-case analyses of issues. Journalists coined the term "o'connorize" to describe her approach. During her first decade on the Court, she tended to be on the same side as the conservatives. However, with the departure of the last liberals of the Warren Court, she increasingly found herself agreeing with the more liberal justices.

Because she was a centrist often searching for a compromise, O'Connor was frequently the swing vote in controversial cases that were decided by 5-4 majorities. For this reason, especially during the last fifteen years of her tenure, some observers said that she was the most influential person in the United States.

In the matter of states' rights, Justice O'Connor was a strong defender of the Tenth Amendment, which recognizes that all unmentioned powers are reserved to the states. In the 1987 case of *South Dakota v. Dole*, she dissented from the majority, which upheld a federal law that required states to have a minimum drinking age of twenty-one in order to receive federal highway funds. Although she noted that the intention of this law was laudable because of its goal of reducing drunken driving, she believed that the law violated both the Tenth Amendment and the Twenty-first Amendment, which granted to the states alone the right to regulate alcoholic beverages.

In the opinion for the Court in *Tafflin v. Levitt* (1990), O'Connor reasserted the doctrine of dual sovereignty, writing that the states' sovereignty was "subject only to limitations imposed by the supremacy clause." In *New York v. United States* (2002), she wrote the majority opinion, which invalidated a federal case intended to force states to either reach an agreement with another state to accept radioactive waste or to keep it in their own disposal facilities. In *Seminole Tribe v. Florida* (1996), she joined the 5-4 majority to sustain the Eleventh Amendment claim that Congress could not use the commerce power to abrogate the states' sovereign immunity from suits.

When she was first appointed by President Reagan, O'Connor was apparently in favor of overturning the right to abortion as had been recognized in *Roe v. Wade* (1973). Her views on the issue changed over the years, in large part because of her deference for previous Court decisions—the doctrine of *stare decisis*. Writing her first major abortion opinion in *Akron v. Akron Center for Reproductive Health* (1983), she criticized *Roe*'s trimester approach while recognizing that a woman's "liberty interest" included the right to terminate an unwanted pregnancy. It was in this case that she proposed her influential "undue burden" standard for evaluating restrictions on abortion. In *Webster v. Reproductive Health Services* (1989), she joined a plurality in approving a number of state restrictions on abortion. However, when the Court seemed poised to overturn *Roe v. Wade*, she joined a 5-4 majority to preserve the precedent in the case of *Planned Parenthood of Southeastern Pennsylvania v. Casey* (1992). O'Connor justified her vote primarily in terms of *stare decisis* and the need for continuity in the law. When the decision was announced, the justices did not try to hide their intense disagreement.

In cases dealing with the establishment clause, O'Connor often sought a middle position. In *Lynch v. Donnelly* (1984), for example, she joined the 5-4 majority in approving a city-sponsored Christmas nativity display that included nonreligious symbols such as Santa's sleigh and a Christmas tree. In a separate concurring opinion, she suggested the use of an endorsement test, considering whether the display conveys "a message of approval or disapproval" of a specific religion. In the case of *Wallace v. Jaffree* (1985), O'Connor applied her endorsement test in ruling that a moment of silence in the schools was an indirect way to reintroduce prayers. The Court used O'Connor's endorsement test in several later cases, including *Zelman v. Simmons-Harris* (2002), in which O'Connor joined another 5-4 majority in upholding the use of state-funded vouchers that could be used for attendance at parochial schools.

O'Connor helped shape constitutional law in affirmative action cases. In *Wygant v. Jackson* (1986), examining a policy of using race in layoffs, she emphasized that race-based classifications were inherently suspect and insisted that programs must be narrowly drawn and defensible in terms of a compelling government interest. In *Adarand Constructors v. Peña,* she wrote the opinion for the 5-4 majority, insisting that both federal and state programs must undergo this "strict scrutiny" analysis in order to be approved. Some observers believed that *Adarand* would result in an end to preferences based on race. However, in another 5-4 decision, *Grutter v. Bollinger* (2003), O'Connor wrote the opinion that recognized diversity as a compelling interest of higher education institutions, thereby allowing some race preferences in admissions so long as each applicant was assessed individually.

O'Connor also provided the swing vote in several cases dealing with gay rights. In *Boy Scouts of America v. Dale* (2000), O'Connor joined the majority in ruling that New Jersey had violated the Boy Scouts' freedom of association in prohibiting the organization from discriminating against adult leaders on the basis of sexual orientation. In *Lawrence v. Texas* (2003), however, she agreed that states had no constitutional authority to prohibit homosexual sodomy among consenting adults. Rather than basing the decision on privacy rights, which was the position of the majority opinion, she wanted to base the case on the principle of equal protection, which would have had more far-reaching consequences as a precedent.

On July 19, 2005, Justice O'Connor announced her retirement from the Court, primarily in order to care for her sick husband. She received much praise from both liberal Democrats and conservative

Republicans, and many people expressed the desire that she should reconsider. President George W. Bush named John G. Roberts as her replacement, but after the death of Chief Justice Rehnquist on September 3, Roberts was named his replacement, and Samuel A. Alito, Jr., was sworn in to replace O'Connor on January 31, 2006. O'Connor used her departure to deliver high-profile speeches expressing concern and sadness for the attacks on the independent judiciary, and she announced that she would work with the American Bar Association on a commission to help educate the public about the role of judges and the principle of separation of powers.

Edmund J. Campion
Revised and updated by the Editor

FURTHER READING

Biskupic, Joan. *Sandra Day O'Connor: How the First Woman on the Supreme Court Became Its Most Influential Member.* New York: ECCO, 2005.

Hensley, Thomas R. *The Rehnquist Court: Justices, Rulings, and Legacy.* Santa Barbara, Calif.: ABC-Clio, 2006.

Huber, Peter W. *Sandra Day O'Connor: Supreme Court Justice.* New York: Chelsea House, 1990.

McFeatters, Ann Carey. *Sandra Day O'Connor: Justice in the Balance.* Albuquerque: University of New Mexico Press, 2006.

Maveety, Nancy. *Justice Sandra Day O'Connor: Strategist on the Supreme Court.* Lanham, Md.: Rowman & Littlefield, 1996.

O'Connor, Sandra Day. *The Majesty of the Law: Reflections of a Supreme Court Justice.* New York: Random House, 2003.

Zelnick, Robert. *Swing Dance: Justice O'Connor and the Michigan Muddle.* Stanford, Calif.: Hoover Institution Press, Stanford University, 2004.

SEE ALSO Abortion; Alito, Samuel A., Jr.; *Gratz v. Bollinger/Grutter v. Bollinger*; *Lawrence v. Texas*; *Planned Parenthood of Southeastern Pennsylvania v. Casey*; Rehnquist, William H.; Religion, establishment of; Resignation and retirement; Tenth Amendment; *Webster v. Reproductive Health Services.*

Writing of Opinions

DESCRIPTION: Written statements explaining the Supreme Court's decision in a case. Opinions fall into four types: opinions of the Court (majority opinions), judgments of the Court (plurality opinions), concurring opinions, and dissenting opinions.

SIGNIFICANCE: Because Court opinions state the rule of law in the case and the writer substantially controls their content, the assignment and writing of opinions is an important matter.

Many of the modern procedures regarding the assignment and writing of opinions were initiated shortly after 1801, when Chief Justice John Marshall assumed office. Marshall preferred that the Supreme Court issue a majority opinion, believing that a more unified presentation of the rule of law would strengthen its impact.

THE PROCESS

After hearing oral argument in a case, the justices meet in secret conference to decide, by formal vote, whether to reverse or to affirm the decision of the lower court. This vote is known as the conference vote on the merits. If a chief justice is in the majority at the conference vote on the merits, he or she assigns the writing of the opinion of the Court. Chief justices can write the opinion themselves or select any justice in the majority. If the chief justice is in the minority or fails to vote, the senior associate justice in the majority assigns the majority opinion. Fred M. Vinson assigned 80 percent of the majority opinions while he was chief justice. Chief Justice Earl Warren assigned 86 percent, as did Chief Justice Warren E. Burger. Chief Justice William H. Rehnquist assigned 82 percent of the majority opinions through the 1990 term of the Court.

In the late 1980's, Justice William J. Brennan, Jr., introduced the same assigning procedures for dissenting opinions when more than one justice was in dissent at the conference vote on the merits. Before that time, justices in dissent would write dissenting opinions at will.

After receiving the assignment to write the opinion of the Court, the justice prepares a preliminary draft. This draft is circulated to all the justices participating in the case. The other justices send back memos in which they indicate that they join the Court's opinion, request substantive changes to be made to the opinion, state that they will not be joining the opinion of the Court, or inform the opinion writer that they will decide whether to join after they have read the other opinions in the case. The opinion writer might revise the opinion and redistribute several drafts of it.

The justices are free to change the vote they cast at the conference at any time before the handing down of the decision of the Court. As a result, the Court at conference might vote to reverse the decision of the lower court but vote to affirm that decision at the final vote on the merits.

It takes a majority vote to generate an authoritative opinion of the Court. If such a vote is not obtained, the opinion will be a judgment of the Court (also known as a plurality opinion), which lacks full precedent power. In addition to majority, plurality, and dissenting opinions, the justices on the Court can write concurring opinions. A justice who writes such an opinion agrees with the outcome favored by the majority or plurality opinion writer but disagrees with one or more of the statements set forth in that opinion. A concurring opinion writer may or may not join the opinion of the Court.

A STATISTICAL VIEW

Researcher Elliott Slotnick inspected all 6,275 opinion assignments made by the chief justices from the beginning of the Court under William H. Taft in 1921 until the end of the 1973 term of the Burger Court. Slotnick discovered that from the last four terms of the Vinson Court (1949-1952) until the end of the 1973 term, the chief justices tended to assign to each justice approximately the same number of opinions of the Court. In "important" cases, however, the equality norm was not followed. Instead, the chief justices tended to assign the majority opinions to themselves or to those justices who usually vote with them. The chief justices were more likely to self-assign in cases involving a unanimous or highly cohesive Court than in cases involving a highly divisive Court. In addition, Slotnick found that new justices were not disadvantaged in opinion assignment.

Subsequent researchers discovered that specialization took place in opinion assignment on the Warren and Burger Courts. Justices ranked as "failures" by law professors were assigned fewer opinions of the Court. Justices on the Vinson Court who wrote more quickly were favored in opinion assignment, and in cases decided by a 5-4 or 4-3 vote at the conference vote on the merits on the Warren Court, the justice ideologically closest to the dissenters was assigned approximately twice the number of opinions of the Court as could be expected based on chance.

CONTENT OF THE MAJORITY OPINION

In an innovative 1991 study, Glenn Phelps and John Gates compared the constitutional arguments made by conservative justice Rehnquist and liberal justice Brennan in their majority opinions. They expected Rehnquist to advance arguments based on the text of the Constitution and the intent of the Framers and Brennan to present arguments based on what is just or what is good for society. They discovered, however, that there were only minor differences between the justices regarding how often they advanced these kinds of arguments. Both justices overwhelmingly advanced arguments based on precedent.

Saul Brenner

FURTHER READING

Blanc, D. Ellsworth. *The Supreme Court: Issues and Opinions.* Huntington, N.Y.: Nova Science Publishers, 2001.

Phelps, Glenn A., and John B. Gates. "The Myth of Jurisprudence: Interpretative Theory in the Constitutional Opinions of Justices Rehnquist and Brennan." *Santa Clara Law Review* 31 (1991): 567-596.

Sekulow, Jay. *Witnessing Their Faith: Religious Influence on Supreme Court Justices and Their Opinions.* Lanham, Md.: Rowman & Littlefield, 2006.

Slotnick, Elliott E. "Who Speaks for the Court? Majority Opinion Assignment from Taft to Burger." *American Journal of Political Science* 23 (1979): 60-77.

Van Geel, Tyll. *Understanding Supreme Court Opinions.* 4th ed. New York: Longman, 2005.

SEE ALSO Advisory opinions; *Boy Scouts of America v. Dale;* Chief justice; Conference of the justices; Dissents; Marshall, John; Reporting of opinions; Seriatim opinions.

Oral Argument

DESCRIPTION: Spoken presentation to the Supreme Court given by the litigants' lawyers.

SIGNIFICANCE: Justices question the litigants' lawyers during the oral argument, clarifying statements made in the briefs and testing the soundness of the arguments brought before them.

During oral argument, the justices question the lawyers about any arguments in the written briefs that may need further clarification before the argument receives the full confidence of the Court. In a few cases, oral arguments leave justices with a different impression of the case from that formed by reading the written briefs.

Oral arguments are scheduled on Mondays, Tuesdays, and Wednesdays during the Court's term between October and April. The justices hear about 168 arguments during that time, about four each day. Arguments before the Court begin with the clerk of the Court's traditional cry:

> Oyez, oyez, oyez! All persons having business before the Honorable, the Supreme Court of the United States, are admonished to draw near and give their attention, for the Court is now sitting. God save the United States and this Honorable Court.

The chief justice then calls the name and number of the case, and the first lawyer to speak traditionally opens with "Mr. Chief Justice, and may it please the Court." Once argument begins, the advocate is interrupted frequently with questions from the bench.

An effective oralist answers questions from the bench while weaving the argument's major points into the presentation. The respondent, who speaks after the petitioner, must address the concerns already addressed by the bench, incorporating that response into his or her major arguments. The justices do not allow advocates to read at any length. Advocates do not speak when the justices are asking questions and always remain respectful of the Court.

In the nineteenth century, oral arguments could last for two or three days. The flamboyant styles of such advocates as Daniel Webster and Henry Clay made Court hearings popular with the public. In 1849

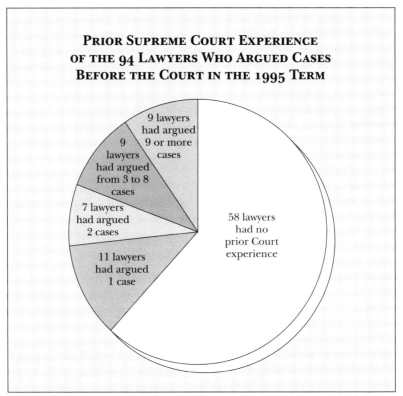

PRIOR SUPREME COURT EXPERIENCE OF THE 94 LAWYERS WHO ARGUED CASES BEFORE THE COURT IN THE 1995 TERM

9 lawyers had argued 9 or more cases

9 lawyers had argued from 3 to 8 cases

7 lawyers had argued 2 cases

11 lawyers had argued 1 case

58 lawyers had no prior Court experience

Source: Lawrence Baum, *The Supreme Court* (6th ed. Washington, D.C.: Congressional Quarterly, 1998), p. 89.

arguments were limited to two hours for each side. In 1971, during Chief Justice Warren E. Burger's tenure (1969-1986), oral arguments were reduced to thirty minutes for each side in response to the increasing caseload that faced the Court. The appellant is allowed to reserve some of that time for rebuttal after hearing the appellee's argument. Time limits are strictly enforced. A white light on counsel's lectern indicates five minutes remain, and a red light signals time has ended.

Oral arguments are not broadcast; therefore, the only way to hear them is to attend the Court's sessions. However, transcripts of the arguments are available.

Paul Bateman

SEE ALSO Briefs; Conference of the justices; Opinions, writing of; Review, process of; Rules of the Court; Solicitor general; Workload.

Palko v. Connecticut

CITATION: 302 U.S. 319
DATE: November 12, 1937
ISSUE: Double jeopardy
SIGNIFICANCE: When the Supreme Court refrained from incorporating the Fifth Amendment's protection against double jeopardy into the due process clause of the Fourteenth Amendment, Justice Benjamin Cardozo's opinion for the Court articulated the influential "fundamental fairness" standard of selective incorporation.

The state of Connecticut indicted a man named Palko for the capital offense of first-degree murder, but the jury convicted him only of second-degree murder and sentenced him to life imprisonment. Connecticut's constitution and laws permitted a second trial, and the state again tried and convicted him, this time for the more serious capital offense. In the same circumstances, the federal government would not have been allowed to retry Palko because of the Fifth Amendment's ban on double jeopardy. Facing execution, Palko appealed, arguing that the due process clause of the Fourteenth Amendment incorporated the double jeopardy ban, thereby making it applicable to the states.

By an 8-1 vote, however, the Supreme Court disagreed, finding against Palko. In the opinion for the Court, Justice Benjamin N. Cardozo ruled that the Fourteenth Amendment's due process clause did not include the Fifth Amendment's principle that no person can be tried twice for the same offense. His opinion was noteworthy primarily because of its proposal for a "fundamental fairness" standard of selective incorporation as a basis for deciding which provisions of the Bill of Rights would apply to the states. In his words, the standard was whether a particular right "represented the very essence of a scheme of ordered liberty" and whether it was a "principle of justice so rooted in the traditions and conscience of our people as to be ranked fundamental." In subsequent years, the majority of the justices would adopt Cardozo's *Palko* standard. Although Palko was executed, decades later in *Benton v. Maryland* (1969) the Court would utilize this standard in reversing the *Palko* ruling, thereby making the prohibition on double jeopardy one of the provisions in the Bill of Rights that is binding on the states.

Richard L. Wilson
Revised by the Editor

SEE ALSO Cardozo, Benjamin N.; Double jeopardy; Due process, procedural; Fifth Amendment; Fourteenth Amendment; Fundamental rights; Incorporation doctrine; Jury, trial by.

William Paterson

IDENTIFICATION: Associate justice (March 11, 1793-September 9, 1806)
NOMINATED BY: George Washington
BORN: December 24, 1745, County Antrim, Ireland
DIED: September 9, 1806, Albany, New York
SIGNIFICANCE: While serving on the Supreme Court, Paterson participated in several important cases in American jurisprudence that established the Constitution as the law of the land.

Born in Ireland, William Paterson is one of only six Supreme Court justices born in a foreign country. Paterson graduated from the College of New Jersey (later Princeton) in 1763 and earned a graduate degree in 1766. He studied law under Richard Stockton and was admitted to the bar in 1769, establishing a practice in New Bromley, New Jersey. During the Revolutionary War, Paterson was an officer in the Somerset County Minutemen and also served as a member of the Council of Safety.

In 1775 Paterson was selected as a delegate to the First Provincial Congress of New Jersey. He was elected to the State Constitutional Convention in 1776, where he helped draft the New Jersey constitution. He was named the first attorney general of New Jersey in 1776 and actively prosecuted Loyalists. In the Constitutional Convention held in Philadelphia in 1787, Paterson represented New Jersey. He was the architect of the famous New Jersey plan, which supported the interests of the smaller states by calling for a federal legislature with

William Paterson.
(Max Rosenthal/
Collection of the
Supreme Court of
the United States)

equal representation for each state. The Virginia and New Jersey plans were consolidated to form the American legislative structure.

In 1788 Paterson was elected by the New Jersey legislature to serve in the first U.S. Senate. He and his colleague, Oliver Ellsworth, drafted the Judiciary Act of 1789 that established the federal court system, a three-tiered system of courts, consisting of the Supreme Court, circuit courts, and district courts. In 1790 Paterson was elected governor and chancellor of New Jersey.

On March 4, 1793, President George Washington appointed Paterson to the Supreme Court. He became well known for his decision in *Van Horne's Lessee v. Dorrance* (1795), a circuit court case, which helped to establish the nature of constitutional governments. Paterson's opinion in the *Van Horne* case served as a precedent in the *Marbury v. Madison* (1803) decision, one of the most significant Court decisions. Chief Justice John Marshall cited Paterson's *Van Horne* opinion in the *Marbury* decision, thus establishing the right of the judicial branch to review and void acts of the executive and legislative branches if the acts violate the Constitution.

In 1796 Paterson wrote one of the separate majority opinions in *Hylton v. United States.* Paterson argued that a federal tax on carriages was legal because it was an indirect tax, not a direct tax. The sustaining of the carriage tax proved pivotal some one hundred years later when the Court declared the federal income tax was unconstitutional, eventually leading to the Sixteenth Amendment.

Alvin K. Benson

SEE ALSO Constitutional law; Ellsworth, Oliver; Jay, John; *Marbury v. Madison*; Marshall, John; Rutledge, John.

Payne v. Tennessee

CITATION: 501 U.S. 808
DATE: June 27, 1991
ISSUE: Capital punishment
SIGNIFICANCE: The Supreme Court allowed victim impact statements to be included in the capital sentencing phase of trials.

After convicting Payne of murder, the prosecutor called some of the victim's family to testify in the penalty phase and referred to those statements during closing arguments. Upon being sentenced to die, Payne appealed to the Supreme Court, citing existing precedents against allowing testimony regarding the impact of his crime, but the Court upheld the conviction and the sentencing. Chief Justice William H. Rehnquist wrote the opinion for the 6-3 majority, overturning *Booth v. Maryland* (1987), which prohibited victim impact testimony, and *South Carolina v. Gathers* (1989), which prohibited prosecutors from mentioning the crime's impact on the victim or the family. The Court ruled that the Eighth Amendment did not bar such testimony.

Richard L. Wilson

SEE ALSO Capital punishment; Due process, procedural; Eighth Amendment; *Furman v. Georgia*; *Gregg v. Georgia*; *McCleskey v. Kemp*; Rehnquist, William H.

Rufus W. Peckham

IDENTIFICATION: Associate justice (January 6, 1896-October 24, 1909)
NOMINATED BY: Grover Cleveland
BORN: November 8, 1838, Albany, New York
DIED: October 24, 1909, Altamont, New York
SIGNIFICANCE: During his Supreme Court tenure, Peckham wrote
some of the major opinions protecting the liberty to contract and
consistently voted to strike down government regulation of eco-
nomic freedoms.

Born in New York, Rufus W. Peckham followed in his father and
brother's footsteps when choosing a law career. He rose through the
New York Democratic Party ranks. He became friendly with the Democratic governor, Grover Cleveland, who supported him in his bid to be
elected to the state's highest court. During Peckham's tenure on the
state supreme court, he was introduced to a conservative property
rights agenda. It was during this time that his legal views solidified.

After Cleveland was elected president of the United States, he
sought to reward his loyal New York supporters through government
appointments. During his first term, Cleveland chose Peckham's older
brother, Wheeler H. Peckham, for one of his early Supreme Court appointments. The older Peckham, however, was rejected by the Senate,
opening the way for his brother to be appointed. In 1895 Cleveland
nominated the younger Peckham, who was easily confirmed.

FREEDOM OF CONTRACT

Justice Peckham immediately joined the conservative wing of the
Court, which included Chief Justice Melville W. Fuller and Justice
David J. Brewer, and expressed strong support for property rights. In
one of his early opinions, *Allgeyer v. Louisiana* (1897), Peckham spoke
for a unanimous Court in striking down a Louisiana insurance law as
a violation of the freedom of contract. In *Allgeyer,* Peckham defined
this new right as constitutional protection for an individual's ability
to choose an occupation freely and employ his or her faculties and
skills without burdensome government regulation. This placed the
Court and Peckham in direct confrontation with Progressive politi-

cians who wanted to use legislation to alleviate some of the problems associated with the new industrial society. Peckham, though, saw such legislation as a threat to the continued development of the economy and a clear violation of liberty rights under the U.S. Constitution. For the next forty years, Peckham's broad definition of freedom of contract held sway over the Court's jurisprudence.

As one of the creators of this new right, Peckham was unwavering in his support. He was one of two dissenters in *Holden v. Hardy* (1898), which upheld a ten-hour workday for miners and allowed regulation of the freedom of contract when the state was acting to protect the public's health, safety, and welfare.

He also wrote the well-known *Lochner v. New York* (1905) opinion. *Lochner* dealt with a New York state law that limited bakers to ten-hour workdays and placed other restrictions on the baking industry within the state. Lochner, a bakery owner, was found to have violated the law and fined. He appealed the fine through the courts, claiming that his

Rufus W. Peckham.
(Library of Congress)

freedom to contract with his workers had been violated. Peckham agreed and wrote for a narrowly divided Court that struck down the law as unconstitutional. Peckham accused the legislature of engaging in special interest legislation rather than protecting workers' health, safety, and welfare. He noted that baking was not a dangerous occupation and that only a small group of workers rather than the entire public benefited from the regulation.

Although the *Lochner* decision was subsequently denounced as judicial activism at its worst, Peckham's opinion adhered to the Court's established precedent and remained good law into the 1930's. *Lochner* bolstered Peckham's reputation as a defender of individual economic rights.

ELEVENTH AMENDMENT

Peckham's effect on the Court's jurisprudence stretches beyond his opinions on freedom of contract, all of which were overruled by later courts. He also sought to expand the power of the federal courts in ruling on state legislation. However, he was faced with the strictures of the Eleventh Amendment, which prohibited individuals from suing state governments in federal courts. In one of his most long-standing opinions, *Ex parte Young* (1908), Peckham reinterpreted the amendment to allow lawsuits against states. In *Young*, railroads were required to post rates according to the rate schedule created by the state. Failure to post such a schedule would lead to a hefty fine and possible imprisonment. Young, a railroad executive, appealed and sought to have the law overturned in federal court. His case was thrown out under the Eleventh Amendment. When Young's appeal reached the Court, Justice Peckham was more sympathetic. In his decision, Peckham interpreted the Eleventh Amendment as allowing a state citizen to sue a state official in federal court. He argued that when a state official attempts to enforce an unconstitutional law, that official's immunity from a federal lawsuit no longer exists. Peckham's *Young* decision remained the authoritative interpretation of the amendment, allowing individuals to bring state officials before federal courts.

Justice Peckham, though, was less willing to expand federal power when it involved Congress's ability to regulate commerce. He dis-

Peckham, Rufus W.

sented in *Champion v. Ames* (1903), in which the Court upheld a federal law prohibiting interstate selling of lottery tickets. In *Adair v. United States* (1908), he voted with a six-member majority that struck down as unconstitutional a federal law prohibiting the firing of workers based on their belonging to a union. Peckham agreed that the law exceeded Congress's power to regulate commerce and violated the freedom of contract doctrine.

During his thirteen years on the Court, Peckham left a legacy of unwavering support for individual economic rights and a distrust of government regulation. When he died in 1909, his vision of the Constitution controlled the Court's agenda, and though many of his decisions were subsequently overruled, his effect on the Court during the turn of the century is unquestioned.

Douglas Clouatre

FURTHER READING

Bader, William H., and Roy M. Mersky, eds. *The First One Hundred Eight Justices.* Buffalo, N.Y.: William S. Hein, 2004.

Ely, James W., Jr. *The Chief Justiceship of Melville Fuller.* Columbia: University of South Carolina Press, 1995.

———. *The Fuller Court: Justices, Rulings, and Legacy.* Santa Barbara, Calif.: ABC-Clio, 2003.

Fiss, Owen. *National Expansion and Economic Growth.* New York: Macmillan, 1982.

Friedman, Leon, and Fred L. Israel, eds. *The Justices of the United States Supreme Court: Their Lives and Major Opinions.* 5 vols. New York: Chelsea House, 1997.

Gillman, Howard. *The Constitution Besieged.* Durham, N.C.: Duke University Press, 1993.

Swindler, William. *The Court and the Constitution in the Twentieth Century.* New York: Bobbs-Merrill, 1969.

SEE ALSO *Allgeyer v. Louisiana*; Capitalism; Contract, freedom of; Eleventh Amendment; Fuller, Melville W.; *Lochner v. New York.*

Peonage

DESCRIPTION: Status or condition of involuntary servitude in which one person must work for another in order to pay off a debt.

SIGNIFICANCE: After the Civil War, employers in the rural South used a number of labor practices that had the effect of relegating many African Americans to a state of virtual slavery. In three cases decided between 1905 and 1914, the Supreme Court ruled that these practices violated the Thirteenth Amendment.

Despite the Thirteenth Amendment's command that "neither slavery nor involuntary servitude, except as a punishment for crime . . . shall exist within the United States," forced systems of labor came to dominate the market for African American workers after the Civil War (1861-1865). There were three principal systems or practices used: black codes, sharecropping, and the convict lease system.

Black codes were laws passed in most of the southern states between 1865 and 1866 that applied only to African Americans. Under the codes, African American men who were unemployed or without a permanent residence could be arrested, charged, and fined as vagrants. A person convicted of vagrancy could avoid jail only by contracting to work for a private employer, who would then pay the person's fine. If the person quit his job before his contract term expired, he would be arrested and returned to the employer. The codes gave the employers the right to use physical force to discipline contract workers.

SHARECROPPING

Along with the contract labor system that developed under the black codes, the southern states also used a system of farm tenancy known as "sharecropping." Although the sharecropping system exploited poor whites as well as African Americans, an overwhelming number of sharecroppers were African Americans. Under this system, a farmer leased a plot of land from a plantation owner. As rent for the land, the sharecropper-farmer agreed to pay the planter a certain portion of the cotton crop produced at the end of the harvesting season. However, the sharecropper was also compelled to purchase all seeds, food, clothing, and other necessities from the planter's store. These purchases were usually made on credit, at extremely high interest rates. Moreover, the planter determined how much crop the sharecropper had produced and what that crop was worth. The sharecropper was rarely able to pay what was owed for items purchased from the store and the rent for the leased land. As a result, year after year, the sharecropper had no choice but to purchase more items on credit. Sharecroppers caught up in this continuous cycle of debt soon found themselves in a position that came to be known as "debt peonage," in which the sharecropper was required by law to work for the planter until the debt was paid off—an event that never occurred.

CONVICT LEASE SYSTEM

The convict lease system was perhaps the most exploitative of the peonage practices. Under this system, a person convicted of a crime would be lent by the state to work for a private employer. The employer would pay the state a fee for each convict worker. The demand for leased convict workers was nearly insatiable, and states received large amounts of revenue from the leasing system. As a result, large numbers of people became ensnared in the southern criminal justice system. The overwhelming majority of these people were African American men, most of whom had been convicted of petty offenses such as vagrancy or on trumped-up charges.

The convict lease system was exceedingly brutal. Leased convicts were subject to frequent whippings that rivaled the treatment of slaves in their viciousness. The prisoners lived in inhumane conditions and were worked ceaselessly, sometimes literally being worked to death. Indeed, the cruelty of the system is evidenced by its death toll—reaching an average annual rate of 20 percent and in some places rising as high as nearly 50 percent.

CONGRESS AND THE COURT ACT

Congress first acted against peonage by passage of the Peonage Act of 1867. Under the act, any person who held another in peonage was subject to a fine and term of imprisonment. In *Clyatt v. United States* (1905), the Supreme Court upheld the constitutionality of the act. The case involved the conviction of Samuel M. Clyatt who, in 1901, led a party of three armed white men into Florida and took back to Georgia two black men to work off debts that Clyatt claimed the men owed him. In arresting the two men, Clyatt acted under the authority of Florida law.

Writing for a unanimous Court, Justice David J. Brewer stated that the justices had no doubt that the Peonage Act was within Congress's authority under the Thirteenth Amendment. Moreover, the Court held, the act could be applied to "any person holding another in a state of peonage," even where the person acted pursuant to "a municipal ordinance or state law sanctioning such holding."

The most important legal blow to peonage came six years after *Clyatt* in *Bailey v. Alabama* (1911). In *Bailey*, the Court held that Alabama could not punish a person for breaching a labor contract. The case arose from the conviction of Alonzo Bailey under an Alabama statute that made it a crime to enter into a labor contract with the intent to defraud the employer. Under the statute, breach of the contract was prima facie evidence of the intent to defraud. Because Bailey had quit his job, the Alabama court held that this was sufficient evidence of his intent to defraud his employer at the time Bailey had entered into the contract.

By a vote of seven to two, the Court reversed Bailey's conviction. The Alabama statute, the Court held, violated both the Peonage Act of 1867 and the Thirteenth Amendment. Justice Oliver Wendell Holmes wrote a vigorous dissent in which he argued that a criminal penalty for breach of a labor agreement was no more unlawful than was a civil damages action for such a breach.

The last peonage case to come before the Court was *United States v. Reynolds* (1914). In this case, the justices unanimously struck down Alabama's criminal surety law. Under such laws, which many southern states had enacted, convicts were released from jail to a private employer. The employer paid the convict's fine, in exchange for which the convict entered into an agreement to work for the employer for a fixed term. If the person quit his job before the term of the surety contract expired, he was subject to additional criminal penalties. In an opinion by Justice William R. Day, the Court held that state surety laws violated the Thirteenth Amendment and the Peonage Act.

The Court's three peonage decisions established that peonage violated the constitutional prohibition on slavery and involuntary servitude. However, as important as these decisions are to the jurisprudence of the Thirteenth Amendment, the decisions had no discernible effect on the existence of peonage, as these exploitative labor practices continued long after the Court's ruling in the *Reynolds* case.

Barbara Holden-Smith

FURTHER READING

Bickel, Alexander M., and Benno Schmidt, Jr. *The Judiciary and Responsible Government, 1910-21*. New York: Macmillan, 1984.

Daniel, Pete. *The Shadow of Slavery: Peonage in the South, 1901-1969*. Urbana: University of Illinois Press, 1972.

Klarman, Michael J. *From Jim Crow to Civil Rights: The Supreme Court and the Struggle for Racial Equality*. New York: Oxford University Press, 2006.

Novak, Daniel. *The Wheel of Servitude: Black Forced Labor After Slavery*. Lexington: University Press of Kentucky, 1978.

SEE ALSO Brewer, David J.; Day, William R.; Holmes, Oliver Wendell; Race and discrimination; Slavery; Thirteenth Amendment.

Pierce v. Society of Sisters

CITATION: 268 U.S. 510
DATE: March 17, 1925
ISSUE: Parental rights
SIGNIFICANCE: Reinforcing a 1923 decision, the Supreme Court again applied the doctrine of substantive due process to strike down a law for infringing on a noneconomic liberty.

In 1922 the voters of Oregon approved an initiative that required most children between eight and sixteen to attend public schools. A private parochial school contended that the regulation violated both the right of the school to engage in a useful business and the right of parents to direct the education of their children. In a unanimous decision, the Supreme Court held that the law was inconsistent with the due process clause of the Fourteenth Amendment. Justice James C. McReynolds explained that constitutional liberties "may not be abridged by legislation which has no reasonable relation to some purpose within the competency of the state." Although the case related to religious freedom, the Court did not choose to consider whether the First Amendment might be applicable to the states. Justice Oliver Wendell Holmes, who disliked substantive due process, did not explain why he joined *Pierce* after dissenting in *Meyer v. Nebraska* (1923).

The *Pierce* decision, combined with *Meyer*, meant that the Court firmly recognized that the "liberty clause" protected both economic and noneconomic liberties. When the Court ceased to protect economic liberties after 1937, it did not overturn the *Meyer/Pierce* precedents, and they were important to the Court's recognition of a right to privacy in *Griswold v. Connecticut* (1965).

Thomas Tandy Lewis

SEE ALSO Contract, freedom of; Due process, substantive; *Griswold v. Connecticut*; Holmes, Oliver Wendell; *Lochner v. New York*; McReynolds, James C.; Ninth Amendment; Privacy, right to; *Roe v. Wade*.

Mahlon Pitney

IDENTIFICATION: Associate justice (March 18, 1912-December 31, 1922)
NOMINATED BY: William Howard Taft
BORN: February 5, 1858, Morristown, New Jersey
DIED: December 9, 1924, Washington, D.C.
SIGNIFICANCE: During his tenure on the Supreme Court, Pitney was noted for his meticulously crafted and staunchly conservative opinions, particularly those in the area of labor organization.

Mahlon Pitney was the son of a prominent attorney who eventually became vice chancellor of New Jersey. Pitney entered Princeton (then called the College of New Jersey) in 1875. He thus was a classmate of Woodrow Wilson, and although they joined opposing political parties, the two maintained a cordial relationship. Upon his graduation in 1879, Pitney studied law in Morristown with his father, was admitted to the bar, and opened his own practice in nearby Dover, a growing industrial city. When his father became vice chancellor, Pitney took over the Morristown practice and prospered both professionally and politically.

In 1894 Pitney became the Republican nominee for Congress. He won a close election but was reelected in 1896 more substantially—partly because his conservative stand against the free coinage of silver attracted "gold Democrats" as well as Republicans. A year before the end of his second term, however, Pitney resigned from Congress to enter the state senate. Soon he was the senate president. He rose in New Jersey Republican circles because of his ability, his steadfast conservatism, and his willingness to cooperate with the state's Republican "boss," William Sewall. He probably had his eye on the governorship. However, in 1901, his life suddenly changed course. When Governor Foster Voorhees nominated him to the New Jersey Su-

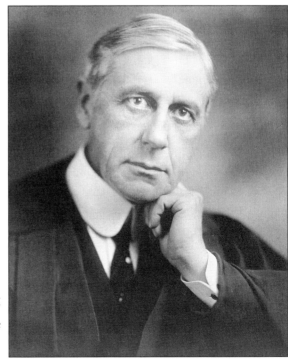

Mahlon Pitney. (Harris and Ewing/ Collection of the Supreme Court of the United States)

preme Court, Pitney turned his back on politics and devoted the rest of his career to the judiciary.

From February, 1901, until January, 1908, Pitney was a justice of the New Jersey Supreme Court, but then he was offered the chancellorship of New Jersey. He held that position at the apex of the state's appellate system until his appointment to the U.S. Supreme Court. His nomination came from William H. Taft—apparently on the strength of a single dinner meeting between the two, one week before Taft announced his choice. Pitney's antilabor views were well known, and they sparked a short Senate debate during which some progressive Republicans deserted Taft and voted against the nominee. The party loyalists were able to carry the nomination, however, by a vote of fifty to twenty-six.

During his tenure of nearly eleven years, Pitney authored 244 majority opinions for the Court and only 19 dissents. Consistent with his earlier views, Pitney wrote a number of strongly antiunion opinions, the most important of which were *Coppage v. Kansas* (1915), upholding the right of employers to fire employees who refused to resign from their unions, and *Hitchman Coal and Coke Co. v. Mitchell* (1917), ruling that employers could get an injunction to prevent unionization if the workers had previously agreed not to organize. These and other decisions provoked spirited dissents from the shifting group of moderates and liberals on the Court—Oliver Wendell Holmes, Louis D. Brandeis, Charles Evans Hughes, John H. Clarke, and William R. Day.

In August, 1922, a serious stroke left Pitney unable to continue, and he resigned his position effective December 31. Two years later, he died at his home in Washington, D.C.

David W. Levy

SEE ALSO Contract, freedom of; Taft, William H.; White, Edward D.

Planned Parenthood of Southeastern Pennsylvania v. Casey

CITATION: 505 U.S. 833
DATE: June 29, 1992
ISSUE: Abortion
SIGNIFICANCE: Although the Supreme Court reaffirmed a woman's constitutional right to terminate a pregnancy before the fetus attains viability, it rejected the trimester framework and allowed states to enact abortion restrictions that did not place an "undue burden" on the woman's right.

In the landmark case *Roe v. Wade* (1973), the Supreme Court ruled that a woman has a constitutional right to privacy that includes a right to abortions. By the early 1990's, because of several appointments by Presidents Ronald Reagan and George H. W. Bush, the Court increasingly approved of regulations that made it more difficult for women to obtain abortion services. The suit against Pennsylvania governor Robert Casey challenged a statute that required spousal notification, the consent of one parent in the case of an unmarried minor, a twenty-four-hour waiting period before abortion procedures, and the obligation of providers to give patients information about adoptions and the health risks of abortions. In previous cases, the Supreme Court had struck down similar restrictions. Before the *Casey* decision was announced, many observers expected that a conservative majority might overturn the *Roe* precedent.

In *Casey*, the Court was extremely fragmented. Five justices voted to reaffirm a woman's right to an abortion during the early stages of pregnancy. Three of the five, however, emphasized *stare decisis* (precedent) rather than constitutional principle. Five justices voted to invalidate the spousal notification requirement, and seven justices voted to uphold the other statutory regulations. In addition, a joint opinion of the controlling plurality accepted two ideas that Justice Sandra Day O'Connor had advocated for several years: the rejection of *Roe*'s trimester framework as unworkable and the recognition of an undue burden standard for evaluating whether regulations were acceptable. The opinion spoke of a woman's "liberty" rather than her "privacy."

Two members of the Court wanted to strike down all the Pennsylvania restrictions. Four of the justices entirely rejected the idea that the Constitution protects a right to abortions. The compromises in Casey's controlling opinion did not please either pro-choice or pro-life organizations.

Thomas Tandy Lewis

SEE ALSO Abortion; Birth control and contraception; Due process, substantive; Fundamental rights; Judicial scrutiny; Privacy, right to; *Roe v. Wade.*

Plea Bargaining

DESCRIPTION: Process of negotiations through which criminal cases are adjudicated without the defendants exercising their right to trial.

SIGNIFICANCE: In the last third of the twentieth century, the Supreme Court formally sanctioned the process of plea bargaining, which had been practiced for many years, and ruled on the acceptability of procedures governing it.

Plea bargaining is the process engaged in by prosecutors and defense attorneys in criminal cases to attempt to arrive at satisfactory dispositions of cases without the need to conduct trials. Such dispositions may result in tangible benefits for prosecutors, defendants, and the criminal justice system as a whole. Prosecutors gain certainty that defendants will be convicted, reduce their caseloads, and avoid having to put the victims of crimes and other witnesses through the ordeal of trials. Defendants usually receive reductions in the charges they face or sentences they receive in return for their agreement to plead guilty. The criminal justice system saves a great deal of time and money in avoiding trials, especially jury trials.

Critics argue that plea bargaining turns the justice system into a marketplace in which such fundamental protections as the right to cross-examine one's accuser, the right to a jury trial, and the requirement that the prosecution prove guilt beyond a reasonable doubt are largely ignored. They claim that plea bargaining is tantamount to punishing defendants who exercise their constitutional right to trial, because such defendants incur heavier sentences than those who plead guilty.

Beginning in the latter part of the twentieth century, the Supreme Court made clear that, done properly, plea bargaining was an accepted part of the criminal justice system. Although invalidating the plea of guilty in the particular case before it, the Court, in *Boykin v. Alabama* (1969), suggested that adjudications of guilt based on guilty pleas were constitutional if adequate safeguards for protecting defendants' rights were present. The Court declared in *Santobello v. New York* (1971) that plea bargaining is an "essential component of the administration of justice" and something to be "encouraged." In *Brady v. United States* (1970), the Court held that even when a defendant pleads guilty to avoid the possibility of receiving the death penalty if convicted at trial, such a plea is not unconstitutionally coercive.

PLEA BARGAINS AS CONTRACTS

Plea bargains have often been compared to contracts, and the Court has been confronted with plea bargaining issues that mirror to some extent contractual questions. Still, the Court's decisions reflect the view that there are differences between the correct legal approach to contracts that are breached and to plea bargains that are not honored. In *Santobello*, the defendant, in exchange for his plea of guilty, had bargained for the prosecutor to make no recommendation at the time of sentencing. However, a different prosecutor, unaware of his colleague's earlier promise, recommended to the judge that the defendant receive one year in jail. The judge imposed the one-year sentence and claimed his decision was made independent of the prosecutor's improper recommendation. The Court invalidated the plea, holding that the defendant was entitled to what he had bargained for, a sentence absent any prosecutor's recommendation. Unlike most contract cases, however, the Court did not require that the victim of the broken promise be allowed to choose his remedy. Instead, the Court left it to the state court to decide if the interests of justice would be best served by allowing the defendant to withdraw his plea, as he preferred, or only to have the defendant resentenced before a different judge. In *Mabry v. Johnson* (1984), the Court held that the prosecutor was able to withdraw an offer that he made and that was accepted by the defendant as long as the plea of guilty had not yet been formally taken in court.

KNOWING AND VOLUNTARY PLEAS

The Court expressed a strong interest in ensuring that defendants who plead guilty and waive their right to trial do so in a manner that is voluntary and knowing. In *Boykin*, the Court held that if defendants are not informed that their guilty pleas waive their rights against compulsory self-incrimination, to confront their accusers, and to a jury trial, that their pleas are unconstitutional. Boykin and the judge who accepted his plea did not discuss these issues. Even when such a discussion takes place, the plea may be invalidated as being involuntary or unknowing. In *Blackledge v. Allison* (1977), the Court held that even when defendants waive their rights in court, such waivers may be deemed invalid if they are merely a formulaic series of responses that fail to show that defendants understand an important component of the bargaining process.

Another aspect of the requirement that a guilty plea be knowing and voluntary relates to the connection that must be shown between the criminal conduct admitted by the defendant and his understanding of the elements of the crime to which he is pleading guilty. In *Henderson v. Morgan* (1976), the Court held a guilty plea to be involuntary when the defendant admitted he stabbed the victim to death but never acknowledged that he *intended* to kill her. An intent to kill was a required element for the second-degree murder charge to which the defendant pleaded guilty.

TRIUMPH OF THE MARKETPLACE

Some claim that in a desire to encourage guilty pleas, the Court has traveled a long way in allowing the values of the marketplace to govern the bargaining process. In *Bordenkircher v. Hayes* (1978) the Court upheld the decision of a prosecutor to have a defendant reindicted so as to face a heavier sentence after the defendant rejected the prosecutor's offer of a plea agreement. The Court, in a 5-4 decision, held that such practices are merely legitimate aspects of the bargaining process. In *North Carolina v. Alford* (1970), the Court permitted a plea to stand even when the defendant claimed to be innocent of the crime to which he pleaded guilty. Where the prosecutor, the defendant, and the judge all agree to a certain disposition, the Court is unlikely to intervene.

Steven P. Grossman

FURTHER READING

Fisher, George. *Plea Bargaining's Triumph: A History of Plea Bargaining in America.* Stanford, Calif.: Stanford University Press, 2003.

Herman, G. Nicholas. *Plea Bargaining.* Charlottesville, N.C.: Lexis Law, 1997.

Heumann, Milton. *Plea Bargaining: The Experiences of Prosecutors, Judges, and Defense Attorneys.* Chicago: University of Chicago Press, 1978.

McCoy, Candace. *Politics and Plea Bargaining.* Philadelphia: University of Pennsylvania Press, 1993.

McDonald, William F., and James Craven. *Plea Bargaining.* Lexington, Mass.: Lexington Books, 1980.

Vogel, Mary E. *Coercion to Compromise: Social Conflict and the Emergence of Plea Bargaining, 1830-1920.* Rev. ed. New York: Oxford University Press, 2005.

SEE ALSO Capital punishment; Contract, freedom of; Habeas corpus; Jury, trial by; Self-incrimination, immunity against.

Plessy v. Ferguson

CITATION: 163 U.S.
DATE: May 18, 1896
ISSUE: Segregation
SIGNIFICANCE: The Supreme Court held that the equal protection clause of the Fourteenth Amendment did not prohibit government-mandated segregation as long as accommodations were equal for both races.

During the late nineteenth century, southern state legislatures enacted many laws requiring segregation. Louisiana's Separate Car Act of 1890 provided for "equal but separate accommodations for the white and colored races" on passenger railways within the state. In a test case, Homer Plessy, who was classified as "colored" because of his one-eighth African ancestry, was arrested for refusing to leave a car reserved for whites. Plessy claimed that the law was unconstitutional under both the Thirteenth and Fourteenth Amendments.

By a 7-1 vote, the Supreme Court sustained the Louisiana law. Writing for the majority, Justice Henry B. Brown narrowly interpreted the words of both amendments. Although the Fourteenth Amendment was designed to guarantee "the absolute equality of the races before the law," it did not require social equality or racial intermingling. Brown could see no evidence that segregation "stamps the colored race with a badge of inferiority," and he assumed that the laws were incapable of changing long-established customs. The lone dissenter, former slave owner Justice John Marshall Harlan, argued that racial

Justices of the Court that ruled in Plessy v. Ferguson. (Library of Congress)

separation amounted to imposing "a badge of servitude" on African Americans, and he wrote, "Our Constitution [1789] is color blind and neither knows nor tolerates classes among its citizens."

The *Plessy* doctrine of separate but equal provided the constitutional foundation for the Jim Crow system. Beginning in the 1930's, the Court began to chip away at the doctrine and to demand that public facilities really be equal. It was not until *Brown v. Board of Education* (1954) that the Court repudiated the *Plessy* precedent.

Thomas Tandy Lewis

SEE ALSO *Brown v. Board of Education*; Civil Rights movement; Equal protection clause; Fourteenth Amendment; Harlan, John Marshall; Race and discrimination; Reconstruction; Segregation, de jure; Taney, Roger Brooke.

Police Powers

DESCRIPTION: Powers to legislate to promote public health, safety, morality, or welfare.

SIGNIFICANCE: State governments use police powers to adopt numerous laws that regulate economic and social behavior. These state laws sometimes limit protected civil liberties or conflict with federal efforts to create uniform national economic regulation. The resulting disputes are resolved in the Supreme Court.

As the Supreme Court ruled in *Jacobson v. Massachusetts* (1905), state governments possess police powers, presumably having inherited them from the British government at independence. Sometimes states authorize local governments to make police power laws, usually with significant restrictions. Police powers are very extensive. Through exercise of these powers, states have created traffic safety codes, compulsory vaccination laws, building and housing codes, labor regulations, air pollution abatement laws, restaurant inspection ordinances, and many similar laws. Indeed, few state laws that regulate the economy are not based at least partly on police powers. Some of these laws may dramatically control behavior. Laws that require strict quarantines for people with contagious diseases, for example, may even limit otherwise federally protected civil liberties. The Court consistently gave states broad latitude to use their police powers, usually requiring only that a state regulatory law be reasonably related to some legislatively determined health or safety goal to be constitutional.

The *Jacobson* court explicitly ruled that the states did not surrender police powers when the federal government was formed. The federal government has no general police power, except what is necessary to make health and safety regulations for the District of Columbia and for those territories, not part of any state, that are governed directly by Congress. As a result, federal laws that regulate economic or social behavior must be based on some other power, something explicitly granted to Congress in the Constitution.

THE POTENTIAL FOR CONFLICT

The Constitution gives the federal government the power to regulate that part of the economy that concerns more than one state. Knowing that people would not be able to do business across state lines without such standard elements as a single national currency, the Founders looked to Congress to "foster and protect" interstate commerce by making those necessary national rules. Particularly after the New Deal in the mid-1930's, Congress regulated many parts of the economy, being especially active in those areas where there were national problems (such as the farm economy) or where states were naturally unable to deal with problems (such as interstate transportation).

As a result, many areas of the economy became governed by national regulatory codes. For example, Congress created a single national system of airline and airport safety regulation. All air-traffic controllers are federal employees who are located at airports and other facilities as determined by the national government and who use the same equipment, which was bought by Congress. As a result, regardless of their location, these important safety officials can communicate with each other. Nationwide, airport runways and lighting systems must meet a single set of standards. U.S. pilots must meet the same health standards wherever they are based.

However, these uniform national rules sometimes conflict with state regulations that are designed to deal with local problems. For example, if Congress protects public safety by regulating airlines and airports, can a state additionally require airlines to cease takeoffs and landings at an in-state airport at ten each night to promote the local health interest of noise abatement? If Congress requires certain air pollution control devices to be installed on new automobiles, can a state such as California, which has unusually severe pollution problems, require cars sold in that state to be equipped with even more (and more expensive) pollution control equipment? The development of uniform national rules prevents attention to local problems, but dealing with local problems destroys uniformity.

THE COURT AS REFEREE

Because the conflicts in such cases are between constitutional powers—state police powers versus the interstate commerce clause of the Constitution—it becomes the Court's job to resolve them. The Court serves as referee of the federal system, determining, in individual cases, how much states may interfere with federal uniformity. Traditionally, the Court balanced a state's interest in its local regulation against the national interest in uniformity.

In doing so, the Court considered many variables. As a general rule, police power regulations are likely to be upheld if they cover areas of the economy in which state interest is traditionally paramount, if they further important local health or safety concerns, and if they affect interstate commerce only slightly. As the Court noted in *Cooley v. Board of Wardens of the Port of Philadelphia* (1852), the harbor of the city of Philadelphia is different from any other harbor and poses unique hazards to navigation. Because the requirements for safe shipping in the port are so directly related to these unique conditions, Pennsylvania can legitimately make interstate and international ships meet its local safety codes while in the harbor, even though those ships are in other respects regulated by Congress.

However, as Chief Justice John Marshall observed in *Gibbons v. Ogden* (1824), some parts of the economy, by their natures, require single, uniform national regulation. In such cases, only Congress can provide the necessary comprehensive laws. By tradition, some parts of the economy have become identified with such national regulation. Included are nuclear power plants, which are closely associated with national supplies of radioactive fuel and pose national hazards; modern commercial airlines, which must simultaneously operate in numerous states; and, as the Court ruled in *Southern Pacific Co. v. Arizona* (1945), freight railroad systems.

In *South Carolina v. Barnwell Brothers* (1938), the Court ruled that interstate trucking companies could be subjected to local safety regulation, even when the regulation made it difficult to operate across state borders. In this case, the Court emphasized the existence of distinctly local safety problems that justified lower speed limits, smaller truck-size requirements, and lighter load restrictions. As a result of this litigation, for many years states had much greater control over trucking companies operating within their borders than they had over railroads or airlines.

GENERAL TRENDS

After the mid-1930's, when the Court became more receptive to the increased federal control over the economy represented by New Deal programs, the Court generally tended to reinforce the development of national standards. Part of this trend toward national control was a response to the increasing nationalization of the economy itself, following the building of the interstate highway system and the growth of huge corporations that do business in every state. Coalfired or water-driven power plants are local factories, but nuclear power plants are part of the interstate distribution network for carefully controlled radioactive fuel supplies. Because they are more expensive, they must be financed nationally, and because they are larger and more dangerous, they pose interstate—indeed, national—safety problems. Therefore, it is appropriate to make them meet national uniform construction and safety regulations.

Perhaps in response to this trend, the Court reinterpreted some constitutional rulings that previously had favored states. For example, after the development of the interstate highway system, the *Barnwell Brothers* case was overruled in *Kassel v. Consolidated Freightways* (1981). Because of the history of Prohibition and repeal, states exercised broader powers over alcoholic beverages than they could exercise over other consumer goods. Indeed, the Twenty-First Amendment gives states the power to block interstate commerce in alcohol entirely in order to maintain statewide prohibitions. However, *South Dakota v. Dole* (1987) limited state power to regulate access to alcohol even in the interest of highway safety.

Finally, in the twentieth century, the Court developed the doctrine of federal preemption: If an area seems, by its nature, appropriate for national regulation, and Congress adopts a law that is meant as a comprehensive regulation, then states are forbidden to regulate in the area Congress has occupied—or preempted—no matter how severely local problems cry out for local regulation. For example, in *Burbank v. Lockheed Air Terminal* (1973), the Court held that the federal government's adoption of comprehensive airport regulation preempted that field and kept states from passing even urgently needed noise abatement regulations.

STATES' RIGHTS

Deference to the federal government became so extensive that scholars argued that the federal balance itself was being altered. However, in the latter part of the twentieth century, the Court showed some signs of letting the pendulum swing back the other way. In *Pacific Gas and Electric Co. v. State Energy Resources Conservation and Development Commission* (1983), the Court suggested that it might construe the preemption doctrine narrowly. Specifically, the Court held that it would not assume that just because Congress had preempted the field of nuclear power plant safety it had also meant to preempt all state regulation designed to make sure that power companies that operated such plants were financially solvent. The Court seemed to be saying that Congress would have to specify precisely what it was preempting. If there was uncertainty, Congress could not count on the Court automatically resolving the uncertainty in favor of the federal government. This was quite a change of tone from the *Burbank* case. A similar narrow construction of the federal cigarette labeling requirements allowed people made ill by smoking to sue cigarette manufacturers in state courts, in *Cipollone v. Liggett Group* (1992).

States were given a freer hand to develop their own health and safety rules as a result of decisions that protected them from being forced to participate in federal programs. In *Printz v. United States* (1997), the Court held that the Tenth Amendment forbids the federal government from assigning state officials any duties to implement a national program. Specifically, *Printz* held that local sheriffs did not have to perform the background checks of gun buyers required by federal handgun control legislation. Subsequently, some states developed their own safety regulations governing handgun sales.

Paul Lermack

FURTHER READING

One possible way to begin a study of this subject is by looking at general works on legal aspects of policing, such as John C. Klotter's *Legal Guide for Police: Constitutional Issues* (6th ed. Cincinnati, Ohio: Anderson, 2002) and Barry W. Hancock and Paul M. Sharp's *Criminal Justice in America: Theory, Practice, and Police* (3d ed. Upper Saddle River, N.J.: Prentice-Hall, 2003). Paul Freund's *The Supreme Court of the United States: Its Business, Purposes and Performance* (New York: Meridian Books, 1961) examines the Court's role as referee of the federal system.

The history of police powers is sketched in Ruth Lodge Roettinger's *The Supreme Court and the State Police Power* (Washington, D.C.: Public Affairs Press, 1957) and Howard Gillman's *The Constitution Besieged: The Rise and Demise of Lochner Era Police Powers Jurisprudence* (Durham, N.C.: Duke University Press, 1995). An early comprehensive study is Willis Reed Bierly's *Police Power: State and Federal Definitions and Distinctions* (Philadelphia: R. Welsh, 1907).

Although the scope of police powers is rarely the sole topic of discussion, it often is discussed in works devoted to the proper scope of the congressional commerce power, with which it conflicts. These include Richard Epstein's "The Proper Scope of the Commerce Power," *Virginia Law Review* 73 (1987): 1387, and Vincent A. Cirillo and Jay Eisenhofer's "Reflections on the Congressional Commerce Power," *Temple Law Review* 60 (1987): 901.

SEE ALSO Automobile searches; *Brown v. Mississippi*; *Chimel v. California*; Commerce, regulation of; Federalism; *Florida v. Bostick*; Fourth Amendment; *Gibbons v. Ogden*; Miranda rights; New Deal; States' rights and state sovereignty; *Terry v. Ohio*.

Political Questions

DESCRIPTION: Matters not frequently brought before the Supreme Court because they are considered nonjusticiable and not amenable to judicial resolution.

SIGNIFICANCE: Under Article III of the U.S. Constitution, the Court has jurisdiction over cases concerned with political questions, but it often refuses to hear them, deferring to other branches of government.

Article III, section 2, of the U.S. Constitution presents the categories of federal jurisdiction by outlining fully the types of cases and controversies the Supreme Court may adjudicate. This definitive statement has led the Court to an interpretation that it should hear only "justiciable" cases, that is, cases that are likely to result in a suitable judicial outcome.

The judicial branch of government, although political in many ways, is the least political of the three major governmental branches. Because its justices are appointed rather than elected and serve "during good behavior," which generally means that their tenure is for life, the nine people who serve in this capacity enjoy far greater independence than most public servants do.

EARLY DEFINITION

The first case that forced the Court to define a political question was *Luther v. Borden* (1849), in which the plaintiff sued the defendant for trespass during the Dorr Rebellion in Rhode Island. Citizens of the state, rankling over unjust apportionment and barriers to voting under the state's government, called a constitutional convention of their own and established a new, democratic government with Thomas W. Dorr as governor. When several members of the rebellion, including Thomas Dorr, were arrested under martial law, some of the dissidents attempted to have the charter government declared unconstitutional by citing the clause in Article IV of the Constitution that guarantees a republican form of government to each state. Justice Roger Brooke Taney, writing for the Court, enumerated reasons that the Court could not hear the case and, in this opinion, essentially defined the concept of political questions.

Taney's main concern was that the Court lacked standards on which to base a judgment on the issue posed in *Luther.* He contended that this was a controversy that the Constitution, in Article IV, delegates to other branches of government, thereby removing it from the Court's primary jurisdiction. Taney noted the devastating effect on the entire nation were the judicial branch to replace a legal and existing government with a dissident government. He noted that the Court could not enforce the guarantee of a republican form of government as promised in Article IV, making the matter, in the eyes of the law, a nonjusticiable political question.

Long before *Luther,* Justice John Marshall's opinion in *Marbury v. Madison* (1803) set the groundwork for dealing with nonjusticiable political questions. He wrote, "The province of the court is, solely, to decide on the rights of individuals. . . . Questions in their nature political . . . can never be made in this Court." This statement represented a major step toward addressing the issue of political questions and nonjudiciability.

THE POLITICAL NATURE OF NONJUDICIABILITY

Despite the seeming attempt to elevate the Court above purely political issues, the Court ultimately has total jurisdiction over what cases it will hear. Its deciding to hear or not to hear cases that involve political questions becomes, in itself, a political decision. Its ability to accept or reject petitions to hear cases involving power and influence, its relation to other branches of government as in *Luther,* and its prestige and legal position are inherently political. The decision not to hear *Luther* had as strong political implications as a decision in favor of hearing the case would have had.

The grounds for deciding nonjudiciability of political questions were never precisely drawn. Decisions regarding them were judgment calls, with the Court exercising complete discretion in deciding which cases to hear. It could quite legitimately reject cases that did not suit its convenience or the adjudication of which might cast it in an undesirable light.

More than a century after the *Luther* case, the Court tightened its definition of the political question principle. This principle was articulated in a minority opinion Justice Felix Frankfurter wrote in the case of *Colegrove v. Green* (1946), which challenged apportionment in the congressional districts of Illinois, contending that the Court's refusal to involve itself in *Colegrove* suggested that reapportionment issues were nonjusticiable.

Although a minority opinion, Frankfurter's observations kept the Court out of reapportionment cases until 1960, when it made a decision in the case of *Gomillion v. Lightfoot* (1960). It was virtually forced into doing so because of the nightmare that reapportionment had become, particularly in the southern states, where concerted efforts were afoot to discourage African Americans from voting by redrawing the lines of their districts. Ironically, Frankfurter wrote the opinion in *Gomillion*, which involved gerrymandering for racial purposes. Frankfurter avoided the seeming contradiction between this opinion and his 1946 statement by declaring that *Gomillion* was a Fifteenth Amendment right-to-vote case rather than a reapportionment case. As such, it was justiciable.

REDEFINING THE POLITICAL QUESTION DOCTRINE

Two years after *Gomillion*, in *Baker v. Carr* (1962), a case involving apportionment of the Tennessee legislature, Justice William J. Brennan, Jr., addressed the political question issue and suggested a new method for deciding matters involving it. Because of Frankfurter's minority opinion in *Colegrove*, the Court considered *Baker* under the equal protection clause of the Constitution. Brennan pointed out, however, that because the case involved no issues regarding separation of powers, it met his new guidelines for justiciability. Brennan's redefinition of the political issues doctrine calls for comity, or jurisdictional courtesy among branches of government, for "adherence to a political decision already made," and for a sensitivity to "the potentiality of embarrassment from multifarious pronouncements by various departments on one question."

Justice Frankfurter, who retired from the Court shortly after the *Baker* decision, made his final dissent in regard to it, refuting Brennan's redefinition in the matter of political questions. In his bitter dissent, he reiterated his arguments in *Colegrove*, where he had stated that for the Court to hear reapportionment cases "would cut very deep into the very being of Congress. Courts ought not to enter this political thicket." He now admonished the Court to avoid an entanglement that he considered a violation of the doctrine of judicial self-restraint. Despite his admonitions, Frankfurter's opinions essentially were overruled, largely because of the racial implications of reapportionment.

Two years later, in *Reynolds v. Sims* (1964), the Court reviewed the remedies available in apportionment cases. Where equal protection violations occurred, federal judges were urged to move slowly enough to permit states the opportunity to correct their problem.

An Activist Court

Frankfurter's retirement marked the passing of an old guard that served from the New Deal of the 1930's into the 1960's. The appointment of justices Byron R. White in 1961 and Arthur J. Goldberg in 1962 marked a turning point in the Court's history. The social activism of the Court under Chief Justice Earl Warren, evidenced in such landmark decisions as *Baker*, became increasingly apparent. In this judicial climate, political questions, which were at the forefront of the social dynamism of the Warren Court, could not be disregarded.

In 1969 the Court agreed to hear a case that, perhaps more than any other that had come before it, involved the doctrine of political questions. In *Powell v. McCormick* (1969), Adam Clayton Powell, Jr., sued to regain the seat in the House of Representatives to which he had been duly and legally elected by the citizens of his congressional district in New York City's Harlem. Powell was reelected to Congress in 1966 by a constituency he had served since 1942. Powell, a flamboyant public official and a lightning rod for public criticism, was accused of misusing congressional funds and other transgressions. The Ninetieth Congress that convened in January, 1967, hearing these unsubstantiated accusations, denied Powell his congressional seat.

Had Powell petitioned the Court for a hearing a decade earlier, his petition would surely have been denied. Matters of comity and the issue of the nonjusticiability of political questions would almost automatically have precluded such a case from being heard. Following Justice Brennan's reconsideration and redefinition in the matter of political questions, however, the Court agreed to hear *Powell*, another landmark case that made clear that the only requirements a legally elected member of Congress must meet under the U.S. Constitution are those of age, citizenship, and residence, all of which Powell had met. The Court found in Powell's favor. Further, while this case was pending and while Powell was still being denied his seat, his constituents in 1968 elected him to another term.

EFFECTS OF THE LANDMARK DECISIONS

The landmark decisions in *Baker* and *Powell* cast such doubt on the political questions doctrine that the question of judicial review in impeachment convictions by the Senate, usually considered to be settled negatively, required reconsideration. In the light of these decisions, it became clear that all arbitrary power, such as that which Congress attempted to exercise against Powell, was inimical to constitutional protection. Intrusions by other branches of government in this area, despite the general acceptance of comity, are subject to judicial intervention and decision.

Had President Richard M. Nixon not resigned in 1974, he would probably have been found guilty by the Senate in an impeachment trial. Had this occurred, the question of the nonjudiciability of political questions would have arisen. In all likelihood, a judicial review of his conviction by the Senate would have taken place under the new guidelines regarding political questions.

POLITICAL QUESTIONS IN WAR POWERS CASES

During the late 1960's and early 1970's, under Chief Justice Warren E. Burger, the Court became less activist than it had been under Earl Warren. As the Vietnam War dragged on, several suits were filed to test the constitutionality of U.S. involvement in that conflict. In three test cases, *Mora v. McNamara* (1967), *Orlando v. Laird* (1971), and *Holtzman v. Schlesinger* (1973), lower courts declined to consider the constitutionality of the war, citing the nonjusticiability of political questions or finding these cases unacceptable on other grounds.

In these cases, despite the objections of some justices who claimed the Court should consider the technical question of justiciability as well as the more encompassing question of judicial responsibility, the Court declined to grant hearings. Later, it avoided hearing other such cases, including one brought against President George H. W.

Bush in 1990 questioning his right to engage the United States in military action in the Persian Gulf.

IMPEACHMENTS AND ELECTIONS

The resignation of President Richard M. Nixon in 1974 and the acquittal of President Bill Clinton in his 1999 impeachment trial foreclosed any opportunities for the Supreme Court to review a presidential conviction on charges of impeachment. The Court decided its first impeachment case in *Nixon v. United States* (1993), when federal judge Walter Nixon challenged his own impeachment on the grounds that he had been tried by a senatorial committee rather than before the full Senate. The justices departed somewhat from the *Baker v. Carr* perspective when they unanimously held that issues regarding the legitimacy of impeachment proceedings were better left to the Senate than to the judiciary. Speaking for the majority, Chief Justice William H. Rehnquist argued that the word "try" was sufficiently imprecise to allow the Senate to utilize a variety of procedures. He further found that there were no "judicially discoverable and manageable standards" for assessing an impeachment trial, and that the word "sole" suggested that the Court had no authority to review the Senate's decision in the matter. The *Nixon* ruling appeared to suggest strong judicial deference to the political question doctrine, at least when the issue involved a "textually demonstrable" prerogative of "a coordinate branch of government."

By contrast, the Court's decision in *Bush v. Gore* (2000), which settled the disputed presidential election, demonstrated that the justices would not always pursue judicial restraint in regard to political controversies involving either federalism or separation of powers. When the five-member majority of the Court ordered that the recount of disputed ballots in Florida cease, based on the equal protection clause of the Fourteenth Amendment, the four dissenting justices made several accusations against the majority, including the charge of violating the political question doctrine. Justices John Paul Stevens and Ruth Bader Ginsburg emphasized that the decisions of the Florida's high court were defensible and deserving of respect. Justice Stephen G. Breyer emphasized that the Twelfth Amendment authorized Congress to count the electoral votes. He wrote, "however awkward or difficult it might be for Congress to resolve difficult electoral disputes, Congress, being a political body, expresses the people's will far more accurately than does an unelected Court." If the resolution of the disputed presidential election of 1876 had been less than ideal, he argued, at least the process did not expose the Court to charges of political partisanship. The public expects politicians to act according to partisan motives, but they expect their judges to be fair and as objective as possible.

The political question doctrine will always be controversial. While some scholars view the doctrine as a means for promoting democracy and as a useful antidote against the temptation of judicial activism, especially in regard to controversies relating to the constitutional powers of the three branches, others argue that the doctrine is unconstitutional, because the U.S. Constitution mandates that the Court is to decide all cases and controversies that arise under the Constitution and the laws of the United States. For most justices, however, the main difficulty is choosing principles for assessing which kinds of controversies are best decided judicially and which are better left to other political processes.

R. Baird Shuman
Updated by the Editor

FURTHER READING

One of the best sources for the Court's decisions on the political controversy doctrine and related issues is David M. O'Brien's *Constitutional Law and Politics, Volume One: Struggles for Power and Governmental Accountability* (6th ed. New York: W. W. Norton, 2006). In her *Politics and the Courts: Toward a General Theory of Public Law* (Westport, Conn.: Greenwood Press, 1992), Barbara M. Yarnold offers thorough coverage of the doctrine of political questions, as does John Bell in *Policy Arguments in Judicial Decisions* (New York: Oxford University Press, 1983), which provides detailed information about test cases of the 1960's and 1970's.

Two intriguing books deal in part with how judicial change occurs and with the crucial questions of what determines judiciability and of how the concept of political questions is defined. They are Kenneth M. Holland's *Judicial Activism in Comparative Perspective* (New

York: St. Martin's Press, 1991) and Susan R. Burgess's *Contest for Constitutional Authority: The Abortion and War Powers Debates* (Lawrence: University Press of Kansas, 1992). Burgess's discussion of the war powers debates are of particular interest in showing how the Court can opt to sidestep potentially awkward political issues.

In *The Transformation of the Supreme Court's Agenda: From the New Deal to the Reagan Administration* (San Diego, Calif.: Westview, 1991), Richard L. Pacelle, Jr., traces the course of the Court from a relatively conservative branch of government to one that became notably activist and then again retrenched to a more conservative stand. *Superintending Democracy: The Courts and the Political Process*, edited by Christopher P. Banks and John Clifford Green (Akron, Ohio: University of Akron Press, 2001), is a collection of scholarly essays examining a variety of issues relating to the Court's involvement in politics.

The Court's intervention in the 2000 presidential election raised many political questions, which are the subject of David K. Ryden's *The U.S. Supreme Court and the Electoral Process* (2d ed. Washington, D.C.: Georgetown University Press, 2002) and Alan M. Dershowitz's *Supreme Injustice: How the High Court Hijacked Election 2000* (New York: Oxford University Press, 2002).

SEE ALSO *Baker v. Carr*; Brennan, William J., Jr.; *Bush v. Gore*; Comity clause; Equal protection clause; Frankfurter, Felix; War powers; Warren, Earl.

Poll Taxes

DESCRIPTION: Procedure initially used to raise revenue. Payment of such taxes eventually took the place of property ownership as a stipulation for voting, frequently keeping the poor, both white and black, from voting.

SIGNIFICANCE: From the 1880's to the 1960's, poll taxes were implemented in many southern states to disfranchise African Americans, resulting in congressional involvement and in cases being brought before the Supreme Court.

To get around the Fifteenth Amendment, which guaranteed former male slaves the right to vote, states throughout the South required only African American voters to show payment of the poll tax. In *Williams v. Mississippi* (1898), the Supreme Court upheld the so-called Mississippi solution, which required poll taxes, literacy tests, and residency of black voters. Along with other devices employed to deny the franchise to African Americans, such as white primaries and the grandfather clause, poll taxes persisted. In *Breedlove v. Suttles* (1937), the Court upheld a poll tax as a qualification for voting.

In 1964 the Twenty-Fourth Amendment was passed and ratified, eliminating poll taxes in federal elections. In *Harper v. Virginia State Board of Elections* (1966), the Court declared poll taxes a violation of the equal protection clause of the Fourteenth Amendment in state

During a parade for victory in World War II, the National Association for the Advancement of Colored People displayed a monkey in a cage to protest poll taxes. (Library of Congress)

elections. The Voting Rights Act of 1965, amended in 1970, 1975, and 1982, successfully removed discriminatory voting practices, of which poll taxes were an integral part.

Kevin Eyster

SEE ALSO Civil Rights movement; Equal protection clause; Fifteenth Amendment; Gerrymandering; Grandfather clause; Reconstruction.

Lewis F. Powell, Jr.

IDENTIFICATION: Associate justice (January 2, 1972-June 26, 1987)
NOMINATED BY: Richard M. Nixon
BORN: November 19, 1907, Suffolk, Virginia
DIED: August 25, 1998, Richmond, Virginia
SIGNIFICANCE: During his fifteen years on the Supreme Court, Powell dominated an ideologically balanced court with his pragmatic, centrist views and his kind and courtly personal manner.

The father of Lewis F. Powell, Jr., eventually succeeded in business, but the family as not established socially or economically at the time of Powell's birth. Powell received a bachelor's and a law degree from Washington and Lee University and a master's degree in law from Harvard University. Powell had a long and successful career in private law practice in Richmond, Virginia, worked in the U.S. Army breaking the German codes in World War II, and presided over the American Bar Association and other national professional groups. Powell also led the Richmond School Board in the aftermath of *Brown v. Board of Education* (1954) and served on the state board of education through much of the next decade.

ASSOCIATE JUSTICE

In 1972, at the age of sixty-four, Powell took his seat as an associate justice. If Powell, a Southern gentleman, sustained his aristocratic loyalties without embarrassment, he also appreciated the striking diversity of American traditions and backgrounds. Powell was also noteworthy for a background increasingly rare among Supreme

Powell, Lewis F., Jr.

Court justices: a career without prior judicial experience.

In the next fifteen years until his resignation in 1987, Powell's voice and vote were so critical to constitutional jurisprudence that many might designate this period as the Powell Court rather than by the traditional reference to the presiding chief justice. As the Court and the country swung from the liberalism of Earl Warren's court to the conservatism of the Court under Warren Burger and William H. Rehnquist, Powell often provided the decisive fifth vote. Yet Powell's prominence is as much a matter of his intellectual as his numerical position in close cases. Powell was a "balancer" in both senses. He broke down complex cases into the facts, arguments, and interests arrayed on either side, seeking an equilibrium among them.

Powell's most famous opinion was undoubtedly *Regents of the University of California v. Bakke* (1978). Powell's opinion held that race may be considered in academic admissions but may not preclude full and individual consideration of all candidates. In *San Antonio Independent School District v. Rodriguez* (1973), Powell's opinion for the Court held that disparate funding of public schools was not subject to judicial strict scrutiny because economic class was not a suspect classification nor education a fundamental right. In *McCleskey v. Kemp* (1987), Powell's opinion for the Court held that a statistically significant relationship between the race of the perpetrator and the victim and a capital sentence did not prove that this petitioner's punishment resulted from racial discrimination. However, Powell concurred in striking down a Texas statute that denied state aid to local school districts for illegal alien children in *Plyler v. Doe* (1982).

Moreover, Powell consistently favored proportionality in other criminal process and punishment cases with a strong equality dimension, including *Batson v. Kentucky* (1986), *Rummel v. Estelle* (1980), *Solem v. Helm* (1983), and *Bowers v. Hardwick* (1986). In *United States v. United States District Court* (1972), Justice Powell's majority opinion struck down warrantless wiretaps of suspected domestic subversives. In *California v. Ciraolo* (1986), Powell's dissent expressed the view that a warrantless aerial observation of a fenced-in backyard violated the Fourth Amendment. In *Eddings v. Oklahoma* (1978), Powell's majority opinion forbade the exclusion of individualized, mitigating circumstances in capital sentencing. However, in *Booth v. Maryland* (1987),

870

Powell's opinion for the Court held that victim impact statements at sentencing violated the Eighth Amendment.

Powell's majority opinion in *Gertz v. Robert Welch* (1974) established a middle ground for libel against a private person, allowing states to choose their own standards, except that liability could not be imposed without fault nor punitive damages granted without knowledge of falsity or reckless disregard of truth. In *Gannett Co. v. De-Pasquale* (1979) Justice Powell concurred in upholding a judicial order, agreed to by the prosecution and defense, barring the press and public from a pretrial suppression hearing.

Powell's majority opinion in *Committee for Public Education and Religious Liberty v. Nyquist* (1973) found programs of public assistance to private schools, students, and parents to be unconstitutional. In *Wallace v. Jaffree* (1985), Powell concurred in striking down a "moment of silence" authorization, reserving judgment on a similar practice if undertaken for a secular purpose.

Lewis F. Powell, Jr.
(Library of Congress)

Powell, Lewis F., Jr.

POWELL'S LEGACY

Following Powell's retirement, President Ronald Reagan nominated the controversial Robert H. Bork. Although Powell was confirmed with only one negative vote, Bork's nomination was defeated at least in part because of the contrast between him and Powell both in temperament and in ideological sharpness. Though Anthony M. Kennedy ultimately took Powell's seat, Powell's centrist role was assumed by Sandra Day O'Connor. In the years since, she has frequently controlled a court balanced between liberal and conservative wings. In that role, O'Connor has continued Powell's pragmatism and collegiality.

James E. Lennertz

FURTHER READING

Bader, William H., and Roy M. Mersky, eds. *The First One Hundred Eight Justices.* Buffalo, N.Y.: William S. Hein, 2004.

Freeman, George Clemon, Jr. "Justice Powell's Constitutional Opinions." *Washington and Lee Law Review* 45 (1988): 411-465.

Jeffries, John Calvin. *Justice Lewis F. Powell, Jr.* New York: Fordham University Press, 2001.

Kahn, Paul W. "The Court, the Community and the Judicial Balance: The Jurisprudence of Justice Powell." *Yale Law Journal* 97 (1987): 1-60.

Powell, Lewis F., Jr. "Reflections." *Virginia Magazine of History and Biography* 96 (1988): 315-332.

"A Tribute to Justice Lewis F. Powell, Jr." *Harvard Law Review* 101 (1987): 395-420.

Urofsky, Melvin I. "Mr. Justice Powell and Education: The Balancing of Competing Values." *Journal of Law and Education* 13 (1984): 581-627.

Yarbrough, Tinsley E. *The Burger Court: Justices, Rulings, and Legacy.* Santa Barbara, Calif.: ABC-Clio, 2000.

SEE ALSO Affirmative action; *Batson v. Kentucky*; Judicial self-restraint; *McCleskey v. Kemp*; Race and discrimination; *Regents of the University of California v. Bakke*; *San Antonio Independent School District v. Rodriguez*; School integration and busing.

Presidential Powers

DESCRIPTION: The formal constitutional and legal powers of the U.S. president.

SIGNIFICANCE: The extent of presidential power is often examined by the Supreme Court because of the ambiguity of Article II of the U.S. Constitution, which defines and empowers the presidency.

The first, and in some sense the most important, of Supreme Court actions regarding the presidency arose very early in the constitutional history of the United States. In *Marbury v. Madison* (1803), the seminal case that established the Court's power of judicial review, the Court also had to address relations between the judicial and executive branches. It had to determine whether the secretary of state and, by implication, the president could be subjected to a court order or injunction. Chief Justice John Marshall's opinion distinguished between the legal and political duties of the executive. Where the law requires an executive action, a court order can be issued and enforced; where the president's duty is "political" and discretionary, courts may not intervene. The Court's decision in *Marbury*, often reaffirmed, thus established the fundamental principle that the president and the executive branch of the government are subject to legal restraints. Such a rule is particularly important in governmental systems based on separation of powers, in which conflict between the branches of the government is common.

Article II of the U.S. Constitution is not specific on the extent of the president's powers. The war and foreign affairs powers are shared with Congress; on the domestic side, Article II says that "the executive power shall be vested in a President of the United States" and that "he shall take care that the laws be faithfully executed." However, it does not say exactly what the executive powers are. Consequently, exercises of presidential power have often brought about Court action.

The Court was called on several times to define the president's power to remove federal officials from office. In *Myers v. United States* (1926), the Court held unconstitutional a legislative provision that certain postmasters could not be removed without the consent of the Senate. Chief Justice William H. Taft's opinion held that presidents must be able to select the officers who act under their direction. If they cannot, they could not properly be held responsible for the way in which the laws are executed. The *Myers* rule was later restricted to executive branch personnel in *Humphrey's Executor v. United States* (1935), in which the Court took the position that the president may not remove commissioners of independent regulatory agencies such as the Federal Trade Commission.

President Harry S. Truman (bottom row, center) visited the Supreme Court in 1945, meeting with justices (front row, left to right) Harlan F. Stone, Hugo L. Black, Felix Frankfurter; (second row) Stanley F. Reed, Harold H. Burton, Wiley Rutledge, Jr., Frank Murphy; and (third row, at left) William O. Douglas. During World War II, Truman put U.S. steel mills under federal government control when a strike seemed imminent. In 1952, the Court ruled that he lacked the power to do that.
(Library of Congress)

PRESIDENTIAL POWERS DEFINED

The most important modern case regarding the president's domestic powers is *Youngstown Sheet and Tube Co. v. Sawyer* (1952). During the Korean War, the steelworkers threatened to strike. To avert the possibility that the quantity of steel would be insufficient for military purposes, President Harry S. Truman ordered Secretary of Commerce Charles Sawyer to seize the steel mills and operate them under government control. The steel companies brought action to enjoin the seizure. No law authorized the seizure, and Congress declined to pass one even after President Truman reported his action to it. By means of the Taft-Hartley Act of 1947, Congress had provided a procedure by which the president could seek a court order against the unions to prevent strikes. However, partly for political reasons, President Truman did not wish to invoke this procedure. The government argued that the sum of the executive and war powers of the president authorized the seizure in a national emergency.

The Court disagreed. By a 6-3 vote, the Court held that the seizure was beyond the president's power. The opinion of the Court was delivered by Justice Hugo L. Black, who reasoned that the seizure amounted to lawmaking (the Constitution assigns the power "to raise and support armies" to Congress). Any exercise of presidential power must spring from either the Constitution or a law. Because no law authorized the seizure, Black turned to the Constitution to see if authority could be found there. The claim that the aggregate of presidential power supported the seizure was too broad and open ended; there seemed to be no limit to the powers that could be claimed under the guise of necessity. Consequently the seizure was declared unconstitutional.

Black's analysis of the case was very formal. A more flexible opinion reaching the same result was submitted by Justice Robert H. Jackson. Jackson suggested that claims of presidential power fall into three classes. First, when presidents act in accordance with Congress's will, they have all their own constitutional powers plus whatever powers Congress can delegate. Second, when presidents act in an area in which Congress has not, there is a "grey area" of presidential power, the extent of which may be defined by history, tradition, and the specifics of the situation. Third, when presidents act in contravention of Congress's will, their power is at its minimum; they have only their constitutional powers minus whatever power Congress may have over an area of policy. Jackson saw the steel seizure case as falling into the last category. Consequently the president's act in seizing the steel mills was unlawful. Jackson's opinion has been recognized by subsequent courts as a precedent, almost as if it had been the majority opinion rather than an individual concurrence. Its flexibility and good sense have commended it to later justices, while Black's opinion is sometimes seen as too narrow.

THE NIXON ADMINISTRATION

There were more attempts to increase domestic presidential constitutional power during the administration of President Richard M. Nixon than in any other. Nixon made many new claims of constitutional privilege during his five and a half years in office. All but one of these was eventually decided by the Court, and in every one of these cases, the claim of presidential prerogative was rejected by the Court. The remaining case—involving an attempt by President Nixon to expand the pocket-veto power—was decided by the Court of Appeals for the Federal Circuit against Nixon, and his successor as president, Gerald R. Ford, declined to appeal to the Supreme Court.

In June, 1971, *The New York Times* began to publish the text of a secret Defense Department study—popularly known as the Pentagon Papers—on the origin of the war in Vietnam. The Nixon administration brought action against the *Times*, asking for a court order to suppress the publication of the study. No other president had ever made an attempt to suppress newspaper publication. Other newspapers became involved in publishing portions of the study, and the multiple cases that resulted were quickly consolidated and argued before the Court. Treating the case as an emergency, the Court held, within four days of hearing the oral arguments, that the publication was protected by the First Amendment and that the government did not have the power to impose prior censorship on publication. The vote was six to three.

The Nixon administration also made extraordinary claims to presidential power in what it called "domestic national security" cases. Illegal wiretaps of the defendants in a bombing case had taken place; some of the recorded conversations were between the defendants and their attorneys, which violated attorney-client privilege. The administration refused to disclose these to the defense on the ground that the Fourth Amendment does not forbid warrantless wiretapping when a case involves domestic national security. The Court unanimously rejected this claim in *United States v. United States District Court* (1972).

A claim by the Nixon administration that the president has the power to "impound" funds—to decline to spend moneys appropriated by Congress—was unanimously rejected by the Court in *Train v. City of New York* (1975). Congress later attempted to grant the president that power by establishing a statutory line-item veto in 1996 during the administration of President Bill Clinton. The Court rejected it in *Clinton v. City of New York* (1998) as being beyond the powers granted to the president in the Constitution.

Another broad claim to executive authority was put forward by President Nixon at the time of Watergate. Nixon refused to surrender tapes of presidential conversations to the courts, claiming that they were protected by a broad and self-defined "executive privilege." In *United States v. Nixon* (1974) the Court unanimously rejected Nixon's assertion of an inherent presidential authority to define the scope of his own privileges. Chief Justice Warren E. Burger's opinion invokes the holding from *Marbury v. Madison* that "it is emphatically the province and duty of the judicial department to say what the law is." Nixon was forced to release the tapes, which turned out to contain evidence that he had been part of a conspiracy to obstruct justice. He resigned immediately thereafter.

FOREIGN AND DEFENSE POLICY

In the area of foreign and defense policy, the Court was much more favorable to broad constructions of presidential power. In *United States v. Curtiss-Wright Export Corp.* (1936), Justice George Sutherland, writing for a unanimous Supreme Court, held that the "President alone has the power to speak or listen as representative of the nation." The president's special role in foreign affairs involves some powers implied but not explicitly granted in the Constitution. Many foreign affairs issues may have domestic legal impact, and where they do, the president's decision is dispositive. One example of this is *Dames and Moore v. Regan* (1981), in which the Court held that President Jimmy Carter's agreement with the government of Iran to settle cross-claims by U.S. and Iranian citizens against the two governments by means of an international tribunal had the effect of disqualifying U.S. courts from hearing the cases.

For many years it was thought that presidents had nearly complete personal immunity from lawsuits; indeed, during the Nixon administration, the Court held in *Nixon v. Fitzgerald* (1982) that the president is absolutely immune from civil liability for his official acts. However, in *Clinton v. Jones* (1997), the Court unanimously declined to extend that immunity to nonofficial acts. Consequently, presidents can be sued and forced to give depositions and testify in civil suits. In the Paula Jones case, this liability led directly to the impeachment of President Clinton on charges of perjury and obstruction of justice.

Robert Jacobs

FURTHER READING

A good starting place is the collection of essays in *Presidential Power: Forging the Presidency for the Twenty-First Century*, edited by Robert Y. Shapiro, Martha Joynt Kumar, and Lawrence R. Jacobs (New York: Columbia University Press, 2000).

Although dated, the classic exposition of the president's powers and the role of the Court is Edward S. Corwin's *The President: Office and Powers* (New York: New York University Press, 1957). Henry Abraham's *Justices and Presidents* (New York: Oxford University Press, 1985) has a good discussion of the relation between the appointing process for justices and constitutional outcomes. *The Plot That Failed: Nixon's Administrative Presidency* (New York: John Wiley, 1983) discusses Nixon's claims for increased constitutional power. Robert Scigliano's *The Supreme Court and the Presidency* (New York: The Free Press, 1971) is strong on the pre-Nixon relations between the Court and the presidency, as is Glendon Schubert's *The Presidency in the Courts* (Minneapolis: University of Minnesota Press, 1957).

J. W. Peltason's *Understanding the Constitution* (New York: Harcourt Brace, 1997) has a very clear discussion of some of the leading controversies in the chapter on Article II of the U.S. Constitution. Another good discussion of presidential power may be found in *The Supreme Court and the Powers of the American Government* (Washington,

D.C.: Congressional Quarterly, 1997) by Joan Biskupic and Elder Witt. Henry Paolucci and Richard C. Clark's *Presidential Power and Crisis Government in the Age of Terrorism* (Smyrna, Del.: Griffon House for the Bagehot Council, 2003) looks at the new challenges to presidential power in the twenty-first century.

SEE ALSO *Clinton v. City of New York*; *Clinton v. Jones*; *Curtiss-Wright Export Corp., United States v.*; Elastic clause; Executive agreements; Jackson, Robert H.; *Marbury v. Madison*; Separation of powers; War powers; *Youngstown Sheet and Tube Co. v. Sawyer.*

Printz v. United States

CITATION: 521 U.S. 98
DATE: June 27, 1997
ISSUES: State sovereignty; commerce clause
SIGNIFICANCE: The Supreme Court held that a congressional statute intruded on the rights of the states when it required local law-enforcement officers to conduct background checks on prospective handgun purchasers.

Two law-enforcement officers, Sheriff Jay Printz of Montana and Sheriff Richard Mack of Arizona, challenged the constitutionality of a key provision of the Brady Handgun Violence Prevention Act of 1993. Speaking for a 5-4 majority, Justice Antonin Scalia held that Congress had no power to require the states to enforce a federal regulatory program absent a particularized constitutional authorization. Scalia argued that the Constitution established a system of dual sovereignty, and that the states, as an essential attribute of their retained sovereignty, are "independent and autonomous within their proper sphere of authority." In his dissent, Justice John Paul Stevens argued that the commerce clause authorized Congress to regulate interstate commerce in handguns and that nothing in the Tenth Amendment prohibits Congress from delegating enforcement to the states.

Although the *Printz* decision had many implications for federalism, it did not have much direct impact on the Brady bill. More than half the states had laws requiring background checks consistent with the federal statute, and the federal government planned to conduct its own background checks on gun purchasers in late 1998.

Thomas Tandy Lewis

SEE ALSO Federalism; *Lopez, United States v.*; Police powers; Scalia, Antonin; Second Amendment; States' rights and state sovereignty; Stevens, John Paul; Tenth Amendment.

Right to Privacy

DESCRIPTION: Right to solitude, independence, security in one's own home and possessions, self-determination, and self-definition.

SIGNIFICANCE: Although the right to privacy is not explicitly granted in the U.S. Constitution, the Supreme Court, in various rulings, found that a number of the amendments in the Bill of Rights conveyed this right.

The right to privacy, which is defined in many ways, is not explicitly guaranteed by the Constitution. However, the Supreme Court interpreted many of the amendments of the Bill of Rights as providing some protection to a variety of elements of individual privacy against intrusive government activities. These include the First Amendment freedoms of expression and association, the Third Amendment restriction on quartering of soldiers in private residences, the Fourth Amendment prohibition on unreasonable searches and seizures, the due process clause and guarantee against self-incrimination of the Fifth Amendment, the Ninth and Tenth Amendment reservations of power in the people and the states, and the due process and equal protection clauses of the Fourteenth Amendment.

The Court first applied the term "privacy" to interests protected by the Fourth Amendment in *Boyd v. United States* (1886). More than forty years later, in his dissent in *Olmstead v. United States* (1928), Justice Louis D. Brandeis defined privacy as "the right to be let alone—the most comprehensive of rights and the right most valued by civilized men." The Court adopted Brandeis's reasoning in *Katz v. United*

States (1967). The constitutional concept of privacy requires only the federal government—not the state governments—to refrain from taking actions that would invade protected areas.

The Court found a subjective expectation of privacy encompassed by the Fourth Amendment to exist in calls made from a public telephone booth; it also found reasonable expectations of privacy in homes, businesses, hotel rooms, garages, sealed luggage and packages, and drums of chemicals. It declined to find privacy in bank records, voice or writing samples, telephone numbers, conversations recorded by concealed microphones, and automobile passenger compartments, trunks, and glove boxes. The Court also found no Fourth Amendment protection for abandoned or discarded property or for open fields. The definition of a reasonable expectation shifts, depending in part on the importance of the interest against which it is being measured. When motivated by drug and alcohol crackdowns, for example, individual expectations of privacy are minimized in the name of society's interest in eradicating drug trafficking and driving while intoxicated. The reasonableness standard has been criticized as not keeping pace with the technological revolution.

THE FIRST AND FIFTH AMENDMENTS

The First Amendment right to privacy is balanced against other First Amendment freedoms, resulting in a guarantee of privacy within the home. However, when privacy rights conflict with free expression, the latter always prevails. Any government effort to protect privacy faces significant First Amendment obstacles. Although freedom of association is not specifically mentioned in the First Amendment, it is generally considered to be implicit in its guarantees. In *National Association for the Advancement of Colored People v. Alabama* (1958), the Court found that Alabama could not require the National Association for the Advancement of Colored People to publicize its membership lists under First and Fourteenth Amendment protection of freedom of association.

Privacy is considered an aspect of the Fifth Amendment's protection against self-incrimination. It is also viewed as an element of the takings clause, in that private property cannot be taken without payment of just compensation.

THE FOURTH AMENDMENT

The Fourth Amendment protects citizens' property from seizure by the government and their homes and persons from arbitrary or warrantless searches. The Fourth Amendment recognizes a right of personal privacy and protects against arbitrary intrusions by law-enforcement officials. The Framers were sensitive to the need to insulate people from unlimited governmental powers of search and seizure. Writing for the Court in *Katz v. United States,* Justice Potter Stewart stated that "the Fourth Amendment protects people—not places." He disallowed the placement of a "bug," or listening device, on the outside of a public telephone booth without first obtaining a warrant. The Court later held that the Fourth Amendment extends to any place or thing in which an individual has a "reasonable expectation of privacy."

The Fourth Amendment also states that no warrants should be issued without probable cause, a concept without a precise meaning. As interpreted by the Court, probable cause means that for a search to be valid, a police officer must have good reason to believe that the search will produce evidence of crime. A search warrant is an order issued by a judge or magistrate authorizing a search. To obtain a warrant, a police officer must take an oath or sign an affidavit attesting to certain facts that constitute probable cause to support issuance of a warrant. To maintain the integrity of the Fourth Amendment, the Court charges a neutral and detached magistrate with issuance of warrants that are to describe with particularity the place to be searched and the persons or things to be seized. Police often use tips provided by confidential informants to obtain search warrants. This area is one of the most controversial concerning information provided by anonymous sources. The Court held that a "totality of circumstances" standard would govern permissive reliance by police on anonymous tips.

Under federal law, officers are required to knock and announce their arrival at the place to be searched in order to reduce the potential for violence and to protect the occupants' right of privacy. In *Wilson v. Arkansas* (1995), the Court determined that officers facing exigent circumstances—situations in which they risked losing evidence that is destroyed or disposed of easily—could dispense with the knock and announce requirement. In *Richards v. Wisconsin* (1997), however, the Court ruled unanimously that states may not create a blanket "drug exception" to the requirement that police officers knock and announce before executing a search warrant.

The Court held that certain exceptional situations do not require warrants before conducting a search. Searches in which a warrant is not necessary include searches incidental to a lawful arrest (*Chimel v. California*, 1969), consensual searches (*Schneckloth v. Bustamonte*, 1973), plain view searches (*Coolidge v. New Hampshire*, 1971), searches conducted as part of a hot pursuit (*Warden v. Hayden*, 1967), searches involving evanescent evidence (*Schmerber v. California*, 1966), and emergency searches (*Michigan v. Tyler*, 1978). In *California v. Acevedo* (1991), the Court held that whether the search is of an automobile or any other place, the nature of its object is more important than the nature of the space being searched. Every part of an automobile can be searched, including closed containers.

PERSONAL AUTONOMY

The constitutional right of privacy, which began to take shape in the mid-1960's, came to include the freedom of the individual to make fundamental choices involving sex, reproduction, family life, and other intimate personal relationships. It is this aspect of the right of privacy that is the most intensely disputed and hotly contested. Procreation was ruled a basic civil right by the Court in *Skinner v. Oklahoma* (1942). The marital relationship was viewed as being within a zone of privacy protected by the Ninth Amendment in *Griswold v. Connecticut* (1965). It was that same right of privacy that the Court used to determine that a woman had the right to choose to terminate a pregnancy in *Roe v. Wade* (1973). Claims of reproductive freedom extended to four aspects of reproduction: conception, gestation, labor, and child rearing.

Griswold held that a Connecticut law forbidding use of contraceptives by married couples intruded on the right of marital privacy implicitly guaranteed in the Constitution. In this case, the Court first formally recognized a constitutional right of privacy. It then remained for the Court to define that right. Justice William O. Douglas, writing for the majority, recognized that because the marital relationship lay within a zone of privacy derived from the First, Third, Fourth,

Fifth, Ninth, and Fourteenth Amendments, it should be protected from state and federal interference. Douglas termed marriage "an association that promotes a way of life." A law forbidding use of contraceptives rather than their manufacture or sale, he concluded, seeks to achieve its goals by means that have a maximum destructive impact on the relationship between husband and wife. Such a law was unacceptable. In *Eisenstadt v. Baird* (1972), the Court invalidated a ban on distribution of contraceptives to unmarried people; in *Carey v. Population Services International* (1977), the Court removed limitations on the sale of contraceptives to minors.

Roe v. Wade, a 7-2 decision, extended the right of privacy to a woman's decision to terminate her pregnancy. Because that right was fundamental, the Court reasoned, only the most compelling reasons permit government interference with the exercise of that right. The Court also ruled that an unborn fetus is not a person entitled to Fourteenth Amendment guarantees of life and liberty because the word "person" in that amendment is used in the postnatal sense only. For ease of reference, the Court divided pregnancy into "trimesters," three periods of about three months each. During the first trimester, the woman, in consultation with her physician, can decide whether to terminate her pregnancy, without government interference. During the second, the government can regulate abortion only to preserve and protect the health of the woman. During the third trimester, when the fetus is viable, or capable of meaningful life outside the womb, the government's interest in protecting fetal life becomes more compelling. Only then can the government ban abortion. The Court found that although the government does have an interest in protecting prenatal life, that interest must be balanced against a woman's right to privacy, which is broad enough to protect a woman's exclusive claim to her body.

In the next two decades, the Court reviewed a number of cases in which state and local governments imposed various restrictions on abortion. During the 1970's most of these restrictions were declared unconstitutional. As the composition of the Court grew more conservative in the 1980's, however, many restrictions were viewed more favorably. In *Webster v. Reproductive Health Services* (1989), for example, the Court upheld a Missouri statute imposing significant limitations on the performance of abortions, including a ban on use of public funds, employees, or facilities to counsel a woman about abortion as an option or to perform abortions not necessary to save the mother's life. The future of abortion as an alternative appeared tenuous. However, in *Planned Parenthood of Southeastern Pennsylvania v. Casey* (1992), the Court basically reaffirmed *Roe* but gave the states broader latitude in regulating access to abortion.

OTHER PRIVACY INTERESTS

In *Moore v. City of East Cleveland* (1977), the Court applied the right of privacy in reviewing city ordinances governing residential land use, stressing freedom of choice in matters of marriage and family life. In *Bowers v. Hardwick* (1986), however, in a 5-4 decision, the Court placed limitations on privacy when it declined to extend the right to privacy to homosexuals engaging in consensual sodomy in their homes. Justice Lewis F. Powell, Jr., subsequently expressed reservations about his vote in that case, admitting that he probably "made a mistake."

Marcia J. Weiss

FURTHER READING

An ideal starting point for research into this subject is Kevin M. Keenan's *Invasion of Privacy: A Reference Handbook* (Santa Barbara, Calif.: ABC-Clio, 2005). Kermit L. Hall's *Conscience, Expression, and Privacy* (New York: Garland, 2000) examines how the Supreme Court has treated the concept of the right to privacy. Among other engaging books on the subject are Charles Sykes's *The End of Privacy: The Attack on Personal Rights at Home, at Work, On-Line, and in Court* (New York: St. Martin's Press, 1999), Richard A. Glenn's *The Right to Privacy: Rights and Liberties Under the Law* (Santa Barbara, Calif.: ABC-Clio, 2003), and Suzanne U. Samuels's *First Among Friends: Interest Groups, the U.S. Supreme Court, and the Right to Privacy* (Westport, Conn.: Praeger, 2004).

Privacy is extensively treated in constitutional law and civil liberties textbooks. Ellen Alderman and Caroline Kennedy's *The Right to Privacy* (New York: Alfred A. Knopf, 1995) treats privacy in the context of various scenarios and is well written and easy to understand. In *The Limits of Privacy* (New York: Basic Books, 1999), Amitai Etzioni argues that privacy should not be regarded as an individual right or given a privileged status in formulation of public policy but be viewed as one good among many. This is a well-written book for those interested in political science or public policy.

In *Privacy in the Information Age* (Washington, D.C.: Brookings Institution, 1997), Fred H. Cate discusses privacy in the United States and compares it with privacy in Europe. The book encompasses the public sector, the private sector, and electronic privacy and contains discussions about notable cases. Priscilla M. Regan's *Legislating Privacy: Technology, Social Values, and Public Policy* (Chapel Hill: University of North Carolina Press, 1995) examines public policy in information privacy (computerization), communication privacy (wiretapping), and psychological privacy (polygraphs).

SEE ALSO Abortion; Automobile searches; Birth control and contraception; *Chimel v. California*; Due process, substantive; *Ferguson v. City of Charleston*; First Amendment; Fourteenth Amendment; Fourth Amendment; *Griswold v. Connecticut*; Ninth Amendment; Search warrant requirement; Takings clause.

Privileges and Immunities

DESCRIPTION: Special rights and exemptions provided by law, which are protected from state government abridgment by Article IV of the U.S. Constitution and the Fourteenth Amendment.
SIGNIFICANCE: The Court made only limited use of these clauses; its reluctance to protect rights with them is a reflection more of the Court's political concerns than of the provisions' substance.

The Supreme Court has given the privileges and immunities clauses varying interpretations according to what it considered the nation's exigent political and economic needs. Opinions addressing these provisions illustrate the political nature of the Court's decision making. Both clauses arise from intergovernmental concerns within the federal system and require that state governments treat citizens with basic equality; litigation about them has also examined the federal courts' role in guaranteeing "fundamental rights."

Article IV, section 2, of the U.S. Constitution provides that "the Citizens of each State shall be entitled to all Privileges and Immunities of Citizens of the other states." In *The Federalist* (1788) No. 80, Alexander Hamilton maintained that this clause was "the basis of the Union." Along with the full faith and credit clause and fugitive felons and fugitive slaves provisions, this clause was designed to ensure interstate comity. Its obvious purpose was to protect citizens of one state from being treated as aliens while in another state. Evidently, the clause did not literally mean what it said. A Georgian has the right to conduct trade in Maryland but not to vote in Maryland's elections. The earliest standard to distinguish between these activities was propounded by Justice Bushrod Washington. Sitting on circuit court, he held that this clause protected out-of-state citizens' fundamental rights, those that "belong, of right, to citizens of all free governments" in *Corfield v. Coryell* (1823).

SUBSTANTIAL REASON TEST

The Court never fully embraced Washington's interpretation. It rarely used the clause to protect fundamental rights, except to ensure some measure of equal treatment by state governments for citizens of other states. Its concern was primarily with the political fallout of interstate relations rather than the rights of individual citizens. The nineteenth century Court limited its use of the clause to protecting the professional, property, and business rights of out-of-state citizens and to providing them access to state courts. The Court's major twentieth century development of the Article IV clause held that lawful state discrimination against citizens of other states must exhibit a "substantial reason for discrimination" beyond their out-of-state citizenship in *Toomer v. Witsell* (1948). The most notable use of the *Toomer* standard was *Doe v. Bolton* (1973), in which the court struck down a statute that allowed only state residents to obtain abortions in Georgia.

After it adopted the *Toomer* "substantial reason" test, the Court returned to the fundamental rights standard in one significant case. It upheld a Montana law that required a higher fee for the hunting licenses of nonresidents than for those for residents. It ruled that equal access to hunting licenses for nonresidents was "not basic to the maintenance of well-being of the Union" in *Baldwin v. Fish and Game Commission* (1978). In all cases, the Court applied the Article IV clause only to unequal treatment of out-of-state citizens, and in most of them, it also based its holdings on the commerce clause.

THE FOURTEENTH AMENDMENT

The Fourteenth Amendment includes the injunction that "No state shall make or enforce any law which shall abridge the privileges or immunities of the citizens of the United States." This clause's primary author, John Bingham, contended that the privileges and immunities referred to "are chiefly defined in the first eight amendments to the Constitution," which he maintained, "were never limitations upon the power of the States, until made so by the Fourteenth Amendment."

The *Slaughterhouse Cases* (1873) presented the first significant litigation concerning the meaning of the Fourteenth Amendment. In that decision, the Court rendered the privileges or immunities clause ineffective as the basis for federal protection of individual rights. The appellants claimed that their right to labor was violated by a Louisiana law that required New Orleans butchers to use a central slaughterhouse. Writing for a 5-4 majority, Justice Samuel F. Miller ruled that the privileges or immunities clause did not protect a right to labor. He maintained that the clause protected only the privileges or immunities granted by the United States and that regulation of the right to labor fell within the authority of the states.

The next day, the Court applied *Slaughterhouse*'s narrow interpretation to hold that the clause did not prevent Illinois from denying women licenses to practice law in *Bradwell v. Illinois* (1873), thus confirming the view of the clause held by the Court ever since. The political and cultural basis of the decision was indicated by Justice Joseph P. Bradley's concurrence, "Women are to fulfill the noble and benign offices of wife and mother." This, he maintained, "is the law of the Creator." A century later, when the Court turned to the Fourteenth Amendment to protect women from discriminatory state laws, it relied on the equal protection clause.

In both *Slaughterhouse* and *Bradwell*, the Court responded to political considerations. It recognized that all citizens' fundamental rights should be secured against infringement. It was also committed to the federal system and determined that the states should retain primary responsibility for governing and protecting the rights of the people. To rule otherwise, the *Slaughterhouse* majority argued, would make "this court a perpetual censor upon all legislation of the states."

Justice Stephen J. Field decried *Slaughterhouse* for reducing the privileges and immunities clause to "a vain and idle enactment, which accomplished nothing." His dissent contained the seeds of the doctrines of freedom of contract and substantive due process that dominated the Court's economic rulings for half a century. Because *Slaughterhouse* emasculated the privileges or immunities clause, when the Court espoused these doctrines, it based them on the Fourteenth Amendment's due process clause. To this day, when the Court chooses to protect individual rights, it turns to the due process, equal protection, or commerce clauses rather than the weakened privileges or immunities clause.

Chuck Smith

FURTHER READING

Olsen, Trisha. "The Natural Law Foundation of the Privileges or Immunities Clause of the Fourteenth Amendment." *Arkansas Law Review* 48 (1995): 347-438.

Perry, Michael J. *We the People: The Fourteenth Amendment and the Supreme Court.* New York: Oxford University Press, 2001.

Rosen, Jeffery. "Translating the Privileges or Immunities Clause." *George Washington Law Review* 66 (1998): 1241-1268.

Scarborough, Jane L. "What If the Butcher in the *Slaughterhouse Cases* Had Won? An Exercise in 'Counterfactual' Doctrine." *Maine Law Review* 50 (1998): 211-224.

Scaturro, Frank J. *The Supreme Court's Retreat from Reconstruction: A Distortion of Constitutional Jurisprudence.* Westport, Conn.: Greenwood Press, 2000.

Simson, Gary J. "Discrimination Against Nonresidents and the Privileges and Immunities Clause of Article IV." *University of Pennsylvania Law Review* 128 (1979): 379-401.

SEE ALSO Bradley, Joseph P.; *Bradwell v. Illinois*; Comity clause; Commerce, regulation of; Fourteenth Amendment; Fundamental rights; Incorporation doctrine; *Slaughterhouse Cases*; Travel, right to.

Progressivism

DATE: 1900-1918

DESCRIPTION: Period characterized by a variety of reforms and legislation aimed at improving the quality of life by regulating commerce and labor.

SIGNIFICANCE: Progressive legislation designed to relieve problems stemming from the rise of big business, including monopolistic practices and exploitative labor conditions, met with frequent challenges in the Supreme Court.

From the end of the Civil War in 1865 until the end of the nineteenth century, Americans devoted their energy to expansion of the urban and industrial segment of the economy at the expense of the worker. By the last decade of the nineteenth century, reformers began to attempt to control or limit the numerous problems that resulted from the rapid industrialization and urbanization.

The growth of big business after the Civil War gave rise to monopolistic practices such as the restraint of trade and price fixing in the oil, sugar, steel, meatpacking, and tobacco industries. The growth and development of the nation's railroads, which spanned the continent and engaged in interstate commerce, enabled the growth of trusts that eliminated competition and drove the small entrepreneur out of business.

Responding to public outcry against these corrupt business practices, Congress passed the Sherman Antitrust Act in 1890. The act protected the public against monopolies by making conspiracies to restrain trade in interstate commerce illegal, providing for triple damages to any person injured by the competition of an unfair business monopoly, and stipulating fines and imprisonment for violations of the act. In effect, the act prohibited every contract, combination in the form of trust or otherwise, or conspiracy that resulted in restraint of trade or commerce among several states or with foreign nations. The majority of business-related cases considered by the Supreme Court during the Progressive era sought relief under the provisions of the Sherman Antitrust Act.

COURT ACTION UNDER PROGRESSIVISM

During the two-term presidency of Theodore Roosevelt, a Progressive Justice Department filed forty-three cases under the Sherman Antitrust Act to restrain or break up monopolistic businesses, including the Northern Securities Company and the beef trust, and questionable practices, including employment contracts and child labor.

In *Northern Securities Co. v. United States* (1904), the Supreme Court decided by a 5-4 vote that a holding company formed by the Great Northern, Southern Pacific, and Union Pacific railroad lines to eliminate competition between two railroad lines was a combination in restraint of trade and therefore a violation of the Sherman Antitrust Act. It ordered the Northern Securities holding company to be dissolved. This ruling was an important departure from the Court's decision in *United States v. E. C. Knight Co.* (1895), in which it made a distinction between commerce and manufacturing and limited the scope of the Sherman Antitrust Act. In *Northern Securities*, the Court held that a holding company sufficiently affected commerce by restraining it even though it was not actually engaged in interstate commerce and therefore came within the purview of the act.

In 1904 the Court adopted the stream of commerce doctrine in which Congress can regulate local commerce (indirect) that is part of the interstate (direct) current of commerce. This stream of commerce doctrine was first enunciated in *Swift and Co. v. United States* (1905), which involved a beef trust. A number of meatpacking houses made agreements among themselves to fix the price of livestock and meat bought and sold in Chicago stockyards and slaughtering houses. Swift claimed that the livestock slaughtered and packed was bought and sold locally and hence was not involved in interstate commerce.

The Court unanimously ruled the meatpackers' agreements violated the Sherman Antitrust Act because meatpacking was a part of the process in which cattle were shipped from out of state to Chicago for slaughter and packing and then shipped out of Illinois to other states for sale. This stream of commerce, which clearly involved more than one state, meant that the act applied in this case. The Court invalidated the price agreements made by Swift and the others. In the opinion for the Court, Justice Oliver Wendell Holmes stated: "When cattle are sent for sale from a place in one state, with the expectation

This early 1900's New York shoe factory relied almost solely on child labor. Progressive legislation, which tried to stop exploitative practices such as that, was often declared unconstitutional by the Supreme Court. (Library of Congress)

that they will end their transit, after purchase, in another, and when in effect they do so, with only the interruption necessary to find a purchaser at the stockyards, and when this is a typical constantly recurring course, the current of commerce among the states, and the purchase of the cattle is a part and incident of such commerce." In subsequent cases, the Court would use the stream of commerce doctrine to regulate the actual production of goods, and it would also use the commerce clause of the Constitution to oversee modern business and industry.

The Court abandoned its literal interpretation of the Sherman Antitrust Act in *Northern Securities*. In an 8-1 decision in *Standard Oil Co. v. United States* (1911), the Court ruled that only unreasonable business combinations and undue restraints of trade were violations of the act. Chief Justice Edward D. White, in the majority opinion, stated that the Sherman Antitrust Act applied only to unreasonable restraints of trade and that the rule of reason should be used in judging whether the act applied in any specific case. Although the Court effectively weakened the act, it upheld a lower court's decision to break up the Standard Oil Trust. In subsequent cases, the rule of reason became the standard for judging violations of antitrust laws.

PUBLIC WELFARE ISSUES

The police powers granted to states allow them to protect the public's health, safety, and morals. During the Progressive period, a number of state and federal laws were passed regulating minimum age and wages of workers, safety, and the number of hours worked in a day. In *Muller v. Oregon* (1908) and other cases, the Court upheld much of this legislation. However, at other times, the Court ruled that Congress had overstepped the bounds of its federal police power. In *Hammer v. Dagenhart* (1918), the Court ruled five to four against the Keating-Owen Child Labor Act of 1916 and held that Congress had overreached its power. It found that labor was an aspect of manufacture and not the product itself. Therefore, although goods produced for interstate commerce had been produced by child labor, the products themselves were not harmful and could not be prohibited from being shipped by interstate commerce. By the end of World War I in 1918, the Court began to retreat from its earlier liberal rulings as the Progressive era came to an end and the Court became more conservative under Chief Justice William H. Taft.

Gregory N. Seltzer

FURTHER READING

Barbuto, Domenica M. *American Settlement Houses and Progressive Social Reform: An Encyclopedia of the American Settlement Movement.* Phoenix, Ariz.: Oryx Press, 1999.

Buenker, John D., and Edward R. Kantowicz, eds. *Historical Dictionary of the Progressive Era, 1890-1920.* New York: Greenwood Press, 1988.

Divine, Robert A., et al. *America Past and Present.* New York: Addison-Wesley, 1998.

Gallagher, Aileen. *The Muckrakers: American Journalism During the Age of Reform.* New York: Rosen, 2004.

Hofstadter, Richard, and Beatrice Hofstadter, eds. *From Reconstruction to the Present Day, 1864-1981.* Vol. 3 in *Great Issues in American History.* New York: Vintage Books, 1982.

Klose, Nelson. *Since 1865*. Vol. 2 in *United States History*. New York: Barrons Educational Services, 1983.
Wingate, Katherine. *Political Reforms: American Citizens Gain More Control over Their Government*. New York: Rosen, 2006.

SEE ALSO Clarke, John H.; Commerce, regulation of; *Hammer v. Dagenhart*; Moody, William H.; Police powers; Rule of reason.

Public Forum Doctrine

DESCRIPTION: Constitutional doctrine relating to attempts by government bodies to control speech activities on public property.
SIGNIFICANCE: Though the Supreme Court initially held that government bodies have the same power to control the use of public properties as private owners, during the twentieth century the Court expanded the rights of citizens to engage in expressive activities in public venues.

Government bodies in the United States own and manage a variety of property, including streets, parks, and public buildings. In their role as property owners, government bodies often seek to exercise control over the activities that occur on government property, including expressive activities. Early in the twentieth century, the Supreme Court interpreted the First Amendment's free speech clause to permit government the same broad discretion to control activities on its property as enjoyed by most private property owners. Over the course of the twentieth century, however, the Court eventually crafted distinctions among *types* of government property that dictated the kinds of control government might exercise over speech-related activities on public property. The Court's elaboration of these distinctions is commonly referred to as the public forum doctrine.

TRADITIONAL PUBLIC FORUMS

The core of the public forum doctrine was the Court's determination that some forms of government property were held by government in trust for its citizens for speech-related purposes. Public streets and parks, for example, have, according to the Court's 1939 ruling in *Hague v. Congress of Industrial Organizations*, "immemorially been held in trust for the use of the public and, time out of mind, have been used for purposes of assembly, communications of thought between citizens, and discussing public questions." The Court designated public properties traditionally held for speech-related properties as "public forums."

Within these public forums, the Court sharply limited government power to regulate speech-related activities. In particular, the public forum doctrine prevents the government from attempting to exclude speech from such forums out of hostility to the views expressed or the subject matters addressed in the speech. Government, however, is not without all power to regulate speech in public forums. It may regulate the timing, placement, or manner of speech in such forums. These kind of regulations—commonly referred to as time, place, and manner restrictions—allow government to control the volume of concerts in public parks, for example, or to schedule appropriate times for parades on public streets. In public forums, then, government may coordinate expressive activities, but it may not censor particular views or subjects. Although government may enforce reasonable time, place, and manner restrictions on speech in these forums, it may discriminate against speech with a particular content only if it demonstrates a compelling justification. This kind of demonstration is rare, but occasionally government will proffer a weighty enough justification, as, for example, in *Frisby v. Schultz* (1988), when the Court upheld a ban on focused picketing on the public streets in front of a particular resident, such as a picket by abortion protesters of the home of a doctor who performed abortions.

DESIGNATED PUBLIC FORUMS AND NONPUBLIC FORUMS

Eventually, the Court had to consider whether other types of public property were subject to the same rules as those it had applied to classic public forums such as public streets and parks. In *Perry Education Association v. Perry Local Educators' Association* (1983), the Court described three categories of public property and the measure of protection to the accorded speech in each of these three types of property. In the first place, the Court reiterated the protection given to speech in "traditional" public forums such as streets or parks. In the second place, the Court identified some types of public property as "designated" public forums. These exist when government opens particular property for a wide range of expressive purposes. In these cases, government must abide by the same rules that apply to traditional public forums. In particular it may not attempt to prevent particular subjects or viewpoints from gaining access to the forum. Thus, in *Widmar v. Vincent* (1981), the Court held that a university could not prevent a Christian student group from meeting in university facilities that had been made generally available to other student groups for speech-related activities.

Finally, the Court ruled in *Perry Education Association* that certain types of public property might be reserved by government for particular purposes and not made available to the public for general expressive activities. Within these "nonpublic forums," government may exercise considerable control over speech, even to the extent of choosing what subjects may be addressed in these forums. Government may not, however, attempt to suppress the expression of particular viewpoints.

Furthermore, at a minimum, any regulations of speech in nonpublic forums must be reasonable. Within these broad parameters government may designate particular uses for its nonpublic forums, including particular expressive uses. Thus, for example, in *United States Postal Service v. Greenburgh Civic Associations* (1981), the Court held that mailboxes are nonpublic forums and that federal law may restrict access to mailboxes to postal material. Similarly, in *Greer v. Spock* (1976), the Court determined that military bases were not public forums and that demonstrations in this venue could be prohibited.

Timothy L. Hall

FURTHER READING

Brzezinski, Matthew. *Fortress America: On the Front Lines of Homeland Security, an Inside Look at the Coming Surveillance State.* New York: Bantam Books, 2004.

Hentoff, Nat. *Free Speech for Me—but Not for Thee: How the American Left and Right Relentlessly Censor Each Other.* New York: HarperCollins, 1992.

Kalven, Harry. *A Worthy Tradition: Freedom of Speech in America.* New York: Harper & Row, 1988.

Kersch, Ken I. *Freedom of Speech: Rights and Liberties Under the Law.* Santa Barbara, Calif.: ABC-Clio, 2003.

O'Neil, Robert M. *Free Speech in the College Community.* Bloomington: Indiana University Press, 1997.

Smith, Norris, and Lynn M. Messina, eds. *Homeland Security.* New York: H. W. Wilson, 2004.

Smolla, Rodney A. *Free Speech in an Open Society.* New York: Alfred A. Knopf, 1992.

Tedford, Thomas L. *Freedom of Speech in the United States.* New York: Random House, 1985.

SEE ALSO Assembly and association, freedom of; Censorship; First Amendment; Fundamental rights; Judicial scrutiny; Speech and press, freedom of; Time, place, and manner regulations.

Ex parte Quirin

CITATION: 317 U.S. 1
DATE: July 31, 1942
ISSUES: Military tribunals; habeas corpus
SIGNIFICANCE: Upholding the secret trials of enemy spies in military tribunals, the U.S. Supreme Court held that the right to trial in regular federal courts, as well as the protections of the Fifth and Sixth Amendments, did not extend to aliens accused of crimes of war.

During World War II, four German saboteurs landed on Long Island, New York, and another four landed at Ponte Verdra Beach, Florida. Agents of the Federal Bureau of Investigation (FBI) captured the eight Germans and turned them over to the military, which quickly tried them on charges of violating the international laws of war. The defendants tried to stop the proceedings with habeas corpus petitions, claiming that the military tribunal had no jurisdiction because regular criminal courts were available. As a precedent, they pointed to precedent in *Ex parte Milligan* (1866). In addition, they objected to the fact that military tribunals utilized juries and did not follow many of the procedures required by the Fifth and Sixth Amendments.

At a special session in July, the Supreme Court unanimously rejected the petition, thus allowing the execution of six of the saboteurs about a week later. Chief Justice Harlan Fiske Stone's opinion for the Court declared that the *Milligan* precedent only applied to U.S. citizens who were not in the armed services. Stone further held that the use of a military tribunal was justified by a combination of the president's powers as commander in chief and a congressional statute, Article of War 15, authorizing military trials for those committing crimes of war. He also pointed to precedents for such tribunals, going back to the trial of John Andre, a British spy, during the Revolutionary War. The justices demonstrated a great deal of deference toward the executive branch's policies in fighting a popular war. They had no desire to make a critical assessment of the principles of due process in the trials, and they ignored the fact that one of the saboteurs had earlier become a naturalized American citizen before returning to Germany. In a similar case involving a Japanese general, *In re Yamashita* (1946), two dissenting justices would argue that the Court was not following the due process requirements of the Fifth Amendment.

In 2001, following the terrorist attacks on the World Trade Center and the Pentagon building, President George W. Bush issued an executive order authorizing military commissions to conduct trials of aliens charged with terrorist acts. In defending the policy, Bush's lawyers quoted from the *Quirin* and *Yamashita* decisions. In the case of *Hamdan v. Rumsfeld* (2006), however, based on the later Uniform Code of Military Justice (UCMJ) as well as the Geneva Convention of 1949, the Court decided that Bush had no authority to set up such commissions.

Thomas Tandy Lewis

SEE ALSO *Hamdan v. Rumsfeld*; Military and the Court; *Milligan, Ex parte*; Stone, Harlan Fiske; War powers.

Race and Discrimination

DESCRIPTION: Practice of treating people differently on the basis of their race, skin color, or ethnicity. Racial discrimination may be perpetrated by governments, private persons, or institutions.

SIGNIFICANCE: After the Civil War and the end of slavery in the United States, the struggle for racial harmony and equality gradually became a contentious issue in the Supreme Court and before the public.

The first African slaves in North America arrived at the English colony of Virginia aboard a Dutch ship in 1619. Slavery grew in the English colonies and continued in the United States after the American Revolution. It was explicitly recognized by the U.S. Constitution. The Thirteenth Amendment, ratified just after the end of the Civil War in 1865, abolished slavery. Two additional constitutional amendments, the Fourteenth and the Fifteenth, were passed in 1868 and 1870, respectively, to protect and enfranchise the newly liberated slaves. The Supreme Court was called on almost immediately to define and interpret the meaning of the new constitutional rules.

In its first Fourteenth Amendment case, *Slaughterhouse Cases* (1873), the Court clearly acknowledged that the purpose of the amendment was to abolish racial discrimination. In *Strauder v. West Virginia* (1880), the Court confronted the first of many black codes, statutes passed in the southern states after the Civil War to deny African Americans their newly recognized rights. A West Virginia statute disqualified African Americans from serving on trial juries. Strauder, a black man charged with murder, asked to have his case removed to a federal court because African Americans could not serve on his jury. The Court granted his request. Justice William Strong wrote, "The words of the amendment . . . contain a necessary implication of a positive immunity, or right, most valuable to the colored race—the right to exemption from legal distinctions implying inferiority in civil society, lessening the security of their enjoyment of the rights which others enjoy, and discriminations which are steps towards reducing them to the condition of a subject race."

SEPARATE BUT EQUAL DOCTRINE

Despite the tone of the first two cases in which the Court had considered the Fourteenth Amendment's command that no state shall "deny to any person within its jurisdiction the equal protection of the laws," its 1896 decision in *Plessy v. Ferguson* established the separate but equal rule. Under this rule, a state did not deny equal protection by establishing racially segregated facilities as long as equal facilities were made available to all.

Apart from its inconsistency with the precedents, *Plessy* also is important because it provided the legal justification for much of the racial segregation that took place in the United States until the 1960's. In reality, the facilities afforded nonwhites were rarely, if ever, equal. The Court may not have been directly responsible for the repression of African Americans, but it did provide the juridical

Four NAACP leaders holding a membership poster for their organization. From left to right: Henry L. Moon, Roy Wilkins, Herbert Hill, and future Supreme Court justice Thurgood Marshall. (Library of Congress)

rationale that permitted both governmental and private racial discrimination.

At the end of World War I, the most visible manifestation of governmental discrimination was the system of segregated public schools that existed pursuant to law in all the former states of the Confederacy and in most of the border states, including Kentucky, Delaware, and Maryland. In 1925 opponents of segregation, most notably the National Association for the Advancement of Colored People (NAACP), devised a strategy to attack the system. By then, *Plessy v. Ferguson* was bolstered by nearly three decades of governmental practice, public acceptance, and by a good many supporting court decisions. Rather than oppose *Plessy* directly, they decided to try to chip away at it, in particular at the equal facilities premise. Because an attack on segregation in elementary and secondary public education was thought to be too threatening to the white majority, the NAACP's legal strategy focused initially on graduate and professional education.

During the 1930's and 1940's a series of cases were brought to the Court in which racial bars had been erected to the admission of African Americans to state university graduate and law schools. In most of these cases, the states had made no provision for African Americans, and the Court was quick to force states to remedy the deficiency. The most significant of these cases was *Sweatt v. Painter* (1950). Homan Sweatt had applied for admission to the University of Texas law school. He was rejected because he was African American. After he brought suit, Texas quickly established a separate law school for African Americans. Sweatt refused to attend the new school and continued his suit. The Court, sensitive to the intangibles in law school education in particular, held unanimously for Sweatt. The opinion's emphasis on intangible criteria provided ammunition for the appellants' briefs in *Brown v. Board of Education* (1954), involving a segregated public school.

THE END OF LEGAL SEGREGATION

Although nothing in the Court's opinion in *Brown* said so explicitly, its thrust went far beyond public education. The Court struck down every state segregation law brought before it within the next few years. Most of these cases were decided by memorandum or *per curiam* (by the entire court) opinions, often with just a brief reference to the authority of *Brown*. Through the remainder of the 1950's and 1960's a long and occasionally violent struggle over segregation took place. The Court's last major opinion in a desegregation case was handed down in *Swann v. Charlotte-Mecklenburg Board of Education* (1971), in which the Court authorized lower federal courts to use "equitable remedies"—court orders—to bring about desegregation. Federal courts mandated school busing, redrafting of district boundaries, and other measures designed to end segregation both legally and practically. By 1980 integration had taken place in many U.S. public schools across the country.

The Court's work also sparked and encouraged the growth and fervor of the Civil Rights movement in other areas in the 1950's and 1960's. Soon private as well as public racial discrimination was under attack. With the passage of the Civil Rights Act of 1964 and subsequent amendments, most private racial discrimination in education, employment, public accommodations, and housing became unlawful. Congress chose to base this statute on the power to regulate interstate commerce rather than on the Fourteenth Amendment. The first important constitutional test of this statute occurred in Georgia in 1964. In *Heart of Atlanta Motel v. United States*, a downtown Atlanta motel challenged the constitutionality of the 1964 Civil Rights Act because it wanted to continue its practice of refusing to rent rooms to African Americans. The Court, in a unanimous opinion written by Justice Tom C. Clark, held that discrimination against African Americans had a substantial effect in discouraging travel. Therefore, barring African Americans from motels placed a burden on interstate commerce, which Congress had the power to control. In a companion case, *Katzenbach v. McClung* (1964), the Court held that Ollie's Barbecue, a small restaurant in Birmingham, Alabama, could also be brought within the scope of antidiscrimination statutes because much of the meat sold there was imported from other states. Within a ten-year period, the law in the United States had changed from permitting government and private discrimination to disallowing both. The Court was a major agent in that change.

PAST DISCRIMINATION

In the 1970's civil rights activists shifted their focus from eliminating racial discrimination to remedying the effects of past discrimination. Amendments to the 1964 Civil Rights Act mandated affirmative action to address this situation. Affirmative action was meant to give preferences to members of traditionally disadvantaged racial groups when the objective criteria for employment or admission to a school were equal between applicants. In practice, it quickly became quota oriented, especially in public institutions where "progress" in bringing an end to discriminatory practices was measured by how many members of minority groups were employed or admitted to programs. Opponents of affirmative action characterized it as reverse discrimination. Supporters saw it as remedial. The practice raised the issue of whether such programs are constitutionally permissible and whether racial classifications could be used to help minorities.

The Court answered this question—albeit in an extremely complex way—in *Regents of the University of California v. Bakke* (1978). The medical school at the University of California, Davis, had established an affirmative action program by which sixteen of the one hundred spots for first-year students were set aside for members of minority groups—blacks, Chicanos, Asians, and American Indians. Allan Bakke, a white applicant, applied to Davis twice and was rejected both times although his grades, Medical College Admission Test scores, and benchmark scores were significantly higher than those of students admitted under the affirmative action program. Bakke's claim was that he had been denied "the equal protection of the laws" required by the Fourteenth Amendment. The opinion of the Court was written by Justice Lewis F. Powell, Jr., for two separate five-justice majorities. The justices saw the case as containing two slightly different questions: first, whether California universities could establish a racial quota system for admission and, second, whether the state could use race as a criterion in any way in shaping its medical school admissions policies. Five members of the Court—Powell, John Paul Stevens, William H. Rehnquist, Potter Stewart, and Chief Justice Warren E. Burger—took the position that quotas may not be used at all. All but Powell would have done away with any use of race. Powell and the remaining four justices—Thurgood Marshall, William J. Brennan, Jr., Harry A. Blackmun, and Byron R. White—took the position that race may be used in admissions decisions; all but Powell would have approved the Davis quota system. The result was that the Davis program was held unconstitutional and Bakke was admitted to the medical school; however, the Court found that affirmative action programs that did not use quotas could still be constitutional, depending on their content.

OTHER RACIAL ISSUES

Although state-mandated segregation raised the most important racial discrimination issues faced by the Court, many other cases involving race were addressed by the justices. Among the most important of these is *Korematsu v. United States* (1944). The Court declared that race is a suspect classification, requiring the most rigorous scrutiny under the equal protection clause. Ironically, *Korematsu* is one of the very small number of cases in which a racial classification survived strict scrutiny by the Court. Toyosaburo Korematsu had disobeyed a military order that excluded all persons of Japanese ancestry from parts of the West Coast at the beginning of World War II. Although the majority sustained the military order as a necessity that the Court should not upset, the strong strictures about racial classifications were to be invoked in many later cases.

In the area of voting rights, the Court found state-mandated all-white primary elections unconstitutional in *Nixon v. Herndon* (1927), and party-run all-white primaries were forbidden in *Smith v. Allwright* (1944). The Voting Rights Act of 1965, which forbade literacy tests for voters, often used in a racially discriminatory way, was upheld by the Court in *South Carolina v. Katzenbach* (1966).

Race-related restrictive covenants in real-estate transactions were ruled unenforceable in *Shelley v. Kraemer* (1948). The restrictive covenant in this case was an agreement in a deed of sale that the property would not be resold to a person "not of the Caucasian race." The Court, in a 6-0 decision, held that the state government would be violating the equal protection clause of the Fourteenth Amendment if such a contract were to be enforced.

In 1967 the court addressed the issue of miscegenation statutes (laws forbidding interracial marriage), which existed in sixteen states, including Virginia. The Court struck down Virginia's law in *Loving v. Virginia* (1967). In defending its statute, Virginia argued that because the law affected whites and nonwhites alike it was not racially discriminatory. Chief Justice Earl Warren, in his opinion for the unanimous Court, wrote that such laws established "invidious discrimination based on race," pointing out that the Virginia statute outlawed interracial marriages when only one of the partners was white.

Thus, by the end of the twentieth century, the Court had established that racial classifications in both federal and state legal systems are unconstitutional except for some benign remedial classifications designed to remedy past governmental discrimination.

Robert Jacobs

FURTHER READING

Just as issues of race and discrimination have continued to challenge American courts, those issues have inspired a large literature. Among the many books looking at race and the Supreme Court are Robert A. Williams's *Like a Loaded Weapon: The Rehnquist Court, Indian Rights, and the Legal History of Racism in America* (Minneapolis: University of Minnesota Press, 2005), Maurice Y. Mongkuo's *Race Preference Programs and the United States Supreme Court Strict Scrutiny Standard of Review* (Lewiston, N.Y.: Edwin Mellen Press, 2005), Michael J. Klarman's *From Jim Crow to Civil Rights: The Supreme Court and the Struggle for Racial Equality* (New York: Oxford University Press, 2004), and Girardeau A. Spann's *The Law of Affirmative Action: Twenty-Five Years of Supreme Court Decisions on Race and Remedies* (New York: New York University Press, 2000). Other useful books include Kevin J. McMahon's *Reconsidering Roosevelt on Race: How the Presidency Paved the Road to Brown* (Chicago: University of Chicago Press, 2004) and Christopher Waldrep's *Racial Violence on Trial: A Handbook with Cases, Laws, and Documents* (Santa Barbara, Calif.: ABC-Clio, 2001).

Among important older works on this subject, the most accessible and useful for the general reader is Richard Kluger's highly readable *Simple Justice* (New York: Alfred A. Knopf, 1976), which traces the Court's role from *Plessy* to *Brown* and the litigation strategies of the NAACP and its opponents. On the origin and meaning of the Fourteenth Amendment, Jacobus tenBroek's *Equal Under Law* (New York:

Collier, 1965) offers an excellent discussion. *Thurgood Marshall: Justice for All* by Roger Goldman, with David Gallen (New York: Carroll & Graf, 1992), offers a good deal of insight into Marshall's role in the later segregation cases.

There are several good biographies of Chief Justice Warren; the one that is strongest on *Brown* is G. Edward White's *Earl Warren: A Public Life* (New York: Oxford University Press, 1982). Justice Frankfurter's role is well explained in *Felix Frankfurter: A Biography* (New York: Coward, McCann & Geoghegan, 1969) by Liva Baker. A good overview of racial discrimination cases may be found in Loren Miller's *The Petitioners: The Story of the Supreme Court of the United States and the Negro* (Cleveland: World, 1966). The history and development of affirmative action is extensively discussed in *The Civil Rights Era: Origins and Development of National Policy, 1960-1972*, by Hugh Davis Graham (New York: Oxford University Press, 1990).

SEE ALSO *Brown v. Board of Education*; Employment discrimination; Fourteenth Amendment; Japanese American relocation; *Loving v. Virginia*; *Plessy v. Ferguson*; *Regents of the University of California v. Bakke*; Restrictive covenants; School integration and busing; Segregation, de facto; Segregation, de jure; Thirteenth Amendment.

Raich v. Gonzales

CITATION: 545 U.S. ____
DATE: June 6, 2005
ISSUES: Commerce clause; controlled substances
SIGNIFICANCE: The Supreme Court recognized the federal government's authority to enforce federal laws outlawing marijuana in all circumstances, even in those states that have legalized the substance for some medical purposes.

In 1996, California legalized the use of marijuana for medicinal purposes in the so-called Compassionate Use Act, which was similar to the statutes in ten other states. All such statutes conflicted with the federal Controlled Substances Act (1970), which criminalized the possession of marijuana for any purpose. After agents of the Drug Enforcement Administration (DEA) destroyed the marijuana and cannabis plants grown by Angel Raich in her garden, Raich joined with other concerned parties to sue the attorney general and the DEA in federal district court.

The Ninth Circuit Court of Appeals ruled that the DEA's application of the federal statute was unconstitutional insofar as it applied to the intrastate, noncommercial possession and cultivation of a substance for medical use as recommended by a physician. The court pointed to the *United States v. Lopez* (1995), in which the Supreme Court had held that federal power did not extend to the regulation of purely local activities.

The Supreme Court, however, upheld the federal government's position by a 6-3 vote. In the opinion for the majority, Justice John Paul Stevens wrote that the commerce claused empowered Congress to prohibit the local cultivation and use of controlled substances, despite state laws to the contrary. He argued that the commerce clause authorized Congress to regulate any "class of activities" that substantially affects interstate commerce. The case was different from *Lopez*, which related to a noneconomic activity having no significant impact on interstate commerce. Because of the difficulty in distinguishing between marijuana cultivated locally and marijuana grown elsewhere, Stevens affirmed that Congress acted rationally in placing this class of activities within the larger regulatory scheme. He also observed that marijuana has a high potential for abuse and no generally recognized medical use.

Thomas Tandy Lewis

SEE ALSO Commerce, regulation of; *Lopez, United States v.*; Stevens, John Paul; Tenth Amendment.

Reconstruction

DATE: 1867-1877

DESCRIPTION: Post-Civil War period during which the Republican-controlled Union government took control of former Confederate state governments and tried to force the southern states to grant African Americans equal rights.

SIGNIFICANCE: Reconstruction gave the Supreme Court a unique opportunity to extend full constitutional rights and protections to African Americans. Instead, however, the Court's conservatism merely worked to undermine congressional Reconstruction plans.

After the Civil War ended in early 1865 the U.S. government faced fundamental constitutional questions. That the Union was indestructible and states had no right to secede had been settled on the battlefield. However, the relation of the former Confederate states to the Union was unsettled, and the meaning of freedom for the former slaves remained to be worked out. Wresting control of Reconstruction from President Andrew Johnson, who was overanxious for reconciliation with the unrepentant white South, the Republican-controlled Congress passed a series of measures designed to secure a broad nationalization of civil rights and establish a rule of law strong enough to protect black Americans for the long haul.

THE BEGINNINGS OF RECONSTRUCTION

While there is no debate about when Reconstruction ended—with the 1877 inauguration of President Rutherford B. Hayes—many dates have been assigned to its beginnings.

Many members of Congress initially believed that the Thirteenth Amendment (1865), which abolished slavery and empowered Congress to enforce its provision with appropriate legislation, would provide sufficient constitutional support for the freed people. However, it soon became evident that northerners and southerners held fundamentally different assumptions about what freedom meant.

When the southern states enacted discriminatory laws—the notorious black codes—designed to keep African Americans in a slavelike condition, Congress imposed further restrictions on the recalcitrant

South. In early 1866 Congress passed a Civil Rights Act that guaranteed basic legal rights to former slaves. President Andrew Johnson vetoed the bill, but Congress overrode his veto. In June Republican leaders in Congress proposed the Fourteenth Amendment, which would define African Americans as citizens and mandate that all federal and state laws apply equally to all citizens. President Johnson urged the states to reject it (which all former Confederate states except Tennessee did), but the Fourteenth Amendment was finally ratified two years later, in 1868. A third "Civil War amendment," the Fifteenth, was proposed in 1869. Ratified the following year, it outlawed denying any citizen the right to vote because of race.

Meanwhile, in 1867, Congress passed a series of laws called the Reconstruction Acts. These laws abolished the South's newly formed state governments and placed every former Confederate state, except Tennessee, a military district governed by federal troops, under martial law. States wishing to qualify for readmission to the Union were required to write new constitutions that would allow for black suffrage. They also had to ratify the Thirteenth and Fourteenth Amendments and democratically elect new state governments. Black voters participated in every step of this process. By 1870 all southern states were readmitted to the Union under reconstituted state governments. However, white southerners never recognized the legality of their integrated state governments.

Nightriders of the Ku Klux Klan terrorized black voters despite the ratification of the Fifteenth Amendment (1870). Congress responded in 1870, and again in 1871, with enforcement acts designed to stop Klan violence and enforce the Fourteenth and Fifteenth Amendments against private acts of violence, as well as illegal state actions. Responsibility for interpreting these new amendments and the laws that supported them eventually fell on the U.S. Supreme Court.

CONSTITUTIONAL ISSUES

The fact that the three Civil War amendments made some changes in the federal system seemed clear. However, the exact nature of those changes was less clear. For example, the question of precisely which privileges and immunities national citizenship conveyed remained. It was not clear whether the Fourteenth Amendment "nationalized" the Bill of Rights, making its provisions apply to the states as well as to the federal government.

It was also unclear whether the national government was empowered to protect black citizens against private interference with their rights. Other questions included the matter of whether the Fourteenth Amendment's state action provision limited federal intervention to cases in which there was statutory discrimination. Was segregation a remnant of slavery outlawed by the Thirteenth Amendment? Did the Fifteenth Amendment provide a positive right to vote? These constitutional issues found their way into the lower federal courts and made their way to the Supreme Court at a time when most northerners had tired of southern questions. The Court's conservative, formalistic answers to these questions effectively eroded the constitutional rights of African Americans living in the South. By the end of the nineteenth century their future was firmly under control of white southerners.

FOURTEENTH AMENDMENT CONTROVERSIES

The Supreme Court first articulated its interpretation of the Fourteenth Amendment in the so-called *Slaughterhouse Cases* (1873). Ironically, these cases involved neither African Americans nor the U.S. government itself as parties. For this reason, the Court was able to construe the Fourteenth Amendment apart from the potentially explosive racial issues of Reconstruction. The cases themselves originated in Louisiana, whose state legislature had granted a meat-slaughtering monopoly in New Orleans that threatened to drive all other butchers out of business. A group of white butchers hurt by this monopoly brought suit, claiming that the monopoly denied them their equal privileges and immunities under the Fourteenth Amendment.

Slaughterhouse presented an opportunity for the Court to recognize that the Fourteenth Amendment had radically altered the federal system, making the U.S. government responsible for protecting the rights of all citizens. However, it was not to be. Justice Samuel F. Miller, speaking for a closely split majority, chose a rigidly narrow interpretation that adhered to a traditional understanding of dual federalism—the notion that state and federal government were

This 1866 editorial cartoon critically examines President Andrew Johnson's Reconstruction policies, which raised a number of issues that were considered by the Supreme Court. (Library of Congress)

sovereign in their separate spheres. National citizenship and state citizenship were separate and distinct, according to *Slaughterhouse*, and only the privileges and immunities of *national* citizenship could be protected by the United States. The states were still responsible for protecting the basic day-to-day rights of their own citizens. The *Slaughterhouse* precedent seriously limited the protections of the Fourteenth Amendment for African Americans, who had hoped to find a federal shelter under the Fourteenth Amendment when the governments of the southern states refused to protect their rights.

The Court's ruling in *United States v. Cruikshank* in 1876 continued to narrow the scope of rights that federal courts could protect under the Fourteenth Amendment. *Cruikshank* involved a race riot in Louisiana, in which perhaps a hundred black Republicans were killed by white Democrats. Closely following Joseph Bradley's circuit court opinion, Chief Justice Morrison R. Waite—recently appointed by President Ulysses S. Grant—announced that the Bill of Rights protected citizens only against actions of the national government. The due process clause, Waite declared, established protection "against arbitrary and unjust legislation," but did not protect blacks from private acts of violence. *United States v. Harris* (1883) made more explicit the state-action concept implicit in *Cruikshank* by overturning portions of the Civil Rights Act of 1871 (also known as the Second Enforcement Act) because they punished private wrongs without reference to state law.

FIFTEENTH AMENDMENT ISSUES

United States v. Reese (1876), a companion case to *Cruikshank*, construed the Fifteenth Amendment for the first time. Waite ruled that this amendment did not establish a positive right to vote but did establish a constitutional right not to be discriminated against because of race. *Reese* declared parts of the First Enforcement Act unconstitutional for overbreadth, while leaving standing sections of the law that explicitly prohibited voter discrimination because of race. This ruling enabled lower federal courts to continue to prosecute voter discrimination cases. Within a few years, however, the southern states devised other, allegedly nonracial, ways of disfranchising African Americans. These included poll taxes, grandfather clauses, and literacy tests.

CIVIL RIGHTS CASES

The *Civil Rights Cases* (1883) tested the constitutionality of the Civil Rights Act of 1875, which made it a misdemeanor to deny equal access to privately owned places of business such as hotels, theaters, and public transportation. The five cases that made their way to the Supreme Court in 1883 originated in New York, California, Kansas, Missouri, and Tennessee, demonstrating that the issue of racial discrimination was not limited to former Confederate states in the

South. Grounding his ruling in the state action concept of the Fourteenth Amendment, Joseph Bradley, speaking for an eight-person majority, declared the Civil Rights Act unconstitutional. The national government could not fix private wrongs under the Fourteenth Amendment; it was limited to cases of overtly discriminatory state law. The Court also ruled that the Thirteenth Amendment did not support the Civil Rights Act. Although there was no state-action limitation in the Thirteenth Amendment, segregation was not a "badge of slavery" prohibited by the amendment.

Justice John Marshall Harlan, a Kentuckian, former slave owner, and opponent of the Fourteenth Amendment, was the only voice of dissent in the *Civil Rights Cases*. Harlan found ample authority for the Civil Rights Act in both the Thirteenth and Fourteenth Amendments. Segregation was a burden of slavery in Harlan's mind, therefore the Thirteenth Amendment's enabling clause gave Congress authority to legislate against it. Moreover, Harlan read the Fourteenth Amendment broadly, finding authority there for the national government to protect the former slaves in all their rights.

PRO-AFRICAN AMERICAN DECISIONS

The Reconstruction-era Court clearly did not champion African American rights, but it did occasionally decide cases in their favor. In *Ex parte Yarbrough* (1884), for example, Justice Miller ruled that Congress had authority, under Article I, section 4 of the Constitution, to protect national elections without benefit of the Fifteenth Amendment. Thus the national government retained broad powers to protect blacks in federal elections against both state officials and private individuals. Under this ruling, the federal courts continued a vigorous prosecution of voting rights offenders through the 1880's.

In a series of jury cases, the Supreme Court again supported African American rights in cases of overt state action. *Strauder v. West Virginia* (1880), for example, overturned a state statute requiring all-white juries as a violation of the Fourteenth Amendment's equal protection clause. *Ex parte Virginia*, decided the same term, upheld the prosecution of a state judge who had systematically excluded blacks from juries in his court. In *Virginia v. Rives* (1880), however, the Court ruled that the mere absence of African Americans on juries in situations in which no discriminatory state law existed did not demonstrate deliberate racial exclusion; the burden of proof was on the aggrieved parties. Southern states were quick to discern that this decision left room for exclusion that was implicit in the system rather than explicit.

WOMEN AND THE FOURTEENTH AMENDMENT

The Reconstruction-era court was even more conservative in addressing women's rights issues than it was African American issues. Women who hoped to use the Fourteenth Amendment to overturn discriminatory state legislation were disappointed. In *Bradwell v. Illinois* (1873), Justice Miller ruled that the amendment's equal protection clause did not remove gender restrictions for admission to the bar. Chief Justice Waite decreed in *Minor v. Happersett* (1875) that the amendment did not extend to women the right to vote.

Joseph Bradley, concurring in *Bradwell*, appears to have summed up the attitude of the Court in his later infamous observation that a woman's "destiny and mission" is to be a wife and mother. While African Americans had made some progress under the Fourteenth Amendment, the status of women remained unchanged.

CONSERVATISM VS. RACISM

Even though the Reconstruction-era Court was not generous to African Americans, its rulings were grounded more in conservative adherence to traditional notions of dual federalism than in overt racism. While the Court insisted on a state-action theory of the Fourteenth Amendment, it moved to protect African American rights in cases of overt state action. Not until two decades after Reconstruction ended did the Court establish a judicial doctrine that explicitly sanctioned racial segregation.

Under Chief Justice Melville W. Fuller, the Court's overtly racist *Plessy v. Ferguson* decision of 1896 upheld a Louisiana statute that outlawed racial mixing on railroad cars. Winking at the differences between black and white cars, Henry Brown for the Court established the notorious separate but equal doctrine, which the Court did not overturn until 1954. Again, as in the *Civil Rights Cases*, Harlan was the Court's only voice of dissent. Harlan decried the "thin disguise of 'equal' accommodations" and prophesied accurately that *Plessy* would eventually prove as damaging to the nation as the Court's 1857 *Scott v. Sandford* decision.

The Supreme Court failed during Reconstruction to establish the constitutional rights of African Americans. The justices' conservatism, racism, and formalistic readings of the law worked against extending federal protections to African Americans. However, it should be kept in mind that the justices reflected the racial and legal values of their time. The Court would not fully support African American rights until the Warren Court instituted what has been called the "second Reconstruction" era during the 1950's and 1960's.

Lou Falkner Williams

FURTHER READING

Literature on Reconstruction is voluminous. Beginners might well begin with overviews of the Reconstruction-era courts. Jonathan Lurie's *The Chase Court: Justices, Rulings, and Legacy* (Santa Barbara, Calif.: ABC-Clio, 2004) and Donald Grier Stephenson, Jr.'s *The Waite Court: Justices, Rulings, and Legacy* (Santa Barbara, Calif.: ABC-Clio, 2003) are comprehensive reference books covering the Supreme Court through the years of Reconstruction.

John R. Howard's *The Shifting Wind: The Supreme Court and Civil Rights from Reconstruction to Brown* (Albany: State University of New York Press, 1999) is accessible and engagingly written. Howard is particularly enlightening on the racial attitudes of individual justices and their impact on Court dynamics, though he may overstate the real impact of Court decisions on life in the South. Donald G. Nieman's *Promises to Keep: African-Americans and the Constitutional Order, 1776 to the Present* (New York: Oxford University Press, 1991) is more balanced.

For an excellent liberal overview see William M. Wiecek's *Liberty Under Law: The Supreme Court in American Life* (Baltimore, Md.: Johns Hopkins University Press, 1988). For a more conservative view of the Court and federal policy, see Michael Les Benedict's "Preserving Federalism: Reconstruction and the Waite Court," *Supreme Court Review* (Chicago: University of Chicago Press, 1978). More detailed information is provided in Harold M. Hyman and William M. Wiecek's *Equal*

Reed, Stanley F.

Justice Under Law: Constitutional Development, 1835-1875 (New York: Harper & Row, 1982); Loren Miller's *The Petitioners: The Story of the Supreme Court of the United States and the Negro* (New York: Pantheon Books, 1966); and Herman Belz's *Emancipation and Equal Rights: Politics and Constitutionalism in the Civil War Era* (New York: W. W. Norton, 1978).

The most detailed and authoritative information available can be found in Charles Fairman's *Reconstruction and Reunion, 1864-88*, 2 vols. (New York: Macmillan, 1987). A detailed analysis of the difficulties of implementing the Fourteenth and Fifteenth Amendments at the state level is Lou Falkner Williams's *The Great South Carolina Ku Klux Klan Trials, 1871-1872* (Athens: University of Georgia Press, 1996). Frank J. Scaturro's *The Supreme Court's Retreat from Reconstruction: A Distortion of Constitutional Jurisprudence* (Westport, Conn.: Greenwood Press, 2000) looks at the continuing legacy of Reconstruction.

SEE ALSO Bradley, Joseph P.; Chase, Salmon P.; Civil War; Fifteenth Amendment; Fourteenth Amendment; Harlan, John Marshall; Hunt, Ward; Incorporation doctrine; Military and the Court; Miller, Samuel F.; Representation, fairness of; State action; Thirteenth Amendment; Waite, Morrison R.; Warren, Earl.

Stanley F. Reed

IDENTIFICATION: Associate justice (January 31, 1938-February 25, 1957)
NOMINATED BY: Franklin D. Roosevelt
BORN: December 31, 1884, Minerva, Kentucky
DIED: April 2, 1980, Huntington, New York
SIGNIFICANCE: As a justice, Reed was a strong supporter of expanded federal authority in New Deal and subsequent cases, but he usually cast conservative votes in civil liberties cases.

Stanley F. Reed grew up in Maysville, Kentucky, the only child of an upper-middle-class family. He graduated from Kentucky Wesleyan

916

Stanley F. Reed.
(Library of Congress)

College and received a second bachelor's degree from Yale. He attended law school at both the University of Virginia and Columbia but did not receive a degree. He practiced law in Maysville with large tobacco cooperatives as his major clients. A Democrat, he was active in Kentucky politics in the 1910-1928 period, serving two terms in the state legislature. He left Kentucky in 1929 to serve as general counsel to the Federal Farm Board and later to the Reconstruction Finance Corporation. President Franklin D. Roosevelt named him solicitor general in 1935, and Reed argued many important New Deal cases before the Supreme Court during the next three years. He was Roosevelt's second appointee to the Court in 1938, retiring nineteen years later. He died in 1980 at age ninety-five, the longest lived of all the Supreme Court justices.

An economic liberal, Reed upheld New Deal legislation by supporting an expansion of Congress's powers under the commerce clause. He usually sided with unions in labor dispute litigation. He supported strong governmental power generally and dissented when the Court voided President Harry S. Truman's seizure of the steel mills during the Korean War in *Youngstown Sheet and Tube Co. v. Sawyer* (1952).

Reed was relatively conservative in freedom of expression cases. Although he gave some support to the preferred freedoms doctrine in freedom of press cases, he did not think free speech claims should override considerations of law and order. He opposed virtually all free speech claims advanced by the Jehovah's Witnesses. Reed's views matched the temper of the Cold War era; he almost always voted to uphold restrictions (for example, denial of passports or government jobs) on those suspected of being communists. Although he voted to overturn convictions obtained by outrageous police behavior, Reed generally opposed expanded claims of defendants' rights. He wrote the Court's opinion in *Adamson v. California* (1947), rejecting the argument that the due process clause of the Fourteenth Amendment incorporated all the criminal justice provisions of the Bill of Rights.

Given his Kentucky origins, Reed was comfortable with racial segregation, but he realized that times were changing. Because he was a southerner, he was assigned the opinion in *Smith v. Allwright* (1944), which held state laws allowing only whites to vote in party primaries to be unconstitutional. (Blacks could vote in general elections, but these were of little importance in the then solidly Democratic South.) Reed was the last colleague whom Chief Justice Earl Warren persuaded to sign the unanimous opinion in *Brown v. Board of Education* (1954).

Despite nineteen years on the Court, Reed was not a memorable justice. He showed little intellectual leadership in any area of the law. His opinions seldom relied on rigorous logic and lacked inspiring rhetoric. He had no clear philosophy of constitutional interpretation, and his opinions turned on facts more often than on doctrines.

Bradley C. Canon

FURTHER READING
Belknap, Michal R. *The Vinson Court: Justices, Rulings, and Legacy.* Santa Barbara, Calif.: ABC-Clio, 2004.

Fassett, John D. *New Deal Justice: The Life of Stanley Reed of Kentucky.* New York: Vantage Press, 1994.

O'Brien, F. William. *Justice Reed and the First Amendment: The Religion Clauses.* Washington, D.C.: Georgetown University Press, 1958.

Parrish, Michael E. *The Hughes Court: Justices, Rulings, and Legacy.* Santa Barbara, Calif.: ABC-Clio, 2002.

Renstrom, Peter G. *The Stone Court: Justices, Rulings, and Legacy.* Santa Barbara, Calif.: ABC-Clio, 2001.

Urofsky, Melvin I. *The Warren Court: Justices, Rulings, and Legacy.* Santa Barbara, Calif.: ABC-Clio, 2001.

SEE ALSO *Adamson v. California*; *Brown v. Board of Education*; Incorporation doctrine; Ninth Amendment; *Smith v. Allwright*; Solicitor general; Stone, Harlan Fiske; Vinson, Fred M.; Warren, Earl; *Youngstown Sheet and Tube Co. v. Sawyer*.

Reed v. Reed

CITATION: 404 U.S. 71
DATE: November 22, 1971
ISSUE: Sex discrimination
SIGNIFICANCE: A landmark case marking the first time that the Supreme Court applied the equal protection clause of the Fourteenth Amendment to strike down a statute because of gender discrimination.

When Richard Reed died, both of his separated parents, Cecil Reed and Sally Reed, petitioned the probate court to administer the estate. The Idaho code required the court to give mandatory preference to the father, without any consideration of the relative capabilities of the applicants. Sally Reed argued that the mandatory preference was unconstitutional.

The Supreme Court, by a 7-0 vote, agreed with her contention. Writing for the Court, Chief Justice Warren E. Burger insisted that any classifications of people must not be arbitrary and must have "a fair and substantial relation to the object of the legislation." Because

there was no rational basis to think that men were always more qualified than women to administer wills, the probate judge must hold a
hearing to determine the relative merits of the two petitioners. Burger refused to consider whether sex might be a suspect classification,
and his endorsement of the rational basis test allowed states considerable discretion in making gender distinctions. In later cases, including *Craig v. Boren* (1976), the Court adopted a more demanding test
requiring a heightened level of scrutiny.

Thomas Tandy Lewis

SEE ALSO *Bradwell v. Illinois*; Burger, Warren E.; Equal protection
clause; Gender issues; Judicial scrutiny; *Virginia, United States v.*

Regents of the University of California v. Bakke

CITATION: 438 U.S. 265
DATE: June 28, 1978
ISSUE: Affirmative action in education
SIGNIFICANCE: The Supreme Court held that educational institutions
may not use rigid quotas in their admissions policies but may take
race into account in order to increase minority enrollment.

By the 1970's many colleges and graduate schools were using affirmative action programs as part of admission policies, usually granting
preferences to members of disadvantaged minority groups in order
to increase their statistical representation. The medical school of the
University of California at Davis instituted a program that reserved
sixteen out of one hundred openings for minority students. Alan
Bakke, a white male, was denied admission, even though his grades
and test scores were significantly higher than those of most students
who were admitted under the set-aside program. Bakke claimed that
the policy violated both the Fourteenth Amendment and the Civil
Rights Act of 1964. The university was unable to certify that Bakke
would not have been admitted without the special admissions policy.
When the controversial case was appealed to the Supreme Court, it

was accompanied by fifty-eight *amicus curiae* briefs.

In *Bakke*, a divided Court made two rulings. By a 5-4 vote, the Court struck down the university's dual system of admissions, which meant that Bakke was accepted into the medical school. In another 5-4 vote, the Court declared that schools could take race into account as one among several factors promoting diversity. Four justices insisted that the 1964 statute prohibited all racial preferences, and four justices found no constitutional or statutory violation in set-aside programs for disadvantaged minorities. Because Justice Lewis F. Powell, Jr., voted with the majority in both rulings, he delivered the controlling opinion in the case. Powell emphasized that each applicant should have the "right to individualized consideration without regard to race." He did not speak for a majority, however, when he advocated use of the compelling state interest test for deciding which racial preferences were permissible.

The *Bakke* case did not provide much guidance on the affirmative action issue. Because of the variety of opinions in the case, it was unclear which level of judicial scrutiny should be used in evaluating programs, and the majority ruling did not explicitly prohibit the use of statistical goals and timetables, which were similar to quotas in result. In the late 1990's there was a strong reaction against the use of racial and gender preferences, and the Court in *Adarand Constructors v. Peña* (1995) held that all preferences must be justified according to the compelling state interest test. Following years of controversy, the Supreme Court reaffirmed the *Bakke* ruling in *Grutter v. Bollinger* (2003).

Thomas Tandy Lewis

FURTHER READING

McNeese, Tim. *Regents of the University of California v. Bakke.* New York: Chelsea House, 2006.

O'Neill, Timothy. *"Bakke" and the Politics of Equality.* New York: Oxford University Press, 1985.

Schwartz, Bernard. *Behind "Bakke": Affirmative Action and the Supreme Court.* New York: New York University Press, 1988.

Spann, Girardeau A. *The Law of Affirmative Action: Twenty-Five Years of Supreme Court Decisions on Race and Remedies.* New York: New York University Press, 2000.

Rehnquist, William H.

SEE ALSO *Adarand Constructors v. Peña*; Affirmative action; Equal protection clause; Gender issues; Judicial scrutiny; Powell, Lewis F., Jr.; Race and discrimination.

William H. Rehnquist

IDENTIFICATION: Associate justice (January 7, 1972-September 26, 1986), chief justice (September 26, 1986-September 3, 2005)
NOMINATED BY: Richard M. Nixon (associate justice), Ronald Reagan (chief justice)
BORN: October 1, 1924, Milwaukee, Wisconsin
DIED: September 3, 2005, Arlington, Virginia
SIGNIFICANCE: Presiding over a conservative shift in the Supreme Court's jurisprudence, Rehnquist participated in the overturning or undermining of many liberal precedents, even though he frequently continued to find himself on the side of the minority.

Born in Wisconsin in 1924, William H. Rehnquist proved to be a formidable presence and an intellectual force before reaching the Supreme Court. After serving as a meteorologist during World War II, he attended Stanford University Law School, where he finished first in his class, two places higher than his future Court colleague Sandra Day O'Connor. During the Supreme Court's 1952 and 1953 terms, he served as a clerk to Justice Robert H. Jackson. After his Washington experience, he began law practice in Arizona and became actively involved in Republican politics, especially during the presidential candidacy of Barry Goldwater. His Republican connections earned him a position as assistant attorney general in the administration of President Richard M. Nixon. During his tenure, he wrote legal briefs in support of Nixon's tough stand against war protesters.

APPOINTMENT TO THE COURT

Rehnquist's loyalty to the Nixon administration was rewarded with an appointment to the Supreme Court as a replacement for the retired Justice John M. Harlan II. Rehnquist's nomination was paired with that of Lewis F. Powell, Jr., who was chosen to replace Justice

Hugo L. Black. Although Powell's confirmation hearings provoked no controversy, Rehnquist was grilled by Senate Democrats. Their main weapon was a Rehnquist memo on the *Brown v. Board of Education* (1954) case written while he was Justice Jackson's clerk. In the memo, Rehnquist presented arguments in favor of upholding the separate but equal doctrine established in *Plessy v. Ferguson* (1896). The memo suggested that school segregation, the issue decided in *Brown*, was constitutional. It was not entirely clear whether Rehnquist designed the memo to analyze the issues for Jackson or to suggest how Jackson should vote. In any case, Jackson joined a unanimous Court in striking down school segregation.

The furor over his memo lengthened Rehnquist's confirmation, but he was able to overcome the issue and won confirmation on January 7, 1972. He then immediately established himself as the most conservative justice on the Court, consistently ruling for government against the individual in civil liberties cases and for state government against the federal government in federalism cases. In his opinions, Rehnquist focused on the misuse of judicial power and carved out a position of judicial restraint as he called for judges to forgo the use of judicial review and to defer to legislative judgments.

Rehnquist took particular aim at the liberal activism of the Court under Earl Warren. He warned that judicial activism harmed the Court as a neutral institution, observing that when conservatives composed a majority on the Court they might engage in similar activism on behalf of their own beliefs. Rehnquist also disagreed with the results reached by the Warren Court. He disagreed with its decisions expanding the rights of criminal defendants. He criticized those decisions that strengthened federal power at the expense of state governments. Rehnquist also disagreed with the recognition of rights such as privacy that were not explicitly mentioned in the Constitution. Upon taking his seat on the Court, Rehnquist set an agenda of restoring traditional law in these areas and overturning the results reached by the Warren Court.

Rehnquist also exhibited a keen sense of humor and the ability to mold personal relationships with even his most liberal colleagues. He maintained close friendships with Justices William J. Brennan, Jr., and William O. Douglas, with whom he had strong disagreements on legal issues. He also exhibited leadership abilities, attracting the votes of his colleagues in support of his views. This ability contributed to President Ronald Reagan's choice of Rehnquist to be chief justice.

A Decade of Dissent

During the 1970's, Rehnquist acquired a reputation as the Court's conservative conscience, earning the nickname "Lone Ranger" because of his willingness to write solo dissents in support of his views. He disagreed with a high percentage of the Court's landmark cases during that decade. Dissenting in the landmark case that recognized the right of women to have abortions, *Roe v. Wade* (1973), he argued that most of the states outlawed abortions at that time that the Fourteenth Amendment was created, and that there was no evidence the framers of the

William H. Rehnquist in 1972. (Library of Congress)

amendment wanted to recognize a right to reproductive privacy. He dissented in *Furman v. Georgia* (1972), in which the Court struck down the death penalty. He also wrote strong dissents in most proaffirmative action rulings, including *Regents of the University of California v. Bakke* (1978) and *United Steelworkers of America v. Weber* (1979).

Rehnquist wrote a particularly important decision during the 1970's espousing his views on state and federal relations. In *National League of Cities v. Usery* (1976), he wrote for a five-member majority that struck down a federal minimum wage for certain state employees. According to Rehnquist, the federal government's intervention on the wages paid to state employees constituted a violation of state sovereignty and those decisions necessary for maintaining that sovereignty. The Tenth Amendment implicitly gave the states the power to determine its employees' wages. The *Usery* decision represented his first successful attempt at turning back federal power to control state policy. His revival of the Tenth Amendment represented a major departure from the Court's consistent precedents since the New Deal.

During the 1970's, Rehnquist established himself as the most doctrinaire conservative on the Court. He was a justice willing to argue his views alone and in dissent. He presented his views forcefully but was frequently unable to convince his colleagues to follow his lead. However, with the aid of new Republican justices appointed during the 1980's, Rehnquist frequently found himself in the majority and able to write his views into the law.

THE CONSERVATIVE COMEBACK

Rehnquist's most loyal ally during his second decade on the Court was his old law school colleague, Sandra Day O'Connor, appointed in 1981. Rehnquist agreed with her on such issues as state and federal relations, the rights of criminal defendants, and the abuse of the federal judicial power. It was in the area of protecting criminal defendants that Rehnquist had his greatest effect.

Rehnquist authored opinions and joined others in limiting protections for criminal defendants. In *Quarles v. New York* (1984), he established the public safety exception to the Miranda rule. He had consistently disagreed with the Court's decision in *Miranda v. Arizona* (1966), which required police to notify suspects of their constitutional rights before custodial interrogations. In *Quarles*, the police asked Quarles about the location of his gun before warning him of his rights. When the Court upheld Quarles's conviction based partly on this evidence, Rehnquist argued that the police, in these exigent circumstances, were acting to protect the public's safety by inquiring about the location of a dangerous weapon. He also joined such opinions as *Michigan v. Long* (1983), *California v. Ciraolo* (1986), and *United States v. Leon* (1984), all of which took narrow interpretations of the Fourth Amendment, thus allowing greater police freedom to conduct warrantless searches.

Rehnquist also joined opinions allowing for greater church and state cooperation and interaction. In *Widmar v. Vincent* (1981), he joined the Court in requiring universities to provide equal access to facilities to religious and secular student groups. In *Lynch v. Donnelly* (1984), he was part of the 5-4 majority that upheld the constitutionality of a publicly funded Christmas nativity scene, provided that the display included non-Christian symbols. However, five years later in *Allegheny County v. American Civil Liberties Union Greater Pittsburgh Chapter*, he was outvoted five to four when the majority found that a more pious nativity scene was unconstitutional.

One of Rehnquist's major setbacks was in the area of federalism. On this issue he saw his opinion in *Usery* overturned in *Garcia v. San Antonio Metropolitan Transit Authority* (1985). With Rehnquist dissenting, the Court refused to disallow the federal government from setting a minimum wage for state and local employees. Rehnquist also occasionally found himself the lone dissenter in other cases. In *Bob Jones University v. United States* (1983), for example, the Court upheld an Internal Revenue Service policy prohibiting tax exemptions to racially discriminatory schools. Rehnquist dissented, agreeing with the Reagan administration that the agency had abused its power.

Years as Chief Justice

Rehnquist's unwavering conservatism made him the first choice of the Reagan administration to replace Chief Justice Warren E. Burger after the latter's retirement in 1986. Rehnquist was nominated to be chief justice and Antonin Scalia was nominated to fill Rehnquist's vacancy as associate justice. Once again Rehnquist faced tough questioning from Senate Democrats, but the Senate's Republican majority easily confirmed him.

From the 1980's, Chief Justice Rehnquist was increasingly, but not always, able to gain majorities in favor of his conservative views on the law. In *Webster v. Reproductive Health Services* (1989), for example, Rehnquist and his four allies upheld a Missouri ban on abortions in state hospitals, as well as other limitations. Many informed observers believed that the right to abortion would likely be overturned. However, surprisingly, in *Planned Parenthood of Southeastern Pennsylvania v. Casey* (1992), a 5-4 majority upheld the basic principles of *Roe v. Wade*, and with Bill Clinton, a Democratic president, in power, it appeared clear that Rehnquist would be unable to achieve his longstanding goal of overturning the precedent.

Although Rehnquist was willing to acknowledge a person's right to die by refusing unwanted medical attention in *Cruzan v. Director, Missouri Department of Health* (1990), he did his best to contain the expansion of these "liberty interests." In *Washington v. Glucksberg* (1997), he wrote for the Court denying the existence of a constitutional right to physician-assisted suicide. The *Glucksberg* decision reflected his refusal to expand the right of privacy based on the substantive due process doctrine. In *Lawrence v. Texas* (2003), as expected, he dissented from the Court's ruling that states may not punish consenting adults for homosexual acts in a private home.

Federalism was always one of Rehnquist's major concerns. In *United States v. Lopez* (1995), Rehnquist spoke for the Court in striking down a federal law prohibiting guns at public schools. According to the chief justice, the law exceeded Congress's power to regulate interstate commerce because gun possession was not considered commerce. *Lopez* strengthened state government control over such local issues as education. In *Seminole Tribe v. Florida* (1996), he restored the states' right to sovereign immunity under the Eleventh Amendment, so that they could not be sued without their consent. Likewise, In *Printz v. United States* (1997), Rehnquist joined the Court's opinion in striking down a federal requirement that local sheriffs conduct background checks before all gun purchases. The Court ruled that the federal government could not require state law-enforcement officials to enforce federal law.

927

Rehnquist placed a high value on private property and wanted to put definite limits on use of the takings clause. In *Dolan v. City of Tigard* (1994), he wrote the majority opinion that struck down a city requirement that a business cede 10 percent of its property in exchange for receiving a building permit. According to Rehnquist, such a requirement constituted a taking of property without compensation, a violation of the Fifth Amendment. In one of the last major cases of his era, *Kelo v. City of New London* (2005), Rehnquist joined the four-member minority that opposed the use of the eminent domain power to transfer property to a private agency for the purpose of economic development.

In interpreting the equal protection clause of the Fourteenth Amendment, Rehnquist's mature view was that government must not treat people differently because of race. Hostile to positive government acts to promote integration, he was almost always on the side of those who opposed court-ordered busing for the purpose of racial balance. Likewise, he was a strong opponent of almost all racial preferences in affirmative action programs. Having written a strong dissent opposing preferences in *Regents of the University of California v. Bakke* (1978), he expressed the same viewpoint when dissenting in *Grutter v. Bollinger* (2003).

Rehnquist appeared to assume that it was in society's interest to interpret the constitutional rights of criminal defendants narrowly. He disliked multiple appeals and long delays in executing convicted murderers. In the case of *Herrera v. Collins* (1993), he wrote for the majority that the claim of innocence did not provide grounds for granting habeas corpus relief. He also remained a determined critic of the exclusionary rule except in especially egregious cases. In *Florida v. Bostick* (1991), for example, he joined the Court's opinion allowing warrantless searches of bus passengers for drugs, a ruling that narrowly defined the concept of an unreasonable search and seizure. In 2000, with the Court's more conservative majority, it appeared that the majority of justices were poised to overturn the requirement that police give Miranda warnings to criminal suspects. Surprisingly, however, Rehnquist wrote for the majority in *Dickerson v. United States*, declaring that it would be mistake to reverse a practice that had become so accepted by the general public.

In 1999, after the House of Representatives impeached President Bill Clinton, Rehnquist became the second chief justice in history to preside over a Senate trial that determined whether a president would be removed from office. Most observers agreed that Rehnquist conducted the proceedings with dignity and in an even-handed manner. During the following year, however, he received harsh criticism for his central role in *Bush v. Gore,* when he joined with four other justices to stop the recount of presidential ballots in Florida, thereby ensuring that George W. Bush would be the next president. Rehnquist's activism in the controversy was widely perceived as being influenced by either ideology or partisan bias. Critics emphasized that the ruling in *Bush v. Gore* was inconsistent with Rehnquist's usual hesitance to expand the equal protection clause and his long-standing deference to the sovereignty of the states.

In October, 2004, it was announced that Rehnquist had been diagnosed with thyroid cancer. Despite his weakened condition, he was able to appear briefly at President Bush's second inauguration to administer the oath of office. Rehnquist continued to participate in many deliberations and decisions, even though he was forced to miss forty-four oral arguments. On September 3, 2005, he died in his home at Arlington, Virginia.

During his long career on the Supreme Court, Rehnquist maintained a consistently conservative vision of the law. Working with his allies on the Court, in particular Justices Antonin Scalia and Clarence Thomas, he had a degree of success in promoting his agenda, especially in the areas of federalism, the establishment clause, court-ordered busing, and the rights of criminal defendants. However, from Rehnquist's perspective, the balance between liberals and conservatives continued to be precarious, and during his last few years he continued to find himself with the minority in key decisions on abortion, affirmative action, and homosexual rights. Almost all scholars agree, nevertheless, that Rehnquist was one of the most influential justices to serve on the Court during the modern period.

Douglas Clouatre
Revised and updated by the Editor

Rehnquist, William H.

FURTHER READING

Bradley, Craig, ed. *The Rehnquist Legacy*. Cambridge, England: Cambridge University Press, 2006. Scholarly collection of essays on Rehnquist's tenure as chief justice.

Friedelbaum, Stanley. *The Rehnquist Court: In Pursuit of Judicial Conservatism*. Westport, Conn.: Greenwood Press, 1994. Emphasizes the conservative direction of the Court under Rehnquist's leadership.

Hensley, Thomas R. *The Rehnquist Court: Justices, Rulings, and Legacy*. Santa Barbara, Calif.: ABC-Clio, 2006. Comprehensive reference handbook on Rehnquist's tenure as chief justice.

Irons, Peter. *Brennan v. Rehnquist: The Battle for the Constitution*. New York: Alfred A. Knopf, 1994. Fascinating comparative study of Rehnquist's and William J. Brennan's opposing ideologies and strategies, written from a liberal perspective.

Lazarus, Edward. *Closed Chambers*. New York: Penguin Books, 1999. Insider's view of the Rehnquist Court and its decision-making processes.

Rehnquist, William H. *Supreme Court*. New York: Barnes & Noble, 2005. Contains first-hand information about Rehnquist's experiences on the Court as well as his views on the Court's history.

Schwartz, Herman, ed. *The Rehnquist Court: Judicial Activism on the Right*. New York: Hill & Wang, 2005. Collection of interesting discussions on many topics from a variety of viewpoints.

Tushnet, Mark. *A Court Divided: The Rehnquist Court and the Future of Constitutional Law*. New York: W. W. Norton, 2005. Argues that the differences between the modern conservative justices and the traditional conservatives made it impossible for Rehnquist to accomplish all he wanted.

SEE ALSO Burger, Warren E.; *Bush v. Gore*; Chief justice; Dissents; Federalism; *Gratz v. Bollinger/Grutter v. Bollinger*; Judicial activism; Kennedy, Anthony M.; *Lopez, United States v.*; O'Connor, Sandra Day; *Printz v. United States*; Roberts, John; *Webster v. Reproductive Health Services*.

Establishment of Religion

DESCRIPTION: An alliance or entanglement between government and religion prohibited by the First Amendment to the U.S. Constitution.

SIGNIFICANCE: In the mid-twentieth century, the Supreme Court settled on a view of the establishment clause that erected a formidable wall between religious and governmental affairs. However, later cases permitted religious symbols and activities in some public contexts and sometimes gave religious groups equal access to government facilities and benefits.

The Supreme Court made a relatively late entrance into the long debate about the appropriate relation between religion and government in the United States, not adding its voice until the 1940's, more than 150 years after the writing of the First Amendment, which restrains Congress from making any laws "respecting an establishment of religion." In 1868 in the wake of the Civil War, the Reconstruction Congress proposed and the states ratified the Fourteenth Amendment to the Constitution. This amendment's due process clause protects citizens from deprivation of life, liberty, or property without due process of law. In the 1940's, the Court ruled that this clause made the provisions of the First Amendment applicable to the states, thus making state and local governments subject to the Constitution's prohibition against establishment of religion.

AID TO RELIGIOUS INSTITUTIONS

In the court's earliest significant interpretation of the establishment clause, it addressed the contentious issue of whether and to what extent the establishment clause limited government aid to private religious schools. In *Everson v. Board of Education of Ewing Township* (1947), the Court considered the constitutionality of state reimbursements to parochial school parents for the expense of transporting their children to the schools. A closely divided Court eventually upheld these reimbursements, characterizing them as only incidentally aiding religious schools in a limited measure comparable to that entailed in police and fire protection for religious institutions. More important, though, in an opinion by Justice Hugo L. Black, the Court set forth the formulation of the establishment clause that would guide its various encounters with church-state problems in the future. At the very least, the Court insisted, the establishment clause means that government can neither establish a particular state or national church, prefer one religion over another, nor aid religion.

Finding principles to transform the sparse words of the establishment clause into a guide for the various intersections between government and religion in modern society was no easy task. Although *Everson* outlined in broad strokes the general contours of the establishment prohibition, it did not settle the many issues that still lay before the Court. The Court made its most enduring attempt to craft a more precise statement in 1971, when it eventually settled on what would thereafter be referred to as the *Lemon* test.

Lemon v. Kurtzman (1971) involved state laws that directly subsidized the salaries of teachers who taught secular subjects in parochial and other nonpublic schools. The Court found these laws unconstitutional on the basis of its conclusion that they offended a three-pronged test of compliance with the establishment clause. To satisfy the clause, a law must have a secular legislative purpose, have a primary effect that neither advances nor hinders religion, and not foster an excessive entanglement between government and religion. The state laws at issue in *Lemon* created an excessive entanglement between government and religious institutions, the Court concluded, since teachers—even of secular subjects—in parochial schools would be inextricably intertwined with the religious mission and activities of those schools. Any surveillance of teachers in parochial schools intended to prevent such an intertwining would itself constitute an impermissible entanglement.

Sustained criticism of the *Lemon* test proliferated in the following years, both on and off the Court. Critics argued that the test was in principle hostile to religion and that in practice it had produced inexplicable results. Under the test, for example, the Court had approved loans of secular textbooks to parochial schools but not loans of maps. Similarly, the Court in *Everson* had approved reimbursements of expenses of parents to transport their children to parochial schools, but it subsequently invalidated state programs that attempted to subsidize the cost of field trips taken by parochial school children. Notwithstanding this criticism, the Court declined to overrule *Lemon* explicitly, although during the 1980's and 1990's it increasingly formulated the establishment prohibition in terms other than those adopted in *Lemon*. Furthermore, a majority of the Court continued to construe the establishment clause as placing significant limits on direct aid to religious institutions.

However, the majority of the justices became increasingly flexible in applying the *Lemon* test, almost abandoning its prohibition against entanglement between government and religious institutions. In *Agostini v. Felton* (1997), the Court overturned a 1985 decision that had barred the use of public school teachers to teach specialized remedial skills in religious schools. Then, in a 5-4 decision, *Mitchell v. Helms* (2000), the justices voted five to four to approve a federal program of providing religious schools with computers and other equipment. The majority concluded that there were sufficient safeguards to prevent the equipment from being used for religious instruction to any significant extent.

FREE SPEECH AND THE ESTABLISHMENT CLAUSE

In early establishment cases, the Court insisted that any significant aid to religion was forbidden by the First Amendment. However, in some contexts, this prohibition against aiding religion collided with notions of fairness and equality. Under the doctrine of free speech, for example, the Court has generally frowned on government laws and policies that discriminate against speech on the basis of its content. Suppose, then, that a university allows a wide assortment of student groups to use university classrooms after hours for meetings and that a group of religious students seek to use a classroom. Allowing the religious students to use university facilities might be characterized as "aiding" religion; nevertheless, refusing to allow this use would clearly constitute discrimination against the religious speech of the students. In *Widmar v. Vincent* (1981), the Court resolved this apparent conflict between the principles of free speech and the establishment clause by ruling in favor of the religious students. The establishment clause, according to the Court, did not prevent the use of university facilities by religious groups on equal terms with other groups. Accordingly, any discrimination against the religious groups in the access to generally available facilities was an impermissible discrimination against them.

The *Widmar* principle was regularly invoked by the Court during the 1980's and 1990's to uphold claims brought by religious believers alleging that they had been discriminated against in the name of the establishment clause. In *Lamb's Chapel v. Center Moriches Union Free School District* (1993), the Court declared unconstitutional a school's discriminatory treatment of a religious group that sought to use school facilities after hours. The Court held that the school's practice of allowing outside groups to use its facilities after hours for social or civic meetings prevented it from barring religious groups from similar uses. In *Good News Club v. Milford Central School* (2001), the Court reaffirmed that ruling and held that it applied to after-hours events at elementary schools as well as at high schools.

Meanwhile, in *Rosenberger v. University of Virginia* (1995), the Court expanded the antidiscrimination principle of *Widmar* to include discrimination in the allocation of student fees. In *Rosenberger*, a Christian student group at the University of Virginia sought to take advantage of the university's practice of paying the printing costs of student organizations who published printed materials. When the Christian student group sought payment for the costs of printing a proselytizing newsletter, the university refused, claiming that the establishment clause prohibited this kind of assistance to a religious organization. A majority of the Court disagreed, however, and concluded that the establishment clause did not bar the payments at issue and that the free speech clause prohibited the university's discriminatory treatment of the religious group.

The Court became even more lenient toward legislation providing indirect tax support for parochial schools, as long as the funds were awarded to students and parents who then freely decided whether to apply the government money at a religious or secular school. A series of such decisions began with *Mueller v. Allen* (1983), when the Court approved a Minnesota law allowing parents to deduct tuition spent at the school of their choice. Although the deduction was open to parents sending their children to private nonreligious schools, 95 percent of the participating parents chose to send their children to religiously sponsored schools. The Court concluded that the statistical data were unimportant because the choices were freely made by the parents without either the encouragement or discouragement of the state.

The *Mueller* rationale was significantly expanded in the 5-4 decision, *Zelman v. Simmons-Harris* (2002), which upheld an Ohio tax-funded voucher plan that allowed parents to use the voucher to pay for tuition at any private school, whether religious or not. Chief Justice William H. Rehnquist, using a "private choice test," argued that the use of vouchers was "entirely neutral with respect to religion." In a strong dissent, Justice David H. Souter countered that the program utilized tax funds to subsidize schools that practiced religious indoctrination. Although the decision was highly controversial, its practical impact was limited because the idea of tax-supported vouchers turned out to be unpopular with the voting public.

RELIGION AND PUBLIC SCHOOLS

The Court's recent enthusiasm for equality concerns has partially breached the so-called "wall of separation" between church and state that once characterized the Court's pronouncements concerning the establishment clause. However, in one area, at least, this wall of separation remains formidable. Beginning with the school prayer decisions in the 1960's, the Court has been especially vigilant in policing alliances between government and religion in the public schools. In *Engel v. Vitale* (1962), the Court invalidated the practice of having public school children recite a prayer composed by state education officials. A year later, in *Abington School District v. Schempp* (1963), the Court extended this holding to prohibit recitations of the Lord's Prayer and devotional Bible readings in public school classrooms. Eventually, the Court would reach a similar conclusion regarding prayers offered at graduation ceremonies, finding in *Lee v. Weisman* (1992) that they also violated the establishment clause.

After the first decisions in the school prayer cases, the Court developed the three-part *Lemon* test, which required that laws and official government policies have secular purposes and effects and not excessively entangle government and religion. When the Court entertained a new series of cases involving religion and public schools in the 1980's, it focused especially on the secular purpose requirement.

In the first case, *Stone v. Graham* (1980), the Court held unconstitutional the posting of copies of the Ten Commandments in public school classrooms. The school district in question argued that it had a legitimate secular purpose in calling attention to an important source of Western law. A majority of the Court concluded, however, that the principal justification behind the display of the Ten Commandments was a religious one and that this purpose offended the establishment clause.

In the second case, *Wallace v. Jaffree* (1985), the Court considered an Alabama statute that had authorized moments of silence in school classrooms for meditation and prayer. Although in separate opinions, a majority of the members of the Court suggested that while moment of silence statutes might be constitutional in principle, the Court nevertheless concluded that the Alabama statute had been supported by an unconstitutional religious purpose of returning prayer to public schools. Finally, in *Edwards v. Aguillard* (1987), the Court turned to the secular purpose requirement once again to invalidate a Louisiana statute that had mandated the teaching of creationism in schools that taught the theory of evolution.

PUBLIC RELIGIOUS CEREMONIES AND SYMBOLS

The vigilance with which the Court patrolled the boundaries of church and state in the public schools did not always manifest itself in other public contexts. The Court wrestled with the long-standing presence in American life of a measure of religiousness in public contexts and sought to harmonize this presence with its establishment doctrine. For example, in *Marsh v. Chambers* (1983), the Court acknowledged that prayers in certain public contexts had been commonplace in U.S. history since its earliest days. The First Congress had appointed chaplains to its sessions with prayers, and Court sessions themselves began with the invocation, "God save the United States and this Honorable Court." Faced with this historical precedent, a majority of the Court—in an opinion by Chief Justice Warren E. Burger—concluded that the Nebraska legislature's practice of beginning its sessions with a prayer offered by a chaplain paid to do so did not offend the establishment clause.

Even more controversial was the Court's decision in *Lynch v. Don-*

nelly (1984), which upheld a city's display of the traditional Christian nativity scene during the Christmas season. Chief Justice Burger again announced the Court's opinion and declared that the city had a secular purpose in sponsoring the nativity scene—to celebrate the Christmas holiday and to depict the origins of the holiday. The decision was closely divided, however, and Justice Sandra Day O'Connor provided the crucial fifth vote needed to reach this result.

Although O'Connor agreed with the result articulated by the chief justice, in her opinion, the presence along with the nativity scene of other holiday symbols inoculated the nativity scene from an establishment violation. Because the nativity scene was set among such items as a Santa Claus house, reindeer and a sleigh, candy-striped poles, a Christmas tree, carolers, and lights, it could not be seen as an endorsement of a particular religious faith, according to Justice O'Connor.

Five years later, in *Allegheny County v. American Civil Liberties Union Greater Pittsburgh Chapter* (1989), the Court would reach a different result concerning a nativity scene displayed alone on public property during the Christmas season. Set in this context, the nativity scene amounted to an endorsement of Christianity according to a majority of the Court and therefore violated the establishment clause.

THE MEANING OF THE ESTABLISHMENT OF RELIGION

Another symbolic controversy involved the displaying of the Ten Commandments in schools, courthouses, and public grounds. When such displays were included with other historical documents to illustrate the history of the American legal system, the Court usually found no constitutional problem with them. However, many displays appeared to convey religious messages. The line separating the two forms of displays was not always easy to draw. In 2005, the Supreme Court issued two simultaneous 5-4 rulings. In *Van Orden v. Perry*, five of the justices held that a six-foot-tall monument that had been on the Texas capital grounds for about forty years did not violate the establishment clause. Several justices were influenced by the age of the monument and others were influenced by the fact that it was only one of seventeen monuments in the large park.

The Court's second 2005 judgment, *McCreary County v. American*

Civil Liberties Union, provided a contrasting decision. Five justices concluded that displays of two relatively recently installed framed copies of the Ten Commandments in Kentucky courthouses were unconstitutional because of evidence that the officials of the counties had desired to promote a religious point of view. The Ten Commandments had originally been displayed alone, but after litigation began, officials added other historical documents. The claim that the displays were secular was, according to Justice David H. Souter, "an apparent sham." The two decisions gave a general indication of how the Court would probably rule on that issue in the future, but without any bright line direction for the lower courts to follow.

The last two decades of the twentieth century saw increasing dissatisfaction on the Court with its establishment doctrine. The three-part *Lemon* test that had governed the Court's resolution of establishment issues for a time seemed less capable of continuing to command assent among a majority of justices. In this state of disarray, individual members of the Court attempted to articulate new understandings of the antiestablishment principle. Justice William H. Rehnquist, for example, suggested in his dissent to the Court's decision in *Wallace v. Jaffree* that the establishment clause should be understood only to prevent government preference for one religion over another. So long as government endorsed or aided religion in general, he contended, rather than endorsing or aiding a particular religion, then the establishment clause was not violated.

During the early 1990's, Justice Anthony M. Kennedy seemed to propose his own key to understanding the establishment clause. In *Lee v. Weisman,* for example, his opinion for the Court focused on the coerciveness of a graduation prayer on those who did not share the religious tenets expressed in the prayer. This emphasis seemed to suggest that noncoercive government alliances with religion might survive an establishment clause challenge.

Finally, and most important, in the mid-1980's Justice Sandra Day O'Connor proposed that the hallmark of an establishment clause violation was its purpose or effect in endorsing religion generally over nonreligion or in endorsing a particular religion over others. She first elaborated this no-endorsement vision of the establishment clause in a series of concurring opinions, beginning with the first nativity scene case, *Lynch v. Donnelly*. By the end of the 1980's, however, her no-endorsement test seemed to have captured a majority view on the Court because the Court applied her test to resolve another nativity scene issue in *Allegheny County v. American Civil Liberties Union Greater Pittsburgh Chapter*. However, during the 1990's, Justice O'Connor's vision of the establishment clause was not featured again in opinions for the Court. All during this decade, no majority ever coalesced to overrule the three-part test of *Lemon*. Instead, the justices were fragmented in their views of the establishment clause, agreeing sometimes on the result in particular cases but seldom agreeing on the broader principles that explained these results.

Timothy L. Hall

FURTHER READING

Religion is a subject well served by studies of every aspect of its place in American history, government, and society. A good starting point for research is Edwin S. Gaustad's *Proclaim Liberty Throughout All the Land: A History of Church and State in America* (New York: Oxford University Press, 2003). Among the many fine examinations of constitutional interpretations of the First Amendment's religion clauses are Melvin I. Urofsky's *Religious Freedom: Rights and Liberties Under the Law* (Santa Barbara, Calif.: ABC-Clio, 2002), Kermit L. Hall's *Conscience and Belief: The Supreme Court and Religion* (New York: Garland, 2000), Daniel O. Conkle's *Constitutional Law: The Religion Clauses* (New York: Foundation Press, 2003), and Phillip E. Hammond's *Religion on Trial: How Supreme Court Trends Threaten the Freedom of Conscience in America* (Walnut Creek, Calif.: AltaMira Press, 2004).

Comprehensive collections of Court decisions relating to the First Amendment's religion clauses are James John Jurinski's *Religion on Trial: A Handbook with Cases, Laws, and Documents* (Santa Barbara, Calif.: ABC-Clio, 2003) and *Toward Benevolent Neutrality: Church, State, and the Supreme Court*, edited by Ronald B. Flowers and Robert T. Miller (Waco, Tex.: Baylor University Press, 1998). Similar, though less inclusive collections of Court cases may be found in *The Believer and the Powers That Are: Cases, History, and Other Data Bearing on the Relation of Religion and Government*, by John Thomas Noonan, Jr. (New York: Macmillan, 1987), and *Religious Liberty in the Supreme Court: The*

Cases That Define the Debate over Church and State, edited by Terry Eastland (Grand Rapids, Mich.: Wm. B. Eerdmans, 1995).

The Court has regularly consulted the history of church-state relations in colonial and revolutionary America to inform its interpretation of the establishment clause. Thomas Curry's *The First Freedoms: Church and State in America to the Passage of the First Amendment* (New York: Oxford University Press, 1986) contains an excellent treatment of these periods. *A Nation Dedicated to Religious Liberty: The Constitutional Heritage of the Religion Clauses,* by Arlin M. Adams and Charles J. Emmerich (Philadelphia: University of Pennsylvania Press, 1990), combines both coverage of the historical background of the religion clauses and their current interpretation by the Court.

For an influential argument that the Court has given too prominent a place to religious skepticism in its interpretation of the religion clauses, see Mark DeWolfe Howe's *The Garden and the Wilderness: Religion and Government in American Constitutional History* (Chicago: University of Chicago Press, 1965). An opposing viewpoint may be found in *The Godless Constitution: The Case Against Religious Correctness,* by Isaac Kramnick and R. Laurence Moore (New York: W. W. Norton, 1996). *Everson Revisited: Religion, Education, and Law at the Crossroads,* edited by Jo Renee Formicola and Hubert Morken (Lanham, Md.: Rowman & Littlefield, 1997), explores the significance and future of the Court's seminal establishment clause decision in *Everson v. Board of Education.*

Robert S. Alley's *School Prayer: The Court, the Congress, and the First Amendment* (Buffalo, N.Y.: Prometheus Books, 1994) provides an evenhanded treatment of one of the most contentious areas of the Court's establishment clause law. The increasing prominence of the principle of equality over that of separation is explored and supported in *Equal Treatment of Religion in a Pluralistic Society,* edited by Stephen V. Monsma and J. Christopher Soper (Grand Rapids, Mich.: Wm. B. Eerdmans, 1998). This movement is contrasted with the case for nearly total separation of government and religion made by Marvin E. Frankel, a former New York federal judge, in *Faith and Freedom: Religious Liberty in America* (New York: Hill & Wang, 1994).

Freedom of Religion

DESCRIPTION: Freedom of religious belief and practice protected, in significant part, by the free exercise clause of the First Amendment.

SIGNIFICANCE: The Supreme Court has generally interpreted the free exercise clause of the First Amendment to protect citizens from unfavorable government treatment on account of their religious beliefs or lack thereof, but the Court has not typically protected religious adherents from conflicts between their conscientious practices and the requirements of generally applicable laws.

The Supreme Court's attention to religious freedom has focused primarily on the meaning of the First Amendment's free exercise clause, though from time to time it has also considered other federal and state laws regarding religious liberty. The First Amendment prevents Congress from making laws prohibiting the free exercise of religion. Although the text of the clause limits its application to congressional infringements on religious liberty, the Court, beginning in the 1940's, declared this liberty to be one of the fundamental rights of free citizens made applicable to state and local governments through the due process clause of the Fourteenth Amendment. Therefore, as currently interpreted by the Court, the constitutional protection of the free exercise of religion applies to government action at every level.

THE WAR AGAINST POLYGAMY

In modern times, government actions specifically targeting unpopular religions for unfavorable treatment have been relatively rare. Far more common are claims by religious believers for exemptions from the requirements of otherwise generally applicable laws. The first significant claim of this sort reached the Court in the last part of the nineteenth century. The Court's resolution of the issue in that context—though briefly repudiated for part of the twentieth century—continues to guide its treatment of free exercise claims.

The case that became *Reynolds v. United States* (1879) grew out of efforts by the administration of President Ulysses S. Grant to stamp out the practice of polygamy in the Utah territory. Relying on a federal antibigamy law that prohibited the marriage of one person to multiple spouses, the Grant administration prosecuted numerous members of the Church of Jesus Christ of Latter-day Saints (Mormons) who, as a matter of religious belief and practice, had consummated bigamous marriages. The Mormon Church attempted to challenge the federal law through a test case brought by George Reynolds, secretary to Mormon leader Brigham Young. After being convicted of bigamy in the Utah territorial district court and having his conviction affirmed in the Utah territorial supreme court, Reynolds appealed his case to the U.S. Supreme Court. The essence of his claim was that the First Amendment's free exercise clause, in guaranteeing religious liberty, prevented the application against him of the federal antibigamy law, since bigamous marriage practices were an essential component of his religion.

The Court unanimously rejected Reynolds's claim. In an opinion by Justice Morrison R. Waite, the Court distinguished between religious beliefs and religious actions, determining that beliefs were immune from legislative prescription but that actions fell within the proper provenance of the law. Reynolds, the Court opined, had been prosecuted not for his beliefs but for his bigamous actions. By the free exercise clause, "Congress was deprived of all legislative power over mere opinion, but was left free to reach actions which were in violation of social duties or subversive of good order." Moreover, the Court readily concluded that the practice of polygamy violated important social duties and was subversive of good order. Congress, then, had acted fully within its constitutional authority.

The Court also determined that the free exercise clause did not guarantee Reynolds an exemption from an otherwise valid exercise of lawmaking authority. Surely the believer in human sacrifice was not entitled to an exemption from the laws of murder nor was the widow who thought it her religious duty to burn herself on the funeral pyre of her husband entitled to an exemption from the laws forbidding suicide. In both cases, the law prohibited such acts, even when motivated by conscientious religious beliefs; and the free exercise clause did not secure any exemptions from these prohibitions. A contrary result was unthinkable to the Court. "To permit this would be to make the professed doctrines of religious belief superior to the law of the land, and in effect to permit every citizen to become a law unto himself."

Eleven years later, the Court lent its aid again to the war against polygamy. In *Davis v. Beason* (1890), the Court upheld an Idaho territorial statute that denied the vote to those who practiced or advocated the practice of polygamy or who belonged to an organization that did so. The Court demonstrated the frailty of the barrier between the absolute protection given to religious beliefs and the lawful regulation of religious practices. Under the statute at issue in the case, mere advocacy of polygamy or membership in an organization—such as the Mormon church—that engaged in such advocacy was sufficient to suffer loss of voting rights. Moreover, the Court adopted a tightly circumscribed notion of religion itself. Religion, the Court declared, had to do with one's relation to the Creator and to the obligations that arose from such a relation. Under this definition, the Court stripped the Mormon practice of polygamy of its claimed religiousness, thus finding additional reason to deny it protection under the free exercise clause.

RELIGION AND THE POLITICAL PROCESS

For almost a hundred years, the interpretation of the free exercise clause adopted in *Reynolds* meant that religious believers were protected against being deliberately targeted by the government for hostile action but not from the burdens occasioned by generally applicable laws. As governments at all levels increased the measure of their lawmaking activity in the twentieth century, inadvertent collisions between religious practice and lawmaking increased in frequency. When legislative policies conflicted with the religious practices of influential segments of the population, lawmakers typically saw fit to craft exemptions for the religious believers in question. For example, when Congress implemented Prohibition's ban on consumption of alcoholic beverages in the early part of the twentieth century, it took care to craft an exemption for the sacramental uses of wine important to many Christian faiths. Similarly, when Congress provided for compulsory military service at various junctures during the twentieth century, it made allowance for certain religious objections to combat by placing the holders of the requisite conscientious beliefs in noncombat positions.

At least in the case of conscientious objector status, the Court consistently took the position that the free exercise clause did not require this accommodation, but the normal workings of the political process were generally sufficient to shield influential religious practices from burdensome encounters with the law. Minority faiths, however, could not be assured of such solicitude from the political process, and the ruling in *Reynolds* deprived them of any constitutional harbor.

THE WARREN COURT REVISION

For a brief interval during the second half of the twentieth century, the Court appeared to reconsider *Reynolds* and adopt an interpretation of the First Amendment far more protective of religious practices. In *Sherbert v. Verner* (1963), the Warren Court turned again to the question of whether a neutral law of general applicability might nevertheless amount to an unconstitutional burden on the free exercise of religion. At issue in *Sherbert* was a state unemployment compensation scheme that refused to pay benefits to a Seventh-day Adventist who, for religious reasons, refused to work on Saturday, the day of her Sabbath. State officials judged that this refusal did not amount to the kind of "good cause" that would otherwise excuse a recipient of unemployment compensation benefits from accepting available work. A majority of the Court, however, in an opinion by Justice William J. Brennan, Jr., ruled that the state's failure to pay the Sabbatarian unemployment benefits amounted to a violation of the free exercise clause. To condition the claimant's receipt of unemployment benefits on her willingness to violate her conscientiously held religious beliefs required that the state demonstrate some overwhelming interest at stake in its legal requirement. Finding no such interest, the Court held that the state was required to pay the claimant the benefits.

The Court's opinion in *Sherbert* seemed to indicate that the free exercise clause protected religious believers from even the unintended effects of otherwise generally applicable laws. The Court's remedy in such cases was not to invalidate the law at issue in its entirety but simply to craft an exemption from the law's demands for the religious claimant. Nine years after the *Sherbert* decision, the Court revisited this issue and seemed to reaffirm its basic holding in *Sherbert*. In *Wisconsin v. Yoder* (1972), the Court considered whether a state compulsory attendance statute could be used to force Amish parents to send their children to school after age fourteen. First, the Court found that the statute imposed a burden on Amish religious beliefs and practices because the Amish insisted that their children would be unfavorably influenced by further schooling after the eighth grade. Second, the Court denied that the state had any compelling purpose for requiring further schooling of Amish children. Accordingly, a majority of the Court held, in an opinion by Chief Justice Warren E. Burger, that the Amish were exempted from the compulsory attendance statute, insofar as it required them to send their children to school beyond the eighth grade.

PRINCIPLE AND PRACTICE

For roughly two decades after its decision in *Yoder*, the Court continued to adhere to the *Sherbert/Yoder* formulation of the free exercise clause: Religious believers were entitled to exemptions from laws that burdened their religious practices unless such laws were justified by some compelling governmental interest. Nevertheless, during these years, the Court routinely ruled *against* religious claimants who asserted free exercise claims. Sometimes, the Court found a significantly weighty public interest at stake, such as when it declined to exempt an Amish employer from the requirement of paying social security taxes for his employees in *United States v. Lee* (1982).

In other cases, the Court found that the government interests involved in particular environments such as prisons or the military warranted greater deference to the government policies. Therefore, in *Goldman v. Weinberger* (1986), the Court upheld an Air Force policy that prohibited an Orthodox Jewish officer from wearing a yarmulke, and in *O'Lone v. Estate of Shabazz* (1987), the Court found that reasonable prison regulations would be upheld even when they conflicted with the sincerely held religious beliefs of prisoners. Finally, in some cases, the Court determined that government decisions about how to conduct its own affairs did not amount to a burden on religious belief or practice. For example, in *Lyng v. Northwest Indian Cemetery Protective Association* (1988), a majority of the Court refused to interfere with government plans to allow the construction of a logging road on government property close to a sacred Native American religious site. Although the logging road would severely impair Native American religious practices, the Court held that the free exercise clause did not prevent the government from using its property as it saw fit.

At issue in *Locke v. Davey* (2004) was whether the free exercise clause permitted states to provide college scholarships for talented students majoring in secular subjects, while excluding from support theology majors studying for the ministry. By a 7-2 vote, the Court found that the exclusion was constitutional. The majority reasoned that the exclusion did not imply an animus toward religion and that states have a "historic and substantial interest" in excluding the public funding of religious activity.

THE PEYOTE CASE

Throughout the 1980's the Court continued to affirm in principle the rigorous standard of protection for religious liberty set forth in *Sherbert* and *Yoder*, but to find in practice any number of reasons for rejecting particular religious claims. In *Employment Division, Department of Human Resources v. Smith* (1990), the Court's principles finally caught up with its practice. At issue in the case were two Native Americans who had been fired from jobs as drug rehabilitation counselors because they had ingested peyote in connection with Native American religious rites. The state of Oregon, where the case arose, classified peyote as a controlled substance and made no exception for sacramental use by Native Americans. After being fired, the two Native Americans sought to obtain unemployment compensation benefits but were refused them on the grounds that they had been fired for job-related misconduct. They, in turn, contested this refusal, claiming that it violated their rights to free exercise of religion. The Court, however, rejected this claim.

An application of the *Sherbert/Yoder* test would have required the state of Oregon to demonstrate some compelling purpose for its peyote law. In fact, Justice Sandra Day O'Connor, agreeing with the result in the case but not in the reasoning of the majority opinion by Justice Antonin Scalia, argued that there was such a compelling purpose and that the Native Americans were thus entitled to no exemption from the Oregon controlled substance law. Nevertheless, a majority of the Court followed Justice Scalia in revisiting the rule in *Sherbert* and *Yoder.* According to Scalia, these cases announced no general rule but merely offered protection for religious believers in certain limited circumstances. The true rule, he declared, was that religious believers normally had no recourse under the free exercise clause against laws that were not targeted at suppressing their religious beliefs or practices but simply had the effect of burdening those beliefs or practices. Because Oregon's peyote law had not been created to target Native American religious practices but simply had the incidental effect of burdening that practice, the law was not subject to a successful free exercise challenge.

THE RELIGIOUS FREEDOM RESTORATION ACT

Reactions to the Court's decision in *Smith* were immediate and stridently critical. Religious groups of all stripes combined with political leaders and legal scholars in denouncing the decision as a betrayal of the principles of religious liberty. In direct response to the *Smith* decision, Congress passed the Religious Freedom Restoration Act (1993) three years later. This law required exemptions for religious believers from federal, state, or local laws that burdened their religious practice unless some compelling reason justified the law and the law was the least restrictive means of furthering the interest. To enact the law, at least as it applied to state and local governments, Congress relied on the Fourteenth Amendment, which authorizes Congress to pass laws to enforce the provisions of this amendment. Congress reasoned that it had power to enforce the protection of religious liberty because this liberty was clearly among those subject to the Fourteenth Amendment's prohibition against depriving persons of "life, liberty, or property without due process of law."

Congress's attempt to invigorate the protections given religious conscience did not go unchallenged. As religious believers sought to wield the Religious Freedom Restoration Act in confrontations with state and local laws, government officials in these cases responded by arguing that Congress lacked the power to pass the Religious Freedom Restoration Act. In the last part of the 1990's one of these cases reached the Court. *Boerne v. Flores* (1997) involved a dispute between a Texas city and a Roman Catholic Church. The church wished to renovate its facilities to accommodate a swelling congregation. The city of Boerne, however, wished to preserve the historic ambience of its downtown district, especially the mission-style Catholic sanctuary, and passed a historical preservation ordinance that blocked the church's plans. When the church filed suit, claiming that the ordinance violated its rights under the Religious Freedom Restoration Act, the city responded by arguing that the federal law was unconstitutional. In a decision that surprised many observers, a majority of the Court agreed with the city and held that Congress's attempt to overrule the effect of the *Smith* decision invaded the Court's prerogatives. Championing its power to define the meaning of constitutional protections for liberty, the Court ruled that Congress lacked power to substitute its own view of free exercise for the view articulated by the Court's opinion in *Smith*.

Timothy L. Hall

FURTHER READING

Perhaps the best place to start any study of this subject is with a comprehensive history of religion in America, such as Edwin S. Gaustad's *Proclaim Liberty Throughout All the Land: A History of Church and State in America* (New York: Oxford University Press, 2003). A next step might be to look at the history of how the courts have interpreted the Constitution's religion clauses in a work such as Daniel O. Conkle's *Constitutional Law: The Religion Clauses* (New York: Foundation Press, 2003) or Kermit L. Hall's *Conscience and Belief: The Supreme Court and Religion* (New York: Garland, 2000). From there, one might go to works such as Melvin I. Urofsky's *Religious Freedom: Rights and Liberties Under the Law* (Santa Barbara, Calif.: ABC-Clio, 2002) and Phillip E. Hammond's *Religion on Trial: How Supreme Court Trends Threaten the Freedom of Conscience in America* (Walnut Creek, Calif.: AltaMira Press, 2004).

Comprehensive collections of Court decisions relating to the First Amendment's religion clauses are James John Jurinski's *Religion on Trial: A Handbook with Cases, Laws, and Documents* (Santa Barbara, Calif.: ABC-Clio, 2003) and *Toward Benevolent Neutrality: Church, State, and the Supreme Court,* edited by Ronald B. Flowers and Robert T. Miller (Waco, Tex.: Baylor University Press, 1998).

Less inclusive collections include *The Believer and the Powers That Are: Cases, History, and Other Data Bearing on the Relation of Religion and Government,* by John Thomas Noonan, Jr. (New York: Macmillan, 1987), and *Religious Liberty in the Supreme Court: The Cases That Define the Debate over Church and State,* edited by Terry Eastland (Grand Rapids, Mich.: Wm. B. Eerdmans, 1995). *The Amish and the State,* edited by Donald B. Kraybill (Baltimore, Md.: Johns Hopkins University Press, 1993), provides useful background for the *Yoder* case and the ongoing conflicts between the Amish and government concerning matters of religious conscience. *Native American Cultural and Religious Freedoms,* edited by John R. Wunder (New York: Garland, 1996), offers similar background to the Court's encounters with Native American religious practices.

Bette Novit Evans's *Interpreting the Free Exercise of Religion: The Constitution and American Pluralism* (Chapel Hill: University of North Carolina Press, 1997) examines the Court's decisions regarding religious liberty, focusing especially on the role of religious freedom in nurturing pluralism. The Catholic perspective of a respected federal appellate judge on religious liberty in the United States may be found in *The Lustre of Our Country: The American Experience of Religious Freedom,* by John T. Noonan, Jr. (Berkeley: University of California Press, 1998). In *The Culture of Disbelief: How American Law and Politics Trivialize Religious Devotion,* by Stephen L. Carter (New York: Basic Books, 1993), the author challenges the Court's religion cases as having undermined religious devotion.

SEE ALSO *Boerne v. Flores; Church of Lukumi Babalu Aye v. Hialeah; Employment Division, Department of Human Resources v. Smith;* First Amendment; Fourteenth Amendment; *Good News Club v. Milford Central School;* Incorporation doctrine; Religion, establishment of; *Reynolds v. United States; Wisconsin v. Yoder.*

Reporting of Opinions

DESCRIPTION: Recording and dissemination of a Supreme Court ruling.

SIGNIFICANCE: For the opinion of the Court to be put into action and have an impact, it must be communicated to the population affected by and charged with enforcing the Court's ruling (including law-enforcement officers, lawyers, lower court judges, and political commentators) as well as the parties to the litigation.

The opinion of the Supreme Court is one of the most complete records of the work of any of the policy-making units of U.S. government. The opinion not only describes the fate of the litigants in the case at hand and the reasons for the Court's decision but also sets guidelines for the resolution of any future disputes arising in the lower courts of the United States that are similar to the case under consideration. The reporting of these decisions, then, is an essential part of the Court's policy-making process.

THE PROCESS

Once the Court reaches its decision in a given case and opinion drafts have been circulated, signed, and finalized, the decision is announced in open court. The author of the majority opinion typically reads a portion of it, and the other justices occasionally offer comment. The dissenters may also read portions of their opinions, although Chief Justice William H. Rehnquist reportedly limited the availability of this outlet. Cases take some time to be reported from their date of public announcement, but usually no more than a year.

After the public announcement of the Court's decision, the opinion goes through a final edit in the office of the reporter of decisions. The reporter of decisions checks all citations, corrects any typographical errors, and adds headnotes and the names of the counsel to the case. He or she then supervises the publication of the decision in the official reporter of the Supreme Court, the *United States Reports*. The *United States Reports* once bore the name of the reporter of decisions in its citation (for example, 123 Wheaton 456), but later adopted the format 123 U.S. 456, where 123 is the volume and 456 the page number. The new citation format began with the ninety-first volume of the *United States Reports*, published in 1874.

The clerk's office provides the press with advance copies of the opinions, and the opinions appear in full form a day or so later in *United States Law Week*, published by the Bureau of National Affairs, and the *Supreme Court Bulletin*, published by Commerce Clearing House. The *United States Reports*, printed under the auspices of the Government Printing Office, publishes both preliminary prints and bound reports of a term's decisions. These appear some time after the announcement of the decisions and include all written opinions of the Court, including dissents and concurrences, unsigned *per curiams*, and orders.

PRIVATE SOURCES

Private organizations also report the decisions of the Court, most of the time with less turnaround time than the Government Printing Office. The West Publishing Company began publishing the *Supreme Court Reporter* in 1883, and the Lawyers Cooperative Company began its *United States Supreme Court Reports, Lawyers' Edition*, in 1901. The *Lawyers' Edition* contains decisions from the Court's beginning, and the *Supreme Court Reporter* begins with the October, 1882, term. These private publishers print the opinions issued by the justices verbatim, adding classifications and notes that aid users in placing the opinions in a larger context. West has a key number system in which cases are classified by subject, allowing for ease in legal research. Supreme Court decisions also appear on several on-line computer services such as WESTLAW and LEXIS-NEXIS (which require purchase to use), where they are published virtually simultaneously with their announcement, as well as on several privately run Web sites including The Legal Information Institute at Cornell University (http://supct .law.cornell.edu), FindLaw Internet Legal Resources (http://www .caselaw.findlaw.com), and Rominger Legal (http://www.rominger legal.com/supreme.htm), all of which are free to the user. All have search engines allowing for easy retrieval of Court case law relevant to any legal inquiry. Many of these report decisions of the lower courts as well.

Sara C. Benesh

FURTHER READING

Baum, Lawrence. *The Supreme Court.* 8th ed. Washington, D.C.: CQ Press, 2004.

Blanc, D. Ellsworth. *The Supreme Court: Issues and Opinions.* Huntington, N.Y.: Nova Science Publishers, 2001.

Epstein, Lee, et al. *The Supreme Court Compendium: Data, Decisions, and Developments.* 3d ed. Washington, D.C.: CQ Press, 2003.

Melone, Albert P. *Researching Constitutional Law.* Carbondale, Ill.: HarperCollins, 1990.

Stern, Robert L., Eugene Gressman, Stephen M. Shapiro, and Kenneth S. Geller. *Supreme Court Practice: For Practice in the Supreme Court of the United States.* 7th ed. Washington, D.C.: Bureau of National Affairs, 1993.

Van Geel, Tyll. *Understanding Supreme Court Opinions.* 4th ed. New York: Longman, 2005.

SEE ALSO Advisory opinions; Dissents; Opinions, writing of; Seriatim opinions.

Fairness of Representation

DESCRIPTION: Each voter's right, in a representative democracy, to have the same opportunity as every other voter to influence the outcome of elections for legislative representatives.

SIGNIFICANCE: The "one person, one vote" principle set forth by the Supreme Court in 1963 required that electoral districts be drawn up with roughly equal populations that do not artificially favor a particular racial or political group.

For many years the Supreme Court refused to become involved in what Justice Felix Frankfurter termed the "political thicket" of legislative apportionment. State legislatures were free to draw their own electoral district boundaries for both state and federal offices. In *Baker v. Carr* (1962), Justice William J. Brennan, Jr., speaking for the Court, stated that failure of a legislature to reapportion its district to reflect population changes could be considered a violation of the equal protection clause. The Court defined the concept of fairness of representation in *Gray v. Sanders* (1963) as the "one person, one vote" principle, which holds that each person's vote should carry the same weight in an election. In *Wesberry v. Sanders* (1964) and *Reynolds v. Sims* (1964), it ruled the principle applicable to both federal and state elections. In *Davis v. Bandemer* (1986), *Shaw v. Reno* (1993), *Bush v. Vera* (1996), and other cases, the Court used the one person, one vote principle, as well as the Fourteenth and Fifteenth Amendments, to ban racial gerrymandering.

Marshall R. King

SEE ALSO *Baker v. Carr*; Delegation of powers; Gerrymandering; *Reynolds v. United States*.

Resignation and Retirement

DESCRIPTION: Relinquishing a position on the Supreme Court either before one is eligible for retirement benefits by tendering a resignation or after serving the requisite period of time to qualify for a pension.

SIGNIFICANCE: Supreme Court justices have lifetime tenure, and many remain on the Court until they die rather than resign or retire. Those who resign frequently pursue other legal careers.

Supreme Court justices may either resign or retire from their positions. Normally, justices who retire from the Court do not engage in further judicial or political activities, although those who resign often do. Resignation or retirement takes on added significance in the case of Supreme Court justices because the U.S. Constitution provides that judges of the supreme and inferior courts are to serve during good behavior. Therefore, unlike members of Congress and the president, federal judges do not have a fixed tenure. The only constitutionally acceptable method by which judges may be removed is through impeachment for and conviction of treason, bribery, or

JUSTICES WHO DIED WHILE SERVING ON THE COURT

Year	Justice	Age	Year	Justice	Age
1798	James Wilson	55	1888	Morrison R. Waite*	71
1799	James Iredell	48	1889	Stanley Matthews	64
1806	William Paterson	60	1890	Samuel F. Miller	74
1810	William Cushing	78	1892	Joseph P. Bradley	78
1811	Samuel Chase	70	1893	Samuel Blatchford	73
1823	H. Brockholst Livingston	65	1893	Lucius Q. C. Lamar	67
1826	Thomas Todd	61	1895	Howell E. Jackson	63
1828	Robert Trimble	51	1902	Horace Gray	74
1829	Bushrod Washington	67	1909	Rufus W. Peckham	70
1834	William Johnson	62	1910	David Josiah Brewer	72
1835	John Marshall*	79	1910	Melville Weston Fuller*	77
1841	Philip P. Barbour	57	1911	John Marshall Harlan I	78
1843	Smith Thompson	75	1914	Horace H. Lurton	70
1844	Henry Baldwin	64	1916	Joseph Rucker Lamar	58
1845	Joseph Story	65	1921	Edward Douglass White*	75
1851	Levi Woodbury	61	1930	Edward T. Sanford	64
1852	John McKinley	72	1938	Benjamin Nathan	68
1860	Peter V. Daniel	76		Cardozo	
1861	John McLean	76	1939	Pierce Butler	73
1864	Roger Brooke Taney*	87	1946	Harlan Fiske Stone*	73
1865	John Catron	79	1949	Wiley B. Rutledge	55
1867	James Moore Wayne	77	1949	Francis W. Murphy	59
1873	Salmon Portland Chase*	65	1953	Frederick M. Vinson*	63
1881	Nathan Clifford	77	1954	Robert H. Jackson	62
1887	William B. Woods	62	2005	William H. Rehnquist*	80

*Asterisked names are chief justices. Edwin M. Stanton died in 1869—after being confirmed by the Senate but before actually serving on the Court.

other high crimes and misdemeanors. Most vacancies on the Court resulted from the death of the incumbent. Indeed, approximately half of the justices who served on the Court died in office.

RESIGNATION

Relatively few justices have resigned from the Court. Some justices elected to leave the Court because they were dissatisfied with some as-

JUSTICES WHO RESIGNED FROM THE COURT

Year	Justice	Age	Reason for resignation
1791	John Rutledge	51	to become chief justice of South Carolina Court of Common Pleas
1793	Thomas Johnson	60	health
1795	John Jay*	49	to enter politics
1796	John Blair, Jr.	64	health
1800	Oliver Ellsworth*	55	health
1804	Alfred Moore	48	health
1835	Gabriel Duvall	82	retirement
1857	Benjamin R. Curtis	47	strained relations with other justices
1861	John A. Campbell	49	to join Confederate government
1870	Robert C. Grier	75	retirement
1872	Samuel Nelson	80	retirement
1877	David Davis	61	to enter U.S. Senate
1880	William Strong	72	retirement
1881	Noah H. Swayne	76	retirement
1882	Ward Hunt	71	disability
1897	Stephen J. Field	81	health
1903	George Shiras, Jr.	71	retirement
1906	Henry B. Brown	70	health
1910	William H. Moody	56	disability
1916	Charles Evans Hughes	54	to enter politics (later returned as chief justice)
1922	Mahlon Pitney	64	disability
1922	John H. Clarke	65	to advocate U.S. entry into League of Nations
1922	William R. Day	73	health
1925	Joseph McKenna	81	retirement
1930	William Howard Taft*	72	health
1932	Oliver Wendell Holmes, Jr.	90	retirement
1937	Willis Van Devanter	78	political opposition to president

*Asterisked names are chief justices

(continued)

JUSTICES WHO RESIGNED FROM THE COURT—CONTINUED

Year	Justice	Age	Reason for resignation
1938	George Sutherland	75	political opposition to president
1939	Louis D. Brandeis	82	retirement
1941	Charles Evans Hughes*	79	retirement
1941	James C. McReynolds	78	retirement
1942	James F. Byrnes	63	to take wartime job
1945	Owen J. Roberts	70	retirement
1956	Sherman Minton	65	retirement
1957	Stanley F. Reed	72	retirement
1958	Harold H. Burton	70	retirement
1962	Charles E. Whittaker	61	disability
1962	Felix Frankfurter	79	retirement
1965	Arthur J. Goldberg	56	to become ambassador to the United Nations
1967	Tom C. Clark	67	to avoid conflicts of interest when his son was appointed attorney general
1969	Abe Fortas	58	reputation damaged by charges of unethical conduct
1969	Earl Warren*	78	age
1971	John M. Harlan II	72	age and health
1971	Hugo L. Black	85	age and health
1975	William O. Douglas	77	age and health
1981	Potter Stewart	66	age
1986	Warren E. Burger*	79	to chair Commission on Bicentennial of Constitution
1987	Lewis F. Powell, Jr.	79	age and health
1990	William J. Brennan, Jr.	84	age and health
1991	Thurgood Marshall	82	age and health
1993	Byron R. White	76	retirement
1994	Harry A. Blackmun	85	age
2006	Sandra Day O'Connor	75	retirement

*Asterisked names are chief justices

pect of their work on the Court. For example, Thomas Johnson (1791-1793) and Alfred Moore (1800-1804) were unhappy with the requirement that members of the Court perform duties as circuit judges simultaneously with their Court duties.

Other justices have resigned to accept or to seek another office. John Rutledge (1790-1791), one of George Washington's initial appointees to the Court, resigned without ever having sat on a case to become chief justice of the Court of Common Pleas in South Carolina. Chief Justice John Jay (1789-1795) left the Court upon being elected governor of New York. Similarly, David Davis (1862-1877) terminated his judicial career to accept election to the U.S. Senate from Illinois, and Charles Evans Hughes (1910-1916) resigned his associate justice position upon receiving the Republican nomination for the presidency. Hughes was defeated by Woodrow Wilson. Later Hughes was appointed chief justice (1930-1941) by President Herbert Hoover, becoming the only person to serve at two different times on the Court.

James F. Byrnes (1941-1942) and Arthur J. Goldberg (1962-1965) left the Court to accept positions in the Franklin D. Roosevelt and Lyndon B. Johnson administrations, respectively. Byrnes appears to have found the work on the Court less interesting than he had anticipated and desired to return to the more challenging political life he had abandoned when he accepted Roosevelt's appointment some months earlier. President Johnson prevailed on Goldberg to accept an appointment as U.S. ambassador to the United Nations, a position that had become vacant after the death of Adlai Stevenson.

Ill health led to the decisions of John Blair, Jr. (1790-1795), Oliver Ellsworth (1796-1800), Gabriel Duvall (1811-1835), and Charles E. Whittaker (1957-1962) to leave the Court. Benjamin Curtis (1851-1857) apparently resigned over dissatisfaction with the *Scott v. Sandford* (1857) decision, and John A. Campbell (1853-1861) resigned when his native state of Alabama seceded from the union. John H. Clarke (1916-1922) abbreviated his career after only six years on the Court to devote his time to securing the entry of the United States into the League of Nations. Finally, Justice Abe Fortas (1965-1969) resigned because of alleged ethical improprieties while serving on the Court.

RETIREMENT

Before 1869, there was no statutory provision for pension benefits for Court justices. In that year Congress enacted legislation permitting justices to retire at age seventy with ten years of service on the judiciary. Between 1869 and 1921, seven retirements occurred; fourteen between 1921 and 1969; nine after 1969. In 1937 President Franklin D. Roosevelt proposed that for every justice over the age of seventy who did not retire within six months, an additional justice would be appointed to a maximum of fifteen. Although the Court-packing plan was not approved, Congress did liberalize pension benefits for federal judges. Under the law, judges might retire as early as age sixty-five provided they met certain length of service requirements.

Within four years of the enactment of this legislation, four members of the Court retired. Advanced age or physical infirmities often prompted retirement. No doubt these factors were instrumental in the retirements of Justices Lewis F. Powell, Jr. (1972-1987), William J. Brennan, Jr. (1956-1990), Thurgood Marshall (1967-1991), and Harry A. Blackmun (1970-1999). Justice Tom C. Clark (1949-1967) retired when his son, Ramsey Clark, was nominated as attorney general of the United States. The elder Clark recognized the awkward situation presented by his continuance on the Court under these circumstances. When Justice Sandra Day O'Connor announced her retirement in 2005, the primary reason she cited was her need to care for her ailing husband.

Finally, there is some evidence that justices may try to time their retirement so as to permit a president of their own party or philosophically compatible with them to name their successor. Nathan Clifford (1858-1881) stayed on the Court as long as he could in the hope that a Democratic president would appoint his successor. He died in 1881 with a Republican in the White House. Earl Warren (1953-1969) may have timed his retirement to allow Johnson to choose his successor as chief justice rather than permit Richard M. Nixon, the Republican likely to follow Johnson in office, to make the appointment. If that was Warren's motivation, it did not succeed; Johnson's choice of Fortas to succeed him failed to win approval in the Senate, and Nixon later named Warren's successor, Warren Burger.

The modern pattern is for justices to remain on the Court until death or retirement. No member of the Court died in office between 1954 and William H. Rehnquist's death in 2005, and through 2006, no justice had resigned—as opposed to retiring—since 1965. With the stature of the Court firmly established, the prestige of membership on the Court widely recognized, and the conditions of service more attractive than in the nineteenth century, resignation to pursue other endeavors is unlikely.

Robert Keele

FURTHER READING

Abraham, Henry. *Justices and Presidents: A Political History of Appointments to the Supreme Court.* New York: Oxford University Press, 1985.

Baum, Lawrence. *The Supreme Court.* 8th ed. Washington, D.C.: CQ Press, 2004.

Cramton, Roger C., and Paul D. Carrington, eds. *Reforming the Court: Term Limits for Supreme Court Justices.* Durham, N.C.: Carolina Academic Press, 2006.

Friedman, Leon, and Fred Israel, eds. *The Justices of the Supreme Court: Their Lives and Opinions.* 5 vols. New York: Chelsea House, 1997.

Savage, David G., ed. *Guide to the United States Supreme Court.* 4th ed. Washington, D.C.: Congressional Quarterly, 2004.

Schwartz, Bernard. *A History of the Supreme Court.* New York: Oxford University Press, 1993.

Ward, Artemus. *Deciding to Leave: The Politics of Retirement from the United States Supreme Court.* Albany: State University of New York Press, 2003.

SEE ALSO Byrnes, James F.; Campbell, John A.; Clark, Tom C.; Clifford, Nathan; Davis, David; Fortas, Abe; Goldberg, Arthur J.; Hughes, Charles Evans; Johnson, Thomas; Nominations to the Court; O'Connor, Sandra Day; Salaries of justices.

Restrictive Covenants

DESCRIPTION: Private agreements or contracts meant to deny a privilege, usually housing, on the basis of race, gender, or ethnicity.

SIGNIFICANCE: The Supreme Court limited, then banned, restrictive covenants, helping reduce housing discrimination.

A common practice in Northern and Western cities, restrictive covenants were a prime example of de facto segregation practices. Typically the covenants required buyers not to resell their homes to African Americans, Latinos, Asians, Jews, or other ethnic/racial groups not wanted in the neighborhood or community, allowing builders to create all-white suburbs and schools. Initially, the Supreme Court permitted restrictive covenants on the grounds that the court had no jurisdiction over private property transfers. The Court took its first step toward limiting restrictive covenants in *Shelley v. Kraemer* (1948), in which it ruled that states that enforced restrictive covenants were liable to be prosecuted for civil rights violations even if the individual homeowners

Contemporary Harper's Weekly *illustration of celebrations outside the galleries of the House of Representatives after passage of the Civil Rights Act of 1866. A clause in that law outlawed housing discrimination.* (Library of Congress)

were not. In *Jones v. Alfred H. Mayer Co.* (1968), the Court rejected the legality of restrictive covenants under the provisions against discrimination in sale or rental of property to African Americans found in the Civil Rights Act of 1966. In banning covenants, *Mayer* also cited the enforcement clause of the Thirteenth Amendment, which gave Congress the authority to determine and eliminate the "badges and incidents of slavery." The case also legitimized the Title VIII fair housing provisions of the Civil Rights Act of 1968, which guaranteed housing rights regardless of race or ethnicity.

Steven J. Ramold

SEE ALSO Housing discrimination; Race and discrimination; Segregation, de facto; *Shelley v. Kraemer*; Thirteenth Amendment; Zoning.

Process of Review

DESCRIPTION: Procedure whereby the Supreme Court accepts a case to hear and then determines the outcome.

SIGNIFICANCE: The Court is bound by procedural rules and conventions intended to ensure fairness during the review process as well as consistent treatment of all parties.

The Supreme Court is primarily a court of appellate jurisdiction, although it has original jurisdiction to hear trials in cases that involve conflicts between two or more states or between states and the federal government. To ask the Court to hear an appeal, a party must file a petition for a writ of *certiorari*, which usually occurs after judgment was entered against that party in a lower court. The Court will grant *certiorari* if, in its discretion, the Court decides that the party meets one of the criteria required by the rules of the Supreme Court of the United States. Although no rule requires it, generally, four out of the nine justices must vote to grant *certiorari* (cert) before an appeal is accepted. *Certiorari* is granted in a very small percentage of the cases that are actually filed; moreover, the Court's conferences regarding the *certiorari* decision are private. Only the ultimate decision is released to the public record.

If *certiorari* is granted, the Court might decide to hear the appeal on its merits with briefs and oral argument, or the Court might rule on the appeal without oral argument issuing an opinion from the Court as a whole, referred to as a *per curiam* decision. In the event the Court decides to hear an appeal on its merits, parties must file briefs presenting their positions for the Court and an oral argument is scheduled. Also, the portions of the trial and previous appellate records are sent to the Court for its use.

As the Court confers privately to reach a decision, the Court is limited by the deference it must afford the lower court decision, the standard of review. The standard of review is determined by whether the issue appealed is a legal issue, a factual issue, or a discretionary issue.

A clerk of the Supreme Court examining docketed cases for a single week in 1970. The growing number of cases that the Court reviews led to creation in 1972 of the cert pool, a process by which clerks screen petitions before they reach the justices.
(Library of Congress)

Furthermore, the Court will affirm a lower court decision if the error complained of is harmless. An error is harmless if the judgment would have been the same absent the error.

Finally, once the justices reach a decision, one justice is assigned the task of writing the opinion. Drafts are circulated among the justices until all revisions, comments, and corrections are complete. A decision is not announced until the opinion is released to the public record.

Joanne LeBlanc Verity

SEE ALSO Appellate jurisdiction; Briefs; *Certiorari,* writ of; Clerks of the justices; Judicial review; Opinions, writing of; Oral argument.

Reynolds v. Sims

CITATION: 377 U.S. 533
DATE: June 15, 1964
ISSUE: Reapportionment
SIGNIFICANCE: The Supreme Court clearly established the one person, one vote principle for all legislative districting except the U.S. Senate.

Many states had state senates apportioned on a geographical basis, providing an equal number of senators to each county no matter how widely the population varied, just as the U.S. Senate was apportioned. The Supreme Court, by an 8-1 vote, ruled that both houses of a state legislature had to be apportioned according to the one person, one vote principle that the Court laid down in *Gray v. Sanders* (1963). However, the Court did not accept that counties stood in relation to their state as the states did in relation to the nation and allowed an exception to the one person, one vote principle in apportionment for the U.S. Senate. This decision led to widespread protests and an unsuccessful attempt to overturn the decision through constitutional amendment.

Richard L. Wilson

SEE ALSO *Baker v. Carr;* Representation, fairness of.

Reynolds v. United States

CITATION: 98 U.S. 145
DATE: May 5, 1879
ISSUES: Freedom of religion; marriage
SIGNIFICANCE: Upholding a congressional prohibition on polygamy, the Supreme Court ruled that the First Amendment protects all religious beliefs but does not protect religiously motivated practices judged harmful to the public interest.

George Reynolds, an active member of the Church of Jesus Christ of Latter-day Saints (Mormons) in the territory of Utah, was convicted of the crime of bigamy, contrary to a federal statute of 1862. All parties agreed that Mormon church doctrine required male members to practice plural marriage when circumstances permitted. The justices of the Supreme Court unanimously ruled that Reynolds's conviction was not a violation of the free exercise clause of the First Amendment. In the official opinion, Chief Justice Morrison R. Waite made a distinction between beliefs and conduct. Although the U.S. Congress could place no restraint on religious opinions, it had the authority to punish "actions which were in violation of social duties or subversive of good order." Waite pointed to the long-standing common-law prohibition of bigamy and quoted respected jurists who believed that the practice promoted despotic government and disrespect of women.

Reynolds is considered a landmark because it was the Court's first major pronouncement on the topic of the free exercise clause in relation to an unconventional religious practice. Waite's formulation of a belief-conduct distinction was important for later cases, as was his reference to the Jeffersonian metaphor of "a wall of separation between church and state." Although the opinion recognized that Congress could not prohibit a religious practice without a reasonable basis, it did not demand a very compelling justification. During this period, rights under the First Amendment were not applicable to the states, but *Reynolds* was in total conformity with state laws on marriage and religion.

Thomas Tandy Lewis

SEE ALSO *Employment Division, Department of Human Resources v. Smith*; First Amendment; Religion, freedom of; Waite, Morrison R.

John Roberts

IDENTIFICATION: Chief justice (September 29, 2005-   )
NOMINATED BY: George W. Bush
BORN: January 27, 1955, Buffalo, New York
SIGNIFICANCE: When he replaced William H. Rehnquist as chief justice, Roberts was expected be a conservative force but more moderate and conciliatory than his predecessor.

The son of a steel executive, John Glover Roberts, Jr., was born in Buffalo, New York. When he was at a young age, his family moved to the affluent town of Long Beach, Indiana. He and his three sisters grew up in a devoutly Roman Catholic, upper middle-class family. He attended a Roman Catholic boarding school in La Porte, Indiana, where he graduated first in his class in 1973. In addition to his studies, he was captain of the football team, coeditor of the school newspaper, and enthusiastic participant in wrestling, choir, and drama.

Roberts was an outstanding undergraduate student at Harvard University, where he won a competitive award for an essay on Marxism and Bolshevism. During the summers he worked in a steel mill. Afer graduating summa cum laude in 1973, he studied at Harvard Law School, where he was managing editor of the law review. Again, he graduated summa cum laude in 1979.

After his graduation, he worked one year as a law clerk at the Court of Appeals for the Second Circuit. During 1980 and 1981, he served as law clerk for Associate Justice William H. Rehnquist. From 1981 to 1986, he worked for the Reagan administration, first as special assistant to the U.S. attorney general and then as associate counsel to the president. After working at the private law firm Hogan & Hartson, he spent the next four years as principal deputy solicitor general. He argued thirty-nine cases before the Supreme Court and prevailed in twenty-five of them. From 1993 to 2003, he returned to Hogan & Hartson, in which he became a partner; in 1995, he reported an income of $1,044,399. In May, 2001, President George W. Bush nominated him to the Circuit Court of Appeals for Washington, D.C., and the Senate finally gave its approval on June 2, 2003.

During his two years on the District of Columbia Circuit, Roberts authored forty-nine opinions, including three dissents. In his analysis of these opinions, law professor Cass Sunstein observed that Roberts was a "judicial minimalist" who emphasized precedent and generally wrote narrow case-based decisions while avoiding doctrinaire pronouncements. In the case of *Hedgepeth v. Washington Metro Authority*, Roberts wrote that an "unwise or even asinine" law does not necessarily violate the Constitution.

APPOINTMENT TO THE SUPREME COURT

On July 19, 2005, shortly after Sandra Day O'Connor announced her retirement, President Bush nominated Roberts to the Supreme Court to fill her seat. However, with the sudden death of Chief Justice Rehnquist in September, Bush quickly chose Roberts to become chief justice. During the Senate confirmation hearings, Roberts convinced most observers that although he was a conservative, his views were more moderate than those of his predecessor. He declared that he did not have an agenda, defended broad congressional powers under the commerce clause, and generally defended a perspective of judicial self-restraint. In answering a question, he observed that the Constitution contained no "bad idea clause." Acknowledging that *Roe v. Wade* "is the settled law of the land," he said that his personal views would not prevent him from "fully and faithfully applying that precedent." The Senate Judiciary Committee approved Roberts's nomination by a 13-5 vote. On September 29, the full Senate gave its consent by a 78-22 margin. At the age of fifty, Roberts became the youngest chief justice since John Marshall.

While presiding over the Supreme Court on October 3—the first day of the 2005-2006 session—Roberts wore a plain black robe without the gold sleeve-bars of the former chief justice. During the course of his first session, he made a favorable impression on most observers. He was consistently prepared and extremely polite, and he avoided polemics. Although many decisions under Roberts were settled by 5-4 margins, as was true of the Rehnquist Court, Roberts's conciliatory tone appeared to promote more of a spirit of collegiality. During his first year on the Court, there was not much evidence that he was having much influence on the convictions of the other justices, and he voted with the minority about as often as he was on the side of the majority.

Roberts appeared to take a broad view of the prerogatives of government, especially in the area of criminal justice. For example, while the Court was examining the case dealing with Oregon's doctor-assisted suicide law, *Gonzales v. Oregon*, Roberts was one of three dissenters who believed that the federal government had statutory authority to prosecute physicians who prescribed lethal doses. In *Garcetti v. Ceballos* he joined a 5-4 majority to rule that whistle blowers did not enjoy any special protection from the First Amendment. In *Hudson v. Michigan* (2006), he joined a five-member majority to allow use of criminal evidence obtained in violation of the knock-and-announce rule.

Chief Justice John Roberts (right) with justices (left to right) Stephen Breyer, Ruth Bader Ginsburg, Clarence Thomas, and John Paul Stevens at a memorial service for former chief justice William H. Rehnquist in June, 2006. (AP/Wide World Photos)

Roberts usually voted with the more conservative wing of the Court, although not as consistently as Justice Samuel Alito. Whenever the court divided into 5-4 votes, Roberts almost invariably voted with the conservatives (with Anthony M. Kennedy being the swing vote). During his first session, Roberts was on the same side as conservative justice Clarence Thomas in 82 percent of the decisions, whereas he only agreed with liberal justice John Paul Stevens in 35 percent of the cases.

Thomas Tandy Lewis

FURTHER READING

Dworkin, Ronald. "Judge Roberts on Trial," *New York Review of Books* 52 (October 20, 2005): 14-17.

"John Roberts's Biography," *Supreme Court Debates* 8 (November, 2005): 197-224.

Neubauer, David. *Battle Supreme: The Confirmation of Chief Justice John Roberts and the Future of the Supreme Court.* Belmont, Calif.: Thomson/Wadsworth, 2005.

O'Connor, Sandra Day. "The New Face of America's High Court," *Time*, May 8, 2006, 64.

Taylor, William L. "The Nominee," *New York Review of Books*, October 6, 2005, 30-35.

Thomas, Evan, and Stuart Taylor, Jr. "John Roberts," *Newsweek*, August 1, 2005, 23-34.

SEE ALSO Alito, Samuel A., Jr.; Burger, Warren E.; Chief justice; *Hudson v. Michigan*; Nominations to the Court; Rehnquist, William H.; Senate Judiciary Committee.

Owen J. Roberts

IDENTIFICATION: Associate justice (June 2, 1930-July 31, 1945)
NOMINATED BY: Herbert Hoover
BORN: May 2, 1875, Germantown, Pennsylvania
DIED: May 17, 1955, West Vincent Township, Chester County, Pennsylvania
SIGNIFICANCE: During fifteen years on the Supreme Court, Roberts was the swing vote in the struggle between President Franklin D. Roosevelt and the Court, particularly over New Deal legislation. His critics cite a lack of jurisprudential consistency in his decisions.

Born in southeastern Pennsylvania, Owen J. Roberts studied at the University of Pennsylvania, receiving a law degree in 1898. He worked first as a private attorney and then as an assistant district attorney in Philadelphia. In 1924 President Calvin Coolidge appointed Roberts a special U.S. attorney to investigate the Teapot Dome scandal. President Herbert Hoover nominated Roberts to the Supreme Court in 1930 after Hoover's first nominee, Judge John J. Parker, was not confirmed by the Senate.

Roberts joined a conservative Court noted for its skepticism of governmental regulation of business. The Court regularly overturned New Deal legislation proposed by President Franklin D. Roosevelt. Roberts's vote often was the swing vote in the conflict between the Court and the president. His positions seemed to defy a consistent jurisprudential philosophy. In *Nebbia v. New York* (1934), Roberts upheld the state regulation of commerce. In a number of cases, including *Panama Refining Co. v. Ryan* (1935), *Schechter Poultry Corp. v. United States* (1935), and *United States v. Butler* (1936), he joined the Court in voicing opposition to federal economic regulation. The Court's opposition to Roosevelt's programs led the president to propose enlarging the Court, the famous Court-packing plan.

In response to public criticism of the Court, Roberts changed his position on the New Deal. In *West Coast Hotel Co. v. Parrish* (1937), for example, he voted to uphold a state minimum-wage plan. He also voiced his opinion in civil liberties cases, again exhibiting little consistency. In *Grovey v. Townsend* (1935), Roberts wrote the opinion up-

Roberts, Owen J.

Owen J. Roberts.
(Harris and Ewing/
Collection of the
Supreme Court of
the United States)

holding the white primary and dissented when the Court struck it down in *Smith v. Allwright* (1944). He wrote the Court opinion in *Cantwell v. Connecticut* (1940), freeing a Jehovah's Witness convicted for soliciting contributions without a permit. In *Korematsu v. United States* (1944), Roberts's dissent indicated his opposition to the forced relocation of Japanese Americans during World War II.

John David Rausch, Jr.

FURTHER READING

Bader, William H., and Roy M. Mersky, eds. *The First One Hundred Eight Justices.* Buffalo, N.Y.: William S. Hein, 2004.

Friedman, Leon, and Fred Israel, eds. *The Justices of the Supreme Court: Their Lives and Major Opinions.* 5 vols. New York: Chelsea House, 1997.

Hendel, Samuel. *Charles Evans Hughes and the Supreme Court.* New York: King's Crown Press, Columbia University, 1951.

Leonard, Charles A. *A Search for a Judicial Philosophy: Mr. Justice Roberts and the Constitutional Revolution of 1937.* Port Washington, N.Y.: Kennikat Press, 1971.

Parrish, Michael E. *The Hughes Court: Justices, Rulings, and Legacy.* Santa Barbara, Calif.: ABC-Clio, 2002.

Pearson, Drew, and Robert Allen. *The Nine Old Men.* Garden City, N.Y.: Doubleday, Doran, 1936.

Renstrom, Peter G. *The Stone Court: Justices, Rulings, and Legacy.* Santa Barbara, Calif.: ABC-Clio, 2001.

SEE ALSO Court-packing plan; Hughes, Charles Evans; *Korematsu v. United States*; New Deal; *Schechter Poultry Corp. v. United States*; *Smith v. Allwright*; Stone, Harlan Fiske; *West Coast Hotel Co. v. Parrish.*

Rochin v. California

CITATION: 342 U.S. 165
DATE: January 2, 1952
ISSUES: Due process, procedural; incorporation doctrine
SIGNIFICANCE: Although the Supreme Court did not make the Fifth Amendment or the exclusionary rule binding on the states, it held that evidence obtained in a shocking and grossly unfair manner cannot be used in a criminal trial.

Based on information that Antonio Rochin was selling drugs, the police entered his home without obtaining a search warrant. After observing Rochin swallow two capsules, the police rushed him to a hospital, where a doctor used an emetic solution and a stomach pump to force him to vomit the pills into a pail. The pills, which contained morphine, were used as evidence in his trial. He was found guilty and sentenced to sixty days in jail.

By an 8-0 vote, the Supreme Court overturned Rochin's conviction. Speaking for a majority, Justice Felix Frankfurter declared that breaking into the defendant's house and then forcibly extracting his stomach's content was "conduct that shocks the conscience." Quoting *Palko v. Connecticut* (1937), Frankfurter interpreted the due process clause as protecting those personal immunities that "are implicit in the concept of ordered liberty." In concurring opinions, Justices Hugo L. Black and William O. Douglas argued in favor of deciding the case on the basis of the Fifth Amendment, which should have been made binding on the states through the Fourteenth Amendment. Black criticized Frankfurter for using a subjective natural law approach.

The Court finally ruled that the Fifth Amendment applied to the states in *Malloy v. Hogan* (1964), and it ruled that in Fourth Amendment cases, the exclusionary rule is binding on the states in *Mapp v. Ohio* (1961). Even though states are now required to respect most of the principles in the Bill of Rights, the subjective "shock the conscience" standard reappears from time to time in a variety of different contexts.

Thomas Tandy Lewis

SEE ALSO Due process, procedural; Exclusionary rule; Frankfurter, Felix; *Hudson v. Michigan*; Incorporation doctrine; *Mapp v. Ohio*; *Palko v. Connecticut*; Search warrant requirement; Self-incrimination, immunity against.

Roe v. Wade

CITATION: 410 U.S. 113
DATE: January 22, 1973
ISSUE: Abortion
SIGNIFICANCE: The Supreme Court ruled that a woman has a constitutional right to terminate an unwanted pregnancy before the fetus acquires viability and that a fetus is not a person under the Fifth and Fourteenth Amendments.

By the early 1970's, a great deal of controversy had arisen about abortion laws. The majority of states permitted abortions only when necessary to save the life of the pregnant woman. Some sixteen states allowed abortions under other circumstances, such as pregnancies resulting from rape and incest. In 1970 three states enacted liberal laws that allowed some form of abortion on demand. As American culture placed greater emphasis on individual freedom, the number of illegal abortions appeared to be growing, often using primitive methods in unsanitary conditions. With the revitalized feminist movement, the right to terminate unwanted pregnancies was increasingly defined as an issue of gender equality.

The Supreme Court gradually accepted the theory of a constitutionally protected right to generic privacy, emphasizing personal choice in marriage, child rearing, and procreation. The Court significantly expanded privacy rights in *Griswold v. Connecticut* (1965), which struck down a state law prohibiting the sale of contraceptives. The *Griswold* majority located the right to privacy in three main places: the "penumbras" of the Bill of Rights, the substantive "liberty" protected by the Fifth and Fourteenth Amendments, and the unenumerated rights of the Ninth Amendment. In *Eisenstadt v. Baird* (1972), the Court explicitly recognized that the right to privacy included an individual's reproductive freedom. Although *Eisenstadt* specifically dealt with the right to use contraceptives, the language in the majority's opinion appeared broad enough to subsume the abortion issue.

TWO CASES

In 1969 Norma McCorvey, an unmarried pregnant woman living in Texas, was unhappy to discover that the state criminalized abortions except when necessary to protect the life of the woman. She consulted two attorneys, Sarah Weddington and Linda Coffee, who were young and energetic feminists strongly dedicated to the cause of reproductive freedom for women. McCorvey, using the pseudonym Jane Roe, filed a class-action suit in federal court against Dallas district attorney Henry Wade, asking for an injunction to stop enforcement of the abortion law. A three-judge district court declared the Texas law unconstitutional but refused to issue an injunction because the constitutional issue remained unresolved. Weddington and Coffee, assisted by the American Civil Liberties Union (ACLU), appealed the case directly to the Supreme Court in 1971. That same year, *Doe v. Bolton*, challenging Georgia's less restrictive abortion law, was also appealed to the Court.

When the Court agreed to hear the two abortion cases, numerous pro-choice and pro-life organizations presented *amici curiae* briefs. On December 13, 1971, the Court, composed of only seven justices, heard oral arguments on the cases. At conference three days later, at least four of the justices agreed that the laws of Texas and Georgia were unconstitutional, but there was almost no agreement about the constitutional rationale or about whether the woman's right to an abortion would apply to the entire period of the pregnancy. The chief justice assigned the cases to Justice Harry A. Blackmun. Six months later, Blackmun circulated a first draft that ruled only on the narrow issue of vagueness. For several reasons, the cases were reargued before a nine-member Court on October 11, 1972.

A RIGHT TO PRIVACY

By a 7-2 vote, the Court struck down the abortion laws of Texas and Georgia. Speaking for the majority, Justice Blackmun declared that a right to privacy, which derives primarily from the "concept of personal liberty" in the due process clause of the Fourteenth Amendment, "is broad enough to encompass a woman's decision whether or not to terminate her pregnancy." Her right to an abortion, although a fundamental right, is not unqualified and must be considered in relation to the state's important and legitimate interests in protecting maternal health and the "potentiality of human life."

Blackmun's opinion outlined abortion rights in three trimesters. During the first three months of pregnancy, the abortion decision is entirely a private decision left up to the woman. After the end of the first trimester, the state may regulate procedures "in ways that are reasonably related to maternal health." After the second trimester, as the fetus acquires the ability to survive independently of its mother, the state may proscribe abortions except when necessary "for the preservation of the life or health of the mother." Presenting a survey of the historical record, Blackmun concluded that abortion laws at common law and throughout the nineteenth century had been less restrictive than those in effect in 1973. Finally, he concluded that there was no evidence that the word "person" in the Constitution referred to prenatal life.

Justices Byron R. White and William H. Rehnquist dissented.

White criticized the Court for giving greater value to the "convenience" of the pregnant woman than to "the continued existence and development of the life or potential life that she carries." Finding the constitutional issues ambiguous, he wrote that the matter "should be left with the people and to the political processes the people have devised to govern themselves." Justice Rehnquist wanted to evaluate abortion laws according to the rational basis test rather than the stricter compelling interest test. Observing that the majority of states had restrictive abortion laws on the books when the Fourteenth Amendment was ratified, he could find no evidence that the right to an abortion was "so rooted in the traditions and conscience of our people as to be ranked as fundamental."

Roe was one of the most controversial decisions in the history of the Court. As the Court became more conservative in the 1980's, a bare majority of the justices continued to uphold the woman's right to an abortion before viability, but they increasingly allowed state and local governments to place restrictions on abortion practices. In *Planned Parenthood of Southeastern Pennsylvania v. Casey* (1992), a highly fragmented Court abandoned the trimester framework and accepted an "undue burden" standard for determining whether regulations were acceptable.

Thomas Tandy Lewis

FURTHER READING

Baird, Robert M., and Stuart E. Rosenbaum, eds. *The Ethics of Abortion: Pro-Life v. Pro-Choice.* Amherst, N.Y.: Prometheus, 2001.

Dworkin, Ronald. *Life's Dominion: An Argument About Abortion, Euthanasia, and Individual Freedom.* New York: Alfred A. Knopf, 1993.

Faux, Marian. *"Roe v. Wade."* New York: New American Library, 1988.

Garrow, David. *Liberty and Sexuality: The Right to Privacy and the Making of "Roe v. Wade."* New York: Macmillan, 1994.

Hull, N. E. H., and Peter Charles Huffer. *"Roe v. Wade": The Abortion Rights Controversy in American History.* Lawrence: University of Kansas Press, 2001.

Lively, Donald E., and Russell L. Weaver. *Contemporary Supreme Court Cases: Landmark Decisions Since "Roe v. Wade."* Westport, Conn.: Greenwood Press, 2006.

Tribe, Lawrence. *Abortion: The Clash of Absolutes.* New York: W. W. Norton, 1990.

Williams, Mary E., ed. *Abortion: Opposing Viewpoints.* San Diego: Greenhaven Press, 2002.

See also Abortion; Birth control and contraception; Due process, substantive; Fourteenth Amendment; Fundamental rights; Gender issues; *Griswold v. Connecticut*; Judicial scrutiny; *Planned Parenthood of Southeastern Pennsylvania v. Casey*; Privacy, right to; *Webster v. Reproductive Health Services.*

Rompilla v. Beard

CITATION: 542 U.S. ___
DATE: June 20, 2005
ISSUE: Right to counsel
SIGNIFICANCE: The Supreme Court reaffirmed that criminal defendants have a right to effective assistance of counsel and also provided additional clarification about practices that constitute ineffectiveness.

Rompilla v. Beard expanded and clarified the principles of *Strickland v. Washington* (1984), recognizing that the Sixth Amendment's right to counsel can be infringed by an incompetent lawyer. In overturning a verdict, *Strickland* required that a defendant must demonstrate a "reasonable probability" that except for the deficiency the outcome would have been different. Although it was difficult for defendants to meet this standard, one defendant had his conviction overturned in Wiggins v. Smith (2003), which held that a defense attorney's failure to investigate his troubled background as mitigating evidence amounted to ineffective assistance of counsel.

A Pennsylvania jury found Ronald Rompilla guilty of first-degree murder. At the sentencing phase, the prosecutor informed the jury of Rompilla's previous convictions of assault and rape, which were aggravating factors. The jury sentenced him to death. Rompilla then obtained a new lawyer, who appealed the verdict with the argument that the earlier defense attorney had failed to present mitigating evidence that might have produced a different sentence. Although a district court rejected the argument, the Third Circuit Court of Appeals ruled in Rompilla's favor.

The Supreme Court agreed with the Third Circuit's decision. Speaking for a 5-4 majority, Justice David H. Souter argued that Rompilla's trial attorney had acted ineffectively when not looking for mitigating circumstances, especially his early life experiences with mental illness, alcoholism, and abuse. The attorney had even failed to read the file on Rompilla's criminal record, which contained evidence of these mitigating considerations. In conclusion, Souter noted that knowledge of this evidence might have influenced the jury's perception of culpability, so that there existed a "likelihood of a different result" with effective counsel.

Thomas Tandy Lewis

SEE ALSO Bill of Rights; Exclusionary rule; Fourteenth Amendment; *Gideon v. Wainwright;* Incorporation doctrine; Miranda rights; Self-incrimination, immunity against; Sixth Amendment.

Roper v. Simmons

CITATION: 543 U.S. 551
DATE: March 1, 2005
ISSUES: Capital punishment; cruel and unusual punishment
SIGNIFICANCE: The Supreme Court decided that it is unconstitutional to execute any person who is younger than eighteen at the time of committing a capital offense.

Since the 1950's, the Supreme Court has recognized that the meaning of "cruel and unusual punishment" is determined by "evolving standards" of decency that reflect societal values. In *Stanford v. Kentucky* (1989), the justices allowed the imposition of capital punishment on an offender who was only sixteen years old at the time of the crime. A few years later, however, in *Atkins v. Virginia* (2003), they decided that society's standards of decency had evolved to the extent that the execution of the mentally retarded had become unconstitutional.

Christopher Simmons was sentenced to death for a murder he committed at the age of seventeen. Based on the reasoning used in the *Atkins* decision, however, the Missouri Supreme Court ruled that the execution of minors was unconstitutional. The ruling was then appealed to the U.S. Supreme Court.

By a 5-4 vote, the Court upheld the ruling of Missouri's high court. Writing for the majority, Justice Anthony M. Kennedy based the ruling on four major considerations. First, Kennedy inferred a national consensus, given that three-fifths of the states no longer utilize the death penalty against minors, whereas only three states in the last ten years had actually executed minors. Secondly, a large body of scientific evidence finds that in comparison with adults, juveniles lack maturity and a sense of responsibility, and that they are much more vulnerable to outside pressures and negative influences. Thirdly, international opinion is overwhelmingly against the execution of juveniles. Finally, Kennedy found that drawing the line at eighteen was reasonable because it is where government draws the line at adulthood for numerous other purposes. The four dissenting justices were particularly unhappy with Kennedy's references to foreign sources for references.

Thomas Tandy Lewis

SEE ALSO Capital punishment; *Furman v. Georgia*; *Gregg v. Georgia*; *McCleskey v. Kemp*.

Roth v. United States/Alberts v. California

CITATION: 354 U.S. 476
DATE: June 24, 1957
ISSUE: Obscenity
SIGNIFICANCE: While reaffirming that obscene material is not protected by the First Amendment in these two simultaneous rulings, the Supreme Court for the first time defined obscenity narrowly and put strict limits on the kinds of obscenity that may be proscribed by either federal or state laws.

A man named Samuel Roth conducted a New York business that published and sold books, magazines, and photographs. The federal government's Comstock statute made it a crime to send through the U.S. mail publications that are "obscene, lewd, lascivious, or filthy" or "of an indecent character." Roth was found guilty in district court for violating four counts of the statute. At the same time, David Alberts was convicted under a California statute that criminalized the advertising of "obscene or indecent" materials. When Roth and Alberts each petitioned the U.S. Supreme Court for review, the Court accepted both cases and consolidated them into one decision. The major issue was whether the state stutures, as interpreted, were consistent with the First Amendment's freedom of speech and press.

Historically, both the federal and state governments had long criminalized most forms of pornography; time and again the Supreme Court had consistently endorsed such laws as a reasonable means to promote the state's legitimate interest in "decency." Between 1842 and 1956, the U.S. Congress had enacted twenty anti-obscenity laws, and at least six times the Supreme Court had upheld prosecutions under these laws. Many American courts continued to follow *Regina v. Hicklin* (1868), which looked to the effects of isolated passages on the most susceptible persons of society. Under what became known as the *Hicklin* test, the works of authors such as D. H. Lawrence and James Joyce were often prohibited from public sale. Roth and Alberts, however, had been convicted under a less restrictive standard, promoted by Judge Learned Hand and other liberal jurists, which considered the work as a whole and its impact on the average adult. Given the Court's precedents, the prospects for Roth and Alberts did not appear very promising.

The Court voted six to three to uphold Roth's federal conviction and seven to two to uphold Alberts's conviction under California law. Writing for the majority, Justice William J. Brennan, Jr., summarized the Anglo-American tradition of proscribing obscenity, and he concluded that obscenity enjoyed no constitutional protection because it had been historically recognized as "utterly without redeeming social importance." Making a distinction between sex and obscenity, Brennan rejected the *Hicklin* test as "unconstitutionally restrictive." As an alternative, he endorsed the alternative test of "whether to the aver-

979

age person, applying contemporary community standards, the dominant theme of the material taken as a whole appeals to the prurient interest." Curiously, Brennan did not discuss whether there was any distinction between indecent and obscene material—a distinction that would later become important.

Two liberal members of the Court, Justices William O. Douglas and Hugo L. Black, dissented and asserted that the First Amendment protected all forms of expression. One member of the Court, John Marshall Harlan, distinguished between federal and state prosecution of obscenity, arguing that due process in the Fourteenth Amendment allowed the states greater discretion than the provision of "no law" in the First Amendment.

The *Roth/Alberts* decision was a major landmark case for four reasons. First, it established a new precedent of restricting government's prerogative to criminalize obscene or indecent materials. Secondly, it proposed a narrow definition of obscenity. Thirdly, *Roth/Alberts* declared that all ideas were protected unless they were "utterly without redeeming social importance." Finally, it explicitly rejected the *Hicklin* test, thus making it much more difficult for prosecutors to obtain criminal convictions. In post-*Roth* cases, the Court would often be divided over whether the First Amendment protects a right to traffic in indecent or obscene materials—even more over how these subjective terms should be defined. The Court's majority would eventually agree to accept the compromises found in *Miller v. California* (1973) and *New York v. Ferber* (1982).

Thomas Tandy Lewis

SEE ALSO *Alberts v. California*; Censorship; First Amendment; *New York v. Ferber*; Obscenity and pornography; Speech and press, freedom of; Warren, Earl.

Rule of Reason

DESCRIPTION: A rule established by the Supreme Court for examining the reasons for certain business activities before deciding whether a corporation has violated antitrust statutes.

SIGNIFICANCE: Under the Sherman Antitrust Act (1890) not all monopolies are illegal—only those that obtain monopoly power using abusive strategies. The Court's application of the rule of reason made it the arbiter of monopolistic business practices in extremely complex and time-consuming cases.

The rule of reason was first enunciated by the Supreme Court in the antitrust case of *Standard Oil Co. v. United States* (1911). Standard Oil had been accused of monopolistic practices that were said to violate the Sherman Antitrust Act of 1890. The act made illegal "every contract, combination . . . or conspiracy in restraint of trade or commerce." The second section of the Act was directed against "every person who shall monopolize or attempt to monopolize . . . or conspire . . . to monopolize any part of trade or commerce among the several States." The language of the act is extraordinarily broad.

The Court dealt with this problem by formulating the rule of reason. The justices attempted to draw together several diverse strands of common-law jurisprudence as well as earlier American cases. Chief Justice Edward D. White's opinion for the majority held that competition is the central rule of trade and cannot be put aside. Some business practices, such as price fixing, are always anticompetitive and thus come under the Sherman Antitrust Act. However, some things on which competing businesses might agree are "reasonable" are not necessarily anticompetitive. An example might be common physical or electrical standards for products. In each case, the Court must scrutinize the agreement between companies to see whether it is more in the public interest than competition would be and if the terms of the agreement are in fact reasonable. The Court concluded that restraints on trade become unlawful only if they are undue or unreasonable. Both sections of the Sherman Antitrust Act were held to be subject to this qualification.

In the face of evidence that Standard Oil (and, in a similar 1911 case, the American Tobacco Company) had engaged in industrial espionage, local price cutting, price fixing, and secret rebates, the Court held that Standard Oil had engaged in predatory practices and the company was ordered to be dissolved.

SUBTLE JUDGMENTS AND DIFFERENCES

The Court's subsequent cases establish that there are two kinds of considerations in an antitrust case. Some business practices are unreasonable per se (in themselves) and are not subject to the rule of reason. Price fixing and market-sharing arrangements are examples of these. Other concerted business practices must be analyzed in the light of the rule of reason, in which case the Court must ask itself whether the public interest is better served by the business agreement or by completely free competition. The final question is whether competition is substantially impeded.

The kinds of judgments that courts—and the Supreme Court in particular—must make in this area are very complex and subtle, in large part because every case requires separate analysis in both legal and economic terms. Antitrust cases are almost always extremely technical and tend to divide the Court along liberal-conservative lines.

In general, business groups favor the rule of reason. Over the years, they have attempted to persuade the Court to expand the scope of the rule and to simultaneously limit the number of practices that fall under the per se rule. Critics of the rule of reason, including many consumer-oriented groups, argue that the rule emasculated the Sherman Antitrust Act. Although on its face the law appears to make any restraint of trade unlawful, some restraints are lawful under the rule of reason. Critics complain in particular that the size of a business alone is not, according to the Court, analyzed under the per se rule. Thus even when monopoly power can be exercised by a very large firm, unless the government can show that actual anticompetitive practices took place, a Sherman Antitrust Act conviction may not stand. This was one of the issues in the great antitrust action brought by the government against Microsoft in the late 1990's.

Robert Jacobs

FURTHER READING

Cefrey, Holly. *The Sherman Antitrust Act: Getting Big Business Under Control.* New York: Rosen Publishing Group, 2004.

Ely, James, Jr. *The Guardian of Every Other Right: A Constitutional History of Property Rights.* New York: Oxford University Press, 1992.

Gellhorn, Ernest, William E. Kovacic, and Stephen Calkins. *Antitrust Law and Economics in a Nutshell.* St. Paul, Minn.: West Publishing, 2004.

Price, Polly J. *Property Rights: Rights and Liberties Under the Law.* Santa Barbara, Calif.: ABC-Clio, 2003.

Thompson, George C., and Gerald P. Brady. *Antitrust Fundamentals: Test Cases and Materials.* St. Paul, Minn.: West Publishing, 1974.

SEE ALSO Antitrust law; Capitalism; Commerce, regulation of; Progressivism.

Rules of the Court

DESCRIPTION: Internal guidelines adopted by the Supreme Court that set forth its jurisdictional and procedural processes.

SIGNIFICANCE: The rules of the Court stipulate practice and procedure before the Court and how the Court accepts and disposes of litigation.

The Supreme Court has operated by an internal set of rules since the first rulebook was adopted on February 3, 1790. Rule 1 established a clerk of the Court, requiring this person to reside at the seat of government but restricting him or her from practicing law while serving the Court. The rule even forbade the clerk from taking the original record of the Court out of the courtroom or from the office without an order from the Court. The early rules reflected the colonial experience of using the British high courts as a model. Rule 7 says "the Court will follow the practice as stipulated by the Courts of King's Bench, and of chancery, in England." The Court originally had several rules concerning equity and admiralty cases, once a large portion of its docket.

The Court's internal rules stipulate how appeals proceed, the swearing in of counsel to the Court bar, and even particulars of appendices to briefs and filing fees. Rules of procedure have been modified as the role of the institution in American life altered. Over time the rules of the Court changed to reflect the current content and volume of the docket.

DEALING WITH THE WORKLOAD

The first one hundred years of the Court saw the justices deciding federal appeals at about the same rate. After the Civil War, the volume of appeals to the Court rose dramatically. Congress responded in 1891 and again in 1925 by allowing the Court to determine what cases it would review. Again in 1997 discretion was granted to the justices to set their docket, so much so that by the late 1990's the Court had almost complete discretion over what cases it hears or denies by writ of *certiorari*.

One of the more notable rules, the rule of four, was adopted by the Court in 1925. This rule stipulates that if four of the nine justices want to take a case on appeal, it is placed on the docket for review. The justices have stated both in the rules of the Court and in other forums that the rule of four is strictly a procedural threshold, not a vote on the merits of a case. However, litigants realize when writing their briefs that they must convince at least four of the justices that their case is important enough for the Court to grant review. The result is that the procedural rule of four creates a strategic hurdle for litigants wishing to be heard.

Other rules of the Court have changed over time, again reflecting the rising workload of the Court and its increased importance as a governmental institution. For example, the length of time allotted for oral arguments has changed dramatically. When the Court first began operating, the time for oral arguments was unrestricted. Lawyers would argue their side of the case, often going on for several days before yielding. Historians note that the local press at the time commented on the lengthy oral arguments in cases such as *McCulloch v. Maryland* (1819) and *Dartmouth College v. Woodward* (1819). Oral arguments were a form of entertainment, and leading lawyers of the day such as Daniel Webster and Charles Lee were notable for their lively presentations in Court. By 1849 limitations were placed on counsel, giving each side two hours to present its case before the justices. In 1917 oral arguments shrunk to one and one-half hours for each side. In 1919 arguments were reduced to only one hour per side. By 1970 oral arguments were tightly controlled, giving only one-half hour to each side for presentation and argument. Oral arguments can still be entertaining, but the performance is a much briefer version than when the Court first began.

Changes in other rules such as the length of the Supreme Court's term reflect the workload constraints on the justices. The timeliness of appeals, procedure for filing, the content of briefs, stipulations placed on the content of oral arguments as well as other rules have been altered over time in response to the volume of appeals and the importance of Court decisions in dispensing justice.

The rules of the Court reflect both statutes and custom in governing how the Court proceeds. They have contributed to the institutionalization of the Court and made its operation more efficient and effective.

Priscilla H. Machado

FURTHER READING

Federal Criminal Code and Rules. St. Paul, Minn.: West Group Publishing, 2003.

Frankfurter, Felix, and James Landis. *The Business of the Supreme Court: A Study of the Federal Judicial System.* New York: Macmillan, 1928.

Hall, Timothy L., ed. *The U.S. Legal System.* 2 vols. Pasadena, Calif.: Salem Press, 2004.

Savage, David G., ed. *Guide to the United States Supreme Court.* 4th ed. Washington, D.C.: Congressional Quarterly, 2004.

Sterns, Robert L., and Eugene Gressman. *Supreme Court Practice.* Washington, D.C.: Bureau of National Affairs, 1969.

United States Supreme Court. *Rules of the Supreme Court of the United States.* Washington, D.C.: Author, 1997.

SEE ALSO Briefs; *Certiorari,* writ of; *McCulloch v. Maryland*; Opinions, writing of; Oral argument; Review, process of; Workload.

John Rutledge

IDENTIFICATION: Associate justice (February 15, 1790-March 5, 1791), chief justice (unconfirmed; 1795)
NOMINATED BY: George Washington
BORN: c. September, 1739, Charleston, South Carolina
DIED: June 21, 1800, Charleston, South Carolina
SIGNIFICANCE: Rutledge's criticisms of Jay's Treaty most likely caused the Senate to fail to confirm his nomination as chief justice of the United States.

John Rutledge was a patriot whose nationalist loyalties contributed to his political demise. His father, Andrew Rutledge, came to South Carolina in 1720 via New York with a law degree from Trinity College, Dublin. He arrived in the southern colony and quickly became a member of the Episcopal Church, satisfying the law requiring all landowners to be Christian communicants. His marriage to a wealthy widow provided the family with financial resources and status. The younger Rutledge's early years, including a legal education at the Inns of Court, are replete with service to the Crown and Colony. He initially manifested Loyalist views and sought to prevent a break with the Crown. His legal education proved germane to his future conduct and opinions about how the colony and later, the state, should operate.

Rutledge was one of South Carolina's more conservative delegates to the First and Second Continental Congresses. He helped draft South Carolina's constitution and was elected to its first general assembly. He was strongly nationalistic in expressing his political views.

Rutledge was nominated to the Supreme Court by George Washington and was one of the Court's original members. He presided over the first session of the first circuit court as part of his duties as a supreme court justice. Bored by the Court's lack of activity and apparently unhappy over not being made chief justice, Rutledge resigned in March, 1791.

Upon his resignation, Rutledge became chief justice of South Carolina. For the next four years, he presided with distinction over the courts of common pleas and general sessions. In 1795 he heard rumors that Chief Justice John Jay was considering resigning to become

John Rutledge.
(Robert Hinkley/
Collection of the
Supreme Court of
the United States)

governor of New York. Rutledge wrote Washington expressing interest in Jay's position. On July 1, 1795, he resigned from the South Carolina bench when Washington offered him Jay's position, an interim appointment subject to congressional confirmation. Rutledge presided over the August term in 1795.

The day before he was notified of his appointment as chief justice, Rutledge, while speaking in Charleston, had expressed his opposition to Jay's Treaty (1794) and called Jay a traitor. Whether Rutledge understood the need for Jay's conduct in negotiating the treaty is not as important as the fact that the Senate had ratified the document. His criticisms were aimed at the same people who were to decide on his fitness to be chief justice of the United States. Rutledge denounced the treaty as demeaning to an independent state. The Federalist Party, commanding the Senate, opposed Rutledge's nomination because of his political statements. On December 15, 1795, the Senate rejected his nomination. During his recess appointment as chief justice, he heard only two cases: *Talbot v. Jansen* and *United States v. Peters.*

The reasons given for the Senate's rejection included Rutledge's alleged health problems and age; some senators said that he was mentally unstable. However, no evidence indicates that his rejection was anything other than political. He changed the Court by introducing a precedent: Justices had to be publicly apolitical, a warning that later justices have found fruitful.

Arthur K. Steinberg

FURTHER READING

Bader, William H., and Roy M. Mersky, eds. *The First One Hundred Eight Justices.* Buffalo, N.Y.: William S. Hein, 2004.

Cushman, Clare, ed. *The Supreme Court Justices: Illustrated Biographies, 1789-1995.* 2d ed. Washington, D.C.: Congressional Quarterly, 1995.

Friedman, Leon, and Fred L. Israel, eds. *The Justices of the United States Supreme Court: Their Lives and Major Opinions.* 5 vols. New York: Chelsea House, 1997.

Harrington, Matthew P. *Jay and Ellsworth, The First Courts: Justices, Rulings, and Legacy.* Santa Barbara, Calif.: ABC-Clio, 2007.

SEE ALSO Jay, John; Nominations to the Court.

Wiley B. Rutledge, Jr.

IDENTIFICATION: Associate justice (February 15, 1943-September 10, 1949)

NOMINATED BY: Franklin D. Roosevelt

BORN: July 20, 1894, Cloverport, Kentucky

DIED: September 10, 1949, York, Maine

SIGNIFICANCE: The ninth and final appointee of Franklin D. Roosevelt, Rutledge played a pivotal role in moving the Supreme Court on a course from economic to social liberalism. However, his untimely death in 1949 had the effect of blunting liberal reform until the rise of the Warren Court four years later.

Wiley B. Rutledge, Jr., was the son of a circuit-riding Baptist preacher. Receiving a preliminary education at Marysville College in Tennessee, he subsequently received his B.A. degree at the University of Wisconsin in 1914. Rutledge spent the next three years teaching high school in Indiana before relocating for reasons of health to Albuquerque, New Mexico.

Named secretary to the Albuquerque City school board in 1917, Rutledge that same year began studying law. In 1922 he received his juris doctorate from the University of Colorado, which subsequently hired him as a professor of law. He later taught at Washington University in St. Louis before moving on to the University of Iowa, where he became dean of the law school in 1930.

During the next six years, Rutledge became known for his liberal views. His enthusiastic support for Franklin D. Roosevelt's New Deal programs eventually brought him to the attention of Nebraska Senator George W. Norris, and in 1936 Rutledge was appointed associate

Wiley B. Rutledge, Jr.
(Library of Congress)

justice of the U.S. District Court of Appeals for the District of Columbia. His most famous ruling at this time was to vote to convict the American Medical Association for violating the Sherman Antitrust Act (1890).

In 1939 Rutledge was considered twice for the Supreme Court for seats that were ultimately filled by Felix Frankfurter and William O. Douglas. With the resignation of Justice James F. Byrnes in late 1942, however, Rutledge was named Roosevelt's ninth and final appointee to the Court on January 11, 1943.

Rutledge faced little trouble with his confirmation. Overcoming criticism that he had no real courtroom experience, Rutledge was overwhelmingly approved by the Senate on February 8 and formally took his seat on the Court one week later. Almost immediately, he became a member of the Court's liberal bloc along with Hugo L. Black, William O. Douglas, and Frank Murphy.

An ardent believer in the concept of economic liberalism, Rutledge readily supported almost all efforts at administrative regulation of the economy—even at the expense of judicial review. Over time, however, Rutledge became better known for his untiring support of civil liberties, especially involving the First and Fifth Amendments.

Participating in the controversial labor law case of *United States v. United Mine Workers* (1947), Justice Rutledge joined Murphy in a dissent that would ultimately be the beginning of the end of what was sometimes called the "Roosevelt Court." With the death of Justice Murphy on July 19, 1949, and Rutledge's unexpected demise less than two months later, President Harry S. Truman was able to appoint more socially conservative jurists to the bench to transform the Court.

Harvey Gresham Hudspeth

FURTHER READING

Bader, William H., and Roy M. Mersky, eds. *The First One Hundred Eight Justices.* Buffalo, N.Y.: William S. Hein, 2004.

Belknap, Michal R. *The Vinson Court: Justices, Rulings, and Legacy.* Santa Barbara, Calif.: ABC-Clio, 2004.

Ferren, John M. *Salt of the Earth, Conscience of the Court: The Story of Justice Wiley Rutledge.* Chapel Hill: University of North Carolina, 2004.

Harper, Fowler. *Justice Rutledge and the Bright Constellation*. Indianapolis, Ind.: Bobbs-Merrill, 1965.

Harrington, Matthew P. *Jay and Ellsworth, The First Courts: Justices, Rulings, and Legacy*. Santa Barbara, Calif.: ABC-Clio, 2007.

Renstrom, Peter G. *The Stone Court: Justices, Rulings, and Legacy*. Santa
Barbara, Calif.: ABC-Clio, 2001.

SEE ALSO Black, Hugo L.; Byrnes, James F.; Douglas, William O.; Incorporation doctrine; Murphy, Frank.

Salaries of Justices

DESCRIPTION: Compensation received by the justices for performing
their Supreme Court duties.

SIGNIFICANCE: Justices have historically been dissatisfied with their
compensation, and the absense of a pension plan in the past discouraged their retirement.

The Judiciary Act of 1789 allowed the chief justice to draw a salary of
$4,000, while the associates received $3,500. Salaries were not increased again until 1819. The $500 difference in salaries between the
chief justice and associates continued until 1969, after which the difference was increased to compensate for the chief justice's increasing
administrative obligations.

Congress, which is in charge of adjusting the salaries of the justices, did not increase salaries for long periods of time during the
1800's and 1900's. Raises occurred more often after 1955. The Ethics
Reform Act of 1989 set the chief justice's 1990 salary at $124,000 and
the associates' salaries at $118,600, a raise of 7.9 percent. In 1991 sala-
ries were raised another 25 percent. Beginning in 1992 and continuing with subsequent years, salaries reflected a cost-of-living adjustment. In January 2006, the chief justice's annual salary was $212,100,
and associate justice salaries were $203,000.

Over the years, several judges have publicly voiced complaints regarding their salaries. In 1816 Justice Joseph Story argued that the
"cost of living had doubled and that the expenses of the justices had

quadrupled" since 1789. Salary was a minor consideration in Justice Benjamin R. Curtis's decision to leave the Court, and decades later Justice Salmon P. Chase recommended that the court reduce the number of justices so the salaries for the remaining justices could be raised. Congress did reduce the size of the Court but did not adjust salaries. In 1989 Chief Justice William H. Rehnquist made history by testifying before Congress regarding salaries of federal judges and justices.

PENSIONS

No law provided justices pension benefits. In 1869 Congress enacted legislation permitting justices to retire with benefits at age seventy with ten years of service on the judiciary. Seven justices retired between 1869 and 1921. Over the next six decades, fourteen more justices retired. Nine justices retired between 1969 and 1999. After President Franklin D. Roosevelt proposed his court-packing plan in 1937, Congress liberalized pension benefits for federal judges. Under a new law, judges could retire as early as age sixty-five if they met certain length of service requirements.

Andrea E. Miller

SEE ALSO Chase, Salmon P.; Chief justice; Court-packing plan; Curtis, Benjamin R.; Judiciary Act of 1789; Rehnquist, William H.; Resignation and retirement; Workload.

San Antonio Independent School District v. Rodriguez

CITATION: 411 U.S. 1
DATE: March 21, 1973
ISSUES: Suspect classifications; fundamental rights
SIGNIFICANCE: The Supreme Court held that wealth was not a suspect classification and that education was not a fundamental right. Therefore, the Court used the minimal scrutiny test and concluded that the U.S. Constitution did not require states to provide school districts with equal funding for public education.

Like many other states, Texas financed its public schools largely through local property taxes. As a result, wealthy school districts were able to spend significantly more money on public education than poor districts. Demetrio Rodriguez lived in a relatively poor district in San Antonio, where per capita expenditures were about half those in the city's most affluent district. Filing a class-action suit, Rodriguez claimed that the Texas system of school finance discriminated on the basis of wealth and that education was a fundamental interest that the state should provide to all its citizens without regard to their ability to pay for it.

By a 5-4 vote, the Supreme Court upheld the Texas system of finance. Justice Lewis F. Powell, Jr.'s majority opinion employed the minimal scrutiny test, inquiring whether the system bore "some rational relationship to legitimate state purposes." Powell noted that no claim was being made that poor children were being denied a free public education and that the state provided enhancement funds to maintain minimum standards for each school district. Taking all relevant facts into account, he reasoned that a system using local taxation promoted the state's legitimate interest in encouraging local participation in public education.

In a long and memorable dissent, Justice Thurgood Marshall insisted that the Court had previously recognized that certain unenumerated rights were fundamental and that Texas's system had a discriminatory impact on an identifiable "class." In addition, Marshall argued that the use of a two-tier approach to judicial scrutiny was too rigid, and he advocated an alternative sliding-scale approach.

The Court expanded the *Rodriguez* decision in *Kadrmas v. Dickinson Public Schools* (1988), rejecting a poor family's challenge to a North Dakota school district policy that required parents to pay for bus transportation to and from school. Critics of *Rodriguez* sometimes had more success at the state level. In 1989 the Texas supreme court declared that the state's constitution required the legislature to provide relatively equal revenues per student for the financing of public education. Previous to this decision, nine other state supreme courts had issued similar rulings.

Thomas Tandy Lewis

SEE ALSO Due process, substantive; Equal protection clause; Fundamental rights; Judicial scrutiny; Marshall, Thurgood; Powell, Lewis F., Jr.

Edward T. Sanford

IDENTIFICATION: Associate justice (February 5, 1923-March 8, 1930)
NOMINATED BY: Warren G. Harding
BORN: July 23, 1865, Knoxville, Tennessee
DIED: March 8, 1930, Washington, D.C.
SIGNIFICANCE: Sanford served on the Supreme Court for seven years and wrote 130 opinions. A moderate closely allied to Chief Justice William H. Taft, he was overshadowed by his more illustrious colleagues. His most notable contribution was in the widening of free speech rights.

The son of a Tennessee Republican millionaire, Edward T. Sanford received an unusually broad and cosmopolitan education. An excellent and much honored student, he earned two degrees at the University of Tennessee in 1883 and a second bachelor's degree and an M.A. at Harvard in 1884 and 1889. He also spent a year studying in Europe. Sanford graduated from Harvard Law School in 1889, then practiced in his hometown of Knoxville and, after 1898, combined his professional legal work with teaching law at the University of Tennessee.

Sanford came to Washington, D.C., in 1905, at the behest of U.S. attorney general James C. McReynolds (later his colleague on the Supreme Court). McReynolds enlisted Sanford as a special prosecutor, one of President Theodore Roosevelt's "trust busters." After McReynolds moved on, Sanford became assistant attorney general. His work caught the attention of Roosevelt, who, in 1908, appointed him to a federal judgeship in Tennessee. From 1908 until his appointment to the Court in 1923, Sanford was a highly respected federal judge, noted for his civility, tolerance, dignity, charm, and thoughtfulness.

When Justice Mahlon Pitney resigned at the end of 1922, President Warren G. Harding nominated Sanford as his replacement.

Edward T. Sanford.
(Kuaff and Brakebill/
Collection of the
Supreme Court of
the United States)

Sanford's nomination had the support of U.S. attorney general Harry Daugherty and of Chief Justice William H. Taft, who had known Sanford since Justice Department days and was impressed by Sanford's advocacy of U.S. entry into the League of Nations, a cause close to Taft's own heart.

As a Supreme Court justice, Sanford was a moderate who greatly respected judicial precedent and who was an expert in bankruptcy law. Perhaps because of his antitrust efforts, he had considerable sympathy for exercises of state and federal regulation of business, but he was not a friend of organized labor. His record on the rights of African Americans was also mixed. His notable opinion in the *Pocket Veto Case* (1929), one of his last, clarified the use of that presidential power. One researcher noted that Sanford's moderate position placed him in a neutral zone where he drew neither the ire nor the admiration of Court historians.

His lasting contribution was in the area of free speech. In his majority opinions in both *Gitlow v. New York* (1925) and *Whitney v. California* (1927), Sanford declared that the Fourteenth Amendment required the states to uphold First Amendment rights to free speech and a free press. This was a pioneering expression of the view that the Fourteenth Amendment had "incorporated" the guarantees of the Bill of Rights and extended their protections against actions by the states.

David W. Levy

SEE ALSO Fourteenth Amendment; *Gitlow v. New York*; Incorporation doctrine; McReynolds, James C.; Speech and press, freedom of; Taft, William H.

Antonin Scalia

IDENTIFICATION: Associate justice (September 26, 1986-   )
NOMINATED BY: Ronald Reagan
BORN: March 11, 1936, Trenton, New Jersey
SIGNIFICANCE: The first Italian American justice on the Supreme Court, Scalia has been committed to conservative values and has advocated constitutional interpretations based on textual analysis and original understanding. He has endeavored to constrain congressional delegation of power to the federal bureaucracy and to promote moral order through restrictions on expressive liberties, criminal defendants' rights, and affirmative action programs.

The only child of S. Eugene Scalia, a professor of Latin-based languages, and Catherine Panaro Scalia, an elementary teacher, Antonin Scalia attended public schools in Queens, New York, and a Jesuit preparatory school. He earned his bachelor's degree at Georgetown University in 1957 and his law degree at Harvard Law School in 1960. After several years of practice with an elite law firm in Cleveland, Ohio, he joined the faculty of the law school at the University of Virginia.

In 1972, President Richard M. Nixon named Scalia general counsel for telecommunications policy in the executive office of the president. The next year, Scalia was named chairman of the administrative conference of the United States. In 1974, President Gerald R. Ford appointed him as assistant attorney general in charge of the Office of Legal Counsel, a post in which he developed policies on the authority of administrative agencies and other issues of executive power.

Scalia became a scholar in residence at the American Enterprise Institute in early 1977, and later that year he became a law professor at the University of Chicago. While at Chicago, he served as chairman of the American Bar Association section on administrative law, and he published commentary on administrative law and regulatory politics while serving as editor of a journal, *Regulation*, as well as in law reviews.

In July, 1982, President Ronald Reagan nominated Scalia to serve as a judge on the U.S. Court of Appeals for the District of Columbia. Quickly confirmed by the Senate, Scalia served four years on the circuit bench. He wrote opinions in 133 cases, of which ninety addressed the statutory powers of federal agencies.

APPOINTMENT TO THE SUPREME COURT

When President Reagan nominated associate justice William H. Rehnquist to serve as chief justice in 1986, he also nominated Scalia to fill Rehnquist's associate justice seat on the Court. Because Democrats and liberals focused so much energy in attacking and trying to stop Rehnquist's confirmation, Scalia's nomination sailed through the Senate Judiciary Committee with almost no criticism. The senators voted 98-0 in favor of his confirmation, and he took his seat on September 26, 1986.

As an associate justice, Scalia soon voiced a distinctive jurisprudence. A strong critic of the notion of a "living Constitution," he argued that constitutional cases should be decided according to a literal reading of the constitutional text, informed by its original understanding as far as possible. Critics observed that when he rendered decisions, his theories of jurisprudence were often modified by his conservative ideological commitments. An advocate of judicial restraint, Scalia usually supported judicial deference to legislative decisions and expressed disdain for "sociological jurisprudence." In addition, he accepted a broad view of executive prerogatives in matters of national security and foreign relations.

When dealing with separation of powers, Scalia advanced a four-part perspective. First, he argued that judges, when interpreting legislation, should respect the plain meaning of statutes, uphold judicial precedents, and use the doctrine of standing to limit interest group challenges to legislation. Second, he sought expansive presidential direction of federal agencies' policy making. Third, he tried to ensure that agencies not construe statutory language to expand their discretion. Finally, as in his dissenting opinion in *Morrison v. Olson* (1988), he strongly objected to legislation that results in a blurring of the specific boundaries between the powers of the branches that he located in the Constitution.

Although Scalia respected the principle of federal supremacy, his opinions supported the Rehnquist Court's effort to augment the policy-making powers of state governments. Especially he sought to reformulate "dormant" or "negative" commerce clause doctrine and constrain federal prohibition of state policy making and, in *Printz v. United States* (1997), to restrict congressional authority to mandate state policy making. However, through his interpretation of the takings clause, in cases such as *Lucas v. South Carolina Coastal Council* (1992) and *Kelo v. City of New London* (2005), he supported greater protection for the interests of property owners against restrictive state environmental protection legislation.

CONSTITUTIONAL RIGHTS

In matters of criminal procedures, Scalia has consistently voted against defendant rights in cases involving search and seizure, double jeopardy, self-incrimination, and forfeitures. In 2002 and 2005, he wrote dissenting opinions when the Court's majority forbade execution of minors and persons with mental disabilities. Also, he supported a diminishment of habeas corpus relief for prisoners. When the Court's majority continued to require the police to give Miranda warnings in *Dickerson v. United States* (2000), he condemned the ruling and wrote that it gave needless protection to "foolish (but not compelled) confessions." In contrast, when the Court approved a confrontation clause exception for child abuse cases in *Maryland v. Craig* (1990), he denounced the majority for ignoring an explicit constitutional mandate and substituting current opinion.

Scalia has taken complex positions on First Amendment liberties.

In *Employment Division, Department of Human Resources v. Smith* (1990) he replaced strict scrutiny with the criterion of rationality, which diminished protection for religious expression. When interpreting the establishment clause, in contrast, he consistently wanted to allow more governmental support for religious organizations. In *Zelman v. Simmons-Harris* (2002), for example, he endorsed the use of tax-supported vouchers for parochial schools.

Usually Scalia voted to approve restrictions on pornography and obscenity. Dissenting in *McConnell v. Federal Election Commission* (2003), however, he insisted that the political use of money constitutes a form of speech, and he voted to strike down a limit on contributions to political parties. In other freedom of expression cases, including flag burnings, protests at abortion clinics, and regulations of hate speech, he has defended broad constitutional protection for unpopular expressive actions.

Scalia has advocated a "color-blind" approach to racial equality and opposed affirmative steps to counter the continuing effects of racial discrimination. He was especially opposed to preferential policies aimed at increasing racial and gender diversity in employment and education, as seen in his strong dissents in *Johnson v. Transportation Agency* (1987) and *Grutter v. Bollinger* (2003). When dealing with de facto racial segregation of the public schools based on housing patterns, he strongly opposed court-ordered busing and other forms of judicial relief aimed at achieving racial integration. As the use of busing declined, he wrote concurring opinions in support of ending judicial supervision of school systems in which racial segregation persisted. Many of his opinions about legislation designed to end discrimination in employment and voting opposed the government's remedies. In *United States v. Virginia* (1996), moreover, he was the only dissenter, arguing that male-only state-supported education did not violate the equal protection clause.

Scalia unequivocally opposed the development of broad private rights (or liberty interests) under the doctrine of substantive due process. When dealing with abortion cases, as in *Planned Parenthood of Southeastern Pennsylvania v. Casey* (1992) and *Stenberg v. Carhart* (2000), he expressed great animosity to the theory that the due process clause implied that a woman had a right to an abortion. In cases such as *Gon-

zales v. Oregon (2006), he rejected notions about a constitutional right to die or to have the assistance of a physician in hastening death. Likewise, in *Lawrence v. Texas* (2003), when the Court held that states may not outlaw homosexual sodomy, Scalia insisted that states had the authority to validate moral choices and commented that the Court "has largely signed on to the so-called homosexual agenda."

Critics have accused Scalia of promoting a conservative political agenda. This was particularly true in regard to his part in the controversial case of *Bush v. Gore* (2000), which helped ensure the election of President George W. Bush. When the Florida Supreme Court ordered a recount of disputed ballots, which might have added to the votes of Albert Gore, Scalia wrote the emergency injunction that stopped the recount; he explained that the recount might do "irreparable harm" to the country and to President Bush "by casting a cloud upon what he claims to be the legitimacy of his election."

Even Scalia's harshest critics concede his intelligence and verbal skills. He has enjoyed public debates and has not hesitated to use abrasive language when expressing disagreements. Sometimes he has taken public positions that have detracted from a sense of judicial neutrality. However, he has also often made court-watching more enjoyable than it might otherwise be.

Richard A. Brisbin, Jr.
Revised and updated by the Editor

FURTHER READING

Brisbin, Richard A., Jr. *Justice Antonin Scalia and the Conservative Revival.* Baltimore: Johns Hopkins University Press, 1997.

Hensley, Thomas R. *The Rehnquist Court: Justices, Rulings, and Legacy.* Santa Barbara, Calif.: ABC-Clio, 2006.

Rossum, Ralph A. *Antonin Scalia's Jurisprudence: Text and Tradition.* Lawrence: University Press of Kansas, 2006.

Scalia, Antonin. *A Matter of Interpretation: Federal Courts and the Law—An Essay.* Edited by Amy Gutmann. Princeton, N.J.: Princeton University Press, 1997.

_____. "The Rule of Law as a Law of Rules." *University of Chicago Law Review* 56 (1989): 1175-1188.

Staab, James Brian. *The Political Thought of Justice Antonin Scalia: A*

Hamiltonian on the Supreme Court. New York: Rowman & Littlefield, 2006.

Tushnet, Mark. *A Court Divided: The Rehnquist Court and the Future of Constitutional Law.* New York: W. W. Norton, 2005.

SEE ALSO Abortion; Affirmative action; *Bush v. Gore*; Commerce, regulation of; Constitutional interpretation; Die, right to; Dissents; Equal protection clause; First Amendment; Gay and lesbian rights; *Lawrence v. Texas*; *Printz v. United States*; Rehnquist, William H.; Separation of powers; Takings clause.

Schechter Poultry Corp. v. United States

CITATION: 295 U.S. 495
DATE: May 27, 1935
ISSUE: Delegation of power
SIGNIFICANCE: Of the three Supreme Court cases voiding vague delegations of power to executive branch agencies, this ruling regarding the constitutionality of the National Industrial Recovery Act (1933) was the broadest.

The Schechter Poultry Corporation was charged with violating wage and hour provisions of the slaughterhouse industry and selling an "unfit chicken" under the 1933 National Industrial Recovery Act (NIRA). The act was designed to stimulate business recovery and end unemployment, largely through codes of fair competition and other regulations. The Supreme Court unanimously held that the NIRA was essentially unconstitutional because Congress delegated its lawmaking power to the executive branch through excessively vague legislation.

Schechter should be considered along with two other cases: *Panama Refining Co. v. Ryan* (1935) and *Carter v. Carter Coal Co.* (1936). In these three cases, the Court attempted to limit the later widespread congressional practice of transferring its lawmaking responsibility by delegating the hard decisions or the actual wording to executive branch agencies. In *Schechter*, the Court addressed the essence of the

NIRA, unlike its narrow holding in the other cases. In his dissent in *Panama,* Justice Benjamin N. Cardozo argued that the national economic emergency of the Great Depression justified this vague delegation of power, but in *Schechter* he found that the delegation was so extensive that it had "run riot."

Carter, the last Court decision attempting to limit vague delegations of congressional lawmaking power, was supported by only a 5-4 majority. The opinion, written by Justice George Sutherland, used the Tenth Amendment and the indirect-direct commerce distinction as an additional basis for rejecting the NIRA but ended up losing support on the Court. The four dissenters in *Carter* objected to this direct-indirect distinction. The Court never overturned its holdings in these cases but simply ignored them. *Schechter* is currently valid only on the narrow issues of the case.

Richard L. Wilson

SEE ALSO Cardozo, Benjamin N.; Cold War; Commerce, regulation of; Court-packing plan; Delegation of powers; General welfare clause; New Deal; Separation of powers.

Schenck v. United States

CITATION: 249 U.S. 47
DATE: March 3, 1919
ISSUE: Freedom of speech
SIGNIFICANCE: In upholding the conviction of a man for discouraging people from enlisting in the service, the Supreme Court first used the clear and present danger test to determine whether speech could be restricted.

Charles T. Schenck was convicted of violating the 1917 Espionage Act by discouraging enlistments in the armed forces, something that would not have resulted in a prosecution later. Because the key activity was the distribution of leaflets, Schenck protested that his conviction violated his freedom of expression rights under the First Amendment, and he attacked the constitutionality of the Espionage Act.

The Supreme Court unanimously upheld his conviction. In the opinion for the Court, Justice Oliver Wendell Holmes said the leaflet posed a "clear and present danger" to the United States during wartime. It was the first use of this doctrine as grounds on which the government could restrain speech.

Many scholars find it difficult to see how the Schenck leaflet constituted a clear and present danger to anyone. Nonetheless, the clear and present danger test was widely accepted. The test was sometimes abused by justices who said they were following the clear and present danger test when they were really departing from it, using a looser, much more restrictive bad tendency test against speech. The phrase's key limitation is its vagueness, which can be interpreted to be quite intrusive on the free exercise of speech. What is clear to one person may be unclear to another, and what can be a present danger to one can seem quite remote to another. In his opinion, Holmes did state that Schenck's activities in other times and places would have been protected and did clarify the meaning of his test in *Abrams v. United States* (1919) and dissented vigorously when others abused the test in later decisions.

Richard L. Wilson

SEE ALSO Bad tendency test; *Brandenburg v. Ohio*; Espionage acts; *Gitlow v. New York*; Holmes, Oliver Wendell; National security; Seditious libel; War and civil liberties.

School Integration and Busing

DESCRIPTION: Desegregation of public educational institutions so that black and white students have equal access to educational facilities, often through the transportation by bus of school children.

SIGNIFICANCE: The Supreme Court made school integration a major goal of American society. Many of the methods it established to pursue this goal, including busing, have been highly controversial.

In the landmark 1954 decision *Brown v. Board of Education*, the Supreme Court unanimously ruled that the doctrine of separate but equal, established by *Plessy v. Ferguson* (1896), was unconstitutional. Two years earlier, five cases from lower courts in Kansas, South Carolina, Virginia, Delaware, and Washington, D.C., had reached the Court. In all the cases but Delaware, the lower courts had upheld laws prohibiting black children from attending white schools. In deciding *Brown*, the Court decided all these cases.

The *Brown* decision established the principle that separate educational facilities are unequal facilities, a principle that would guide U.S. educational law regarding race in the following decades. The decision did not result in any immediate changes because it was a principle, without guidelines for practical implementation. Therefore, the court followed up the first *Brown* decision with *Brown II* in 1955, when the Court ordered southern school districts to desegregate with all deliberate speed. In *Brown II*, the Court gave responsibility for desegregation to local school authorities. District courts were given the power to enforce the racial desegregation of schools through orders and decrees.

Even after the strict admonition of *Brown II*, nothing happened immediately, other than the mobilization of segregationist forces determined to resist desegregation. In 1957 the *Brown* decision was put to the test when President Dwight D. Eisenhower was forced to activate the Arkansas national guard to escort seven black children through an angry white mob to integrate all-white Little Rock High School. One of the most extreme examples of white defiance against orders to desegregate occurred in Prince Edward County, Virginia, in 1959. Rather than integrate their schools, the white county leaders shut down all schools, both black and white, for five years. Whites who could afford it sent their children to the newly formed Prince Edward Academy. Schools reopened only after the Court ruled, in *Griffin v. County School Board of Prince Edward County* (1964), that it was unconstitutional for any state or local government to close public schools or to contribute in any way to the support of private segregated schools.

THE END OF DE JURE SEGREGATION

In the second half of the 1960's, most legally enforced, or de jure, school segregation ended. However, this did not mean that school populations were suddenly racially balanced to reflect the communities within which they were located. This first phase of school integration following the *Brown* decision is often referred to as "freedom of choice" or "voluntary integration" because blacks and whites were regarded as free to attend the other race's school if they so desired. Other districts had "majority to minority" desegregation policies, where a student in a racial group that made up the majority in a school could transfer to another school where members of that racial group were in the minority. Under these types of desegregation strategies, however, the overwhelming majority of whites chose to continue attending mostly white or all-white schools, while most blacks continued attending either mostly black or all-black schools.

At first, courts went along with the freedom of choice plans, as they seemed reasonable ways of ending de jure segregation. However, when it became obvious that meaningful integration was not going to take place voluntarily, the courts began to change their tactics. In *Green v. County School Board of New Kent County* (1968), the Court ruled that the freedom of choice plan followed by the New Kent County, Virginia, school board was unconstitutional. The Court noted that not a single white student had volunteered to attend the all-black county school, thus maintaining a dual-race system. It ordered the school board to come up with a plan, such as geographic zoning, that would realistically lead to integrated district schools. Following *Green*, the courts increasingly ruled against freedom of choice plans and began to favor geographic zoning without reference to neighborhood racial concentrations as a more forceful approach to school racial integration.

BUSING AND JUDICIALLY ENFORCED INTEGRATION

During the 1970's under the lead of the Court, the federal judiciary became much more involved in attempting to integrate schools in reality as well as in theory. Courts began to make efforts to ensure that black and white students were actually enrolled in the same schools and did not simply have the abstract right to attend school together. The method that received the most public attention was busing. This involved moving students to where members of other races were in order to achieve racial balance. In the 1971 case *Swann v. Charlotte-Mecklenburg Board of Education*, the Court recognized that de facto segregation (actual segregation not supported by law) in schools was linked to residential segregation because children attended schools in the areas in which they lived. The Court ruled that the practice of busing students in order to achieve desegregation was a legitimate remedy.

Not long after the Court sanctioned busing as a desegregation tool, it also made another important ruling in the area of school desegregation, in effect extending the practice of busing to systems outside the South. For the first time, the Court turned its attention northward, where racial segregation was, according to the Court, often just as widespread as it was in the South. In the historic 1973 case *Keyes v. Denver School District No. 1*, the Court found that Denver, Colorado, officials had been intentionally maintaining a dual school system, segregated by race. The Rocky Mountain state capital was ordered by the court to desegregate its public school system, beginning the process of school desegregation outside the South.

Busing was unpopular in many areas. In Boston, white parents and their children overturned and burned buses that were to carry black children to all-white South Boston schools. Other non-Deep-South communities ordered by the courts to bus as a means of forcibly integrating students included Seattle, Tulsa, Oklahoma City, Louisville, Austin, Dallas, Dayton, San Francisco, Los Angeles, and Indianapolis. Though the response was not quite as violent as in Boston, busing often met with opposition in these communities.

Another method of active integration aimed at reducing the effects of residential segregation was school redistricting. This version of redistricting involved redrawing school attendance areas to produce a mixture of students of both races. In some ways, school busing was the right hand of redistricting because some redrawn districts could be quite large, requiring that students be transported long distances to their new schools. Yet another related court-sanctioned method was pairing or clustering schools and distributing students among them with the goal of achieving racial balance.

WHITE FLIGHT AND THE LIMITS OF BUSING

Some experts argue that forced desegregation by the courts was counterproductive. Parents who either opposed desegregation or desegregation by the methods sanctioned by the courts had two options. First, they could leave the public school system, as the early segregationists had done, and enroll their children in private schools. Second, they could leave urban school districts, which tended to contain large numbers of black children, for suburban districts in which whites were clearly the majority population. There is some debate about the extent to which white suburbanization was a result of white flight from urban schools, rather than a population shift occurring for other reasons. Nevertheless, throughout the 1970's American urban school districts grew increasingly poor and black, while suburbs around them grew increasingly prosperous and white. The federal courts were aware of this trend and in several instances intervened to merge predominantly white and black school districts that they contended were the result of deliberate, de jure segregation.

The Court was drawn into the issue and acted for the first time to limit efforts at integration in *Milliken v. Bradley* (1974). This case dealt with the Detroit, Michigan, school district, which was already majority black by 1970. Both the lower federal courts and the court of appeals ruled that it was impossible to integrate Detroit's schools without taking into account the surrounding majority white metropolitan area. Therefore, they ordered the Detroit district merged with the fifty-four predominantly white districts surrounding the city, in effect creating a "super district." On appeal, however, the Court ruled that because there was no evidence or legacy of intentional de jure segregation in the governmental actions creating the surrounding white districts, there was no obligation to dissolve those districts. From 1974 on, school desegregation efforts were limited to within school districts.

THE CONCEPT OF UNITARY STATUS

School officials in many districts trying to satisfy court desegregation orders began to question when they would be considered integrated and thus freed from court supervision. In the *Green* case, the Court suggested that school systems had achieved this goal when discrimination had completely vanished. In *Swann*, the Court elaborated by adding that once desegregation was achieved, school systems would be freed from judicial oversight and the continual racial balancing act, provided that any subsequent racial imbalances in schools were purely demographic and not discriminatory in nature.

Though there had been some activity in district and appellate courts on this issue, the first important Supreme Court decision on unitary status was not handed down until 1991. In the case of *Board of Education of Oklahoma City v. Dowell* (1991), the Court overturned a lower court's ruling and declared that the Oklahoma City school system was at last "unitary." The Court disagreed with the appellate court ruling, which stated that a district could be under court-ordered desegregation for an "indefinite future." Instead, it declared that once a system had achieved unitary status, it no longer needed court approval for student assignment policies provided it did not violate the Fourteenth Amendment equal protection clause.

The second major Court decision regarding unitary status was handed down a year later in the 1992 case of *Freeman v. Pitts*. This case involved the large Atlanta suburban district of DeKalb County, Georgia. The school district filed for unitary status in 1988, which a district court declared had been achieved in the areas of student assignment, transportation, facilities, and extracurricular activities. The district court maintained, however, that the DeKalb County school district needed to do more work in the area of teacher and principal assignment before it could be declared unitary in these two areas. An appellate court overturned the lower court's decision, saying that the school district must be unitary in all six areas before it could be granted any measure of unitary status. The Supreme Court overturned the court of appeals ruling, stating that a district could be declared unitary on a piecemeal basis. Moreover, it reiterated its position in the earlier *Swann* decision that a school district could not be held responsible for racial imbalances caused by demographic factors beyond a school board's control.

In *Missouri v. Jenkins* (1995), the Court prohibited district courts from ordering magnet schools and other expensive educational programs for the purpose of desegregation. With the combination of the *Dowell, Pitts,* and *Jenkins* decisions, it would subsequently be almost impossible for district judges to order new busing plans, and most of the plans in operation would gradually be phased out, except when desired by a local population. A district judge allowed Denver's busing plan to end in 1995. The school boards of Boston and Charlotte stopped assigning students with the goal of desegregation in 1999 and 2002. In effect, court-ordered busing was ceasing to be a major political issue. Resegregation throughout the country, however, was proceeding on a de facto basis. By the early twenty-first century, public schools were racially segregated approximately at the same statistical level they had been in 1968, the date of the *Green* decision. Many communities had some success in promoting desegregation with programs such as magnet schools, but such programs were unlikely to have the statistical impact of busing plans.

Scholars continue to disagree about whether busing plans effectively promoted racial harmony or improved public education. Liberals tend to think that busing plans were necessary to promote contact among the races, and they also argue that integration was necessary because white citizens tend to be indifferent about the quality of predominantly black schools. Conservatives usually assert that the money spent on busing could have been better spent on improving the quality of the schools, and they also deny that court-ordered busing resulted in positive interactions among different racial groups.

Carl L. Bankston III
Updated by the Editor

FURTHER READING

Jeffrey A. Raffel's *Historical Dictionary of School Segregation and Desegregation* (Westport, Conn.: Greenwood Publishing, 1998) is an excellent source of general information on this subject. Charles Clotfelter's *After Brown: The Rise and Retreat of School Desegregation* (Princeton, N.J.: Princeton University Press, 2004) presents a comprehensive account of the history of desegregation from 1954 to the 1990's.

Ronald Formisano's *Boston Against Busing: Race, Class, and Ethnicity in the 1960s and 1970s* (Chapel Hill: University of North Carolina Press, 2004) argues that class resentment, ethnic rivalries, and support of neighborhoods were more important than racism in the protests. Another useful critical study is Sheryll Cashin's *The Failures of Integration: How Race and Class Are Undermining the American Dream* (New York: Public Affairs, 2004). For broader studies of the Supreme Court's involvement in desegregation, see Michael J. Klarman's *From Jim Crow to Civil Rights: The Supreme Court and the Struggle for Racial Equality* (New York: Oxford University Press, 2006), Christine L. Compston's *Earl Warren: Justice for All* (New York: Oxford University Press, 2001), and *Massive Resistance: Southern Opposition to the Second Reconstruction*, edited by Clive Webb (New York: Oxford University Press, 2005).

From "Brown" to "Bakke": The Supreme Court and School Integration, 1954-1978 (New York: Oxford University Press, 1981), by J. Harvie Wilkinson, describes the evolution of Supreme Court policies during the most critical years of school integration. *Swann's Way: The School Busing Case and the Supreme Court* (New York: Oxford University Press, 1986), by Bernard Schwartz, provides a detailed discussion of the case that led to the pursuit of school integration by active means such as busing. *The Court Versus Congress: Prayer, Busing, and Abortion* (Durham, N.C.: Duke University Press, 1989), by Edward Keynes, considers busing one of the controversial issues that have put the Court at odds with elected representatives.

In *Forced Justice: School Desegregation and the Law* (New York: Oxford University Press, 1996), sociologist David J. Armor presents a critical view of the program of forced integration pursued by the courts since the 1970's. On the other hand, the case studies of school desegregation and resegregation presented in *Dismantling Desegregation: The Quiet Reversal of "Brown v. Board of Education"* (New York: New Press, 1997), edited by Gary Orfield, Susan E. Eaton, and Elaine R. Jones, generally suggest that the Court has not been forceful enough in pushing a clear vision of school integration.

SEE ALSO Affirmative action; *Brown v. Board of Education*; Civil Rights movement; Housing discrimination; Judicial activism; Race and discrimination; *Swann v. Charlotte-Mecklenburg Board of Education*.